P9-ARQ-685

The Cambridge Companion to Mendelssohn

The Companion to Mendelssohn is written by leading scholars in the field. In fourteen chapters they explore the life, work, and reception of a composer-performer once thought uniquely untroubled in life and art alike, but who is now broadly understood as one of the nineteenth century's most deeply problematic musical figures. The first section of the volume considers issues of biography, with chapters dedicated to Mendelssohn's role in the emergence of Europe's modern musical institutions, to the persistent tensions of his German-Jewish identity, and to his close but enigmatic relationship with his gifted older sister, Fanny. The following nine essays survey Mendelssohn's expansive and multi-faceted musical output, marked as it was by successes in almost every contemporary musical genre outside of opera. The volume's two closing essays confront, in turn, the turbulent course of Mendelssohn's posthumous reception and some of the challenges his music continues to pose for modern performers.

PETER MERCER-TAYLOR is Associate Professor of Musicology at the University of Minnesota School of Music. He is the author of *The Life of Mendelssohn* (Cambridge, 2000) and has published in a number of journals including *The Journal of Musicology* and *Popular Music*.

Cambridge Companions to Music

Topics

The Cambridge Companion to Blues and
  Gospel Music
Edited by Allan Moore

The Cambridge Companion to Conducting
Edited by José Antonio Bowen

The Cambridge Companion to
  Grand Opera
Edited by David Charlton

The Cambridge Companion to Jazz
Edited by Mervyn Cooke and David Horn

The Cambridge Companion to the Musical
Edited by William Everett and Paul Laird

The Cambridge Companion to the Orchestra
Edited by Colin Lawson

The Cambridge Companion to Pop and Rock
Edited by Simon Frith, Will Straw and John
  Street

The Cambridge Companion to the String
  Quartet
Edited by Robin Stowell

Composers

The Cambridge Companion to Bach
Edited by John Butt

The Cambridge Companion to Bartók
Edited by Amanda Bayley

The Cambridge Companion to Beethoven
Edited by Glenn Stanley

The Cambridge Companion to Berg
Edited by Anthony Pople

The Cambridge Companion to Berlioz
Edited by Peter Bloom

The Cambridge Companion to Brahms
Edited by Michael Musgrave

The Cambridge Companion to Benjamin
  Britten
Edited by Mervyn Cooke

The Cambridge Companion to Bruckner
Edited by John Williamson

The Cambridge Companion to John Cage
Edited by David Nicholls

The Cambridge Companion to Chopin
Edited by Jim Samson

The Cambridge Companion to Debussy
Edited by Simon Trezise

The Cambridge Companion to Elgar
Edited by Daniel Grimley and Julian Rushton

The Cambridge Companion to Handel
Edited by Donald Burrows

The Cambridge Companion to Liszt
Edited by Kenneth Hamilton

The Cambridge Companion to Mendelssohn
Edited by Peter Mercer-Taylor

The Cambridge Companion to Mozart
Edited by Simon P. Keefe

The Cambridge Companion to Ravel
Edited by Deborah Mawer

The Cambridge Companion to Rossini
Edited by Emanuele Senici

The Cambridge Companion to Schubert
Edited by Christopher Gibbs

The Cambridge Companion to Sibelius
Edited by Daniel Grimley

The Cambridge Companion to Verdi
Edited by Scott L. Balthazar

Instruments

The Cambridge Companion to Brass
  Instruments
Edited by Trevor Herbert and John Wallace

The Cambridge Companion to the Cello
Edited by Robin Stowell

The Cambridge Companion to the Clarinet
Edited by Colin Lawson

The Cambridge Companion to the Guitar
Edited by Victor Coelho

The Cambridge Companion to the Organ
Edited by Nicholas Thistlethwaite and
  Geoffrey Webber

The Cambridge Companion to
  the Piano
Edited by David Rowland

The Cambridge Companion to the Recorder
Edited by John Mansfield Thomson

The Cambridge Companion to the
  Saxophone
Edited by Richard Ingham

The Cambridge Companion to Singing
Edited by John Potter

The Cambridge Companion to the Violin
Edited by Robin Stowell

The Cambridge Companion to

MENDELSSOHN

....

EDITED BY
Peter Mercer-Taylor

CAMBRIDGE
UNIVERSITY PRESS

PUBLISHED BY THE PRESS SYNDICATE OF THE UNIVERSITY OF CAMBRIDGE
The Pitt Building, Trumpington Street, Cambridge, United Kingdom

CAMBRIDGE UNIVERSITY PRESS
The Edinburgh Building, Cambridge CB2 2RU, UK
40 West 20th Street, New York, NY 10011–4211, USA
477 Williamstown Road, Port Melbourne, VIC 3207, Australia
Ruiz de Alarcón 13, 28014 Madrid, Spain
Dock House, The Waterfront, Cape Town 8001, South Africa

http://www.cambridge.org

© Cambridge University Press 2004

This book is in copyright. Subject to statutory exception and
to the provisions of relevant collective licensing agreements,
no reproduction of any part may take place without
the written permission of Cambridge University Press.

First published 2004

Printed in the United Kingdom at the University Press, Cambridge

Typeface Minion 10.75/14 pt.   *System* LATEX 2$_\varepsilon$ [TB]

A catalogue record for this book is available from the British Library

ISBN 0 521 82603 9 hardback
ISBN 0 521 53342 2 paperback

Contents

Notes on contributors [*page* vi]
Acknowledgments [ix]
Chronology [x]
List of abbreviations [xv]

Introduction: Mendelssohn as border-dweller *Peter Mercer-Taylor* [1]

Part I • Issues in biography
1 Mendelssohn and the institution(s) of German art music
  Peter Mercer-Taylor [11]
2 Mendelssohn and Judaism *Michael P. Steinberg* [26]
3 Felix and Fanny: gender, biography, and history
  Marian Wilson Kimber [42]

Part II • Situating the compositions
4 Mendelssohn and the rise of musical historicism *James Garratt* [55]
5 Mendelssohn as progressive *Greg Vitercik* [71]

Part III • Profiles of the music
6 Symphony and overture *Douglass Seaton* [91]
7 The works for solo instrument(s) and orchestra *Steve Lindeman* [112]
8 Mendelssohn's chamber music *Thomas Schmidt-Beste* [130]
9 The music for keyboard *Glenn Stanley* [149]
10 On Mendelssohn's sacred music, real and imaginary *R. Larry Todd* [167]
11 Mendelssohn's songs *Susan Youens* [189]
12 Felix Mendelssohn's dramatic compositions: from Liederspiel to
   Lorelei Monika Hennemann [206]

Part IV • Reception and performance
13 Mendelssohn received *John Michael Cooper* [233]
14 Wagner as Mendelssohn: reversing habits and reclaiming meaning in
   the performance of Mendelssohn's music for orchestra and chorus
   Leon Botstein [251]

Notes [269]
Select bibliography [297]
Index [301]

Contributors

Leon Botstein is President and Leon Levy Professor in the Arts and Humanities at Bard College. He is the author of *Judentum und Modernität* and *Jefferson's Children: Education and the Promise of American Culture*. He is also the editor of *The Compleat Brahms* and *The Musical Quarterly*, as well as music director and principal conductor of the American Symphony Orchestra and the Jerusalem Symphony Orchestra, and music director of the American Russian Young Artists Orchestra. He has recorded works by, among others, Szymanowski, Hartmann, Bruch, Toch, Dohnányi, Bruckner, Glière, Reger, Richard Strauss, and Mendelssohn for Telarc, CRI, Koch, Arabesque, and New World Records.

John Michael Cooper is Associate Professor of Music History at the University of North Texas. He is the author of *Felix Mendelssohn Bartholdy: A Guide to Research* and *Mendelssohn's "Italian" Symphony*, and editor, with Julie D. Prandi, of *The Mendelssohns: Their Music in History*. He was also the general editor of a three-volume facsimile edition of the complete surviving autographs for Mendelssohn's A major Symphony.

James Garratt is Lecturer in Music and University Organist at the University of Manchester. His main research interests are in nineteenth-century German music, thought, and culture. His publications include *Palestrina and the German Romantic Imagination: Interpreting Historicism in Nineteenth-Century Music*, as well as several articles on Mendelssohn.

Monika Hennemann has been a member of the Musicology Faculty at Florida State University, the German Faculty at the University of Rhode Island, and most recently a Visiting Assistant Professor of Musicology at the College-Conservatory of Music (University of Cincinnati). She has written extensively on Mendelssohn and also published articles on Webern and on nineteenth-century reception history.

Steve Lindeman is Associate Professor of Music at Brigham Young University. His research interests include Mendelssohn, the concerto genre, and jazz. He is the author of *Structural Novelty and Tradition in the Early Romantic Piano Concerto*, and of articles on Mendelssohn and other composer-pianists in *The Musical Quarterly*, the revised edition of *The New Grove Dictionary*, and *The Cambridge Companion to the Concerto*.

Peter Mercer-Taylor is Associate Professor of Music History at the University of Minnesota. His articles on Mendelssohn, Weber, and various popular music topics have appeared in *19th-Century Music*, *The Journal of Musicology*, *Popular Music*, *Music & Letters*, and *Popular Music & Society*. He is the author of *The Life of Mendelssohn*.

Thomas Schmidt-Beste received his Ph. D. in 1995, with a dissertation on Mendelssohn's musical aesthetics. He served subsequently as Research Associate with the project "Cappella Sistina" of the Heidelberg Academy of Arts and Sciences, and completed his *Habilitation* in 2001 with a thesis on text declamation in the fifteenth-century motet. Schmidt-Beste is currently a Heisenberg Research Scholar of the Deutsche Forschungsgemeinschaft and Lecturer at the University of Heidelberg.

Douglass Seaton is Warren D. Allen Professor of Music at The Florida State University. In addition to Felix Mendelssohn Bartholdy, his research interests center on the interactions between music and literature. He is author of *Ideas and Styles in the Western Musical Tradition* and editor of *The Mendelssohn Companion* and of the critical edition of Mendelssohn's "Lobgesang."

Glenn Stanley is Professor of Music at the University of Connecticut. He edited the *Cambridge Companion to Beethoven*, wrote the article on Schubert's religious music for the *Cambridge Companion to Schubert* and will contribute the chapter on *Parsifal* for the *Cambridge Companion to Wagner*. His most recent work includes essays on the writing of music history in divided Germany after World War II, and discussions of orchestration in nineteenth-century choral music and the Fifth Symphony by Beethoven.

Michael P. Steinberg is Professor of Modern European History at Cornell University and associate editor of *The Musical Quarterly*. He is the author of *Listening to Reason: Culture, Subjectivity, and Nineteenth-Century Music* and *Austria as Theater and Ideology: The Meaning of the Salzburg Festival*. He is the recipient of grants and fellowships from the Guggenheim Foundation and the National Endowment for the Humanities as well as the Austrian State Prize for History and the Berlin Prize of the American Academy in Berlin.

R. Larry Todd, Professor of Music at Duke University, has published widely on music of the nineteenth century, especially that of the Mendelssohns. He is the author of *Mendelssohn: A Life in Music* and *Mendelssohn: The Hebrides and Other Overtures*, and editor of *Mendelssohn and his World* and *Mendelssohn Studies*. Todd has also edited several of Mendelssohn's sacred works, including the oratorios *St. Paul* and *Elijah*.

Greg Vitercik is Chair of the Music Department at Middlebury College where he teaches music history, theory, analysis, interdisciplinary studies, and performance. He is the author of *The Early Works of Felix Mendelssohn: A Study in the Romantic Sonata Style*.

Marian Wilson Kimber is Associate Professor of Musicology at the University of Iowa. She is the author of articles in *19th-Century Music*, *The Journal of Musicology* and *19th-Century Studies*, and chapters in *The Mendelssohn Companion*, *Fanny Hensel geb. Mendelssohn Bartholdy*, *The Mendelssohns: Their Music in History*, and *Nineteenth-Century Piano Music*.

Susan Youens is Professor of Musicology at the University of Notre Dame and the author of seven books on the songs of Franz Schubert and Hugo Wolf, including *Hugo Wolf and his Mörike Songs* and *Schubert's Late Lieder: Beyond the Song Cycles*.

Acknowledgments

I offer my first thanks to John Michael Cooper for his help in identifying potential contributors, and his encouragement throughout the development of this project. Parts of my own contribution to this volume were read – and improved – by Michael Cherlin, Alex Lubet, and Colleen Seguin. I am grateful to Annett Richter for offering a native speaker's insights on a number of German passages, and to Heath Mathews and Kurt Miyashiro, who set the musical examples for this volume, and to Lucy Carolan, at Cambridge University Press, for the keen editorial eye she brought to the whole.

Permission to include facsimiles and text in this volume is gratefully acknowledged to the following:

The Staatsbibliothek zu Berlin – Preußischer Kulturbesitz Musikabteilung mit Mendelssohn-Archiv for permission to reproduce the manuscript pages that appear in Plates 12.1a and 12.1b.

Oxford University Press for permission to include in Chapter 2 material based on Michael P. Steinberg, "Mendelssohn's Music and German-Jewish Culture: An Intervention," *Musical Quarterly* 83 (1999), 31–44. © Oxford University Press.

University of California Press for permission to include in Chapter 3 material based on "The Suppression of Fanny Mendelssohn: Rethinking Feminist Biography," *19th-Century Music* 26 (2002), 113–29. © The Regents of the University of California.

Chronology

1809 Felix Mendelssohn is born in Hamburg on 3 February.

1811 The Mendelssohn family moves to Berlin.

1816 Felix begins two years of elementary school at the Lehr-, Pensions-, und Erziehungsanstalt. On 21 March, the four Mendelssohn children are baptized. During a family visit to Paris, Felix takes lessons with violinist Pierre Baillot and with pianist Marie Bigot.

1818 Fanny and Felix begin lessons with Ludwig Berger. On 28 October, Felix takes part in a concert given by horn player Friedrich Gugel.

1819 Carl Wilhelm Ludwig Heyse begins his seven years of service as children's private tutor. Around this time, Mendelssohn begins violin lessons with Carl Wilhelm Henning, soon replaced by Eduard Rietz. From this year date the earliest documents pertaining to Mendelssohn's lessons in composition with Karl Friedrich Zelter.

1820 Felix and Fanny join the Berlin Singakademie.
Compositions: chamber works and lieder; *Ich, J Mendelssohn* (Lustspiel) and *Die Soldatenliebschaft* (Singspiel).

1821 On 18 June, Mendelssohn attends the premiere of Weber's *Der Freischütz* in Berlin's new Schauspielhaus. He travels with Zelter to Weimar, where, in November, he meets Goethe.
Compositions: *Die beiden Pädagogen* (Singspiel); Piano Sonata in G minor [op. 105]; the first six or seven of twelve string sinfonias (1821–23); *Die wandernden Komödianten* (Singspiel).

1822 Regular Sunday musicales have begun in the Mendelssohn household. The family takes a summer holiday in Switzerland.
Compositions: Magnificat in D; Piano Quartet no. 1 in C minor op. 1 (pub. 1823).

1823 Kalkbrenner plays at one of the Mendelssohn's Sunday musicales. In August Mendelssohn travels with his father to Silesia.

Sources include Wulf Konold, "Chronik," in *Felix Mendelssohn Bartholdy und Seine Zeit* (Laaber, 1981), 10–48; R. Larry Todd, "Mendelssohn; Works," in *The New Grove Dictionary of Music and Musicians* (London, 2001); John Michael Cooper, "Mendelssohn's Works: Prolegomenon to a Comprehensive Inventory," in *MC*, 701–85; Clive Brown, "A Checklist of Mendelssohn's Life and Principal Works," in *A portrait of Mendelssohn* (New Haven, 2003), xv–xxiii; R. Larry Todd, *Mendelssohn: A Life in Music* (Oxford, 2003). The last-named item – the most significant Mendelssohn biography of the last forty years – appeared as this volume was going to press; its impact does not extend beyond the present Chronology and this volume's first chapter.

Square brackets around an opus number indicate posthumous publication (op. 72 was the last work Mendelssohn saw into print). Except where otherwise indicated, works are placed according to their date of completion; where the year of publication differs from this, it is provided in parentheses. A full record of the elaborate revisions to which a large fraction of Mendelssohn's works were subjected is beyond the scope of this chronology. So, too, is an account of every known piece; this Chronology documents only the more consequential events of his compositional career.

Compositions: Concerto for two pianos in E; Violin Sonata in F minor op. 4 (pub. 1824); *Die beiden Neffen oder Der Onkel aus Boston* (Singspiel); Piano Quartet no. 2 in F minor op. 2 (pub. 1824).

1824 Ignaz Moscheles, who will become Mendelssohn's lifelong friend, gives Fanny and Felix several piano lessons.

Compositions: Symphony no. 1 in C minor op. 11 (chamber arr. pub. 1830, parts pub. 1834); Sextet in D [op. 110]; Overture for Wind Instruments op. 24 (first version, rev. version pub. 1839); Concerto for two pianos in A♭.

1825 During a March visit to Paris – bookended by two further visits with Goethe – Mendelssohn and his father call on Luigi Cherubini to gauge Felix's musical promise; Cherubini greets Mendelssohn's Piano Quartet op. 3 with enthusiastic praise. That summer, the Mendelssohns move into their new home at 3 Leipzigerstraße.

Compositions: Piano Quartet no. 3 in B minor op. 3; *Die Hochzeit des Camacho* op. 10 (Singspiel; pub. 1828); Octet in E♭ op. 20 (piano duet arr. pub. 1833).

1826 On 19 November, Felix and Fanny play a four-hand version of the *Sommernachtstraum* Overture op. 21 for Ignaz Moscheles. Carl Maria von Weber dies in London on 25 June.

Compositions: "Trumpet" Overture [op. 101]; Piano Sonata in E op. 6; String Quintet in A op. 18, first version (rev. 1832, pub. 1833); *Ein Sommernachtstraum* Overture op. 21 (pub. 1832); Te Deum.

1827 On 20 February, Mendelssohn's *Sommernachtstraum* Overture and his A♭ concerto for two pianos are performed on the same concert with the north German premiere of Beethoven's Ninth Symphony. Beethoven dies on 26 March. On 29 April, Mendelssohn's opera *Die Hochzeit des Camacho* receives its first and last public performance. Mendelssohn begins his first four semesters of study at the University of Berlin, including Hegel's lectures on aesthetics.

Compositions: pub. of *Sieben Characterstücke* op. 7 (inc. numbers composed as early as 1824); Piano Sonata in B♭ [op. 106]; String Quartet no. 2 in A minor op. 13 (pub. 1830); "Christe, du Lamm Gottes" (the first of eight chorale cantatas that Mendelssohn would compose between 1827 and 1832); completion of pub. of *Zwölf Gesänge* op. 8 (first six pub. 1826, composed c. 1824–27; nos. 2, 3, and 12 are by Fanny Mendelssohn).

1828 After performance of Mendelssohn's cantata for Berlin's 18 April Dürerfest, artist Gottfried Schadow pronounces the young composer an honorary member of the Academy of Art. Schubert dies on 19 November.

Compositions: *Meeresstille und glückliche Fahrt* Overture op. 27, first version (rev. 1834, pub. 1835); *Grosse Festmusik zum Dürerfest*.

1829 On 11 March, Mendelssohn directs the Berlin Singakademie in a revival of J. S. Bach's *St. Matthew Passion*, its first hearing since Bach's death. He travels to England in April, makes several dazzling appearances in the course of London's concert season, then tours Scotland and Wales on foot. He returns to Berlin for the winter. On 3 October, Fanny Mendelssohn marries painter Wilhelm Hensel.

Compositions: String Quartet no. 1 in E♭ op. 12 (pub. 1830); *Trois fantaisies ou caprices* op. 16 (pub. 1831); *Heimkehr aus der Fremde* [op. 89] (Liederspiel).

1830 Mendelssohn is offered the new chair in music at the University of Berlin, which he does not accept. On 8 May, he sets off on his Grand Tour to the south, visiting his grandfather Moses' birthplace, Dessau, and meeting Goethe for the last time in Weimar. He sojourns briefly in Munich, Vienna, Pressburg, and Venice before his November arrival in Rome, where he spends the winter.

Compositions: "Reformation" Symphony in D [op. 107]; *Rondo Capriccioso* in E op. 14 (based on an "étude" of 1828); *Drei Kirchenmusiken* op. 23 (pub. 1832); Psalm 115 op. 31; *Die Hebriden* Overture op. 26 (in its first version, titled *Ouvertüre zur einsamen Insel*; pub., after extensive revision, 1833); pub. of *Zwölf Lieder* op. 9 (composed 1827–30; nos. 7, 10, and 12 are by Fanny Mendelssohn).

1831 Mendelssohn meets Donizetti in Naples and pianist Dorothea von Ertmann, a friend of Beethoven's, in Milan. He tours Switzerland in the summer, and reaches Paris on 9 December.

Compositions: Piano Concerto no. 1 in G minor op. 25 (pub. 1832).

1832 In Paris for the winter, Mendelssohn receives word of the deaths of Goethe and his close friend Eduard Rietz. He performs in London in the spring, where he learns of the death of his teacher, Zelter. Mendelssohn returns to Berlin in late June.

Compositions: *Die erste Walpurgisnacht* op. 60 (first version; rev. 1842–43, pub. 1844); *Capriccio brillant* op. 22; pub. of first volume of *Lieder ohne Worte*, op. 19[b], under the title "Original Melodies for the Pianoforte" (incl. items dating back to 1829).

1833 Mendelssohn's reluctant candidacy for the directorship of the Berlin Singakademie comes to naught; Zelter's long-time assistant Rungenhagen is elected in January. In May, Mendelssohn conducts the Lower Rhine Music Festival, returns to London with his father for much of the summer, then returns to Düsseldorf in October to assume the post of the city's music director, a three-year contract.

Compositions: Fantasia in F# minor op. 28, "Sonate écossaise" (pub. 1834); Symphony no. 4 in A, "Italian" [op. 90] (first version; rev. 1834); *Die schöne Melusine* Overture op. 32 (pub. 1836); pub. of *Sechs Gesänge* op. 19[a].

1834 In Düsseldorf, amid extensive choral and orchestral conducting, Mendelssohn becomes musical intendant for Karl Immermann's new theater, but abandons the project in frustration in early November.

Compositions: *Rondo brillant* op. 29.

1835 Mendelssohn gives his last Düsseldorf concert in July. In August, he arrives in Leipzig, where he assumes his new post as municipal music director and conductor of the Gewandhaus orchestra. Leipzig would remain his home, with occasional hiatuses, for the rest of his life. His father, Abraham, dies on 19 November.

Compositions: pub. of *Lieder ohne Worte* vol. II op. 30;

1836 In March, Mendelssohn receives an honorary doctorate from the University of Leipzig. He directs the Lower Rhine Music Festival in Düsseldorf in late May, where *St. Paul* is premiered to terrific acclaim. During his summer stay in Frankfurt, Mendelssohn courts Cécile Jeanrenaud, to whom he becomes engaged at the end of August.

Compositions: *St. Paul*, op. 36; pub. of *Trois caprices* op. 33 (incl. material dating back to 1833).

1837 In March, *St. Paul* is performed in Boston. Felix and Cécile are married on 28 March, and honeymoon through the summer.

Compositions: String Quartet no. 4 in E minor op. 44 no. 2 (pub. 1839); Psalm 42 op. 42 (pub. 1838); Piano Concerto no. 2 in D minor op. 40 (pub. 1838); Six Preludes and Fugues for piano op. 35 (completed, incl. material dating back to 1827); Three Preludes and Fugues for organ op. 37 (completed, incl. material dating back to 1833); pub. of *Lieder ohne Worte* vol. III op. 38; pub. of *Sechs Gesänge* op. 34.

1838　In February, Mendelssohn begins his first series of "historical" concerts at the Gewandhaus. Carl Wolfgang Paul Mendelssohn, Felix and Cécile's first child, is born on 7 February. In Cologne, Mendelssohn conducts his third Lower Rhine Music Festival.

Compositions: String Quartet no. 5 in E♭ op. 44 no. 3 (pub. 1839); Psalm 95 op. 46 (first version; pub. 1842); *Serenade and Allegro giojoso* op. 43 (pub. 1839); String Quartet no. 3 in D op. 44 no. 1 (pub. 1839); Cello Sonata no. 1 in B♭ op. 45 (pub. 1839); pub. of Three Motets op. 39 (incl. material dating back to 1830); pub. of *Sechs Lieder "Im freien zu singen"* op. 41, his first set of songs for mixed chorus (two more followed in his lifetime: op. 48 in 1840 and op. 59 in 1843).

1839　Mendelssohn conducts the premiere of Schubert's Symphony no. 9 in March. In May, he conducts the Lower Rhine Music Festival in Düsseldorf, then the Brunswick Music Festival in September.

Compositions: *Ruy Blas* Overture [op. 95]; Piano Trio no. 1 in D minor op. 49 (pub. 1840); Psalm 114 op. 51 (pub. 1841); pub. of *Sechs Lieder* op. 47.

1840　All four of Beethoven's overtures to *Fidelio* are performed at a single Gewandhaus concert in January. In August, Mendelssohn offers an all-Bach organ recital at the Thomaskirche to raise funds for the erection of a new Bach monument.

Compositions: pub. of Six Male Choruses op. 50; Symphony no. 2 in B♭ op. 52, *Lobgesang* (pub. 1841).

1841　After repeated overtures from Prussian King Friedrich Wilhelm IV, Mendelssohn reluctantly moves to Berlin for a one-year trial period, during which he is to participate in a vaguely defined plan to revitalize the city's musical life.

Compositions: *Variations sérieuses* op. 54; incidental music to *Antigone* op. 55 (pub. 1843); pub. of *Lieder ohne Worte* vol. IV op. 53.

1842　In May, Mendelssohn conducts the Lower Rhine Music Festival in Düsseldorf, then travels to London, where he is twice welcomed by Prince Albert and Queen Victoria at Buckingham Palace. In October, Friedrich Wilhelm IV frees Mendelssohn to return to Leipzig for the Gewandhaus season, but names him Generalmusikdirektor (on 4 December), with the understanding that he will return to supervise the new cathedral choir the following year. Mendelssohn's mother, Lea, dies on 12 December.

Compositions: Symphony no. 3 in A minor op. 56, "Scottish."

1843　Leipzig's new music conservatory – which Mendelssohn had formally proposed to Saxon King Friedrich August II in 1840 – opens its doors in April under Mendelssohn's leadership. He returns to Berlin in November, where he conducts several concerts and assumes control of the cathedral choir.

Compositions: Cello Sonata no. 2 in D op. 58; incidental music to *A Midsummer Night's Dream* op. 61 (pub. 1844); Psalm 98 [op. 91]; pub. of *Sechs Lieder* op. 57.

1844　Mendelssohn continues his work with the cathedral choir through Holy Week, then journeys to England, where he performs extensively. In September, back in Berlin, he finally succeeds in being released from his duties to that city and returns to Leipzig.

Compositions: Violin Concerto in E minor op. 64 (pub. 1845); pub. of *Lieder ohne Worte* vol. V op. 62; completion of Three Psalms [op. 78].

1845 The early part of the year is spent in Frankfurt with few professional obligations. In the fall, he returns to work in Leipzig, but shares conducting duties with Niels Gade. Compositions: Piano Trio no. 2 in C minor op. 66 (pub. 1846); String Quintet no. 2 in B♭ [op. 87]; Six Sonatas for organ op. 65 (composed 1844–45); pub. of *Lieder ohne Worte* vol. VI op. 67; incidental music to *Oedipus at Colonus* [op. 93], and to *Athalie* [op. 74].

1846 His health declining amid a forbidding schedule of conducting obligations, Mendelssohn works feverishly at *Elijah*, whose 26 August premiere in Birmingham proves one of the greatest successes of Mendelssohn's life. Medical concerns lead to his retirement from piano performance early in the year. Compositions: *Lauda Sion* [op. 73]; *An die Künstler* op. 68; *Elijah* op. 70 (rev. and pub. 1847).

1847 Mendelssohn continues to conduct the Gewandhaus concerts along with Gade. He collapses upon receiving news of his older sister Fanny's death on 14 May. In October, he suffers a subarachnoid hemorrhage and never fully recovers. Mendelssohn dies on 4 November. Compositions: Three Motets op. 69; String Quartet no. 6 in F minor [op. 80]; pub. of *Sechs Lieder* op. 71; pub. of *Sechs Kinderstücke* op. 72 (incl. nos. dating back to at least 1842).

Abbreviations

KBB   Christian Martin Schmidt, ed., *Felix Mendelssohn Bartholdy: Kongreß-Bericht Berlin 1994* (Wiesbaden, 1997)

MC   Douglass Seaton, ed., *The Mendelssohn Companion* (Westport, CT, 2001)

MhW   Todd, R. Larry, ed., *Mendelssohn and his World* (Princeton, 1991)

MNI   Eric Werner, *Mendelssohn: A New Image of the Composer and his Age*, trans. Dika Newlin (London, 1963)

MQ   *The Musical Quarterly*

MSt   Todd, R. Larry, ed., *Mendelssohn Studies* (Cambridge, 1992)

NZfM   *Neue Zeitschrift für Musik*

PM   Carl Dahlhaus, ed., *Das Problem Mendelssohn* (Regensburg, 1974)

TMH   John Michael Cooper and Julie D. Prandi, eds., *The Mendelssohns: Their Music in History* (Oxford, 2002)

Introduction
Mendelssohn as border-dweller

PETER MERCER-TAYLOR

Art Spiegelman's Pulitzer Prize winning 1986 graphic novel *Maus* follows the artist's father, Vladek, through the early years of World War II, tracing the events that culminate in his 1944 arrival at Auschwitz.[1] Though striking in its sense of documentary rigor, the book is animated by a visual conceit that comprises its sole glaring concession to fantasy: Jews are portrayed as mice, Germans as cats, Poles as pigs, Americans as dogs. Though not without its hazards, the image of the Jew as mouse succeeds not only in essentializing the war's governing chain of predatorship, but in encapsulating a broad understanding of the Jews' position among northern Europe's citizenry: mice inhabit walls, having no rooms of their own, consigned to an intersticial realm at once enclosed and excluded by its architectural surroundings. The mouse serves as a shorthand figure for both the Jews' perspective on the world and the anxiety they inspired.

Felix Mendelssohn has proven one of music history's great wall-dwellers. And without wishing to trivialize Spiegelman's subject matter, I suggest that his metaphor might prove a useful point of entry into the essays that follow. Over the last half-century, it has become increasingly customary to see Mendelssohn's life (once thought thoroughly placid) and art (once thought transparently unchallenging) as deeply problematic indeed – the 1974 publication of the provocatively titled essay collection *Das Problem Mendelssohn* was a key moment in this reevaluation. The anxiety Mendelssohn inspires is rooted largely in the peculiar tendency of his life, his career, and his music to make us aware of crucial borders at the same time that he crosses and re-crosses them. Time and again, Mendelssohn succeeds in drawing our attention to the dichotomies through which we make sense of his music and his world, but of which he, himself, inhabits both terms, or neither. Nietzsche's description of Mendelssohn as a "beautiful *episode*" ("schöne *Zwischenfall*"[2]) in German music famously consigned the composer's work to a historical and aesthetic border territory, marking the space between Beethoven and Wagner while fully inhabiting the world of neither. But Nietzsche's term, "*Zwischenfall*" – etymologically something like "that which falls between" – resonates more powerfully across the composer's art, life, and legacy than any English counterpart. Indeed, the notion of "falling between" has emerged as something akin to a master trope of Mendelssohn's reception, manifested at times as controversy, often as simply a sense that he does not belong in any of the spaces articulated by music history's standard compartmentalizations.

This volume sets off with three essays on biographical topics, each of which can be understood in terms of an over-arching tension. The question of Mendelssohn's own Jewishness – he was born Jewish, baptized into Protestantism at the age of seven – has been a site of hot contestation since his own lifetime. As Michael P. Steinberg shows in the second chapter of this volume, the composer's biographers and critics are still far from making complete sense of the issue. Eric Werner's landmark 1963 biography, *Mendelssohn: A New Image of the Composer and his Age*, told the story as it seemed most urgently in need of telling in Germany's post-war generation; viewing his subject through the lens of a century's worth of anti-Semitic criticism that ultimately sought to strip Mendelssohn outright of his already tenuous place in the history of German music, Werner places strong emphasis on Mendelssohn's sense of his own Jewish identity, and on his personal humiliation at the hands of anti-Semitic persecutors.[3] Werner's image continues to be filled out through recent studies that have brought increasing resourcefulness to the pursuit of a kind of vestigial Jewish subject position in Mendelssohn's work as both composer and conductor, particularly in the realm of choral music – "the residue," as Leon Botstein has judiciously put it, "of commitments to what Mendelssohn knew to be the heritage of his forebears."[4] Yet recent scholarship has suggested that Werner knowingly overstated the extent of both Mendelssohn's Jewish self-identification and his personal victimization, embellishing and fabricating documentation to get the point across.[5] And no one, in the meantime, has seriously questioned the sincerity of Mendelssohn's personal Christian faith (his wife, Cécile Jeanrenaud, was the daughter of a Protestant pastor), closely bound up as it was with his distinctive eagerness to embed the music of the Christian church in contemporary concert life, both in the non-liturgical performance of religious masterpieces and in the infusion of his instrumental music with chorales and chorale-like material (a central concern of R. Larry Todd's Chapter 10). In short, Mendelssohn sustains a reputation as both the nineteenth century's greatest Jewish composer and one of its most meaningfully Christian ones.

At the same time, the recent explosion in scholarly attention to Felix's older sister, Fanny, has brought an unanticipated twist to his fortunes in the realm of the politics of oppression. Trained alongside Felix in childhood and comparably promising in composition and piano technique alike (perhaps surpassing him in the latter), Fanny might indeed have amounted to one of her generation's major composers had gender politics not stalled her ascent. As it happened, though, she performed almost exclusively in private and semi-private venues, composed a great deal less than Felix, tended toward the composition of smaller forms generally considered more suited to her sex, and undertook the publication of her work only in the last years of her life. Though her father's heart-breaking injunction to the adolescent that the station of housewife was the only one befitting her constituted discouragement enough,[6] the document trail is scarcely more kind to Felix, who also appears to have played a role in holding in check her aspirations to publish.[7] Though some have recently questioned the degree of Felix's culpability in the matter – Marian Wilson Kimber continues this process in Chapter 3 – Felix now plays simultaneously the parts of one of music history's most savagely oppressed figures and one of its more notorious oppressors.

As central a role as the composer/virtuoso played in early nineteenth-century concert life, the relationship between Mendelssohn's activities as a composer and a performer proved extraordinarily complex. Early biographer Julius Benedict clearly meant no disparagement in his laudatory assessment of Mendelssohn's impact: "It would be a matter of difficulty to decide in which quality Mendelssohn excelled the most – , whether as composer, pianist, organist, or conductor of an orchestra."[8] But there is tension even here. As a pianist, an organist, and a conductor of several major choral and instrumental ensembles – a career I survey in Chapter 1 – Mendelssohn played a critical role in solidifying the notion of a "canon" whose maintenance was fast becoming a central priority in German concert life. Though he championed new music as ardently as old in his own lifetime, Mendelssohn's leadership in the formation of the very idea of a stable core repertoire, and the robust condition in which he left the institutions through which it could be sustained, laid the groundwork for a musical world in which a vital concert life could, in principle, be divorced from public interest in contemporary composition. That this principle did not come fully to fruition until the twentieth century does not exculpate Mendelssohn from his role as one of its greatest architects.

In shifting from issues of biography to creative matters – as the present volume does in its fourth chapter – it is clear that no serious stock-taking of Mendelssohn's work is possible without reference to a similarly troublesome cluster of straddled dichotomies and apparent paradoxes. The most striking is the radical discrepancy between Mendelssohn's reputation in his own lifetime and his posthumous reception (explored in this volume's closing section, in John Michael Cooper's and Leon Botstein's chapters – 13 and 14 – on reception and performance, respectively). Henry F. Chorley dedicates much of the closing chapter of his 1854 *Modern German Music* to an argument (if a guardedly circumspect one) for Mendelssohn's "place among the noblest worthies of German music," pointing at the same time to an even more enthusiastic "section of musicians . . . already professing to take leave of Mendelssohn, as one who has closed a great period; and after whom, no more great works shall be produced, save by an utter rearrangement of every known form, principle, and material of Music."[9] Yet Chorley pitches this assessment against the abrupt shift already underway in Mendelssohn's fortunes in Germany, Leipzig in particular: "no sooner was he cold in his grave, than his shallow and fickle townsmen began to question among themselves how far they had been administering to a real greatness, and whether there were not left behind among them some new prophets better than their departed oracle."[10] (One of the most conspicuous of these prophets – Richard Wagner – had issued his landmark anti-Semitic dismissal of Mendelssohn in the pages of Leipzig's *Neue Zeitschrift für Musik* four years earlier).[11] By 1889, George Bernard Shaw – faced with program notes describing Mendelssohn as "a master yielding to none in the highest qualifications that warrant the name" – was prepared to offer his now-famous rejoinder: "compare him with Bach, Handel, Haydn, Mozart, Beethoven, or Wagner; and then settle, if you can, what ought to be done to the fanatic who proclaims him 'a master yielding to,' etc., etc., etc."[12] Shaw doubtless seeks to provoke, but the groundwork for such a denunciation was clearly in place in England and Germany alike.[13] Mendelssohn's star would not ascend again until after the Second World War.

Just as troublesome is the sense, worried over even by some contemporaries, that a fall from greatness occurred in the course of Mendelssohn's own creative life. In the popular rendition of this narrative, he attained, as a teenager, a level of sophistication and originality unrivaled by any other child prodigy in music history, but succumbed, from his mid-twenties onward, to a flagging of energy, creativity, and quality in general. Thus the thoroughgoing engagement with Beethoven's late style in the early string quartets opp. 12 and 13 mellows to the self-assured, unconfrontational language of the three quartets of op. 44, a trajectory traced in Thomas Schmidt-Beste's chapter on Mendelssohn's chamber works (Chapter 8); after several early essays in full-scale piano sonata, Mendelssohn's keyboard output – examined by Glenn Stanley in Chapter 9 – shifts toward smaller forms, many geared toward amateurs in domestic settings; at the same time, the monumentality of Mendelssohn's early concertos is answered, in his mature piano concertos and brilliant single-movement concert pieces, by a forward-looking but persistently lighter-weight engagement with the legacy of Weber's *Konzertstück* (a progression explored in Steve Lindeman's Chapter 7). A most extreme case, of course, is Mendelssohn's operatic output, examined by Monika Hennemann in Chapter 12; after a series of very promising early efforts, and a single rather disappointing performance of his 1825 *Die Hochzeit des Camacho*, Mendelssohn never completed a mature work for the operatic stage.[14]

This narrative of decline has always admitted a rich and diverse body of exceptions, including the D minor Piano Trio op. 49, the *Variations sérieuses* op. 54, the incidental music to *A Midsummer Night's Dream* op. 61, the "Scottish" Symphony op. 56, the Violin Concerto op. 64, and the F minor String Quartet op. 80. These works sit with no special pleading whatever alongside the masterpieces of his early years, and had Mendelssohn composed nothing *but* these later works he would still cut a towering figure among the composers of his generation. Indeed, the idea of a flagging of genius has never seemed to describe as successfully the absence of brilliant works as the increasing proliferation, in Mendelssohn's adulthood, of works whose effectiveness inhered largely in their usefulness, and whose usefulness quickly passed. The *Lieder ohne Worte* and great swaths of Mendelssohn's choral music represent those segments of his oeuvre which flew the highest and fell the farthest. The former offer the fullest embodiment of a creative ideal whose initial triumph and subsequent downfall Charles Rosen's *The Romantic Generation* formulates (in fairly conventional terms) thus:

> If we could be satisfied today with a simple beauty that raises no questions and does not attempt to puzzle us, the short pieces would resume their old place in the concert repertoire. They charm, but they neither provoke nor astonish. It is not true that they are insipid, but they might as well be.[15]

Similar charges have been leveled against Mendelssohn's sizeable output of Lieder, though Susan Youens, in Chapter 11, joins a number of recent scholars who have ascribed a good deal more subtlety to these works than tradition has.[16]

Mendelssohn's large choral works – "formidable and problematic representatives of Victorian profundity," as one recent scholar puts it[17] – pose an even more difficult case. While they too refuse, as a rule, to "provoke [or] astonish," they also offer the clearest locus of the kind of historicizing eclecticism that unnerved many even among Mendelssohn's contemporaries. Franz Brendel, who assumed the editorship of Leipzig's *Neue Zeitschrif für Musik* after Schumann's 1844 retirement from the post, cut straight to this issue in the third instalment of his serial 1845 article "Robert Schumann with Reference to Mendelssohn-Bartholdy and the Development of Modern Music Generally":

> He [Mendelssohn] is in no way a student of Mozart's in the narrow sense, having equally taken up Beethoven and his drive toward the future; but he did not so much fasten decisively on [Beethoven's] last period, the point from which forward development was to begin for a composer of the new ideal, nor, in general, on any single master alone. He took more the entire past, Seb. Bach and Mozart, as his premise . . . and not really to accomplish at once an entirely modern direction.[18]

In his forward to *Das Problem Mendelssohn*, Carl Dahlhaus anchors the conversation firmly around the "problem" of what it means to speak of "classicism" in Mendelssohn's music.[19] This issue continues to lurk behind the two essays comprising the second part of this volume, "Situating the compositions," which examine, in turn, the notions of the "historicistic" (in James Garratt's Chapter 4) and of the "progressive" (in Greg Vitercik's Chapter 5). Yet what has become increasingly clear in the scholarship of the last thirty years is the peculiarly slippery position of Mendelssohn's music along not one but many axes, which either overlap or intertwine so thoroughly as to be distinguishable more in principle than in practice: the conservative and the progressive; the Biedermeier and the Romantic; the comprehensible and the palpably inward; the music of the past and the music of the future; the popular and the elevated; the feminine and the masculine; the superficial and the profound.

The years since the publication of *Das Problem Mendelssohn* have brought forth a particularly rich array of revisionist work on Mendelssohn, in which authors approaching his work from a number of methodological standpoints appear to be pressing toward the common goal of understanding Mendelssohn on his own terms. Leon Botstein's landmark 1991 essay "The Aesthetics of Assimilation and Affirmation" develops a persuasive vocabulary for legitimizing at once the "sentimental" and the retrogressive dimensions of Mendelssohn's art. In Botstein's formulation, the large choral works, for instance, must be judged according to their aim of "engender[ing] two related results: mass participation in music and a heightened ethical sensibility supportive of normative canons of beauty; receptivity to tradition; faith in God; tolerance; and a sense of community."[20] In his 1995 book *Classical Music and Postmodern Knowledge*, Lawrence Kramer has offered a provocative uncoupling of classicism from conservatism in Mendelssohn's work, discerning in Goethe's classicism the roots of the "dynamism" that infuses some of Mendelssohn's most original works: the *Calm Sea, Prosperous Voyage* Overture and *Die Erste Walpurgisnacht* in particular.[21] In a 1999 article in *Music & Letters*, James Garratt laid promising groundwork for reading Mendelssohn's reclamation of older styles against contemporary aesthetics of translation.[22] Thomas Christian Schmidt's 1996 book, *Die ästhetischen Grundlagen der Instrumentalmusik Felix Mendelssohn Bartholdys* – a major achievement still awaiting full digestion by the scholarly community – provides the most systematic account to date of Mendelssohn's compositional aesthetic, particularly of the *Reformwille* at the heart of Mendelssohn's creative world. Schmidt explores the foundations of a compositional impulse that embraced "reform" over "revolution," which "sought not to dethrone the classic or render it superfluous,"[23] but to enter into dialogue with it, appropriating its standards, its greatness of spirit, and – at moments – elements of its styles and forms.

Finally, a site of particular ambiguity in Mendelssohn's work – as his contemporaries well understood – was his approach to what many considered the single most important question facing his generation's composers of instrumental music: the divide between absolute music and program music (a central issue in Douglass Seaton's handling of the symphonies and overtures in Chapter 6). Devotees of both camps can plausibly claim Mendelssohn as an ally. His early concert overtures clearly played a critical role in drawing from the operatic overture (long prone to concert performance in itself) a free-standing instrumental form: if its dramatic frame of reference tended to link the *Midsummer Night's Dream* Overture op. 21 to its operatic forebears, the two that followed (*Calm Sea and Prosperous Voyage* op. 27 and *The Hebrides* op. 26) pressed the genre in new directions, opening paths at the end of which lay the late Romantic tone poem.[24] Mendelssohn's mature symphonies have all passed through history with titles – the "Reformation," the "Italian," and the "Scottish" (though only the last of these three was published in Mendelssohn's own lifetime, then without a title). And the extensive literature that has grown up on the subject attests to the obvious centrality of the question of programmaticism to our understanding of these works. Yet conclusions reached tend to be provisional at best, as often simply speculative, and prone to almost constant revision.[25] And through it all, even Mendelssohn's most robustly programmatic works testify to an unshakable confidence in the continued vitality of Classical motivic and formal procedures that render him a more important positive force in Brahms' nineteenth century than in Liszt's or Wagner's.[26]

These brief introductory remarks do no more, of course, than skim across the surface of Mendelssohn's life, work and reception. It is obvious, too, that this discussion's pervasive focus on "tensions" may mean presenting as straw what more charitable commentators – and doubtless Mendelssohn himself, on certain points – might more profitably seek to spin into the gold of Hegelian dialectical language. This is certainly the promise Schumann holds forth in his often-quoted, if persistently obscure, remark that Mendelssohn was "the most brilliant among musicians; the one who has most clearly recognized the contradictions of the age, and the first to reconcile them."[27] But it is hardly surprising that Schumann's remark should have become such a favorite among Mendelssohn's commentators (and it is not appearing here for the last time in these pages). For the broad trajectory of Mendelssohn studies from then to now might be read, in large measure, as a struggle to establish, on the one hand, the meaning of this statement, and, on the other, its validity.

PART ONE

Issues in biography

1 Mendelssohn and the institution(s) of German art music

PETER MERCER-TAYLOR

By his twenty-first year, Felix Mendelssohn had completed a handful of orchestral and chamber works that placed him among the front ranks of contemporary composers. Yet, as rapidly as a reputation was building around these pieces,[1] it was not as a composer but as a conductor that he made his grand entrance onto the stage of Germany's musical history. On 11 March 1829, he directed the Berlin Singakademie in a revival of Bach's *St. Matthew Passion*, unheard since its composer's death and thought, in Mendelssohn's time, to have been premiered exactly a century before.[2] Upon receiving word of the event, Goethe famously observed to his friend – Mendelssohn's teacher – Karl Friedrich Zelter, "To me, it is as though I have heard the roar of the sea from a distance."[3]

The "Bach revival" that feverishly ensued had hardly been conjured *ex nihilo* by the young conductor: the Singakademie had offered occasional motets and cantatas of Bach's since its 1791 founding, first under the direction of Christian Friedrich Carl Fasch, then, after 1800, under Carl Friedrich Zelter; and by 1829, Bach's generally neglected choral music (his keyboard music had never passed wholly out of currency) had found an important outlet, too, in Frankfurt's Caecilienverein. But there was no question that the 1829 *St. Matthew Passion* revival – abbreviated though the work was through the excision of six of the chorales, some recitative, and all but two of the arias – constituted an event of epoch-making significance in the revitalization of Bach's reputation.[4] And the event serves, for Mendelssohn, as a fitting structural down-beat to a musical career animated as fully by the recovery and consolidation of a musical heritage as by its furtherance through musical composition. Recent scholarship has cast doubt on the historical veracity of Eduard Devrient's oft-repeated account of the dramatic exchange in which he and Mendelssohn persuaded the recalcitrant Zelter to authorize the performance of the passion.[5] But Devrient's rhetoric – his pitting of youthful vision against a calcified status quo – points to a more fundamental truth that cannot be gainsaid: his generation's readiness to embrace the reclamation of the past as a bold new frontier.

The architectural surroundings of the Passion revival were themselves emblematic of the project at hand. The Singakademie's hall, four years old at the time, was based on an 1818 design by Prussia's leading architect, Karl Friedrich Schinkel, conceived as one of a series of neo-classical structures through which Schinkel was systematically implanting the Prussian people's cultural ambitions upon their capital city's increasingly imposing skyline.[6] His Schauspielhaus had opened in 1821 (Mendelssohn himself had attended the first performance there: the epoch-making premiere of Weber's *Der Freischütz*), and his massive Altes Museum was, by 1829, nearing completion at the northern end of the Lustgarten. The lesson of such projects was clear: its music, its drama, and its art mattered to this German audience – for whom the humiliations of Napoleon's onslaught were none too distant a memory, who raced to match economic stride with the more robustly industrialized capitals of France and England – not so much as cycles of commodities created, consumed, and shortly exchanged for newer ones, but as public institutions, victoriously embedded in the cartographies of their city and of their emerging cultural identity.

Where the musical culture of the 1830s and 1840s was concerned, no one played a greater role in this process of embedment than Mendelssohn. Outside the operatic industry, none of his consequential contemporaries – Beethoven, Schubert, Schumann, Berlioz, Liszt, or Chopin – led a life so effortlessly and universally mapped out by biographers in terms of the institutions he served. At the same time, the course of Mendelssohn's career provides a nearly comprehensive catalogue of the venues through which his generation undertook serious music-making, dispersed as his activities were across the realms of choral society, public music festival, professional orchestra, opera house (at least briefly), church, royal court, and beyond. Lurking beneath all is the apparent conviction that what mattered was not only – not even principally – what individuals could create, but what the public could be taught to value. What mattered in the end was what could be institutionalized, woven securely into the cultural, intellectual, economic, spiritual, even architectural fabric that comprised Germany's nascent nationhood. Mendelssohn's professional life was a sustained demonstration that the weaving of this fabric constituted as creative, disciplined a venture as composition itself.

This creative outlook came naturally to the scion of the Mendelssohn family, whose remarkable, generations-long journey seemed impelled by the conviction that there was no greater good than full intellectual, economic, and cultural enfranchisement, and no higher calling than the call to citizenship. Mendelssohn's mother, Lea, was the granddaughter of Daniel Itzig, financial adviser to Friedrich II and one of Prussia's richest inhabitants; Itzig would become the first Jew in Prussia to be granted a patent of naturalization. Felix's father, Abraham – who had made a sizeable fortune of his own in banking – was the son of the celebrated Moses Mendelssohn, who had emerged from a humble childhood in the town of Dessau to become one of the leading philosophers of the Enlightenment, and the first Jew to travel as an intellectual equal among the inhabitants of Berlin's most elite cultural circle. Moses' oldest daughter, Brendel (known in adulthood as Dorothea), played a central role – along with her friends Rahel Levin and Henriette Herz – in the brilliant "salon" culture that had grown up by the turn of the century around homes like her parents', numbering among her acquaintances Friedrich Schleiermacher, Johann Gottlieb Fichte, Alexander and Wilhelm von Humboldt, and Wilhelm and Friedrich Schlegel (the latter she eventually married). Her younger sister, Henriette, hosted a highly successful salon of her own in Paris in the early years of the nineteenth century.

Though salon culture was in a state of general decline in the course of Felix's childhood, one would hardly have guessed as much from the steady stream of intellectual and artistic figures that passed through his Berlin home, particularly after the family's 1825 move to a palatial new property at 3 Leipzigerstraße. As a teenager Felix could boast acquaintance with a host of luminaries that included historical philosopher Georg Wilhelm Friedrich Hegel, natural scientist Alexander von Humboldt, philologist Gustav Droysen, orientalist Friedrich Rosen, and music critic and historian Adolph Bernhard Marx.

At the same time, Abraham and Lea brought every available resource to bear on the educations of their children (Fanny, born 1805; Felix, born 1809; Rebecka, born 1811; and Paul, born 1812). Tradition holds that, by Felix's sixth year, he and Fanny had begun receiving lessons in French and mathematics from their father, and in literature, art, and German from their mother.[7] Felix studied for two years (1816–18) at the *Lehr-, Pensions-, und Erziehungsanstalt*, a private elementary school.[8] Dr. Carl Wilhelm Ludwig Heyse was brought on board as *Hauslehrer* in 1819, directing Felix's studies in geography, mathematics, history, French, and Greek (at which he excelled). By this time, Felix and Fanny – both of them already pianists of staggering achievement – had begun taking lessons at the instrument with Ludwig Berger. Felix's violin lessons with Carl Wilhelm Henning began in 1819, and he would become an accomplished landscape artist under the guidance of painter Gottlob Samuel Rösel.

Nowhere were Felix's industry, creativity, and intellectual acumen more in evidence, though, than in the work in music theory and composition he began under the direction of Singakademie director Carl Friedrich Zelter in 1819. Basing his teaching firmly on J. P. Kirnberger's pedagogical method, which was based in turn on J. S. Bach's, Zelter led Mendelssohn through a rigorous program of study in figured bass, chorale, and counterpoint.[9] By his fifteenth year, Mendelssohn was producing large-scale chamber, orchestral, and piano works of which most professional composers would have been justly proud. With the 1825 completion of the String Octet op. 20, these gave way to masterpieces. He had also, by this point, achieved no small prowess as a conductor through the direction of various ensembles that gathered at the Mendelssohn's Sunday musicales, a tradition that began around 1822.

By the time of the *St. Matthew Passion* revival, the twenty-year-old Mendelssohn thus presented a very impressive package indeed, of which his stunning compositional accomplishments were only a single facet. Throughout his life, Mendelssohn's facility at both piano and organ rarely failed to delight, though his assiduous refusal of bravura display for its own sake left the bulk of contemporary commentators at a loss as to where he ranked among his generation's towering piano virtuosi. A *Harmonicon* review of a performance of 13 May 1833 encapsulates those features of his playing almost universally acknowledged – its accuracy, its faithfulness to the letter of the score, and, where appropriate, his preternatural gift at improvisation:

> The performance of Mozart's concerto by M. Mendelssohn was perfect. The scrupulous exactness with which he gave the author's text, without a single addition or new reading of his own, the precision in his time, together with the extraordinary accuracy of his execution, excited the admiration of all present; and this was increased almost to rapture, by his two extemporaneous cadences [i.e., cadenzas], in which he adverted with great address to the subjects of the concerto, and wrought up his audience almost to the same pitch of enthusiasm which he himself had arrived at. The whole of this concerto he played from memory.[10]

It is hardly faint praise to say that Mendelssohn held his own in the crowded field of piano virtuosi, but the last sentence of this review points to an aspect of Mendelssohn's musical persona – his musical memory – in which he had no peer. The excitement that gathered around the Singakademie's rehearsals for the *St. Matthew Passion* performance centered not only on the epiphanic impression of the gigantic work itself, but on the fact that its meticulous young conductor seemed to know every note by heart, directing rehearsals entirely from memory. At his English keyboard debut, in a concert of 30 May 1829, Mendelssohn electrified the audience by playing Weber's *Konzertstück* (still an unknown piece in England) from memory, a feat he repeated routinely across a range of even the most difficult repertoire. Anecdotes abound of private displays just as amazing to his contemporaries. One, which must stand for many, comes from Ferdinand Hiller's recollections of an event at one of Abbé Bardin's weekly musical gatherings in Paris, during Mendelssohn's visit to the city during the winter of 1832:

I [Hiller] had just been playing Beethoven's E flat Concerto in public, and they asked for it again on one of these afternoons. The parts were all there, and the string quartet too, but no players for the wind. "I will do the wind," said Mendelssohn, and sitting down to a small piano which stood near the grand one, he filled in the wind parts from memory, so completely, that I don't believe even a note of the second horn was wanting, and all as simply and naturally done as if it were nothing.[11]

Mendelssohn was known throughout his life as an exacting conductor, but so consummate in musicianship and so gentlemanly in manner that few complained. His ability to bring forth, on the one hand, the best capacities of an ensemble and, on the other, his vision of a work quickly became the stuff of legends: "Nobody certainly," wrote Julius Benedict, "ever knew better how to communicate, as if by an electric fluid, his own conception of a work to a large body of performers."[12] Though Mendelssohn was not the first to conduct with a baton,[13] he played a substantive role in standardizing the practice, and, indeed, for ushering in the era of the modern conductor as *auteur*.[14]

Yet Mendelssohn's upbringing had equipped him not only with a staggering array of capabilities, but with an extraordinarily robust configuration of professional aspirations: an amalgam of nationalistically tinted intellectualism, a civil service ethos, and the strong desire for financial and geographic stability. And underlying all – largely explaining the occasional misfires that would punctuate his early career – was the drive to achieve the broadest and most lasting possible impact. "I cannot quite agree with you in your not pointing out a positive vocation for Felix,"[15] Abraham's brother-in-law, Jacob Bartholdy, had chafed. "The idea of a professional musician will not go down with me. It is no career, no life, no aim; in the beginning you are just as far as at the end . . ." Felix's whole professional life seemed impelled by the need to prove these sentiments mistaken.

A month after conducting the *St. Matthew Passion* revival, Mendelssohn left for England, the first phase of a three-year period occupied largely in travel. After a brief return to Berlin for the winter and early spring of 1830 – during which he was offered, and declined, the chair of music at the University of Berlin – he set off on the more substantial portion of the Grand Tour, highlighted with stays in Rome, Paris, and, once more, London, from which he returned to Berlin in June 1832. Though he did not conceive of the trip as a professional tour – his stated aim was simply to seek out the proper locale in which to begin his career – he found plentiful opportunities to perform. Indeed, only a few weeks into his initial sojourn in London the English public made it abundantly clear that a brilliant musical career was already underway.[16] He conducted the Philharmonic Society in performances of his

Symphony no. 1 op. 11 and the *Midsummer Night's Dream* Overture to wildly enthusiastic crowds;[17] just as dazzling was the impression he made from the keyboard, in Weber's *Konzertstück* and Beethoven's "Emperor" Concerto. Mendelssohn returned to England nine times before his death, and would maintain close ties with the Philharmonic Society and with a range of English publishers and choral societies for the remainder of his career.[18]

Carl Friedrich Zelter died on 15 May 1832, leaving vacant the directorship of Berlin's Singakademie. Mendelssohn, then in London, had been all but absent from the city's musical life for over three years (he did not perform publicly during his five-month stay in the city between December 1829 and May 1830).[19] Despite the glories of the *St. Matthew Passion* revival, and of his rapidly advancing international reputation, Mendelssohn was not the obvious choice as Zelter's successor: that honor belonged to Karl Friedrich Rungenhagen, who had for nineteen years served capably as Zelter's assistant, and who directed the choir at Zelter's 18 May funeral.[20]

It appears to have been chiefly under pressure from his family, and from friend Eduard Devrient, that Mendelssohn undertook his half-hearted pursuit of the Singakademie directorship. In a letter of 5 September 1832, he expressed to long-time friend Karl Klingemann both his lack of enthusiasm for the post (or, indeed, for Berlin in general) and his certainty that he would not be offered it: "then [comes] the whole motionless, stagnating Berlin backwater, then the negotiations about the Academy, with which they torment me more than is right, in order, in the end, to select their Rungenhagen or God knows whom."[21] The matter came to a vote on 22 January 1833, when Mendelssohn was roundly defeated by Rungenhagen, 148 ballots to 88.[22] Though Eric Werner discerns in Mendelssohn's loss "the severest trauma of his life"[23] – and follows Devrient in supposing anti-Semitism to have played an important role – William Little has pointed judiciously to a host of reasons that the Singakademie might have preferred the established Rungenhagen to the ambitious, yet unsettled, young Mendelssohn, and just as many reasons to rejoice that Mendelssohn did not begin his career tied to this city or this organization.[24]

At the same time, Mendelssohn's stay in Berlin through these months was hardly a total professional loss. His ties to London's Philharmonic Society had been strengthened in November 1832 by a commission for three new works (the "Italian" Symphony would be the first instalment), and he offered a series of highly successful concerts in which his own music figured prominently alongside that of Bach, Beethoven, Weber, and others.[25] Most importantly, however, by the end of the winter he had received an invitation to conduct the fifteenth Lower Rhine Music Festival, being held in Düsseldorf at the end of May. Thus began a relationship that would continue happily through the rest of his life.

By 1833, the Lower Rhine Music Festival was already well on its way toward establishing itself as a pioneering display, in Cecilia Hopkins Porter's terms, of "the process by which an expanding, increasingly affluent, enlightened, and urban bourgeoisie acquired control over the musical establishment and provided the substance of a new mass public."[26] Its participants were almost exclusively amateur musicians, drawn from across Prussia's Rhine Province. Düsseldorf, Cologne, Aachen, and Elberfeld – among various configurations of which the festival had rotated since its 1818 inception – all enjoyed lively, decades-long traditions of civic music-making, an arena with which Mendelssohn was shortly to become well acquainted. Initially a two-day event (it moved toward a three-day format in the course of Mendelssohn's tenure), the festival almost invariably followed a single template: an oratorio was sung on the first day, Handel's outdistancing all others in popularity; a concert followed on the second day, generally setting off with a Beethoven symphony. The 1833 festival was built around Handel's *Israel in Egypt* and Beethoven's "Pastoral" Symphony, a piece that had not yet received a hearing at one of these events. The impression made by the young conductor received ample testimony in the supervisory committee's decision to carry through with their tentative plan to extend the proceedings into a third day, for the first time in the festival's history. The third day's concert, which became an increasingly regular event in the subsequent years, tended toward a *potpourri* of instrumental and vocal music.[27]

The 1833 festival would turn out to be the first of seven that Mendelssohn would conduct, the last coming the year before his death.[28] It was at the 1836 festival that his own first oratorio, *St. Paul*, was premiered; two years later, in Cologne, Mendelssohn programmed J. S. Bach's *Ascension Oratorio*, the first work of Bach's to receive a hearing at one of these events. The festival's prestige built steadily through the years of Mendelssohn's involvement, its directorship, by the time of his death, having emerged as one of Germany's most coveted musical assignments (by the end of the century, its former conductors would include Louis Spohr, Gaspare Spontini, Robert Schumann, Franz Liszt, Johannes Brahms, and Richard Strauss).

Through the late 1830s, particularly in the wake of the *St. Paul* premiere, Mendelssohn became a familiar face at a range of similar gatherings across Germany and England. The year 1837 found him conducting his oratorio at the Birmingham Festival, to which he would return in 1840 and 1846. He conducted *St. Paul* again at the Brunswick Music Festival in 1839, and again at Schwerin's 1840 North German Music Festival. He would take part, too, in the Zweibrücken Music Festival of 1844, and in the 1846 German–Flemish Choral Festival in Cologne.

The most significant immediate result of Mendelssohn's participation in Düsseldorf's 1833 Lower Rhine Music Festival, however, was the offer of work of a more regular kind: the musical directorship of the city. A town of around 24,000,[29] Düsseldorf enjoyed a thriving musical life, if necessarily limited (as Mendelssohn would soon come to understand well) by the rather restricted pool of local talent. The post of musical director had been created in 1812, held by Friedrich August Burgmüller from that year until his death in 1824, and had stood vacant since then.[30] Under the terms of his contract, Mendelssohn was provided a salary of 600 thaler a year, for which he would assume the directorship of the city's orchestral and choral societies, together with the direction of music in the city's churches.

The first task facing Mendelssohn upon his arrival in October (he had spent the summer in England with his father) was the preparation of an entertainment for the visit of Prussian Crown Prince Friedrich Wilhelm, to be undertaken in collaboration with local painters at the Düsseldorf Kunstakademie, Schadow, Hildebrandt, and Schirmer. What materialized was a reprise of choruses from Handel's *Israel in Egypt*, with Mendelssohn at the piano, as accompaniment to a series of *tableaux vivants*.

Handel's oratorios were to play a central role through Mendelssohn's entire stint in Düsseldorf, his work in the city comprising a landmark in the progress of Handel's German reputation.[31] *Alexander's Feast, Messiah, Solomon, Judas Maccabaeus*, and the *"Dettingen" Te Deum* all received hearings, together with Haydn's *The Seasons* and *The Creation*. Overtures by Gluck, Weber, and Cherubini factored importantly among instrumental offerings, together with Mendelssohn's own G minor Piano Concerto op. 25, and ambitious swaths of Beethoven (including the Third, Fourth, and Seventh Symphonies, the "Egmont" Overture, and the C minor Piano Concerto).[32]

Düsseldorf was a predominantly Catholic city; it had been part of the Holy Roman Empire until 1806, when it passed into Napoleon's Rhenish Confederation, thence, under the 1815 terms reached at the Congress of Vienna, into Prussia's Rhine Province. Though the Protestant Mendelssohn could not enter into the direction of Catholic church music with more than an imprecise sense of religious conviction, his artistic convictions served him just as well. His monthly performances of sacred music find him assuming proudly the mantle of the reformer, most significantly in his struggle to give public expression to his own long-time devotion to sacred music of the sixteenth and early seventeenth centuries. Mendelssohn admired Justus Thibaut's influential 1825 book on the subject, *Über Reinheit der Tonkunst*, and had enjoyed a warm personal encounter with the author during an 1827 visit to Heidelberg. In the course of his 1830–31 sojourn in Rome, he had sought out Giuseppe Baini, an expert on Palestrina, and plunged enthusiastically into Fortunato Santini's collection of Italian sacred polyphony.[33] Finding no such music in Düsseldorf's repositories, Mendelssohn struck out, only days after his arrival, for Elberfeld, Cologne, and Bonn, gathering what was to be had of the sacred music of Palestrina, Lotti, Leo, and Lasso. Despite his aversion to Haydn's "skandalös lustig"[34] masses, he pressed these, too, into use, along with masses by Mozart, Cherubini, and Beethoven, and a sampling of Bach's cantatas.[35]

From Mendelssohn's Düsseldorf tenure dates his only period of service to the production of opera, and this period was not, in the balance, a very happy one. He had crossed paths before with the intendant of Düsseldorf's theater, playwright and author Karl Leberecht Immermann: in response to an 1831 commission to provide an opera for the Munich theater, Mendelssohn had turned to Immermann for a libretto, settling on the idea of Shakespeare's *The Tempest*. Though Mendelssohn had ultimately rejected Immermann's work on the project, the author retained sufficient confidence in the young musician to pull for his 1833 appointment in Düsseldorf,[36] and now hoped Mendelssohn would join him in his ambitions to found a new German theater. Their first enterprise was the staging of a series of "model productions" ("Mustervorstellungen" – Immermann's term), initiated with a meticulously rehearsed staging of *Don Giovanni* on 19 December 1833. Those that followed included Weber's *Oberon* and *Der Freischütz* and Mozart's *Die Entführung aus dem Serail* and *Die Zauberflöte*.

Mendelssohn appears to have taken genuine joy in the conducting of opera, recalling to his father the opening night of Cherubini's *Les deux journées* (in March 1834), "[i]t was the most pleasurable evening I have had in the theater in a long time, for I took part in the performance as a spectator, smiling and clapping along, and shouting bravos, yet conducting vivaciously all along."[37] But the administrative duties of the job he did not enjoy in the slightest. As plans for the new theater moved ahead through 1834, increasing turbulence in his relationship with Immermann and Mendelssohn's annoyance with the burdens of assembling a company of musicians from the meager available talent left him less enthusiastic than ever about his involvement in the whole enterprise. Matters came to a head on 2 November, less than a week after the official opening of the new theater, when – to the horror of his father – Mendelssohn cast professional decorum to the wind and summarily resigned all theatrical duties outside of occasional conducting.[38]

He would probably never have taken such an extreme step had he not already arrived at the conclusion that he was meant for greater things than Düsseldorf could provide; he shortly began taking measures to withdraw a year early from his three-year commitment there. The last concert of his tenure took place on 2 July 1835, by which time, however, the twenty-six-year-old had secured the post that would make his career.

In the course of his final winter in Düsseldorf, Mendelssohn had completed negotiations with Leipzig's town council that led to his appointment as that city's musical director and the conductor of its Gewandhaus Orchestra and Thomasschule. His first appearance with the orchestra took place on 4 October 1835, a wildly successful program that included his own *Calm Sea and Prosperous Voyage* Overture and Beethoven's Fourth Symphony. Mendelssohn's work with this orchestra continued in one form or another to the last year of his life.

The city of Leipzig enjoyed a cultural influence well out of proportion to its population (around 45,000); it was home to one of Germany's premier universities, and its dozens of presses produced a substantial fraction of the books published in Germany, including much of its music. The Gewandhaus Orchestra – housed in a city-owned building and governed by a municipal board of directors – had been a noteworthy ensemble for over fifty years.[39] Mozart performed there in 1789, and the orchestra had played a leading role in the early promotion of Beethoven's symphonies. In Mendelssohn's hands, it became Germany's leading orchestra, and one of the most influential musical institutions in Europe.

It became clear at once that Mendelssohn's vision of the conductor's job involved a considerably higher degree of control over the ensemble than previous conductors had sought to exercise. Instrumental music, formerly led by the concertmaster from his desk, was now given over to direction by the conductor himself (though Mendelssohn's concertmaster, Ferdinand David, was one of Europe's most able, and routinely took over conducting duties during Mendelssohn's absences). Mendelssohn also insisted on personally overseeing the direction of as many rehearsals as possible. At the same time, he worked energetically behind the scenes toward insuring better pay for the musicians themselves. What emerged under his guidance was one of the early nineteenth century's clearest models for the modern professional symphony orchestra.

The Gewandhaus concert season, which ran from Michaelmas (29 September) to Easter, was built around twenty subscription concerts, supplemented by benefit concerts for visiting virtuosi, occasional concerts for charitable causes, and chamber concerts. Where repertoire was concerned, Mendelssohn's central objective appears to have been providing the Leipzig public sustained exposure to the music of Mozart and Beethoven; the work of these two proliferates among the overtures, symphonies, concertos, and operatic excerpts (where Beethoven is, to be sure, at something of a disadvantage) that form the core of the orchestra's offerings.[40] In the realm of overture, Cherubini, Spohr, and Weber were also well represented, with Mendelssohn's own concert overtures emerging as perennial favorites. Where concertos were concerned, Mendelssohn was at his most adventurous in the reclamation of a number of J. S. Bach's works in the genre (he also programmed Bach's orchestral suites). At the same time, his commitment to supporting what he considered the worthiest of newer compositions – Ignaz Moscheles, Ferdinand Hiller, and Niels Gade were among those most enthusiastically promoted – yielded an especially impressive crop of symphonic premieres, including the newly discovered C major symphony of Schubert, and Schumann's First, Second, and Fourth. If the vocal components of these concerts tended to draw most heavily on the operas of Gluck, Mozart, Beethoven, Cherubini, and Weber, this did not preclude offerings from Rossini, Bellini, and Donizetti as well. The orchestra also had the opportunity, through Mendelssohn's years, to share the stage with the most eminent touring virtuosi of the day, Franz Liszt, Sigismund Thalberg, Alexander Dreyschock, Clara Schumann, Ignaz Moscheles, and the young prodigy Joseph Joachim among them.

A highlight of Mendelssohn's years in Leipzig were three cycles of "historical concerts," offered during the winters of 1838, 1841, and 1847 (by which time declining health forced him to share some of his conducting duties with Niels Gade). Though each series unfolded chronologically, these were intended not so much to survey the entire consequential history of music as Mendelssohn understood it, but, in Donald Mintz's words, "to demonstrate the continuity of the tradition."[41] Thus Italian polyphony is passed over altogether in favor of a coherent three- or four-concert trajectory that moves from an opening instrumental work of Bach to a symphony of Beethoven and beyond.[42] The 1838 series cast its net wide, sampling the work of Bach, Handel, Gluck, Viotti, Righini, Cimarosa, Haydn, Naumann, Mozart, Salieri, Romberg, Méhul, Vogler, Weber, and Beethoven. While the 1847 series followed a similar design, the four concerts of the 1841 series focused on five canonical composers alone, the first dedicated to Bach and Handel, the next three devoted exclusively to Haydn, Mozart, and Beethoven in turn. In keeping with the spirit of these concerts was Mendelssohn's 6 August 1840 organ recital at the Thomaskirche, comprised entirely of Bach's work (apart from a concluding "*Freie Phantasie*");[43] the proceeds of the event went toward the erection of a new Bach monument.

Though the death of his father only a few weeks into Mendelssohn's Leipzig tenure came as a devastating blow, his first years in the city appear to have been among his life's happiest. During the summer of 1836, while temporarily relieving his ailing friend Johann Nepomuk Schelble of the direction of Frankfurt am Main's Cäcilienverein, Mendelssohn undertook the courtship of Cécile Jeanrenaud, whom he would marry on 28 March of the following year. The marriage produced five children, and appears to have been a remarkably happy one, routinely depicted as flawless in the memoirs and biographical sketches of Mendelssohn's sympathetic contemporaries (Charles Edward Horsley would later enthuse, "In all relations of life, as a son, a husband, and a father, he was humanly speaking perfect.").[44] Though recent scholars tend to look with a kind of patronizing smile toward the image of the Mendelssohns' family life as one of unsullied domestic *Gemütlichkeit*, it has not been proven substantively false.

The June 1840 coronation of Prussia's King Friedrich Wilhelm IV was the first in a series of events that would ultimately pull a reluctant Mendelssohn away from his fortunate situation in Leipzig. Christian Karl Josias von Bunsen, the scholar and diplomat who acted as adviser in the development of Friedrich Wilhelm's grandiose plans for Prussia's intellectual and artistic revitalization, soon arrived at a three-tiered scheme for "reintroducing the most beautiful and noble music into life," calling for a new educational institution, for "really appropriate music for the Divine Services," and for performances of great oratorios, old and new.[45] Bunsen names Mendelssohn as the only logical choice for the job.

A first step in the execution of these plans came that November, when Mendelssohn was offered the directorship of music at the Academy of Arts, together with an invitation to conduct several concerts annually.[46] Though the plan called for the development of a full-blown conservatory from the music section at the Academy, Mendelssohn was skeptical, and dragged his feet in the matter. The following August, he at last moved to Berlin to begin a "trial year," on the understanding that if nothing of consequence had happened by the end of that period – and Mendelssohn strongly doubted that anything would – he would be free to return to Leipzig.[47] He received the title of Kapellmeister in September, by which time he still had only the sketchiest sense of what he had been hired to do.

As Mendelssohn had anticipated, the conservatory failed to materialize in the course of the year that followed. The most rewarding event of his tenure had been the commission to produce incidental music for a staging of Sophocles' *Antigone* (op. 55), premiered in Potsdam on 28 October (the incidental music to Shakespeare's *Midsummer Night's Dream* would follow two years later). By June 1842, Friedrich Wilhelm – aware of Mendelssohn's mounting dissatisfaction – had shifted his focus from his educational agenda to the matter of sacred music, proposing that Mendelssohn be placed "in charge of all Evangelical Church music in the monarchy."[48] Mendelssohn had no interest whatever in such a post, and had resolved, by October, to quit the city once and for all.[49] The king responded to Mendelssohn's resignation with an offer the composer could not bring himself to refuse: a choir and small orchestra were to be assembled to provide music for services in the cathedral, and Mendelssohn was to lead them, but was free to return to Leipzig until this ensemble was actually established. In exchange for this freedom, Mendelssohn happily surrendered half of his 3,000-thaler salary. He wasted no time in quitting Berlin and returning to his duties at the Gewandhaus (where he had little immediate use for his new title of *Generalmusikdirektor* for church music).

Through the summer of 1843, by which time the choir had indeed been organized, negotiations still dragged on as to Mendelssohn's precise duties, particularly as they bore on the musicians of the royal orchestra. In November, he at last moved his family once more to Berlin, where he was charged both to work with the cathedral choir and to share the conducting of symphony concerts with opera director Wilhelm Taubert. Striving to make sense of the musical stipulations of the newly revised Prussian liturgy – Mendelssohn would shortly run afoul of ecclesiastical authorities on the particular question of the orchestra's appropriateness in church music – he provided a number of works for the choir's Christmas, New Year's Day, Passion Sunday, and Good Friday performances, chief among which were several *a cappella* Psalms (published as op. 78) and verse settings (four of which are included in op. 79), and a setting of Psalm 98 with orchestra (op. 91).[50] After Holy Week, Mendelssohn disembarked for several months of travel, including a good deal of concertizing in London through the late spring. When he returned to Berlin in September, it was to chiefly to negotiate for his immediate withdrawal from the city's musical life. Requesting no more than the fulfillment of occasional commissions, and reducing Mendelssohn's salary to 1,000 thaler, Friedrich Wilhelm released the composer from his duties; Mendelssohn left the city at the end of November.

If the situation in Berlin had yielded almost ceaseless frustrations, these years witnessed a much more fortunate series of events in Leipzig. Lawyer Heinrich Blümner had died in February 1839, leaving in the hands of Saxon King Friedrich August II a 20,000 thaler bequest which Blümner had stipulated must go toward the founding or maintenance of a national institute of arts or science. On 8 April 1840, Mendelssohn submitted a petition that the bequest be used for the founding of a music academy.

The petition itself is a rhetorical tour de force, in which Mendelssohn – with the vaguest undercurrent of self-congratulation – takes the full measure of Leipzig's position in the European musical landscape:

[F]or that branch of art that will always remain a principal foundation of
musical studies, for the most elevated instrumental and sacred compositions
in their very numerous concerts and performances in church, Leipzig has
material for the formation (*Bildungsmittel*) of young musical artists in a
supply few other German cities can offer. Through the lively interest with
which the major works of the great masters have, for the last fifty years, been
here (often for the first time in Germany) recognised and taken up, through
the care with which they have continually been brought forth, Leipzig has
assumed an eminent position among the musical cities of the fatherland . . .

[The academy] would give musical activities here an impetus whose
influence would very soon and for ever after be most beneficially
disseminated.[51]

The petition was ultimately granted, and a two-story house erected for the
purpose in the courtyard of the Gewandhaus.[52] In the first week of April
1843, the conservatory officially opened.

The three-year course of study it provided was intended, as the conservatory's prospectus put it, to comprise "all practical and theoretical branches of
music viewed both as an art and as a scholarly discipline."[53] Regular atten-
dance at rehearsals and performances of the Gewandhaus orchestra and
other local music organizations – the *Bildungsmittel* of which Mendelssohn
was so justly proud – was required of all students, symbolically uniting the
specific educational agenda of the conservatory with the broader, public
educational agenda the ensembles had always, in Mendelssohn's view, been
meant to serve.

The faculty was itself a distinguished group, including Robert Schumann
(who taught piano and score reading), Ferdinand David (who taught violin),
and the choirmaster of the Thomaskirche, Moritz Hauptmann (who offered
instruction in harmony and composition). Mendelssohn himself took an
active role in the teaching of composition, singing, and instruments, though,
as Donald Mintz points out, the bulk of his duties where performance was
concerned probably resembled "master classes," in modern parlance, more
than systematic instruction.[54] In the years that followed, Clara Schumann,
Ferdinand Hiller, Niels Gade, and Ignaz Moscheles would join the ranks of
the school's instructors.

After his November 1844 departure from Berlin, Mendelssohn took up
residence in Frankfurt for what amounted to an extended vacation from
professional commitments. His health was declining, and it had become
clear by the time of his August 1845 return to his Gewandhaus duties that he
could no longer sustain his former level of activity. He shared the conducting
of the orchestra with Niels Gade through this season and, acting on the advice
of his physician, retired from piano performance early in 1846. Yet other

conducting obligations continued to press: the end of May found him in Aachen conducting the Lower Rhine Music Festival; two weeks later came the German-Flemish Festival in Cologne; on 26 August, the premiere of *Elijah* in Birmingham.

The conducting of the 1846–47 Gewandhaus concerts was once more divided between Mendelssohn and Gade, though it was clear to all by now that the older man's health was failing. In April, at the season's close, Mendelssohn gathered his remaining strength for a trip to England, where he conducted a series of performances of *Elijah*. In May, in the course of his journey home, he received word of the sudden death of his sister, Fanny, a blow from which he would not recover. Mendelssohn suffered a small stroke on 9 October, another on the 28th, and a third on 3 November; he died the following evening.[55]

In a letter of 28 March 1834, the 25-year-old Mendelssohn had offered his father a glimpse of the optimism that had carried him through his first months in Düsseldorf, and a kernel, surely, of the credo underpinning the brilliant career that was just then beginning to unfold:

> A good performance in the Dusseldorf theater does not, to be sure, spread throughout the world, and scarcely, no doubt, beyond the *Düssels*; but if I please and delight both myself and all those in the house through and through in favor of good music, that is something attractive![56]

Few manifestations of the moody, depressive behavior to which Mendelssohn fell increasingly prone in the final stage of his life are quite as tragic as those intermittent signs that he had fundamentally ceased believing what he once had about the significance of musical performance, or, more broadly speaking, of the institutions he had so labored to build up. As he wrote to his friend, pianist Ignaz Moscheles, on 7 March 1845, "From all this directing and these public musical performances so little is gained even by the public itself, – a little better, a little worse, what does it matter? how easily is it forgotten!"[57]

These final words sound, indeed, like the voice of despair. But where Mendelssohn's own stunning professional achievements are concerned, they could hardly be more wrong.

2 Mendelssohn and Judaism

MICHAEL P. STEINBERG

In 1974 the distinguished musicologist Carl Dahlhaus published an edited
volume called *The Mendelssohn Problem: Das Problem Mendelssohn*.[1] The
book's preface makes reference to the recent increase in attention to the
composer in scholarly as well as performing venues, abetted by the 125th
anniversary of his death in 1972. To speak of a Mendelssohn renaissance,
Dahlhaus emphasizes in his opening sentence, would be a great exaggeration.
This gambit would be equally valid today. The title of this 1974 volume –
as Dahlhaus must have known when he chose it – raises the red flags of
several controversies and confusions, which have likewise remained unre-
solved in the intervening thirty years. Immediately, it conjures a rhetorical,
ideological, and political parallel: the Mendelssohn problem, "the Jewish
problem." If, in other words, there is a "problem" with Mendelssohn the
man or with Mendelssohn the music, the titular phrase works only in the
shadow of the larger cultural issue. Is Mendelssohn a minor composer? In
the present context we must bracket the question. We would not expect
ever to read a book about the Puccini problem, the Mascagni problem, or
the Rimsky-Korsakov problem. The Meyerbeer problem, perhaps. But that
is the point. It is the abiding cultural anxiety of anti-Semitism or about
anti-Semitism that casts an aura over these nineteenth-century composers,
fusing and confusing the judgments of their cultural and aesthetic validity.
Before 1960 and his elevation to canonic status, Gustav Mahler would likely
have appeared as the third man in the group.

Dahlhaus' *Problemstellung* and the arguments of his contributors stick
closely to the realm of the music and its musicological reception. All problems are musical and musicological; the Mendelssohn "problem" involves
first and foremost the legacy of Classicism. Occasionally Dahlhaus' asser-
tions seem to beg for a contextual discussion. For generations, he says,
Mendelssohn reception has suffered from the stereotyping of the composer (8). The source and logic of that stereotyping, Wagner's 1850 essay *Das
Judentum in der Musik*, is mentioned only once in the volume.[2] Dahlhaus
and his contributors share a tacit fear of friction, which accompanies their
wish to rehabilitate Mendelssohn without avowing, let alone opening, the
ideological Pandora's box that made a "problem" of him in the first place.
But perhaps it is unfair to impugn the scholars for their silence; Mendelssohn
himself rarely addressed the issue of his family's Jewish past, obeying what

Arnaldo Momigliano once called "the taboo . . . deeply ingrained" within the converted German Jewish community of Berlin and their discussion of – and their silences about – Judaism.[3] Indeed, the published selections from Mendelssohn's some five thousand surviving letters – as undertaken first by J. G. Droysen and Paul Mendelssohn-Bartholdy in 1860 and again by Rudolf Elvers in 1984 – confirm the general aura of silence and taboo around subjects Jewish. Scholars who have read the five thousand letters (as I have not) may have a different impression of their referential content than I have. But this would surprise me.

A taboo breeds a certain kind of silence: the silence born of the significance and pressure of an issue, precisely not of its irrelevance. Mendelssohn's relation to Judaism, his family's Judaism, the Jewish culture of Biedermeier Germany, indeed to his own Judaism as a dimension of his emotional and symbolic self-definition – all of these refractions should be of abiding interest to his ongoing reception. Mendelssohn's relation to Judaism is a song without many words.

There is no Mendelssohn problem, just as there is no Jewish problem. Like its better-known and more invidious analogue, the "Mendelssohn problem" needs always to wear its scare quotes. Both of them are phantoms; ideological impositions, phantoms of history, invented yet powerful: haunting, violent. The "Mendelssohn" and "Jewish" problems emerge from the anxiety of classification. Classification is an act of authority, of control. Let me state here this essay's central argument: Mendelssohn and modern Jewish experience share a resistance to classification. As I develop my argument, I will try to explore the character and the depth of this parallel. How immanent is it, how inherent to Mendelssohn's aesthetic? Can we understand the Judaism in Mendelssohn's music while removing ourselves from the violence of posterity that Wagner initiated in 1850? Conversely, can we understand the depth and limits of Mendelssohn's Jewish identification while disavowing both the implication that beneath a Lutheran façade lies some kind of authentic or even conventional Jewish essence?

The anxiety of classification is a characteristic of European modernity and hence a catalyst of the thinking that many thinkers call post-modern. The category of the post-modern resists that inheritance of the Enlightenment, at once epistemological and political, that claims the transparency of the knowable world and that responds to such transparency with an agenda of classification and objectification. As the world begins to seem less transparent, more bewildering – a central development of the nineteenth century – the anxiety of classification accumulates. Anti-Semitism figures among its most desperate symptoms. Anti-Semitism involves a hostile classification of a cultural "other." The drive to classification has also a self-objectifying dimension. Thus the European Jews who participated in the making of European modernity found themselves compelled – even apart from the pressure of anti-Semitism – to question their own identity: to assert the immutability of tradition and thereby their own ahistoricity; to invent a new dialectic between tradition and modernity; to define modernity as good and Christian and to join the majority through assimilation and/or conversion.

The philosopher Moses Mendelssohn initiated the new dialectic in the 1780s. His legacy grounds a new Judaism in a new social and political world – before either of them was ready to come into material existence. His seminal work *Jerusalem* (1784) argues first for the rigorous separation of church and state, second for the modern viability of Judaism as a culture of law compatible with such a constitutional separation. Moses Mendelssohn's refusal to provide a system of self-classification (call it "identity" if you like) for modern Jewry seemed to give many of his Jewish readers too little to hold onto. Famously, and symptomatically, his son Abraham morphed his father's rigorous secularity into a path of assimilation and conversion. His move was representative of his generation. In 1815 Abraham Mendelssohn converted his young children Fanny and Felix, and in 1822 entered the Lutheran church himself, together with his wife. Felix Mendelssohn came of age as a Lutheran with a strong and perforce irresolvable appreciation of his family's Jewish history. Two generations too late for his grandfather's Enlightenment, his lifespan unfolded one generation short of the major internal choices and innovations that German Jewry would take in the 1840s – namely, neo-orthodoxy and reform. The historical moment of Felix Mendelssohn is thus especially difficult to classify.

Felix Mendelssohn's Lutheranism is not in dispute. His Jewish legacy remains important and intricate nonetheless, and it is matched by what I would call his Jewish subjectivity. This term requires definition. In my work I understand the term subjectivity to attach to the life of the subject in time, motion, and in relation to the world.[4] As the experience rather than the position of the "I," subjectivity displaces the paradigm of an autonomous subject facing an outside world, but rather a lived experience that is inherently contingent on culture. Subjectivity is thus a mode of experience where self and world are difficult to distinguish. Subjectivity resides at the borders of autonomy and integration, and must be allowed culturally, politically, and discursively to live there. The endless work of subjectivity involves the constant renegotiations of the boundaries between self and world, with the world and history continuously reappearing in the texture of the self in the form of language, other cultural practices, received ideas and ideologies. Subjectivity is a matter not only of and for philosophy, but of politics, psychology, and art. In fact it makes most sense to me to think of subjectivity as an art, and therefore as a mode of being most knowable through art.

Unlike "identity," which involves the desire of the individual to classify and indeed envelope himself or herself within a larger cultural and emotional context, subjectivity resists such fusion. It is thus a psychological and historical partner to modernity, secularity, and other general rubrics that work according to principles of dialogue and distance. The non-classifiability of subjectivity gives it a proximity to aesthetic experience in general. This is perhaps a modernist position: namely, that aesthetic form and subjectivity not be conceived according to a principle of representation, as examples or repetitions of entities external to themselves.

The life of Mendelssohn between Judaism and Protestantism fits into an important historical pattern. Not that of "assimilation," which assumes too much (cultural loss, absorption) but the starker social facts of religious conversion. The relation between emancipation and conversion proved a key controversy in the Enlightenment discourse of Jewish emancipation. Moses Mendelssohn's role in the elaboration of these issues was unparalleled.[5] Like the even more radical Spinoza before him, Mendelssohn sought to affirm the worldly truth of Judaism in its compatibility with modern life. The emancipation of the Jews thus required the modernization of Jewish life. At the same time, his argument resisted the pull of religious conversion, as advocated by the period's best known advocates of Jewish emancipation, including Johann Caspar Lavater and Christian Wilhelm Dohm. *Jerusalem* (1784) offered Mendelssohn's maturest paradigm of intense engagement with the Jewish legacy, secularization, and anti-conversion. The extent to which this lucid but difficult work amounts to a demand for secularization and the extent to which it remains faithful to a traditional assertion of revealed division continues to provoke substantial debate.[6]

Mendelssohn's argument for the social emancipation of the Jews was clear and, to many, convincing. His model for the internal modernization of the Jews proved difficult and even destabilizing. Indeed it was so rigorous in its demand for individualized confrontation with tradition that it resisted all institutionalization. The champion of enlightenment and emancipation, Mendelssohn contributed nonetheless to what Steven Lowenstein has reasonably called the identity crisis of early nineteenth-century German Jewry. For many, modernization meant conversion, and the conversions of four of the six surviving children of Moses Mendelssohn fit this pattern. The actual numbers of Jewish converts remains surprisingly small. They are highest in Prussia, peaking in the decades after 1800, and again between 1880 and 1900. Popular perception would suggest much larger numbers. The historian Heinrich Graetz asserted that half of Berlin Jewry converted. The early nineteenth-century conversion "wave" gained the name *Taufepidemie* (baptism epidemic); the late nineteenth-century wave generated the sobriquet *Taufhaus des Westens* for Berlin's favored baptismal venue: the centrally located and prestigious Kaiser Wilhelm Gedaechtniskirche, a neighbor of the Jewish-owned department store Kaufhaus des Westens (KaDeWe). Between 1800 and 1924, 21,000 Prussian Jews converted to Protestantism, an annual rate of 168 per year. The actual highest number for one year in Berlin is 92, for the year 1829.[7] Deborah Hertz has estimated that 7 percent of Berlin Jews converted between 1770 and 1799.[8] After 1800, several distinguished Berlin families underwent collective conversions, imposing a symbolic as well as a financial burden on the Jewish community, from whose tax rolls they were removed.

Abraham Mendelssohn's decision to convert his children to Lutheranism without doing so himself was not atypical. On the occasion of his daughter Fanny's confirmation, he wrote her a well-known letter of congratulation, describing religious belief in a deistic, universalist manner but classifying the history of world religion according to a strict historical succession:

> The outward form of religion your teacher has given you is historical, and changeable like all human ordinances. Some thousands of years ago the Jewish form was the reigning one, then the heathen form, and now it is the Christian. We, your mother and I, were born and brought up by our parents as Jews, and without being obliged to change the form of our religion have been able to follow the divine instinct in us and in our conscience. We have educated you and your brothers and sister in the Christian faith, because it is the creed of most civilized people . . .[9]

Abraham and his wife themselves converted in 1822. A similar letter to his son Félix will be addressed later. Abraham's brother Nathan converted early and married a converted woman, Henriette Hitzig, of the family of Daniel Itzig, Prussia's first recognized Jewish citizen and Felix Mendelssohn's maternal great-grandfather.

In 1998, *The Musical Quarterly* published an article by Jeffrey Sposato titled "Creative Writings: The [Self-] Identification of Mendelssohn as Jew" and along with it an editorial response by Leon Botstein titled "Mendelssohn and the Jews."[10] The "creative writing" alluded to in Sposato's title refers to the vexed scholarly legacy of Eric Werner's 1963 biography *Mendelssohn: A New Image of the Composer and his Age* (and the German edition that followed in 1980). As is the case with most significant scholarly controversies, there is trouble both at the level of the facts and at the level of interpretation. According to Sposato, Werner factually and interpretively misrepresented the composer as a self-identified Jew.

Werner was the first biographer of Mendelssohn to work with troves of Mendelssohn family letters from the holdings of the New York Public Library, the Library of Congress, the Bodleian Library of Oxford University, the Staatsbibliothek in West Berlin, and others. His own stated purpose was to use these sources toward a correction of the "faulty premises" on which previous biographical treatments had rested. But, according to Sposato and other scholars who have spent time with these same sources, Werner consistently mistranscribed and mistranslated passages from the correspondence. According to Sposato, he did so with particular consistency when the issue at hand involved the composer's relationship to his Jewish heritage and to the climate of anti-Jewish prejudice to which he was exposed. According to Sposato, then, Werner "created" Mendelssohn's Jewish identification.

In a subsequent issue of *The Musical Quarterly*, Peter Ward Jones responded to and seconded Sposato's views.[11] As a Mendelssohn scholar working in the Bodleian Library, one of the principal repositories of Mendelssohn's letters, Ward Jones carries great authority in his negative opinion of Werner's scholarly practice. There is, in addition, an interpretive agreement between Ward Jones and Sposato. They agree that Werner consistently mis- and over-represented Mendelssohn's identification with his Jewish family heritage. Sposato suggests, and Ward Jones speculatively concurs, that Mendelssohn, the man, must be understood as a typical, newly converted Protestant ("Neuchrist").

There are, to my mind, three issues in this controversy that are of fundamental importance to three contiguous discourses: to Mendelssohn studies, to the cultural history of German Jewry in the first half of the nineteenth century, and to the developing discourse that we can call the cultural history of music. First, the same overinvestment in "Mendelssohn Hero" that apparently led Eric Werner to distort the biographical record also produced a measure of constructive and indeed even truthful understanding of a complicated cultural moment and biographical formation. His errors and even his alleged fraudulence notwithstanding, Werner's interpretive shortcomings are quite standard and his biography stands as a major, if dated, milestone in Mendelssohn studies.

Second, Felix Mendelssohn's cultural moment and biographical formation cannot be understood as those of a "typical *Neuchrist*" but rather as a paradigm of a multicultural and uncertain moment in German Jewish history that was available only to the Biedermeier generation, i.e., the generation of 1815–48. The assertion that Mendelssohn should be considered a Protestant rather than a Jew simply replaces one conceptually and historically inadequate label with another and thus duplicates Werner's conceptual and historical limitations, even if it restores the veracity of the source material. As Leon Botstein reflected in his response to Sposato, "[s]elf-identifications are rarely exclusive or stable" (213). In Biedermeier Germany, they were unusually volatile.

Third and finally, if what we would today call "cultural identity" was in flux in general in the Biedermeier period, it was particularly so for a personality such as Mendelssohn's. Felix Mendelssohn was not a "typical" anything. We would have little interest in his life were it not for his exceptionality, much of which obviously resides in his music. Since there is so much cultural and personal engagement evident in the music, we should look there for guidance to significant issues involving the man's mind.

We should look into the mind, moreover, for depth and conflict rather than for sheen and harmony. In doing so, we should dispense, in my view, with three interpretive fallacies: that of authorial intention as a sufficient condition for the understanding of a creative work, that of cultural essentialism in the positing of "identity," and the fallacy specific to post-Wagnerian Mendelssohn reception that recognizes the latter's "brilliance" as an equivalent factor to his musical sheen and harmony and thus as equally suggestive of an alleged mark of superficiality. As practitioners of a cultural history of music, can we not pursue cultural depth and musical depth together?

The "new image" Werner sought to attach to Mendelssohn was that of a "musical focal point" of the nineteenth century. He sought to overcome three obstacles in Mendelssohn reception: musical fashion, as he put it, which could find no place for Mendelssohn among the categories of Wagnerism, impressionism, neo-classicism, and expressionism, and dodecaphony; the "infamous banishment" by the cultural authorities of the Third Reich; and the "equal harm that had been done by the uncritical adulation during a part of the nineteenth century."[12] Although he stated that he wanted to remove Mendelssohn from the hero worship of Victorian listeners and biographers in their shadow, Werner certainly sought to reestablish the importance of Mendelssohn without qualification or apology. He sought also to understand Mendelssohn according to a high degree of cultural complication. He referred to that complication on the first page of the introduction as "the German–Jewish symbiosis."

Werner used this phrase in a general and imprecise manner. It is not clear whether by "symbiosis" he meant a new hybrid formation or a cohabitation of essentially different cultures. (The phrase does not appear in the German edition of 1980, in which these opening pages are quite changed.) The term can be used legitimately to discuss formations within German–Jewish spheres. As a citizen and a thinker, Moses Mendelssohn, for example, was clearly both a Jew and a German. He wrote and published in German and in Hebrew. When, however, "symbiosis" is used to denote relations between Germans and Jews it duplicates by default the very assumptions of essential separateness of spheres that it claims to criticize.

Werner resorted to the term "German–Jewish symbiosis" at precisely
the moment it was falling into conflict. In a now classic letter of December
1962, first published in 1964, Gershom Scholem wrote:

> I deny that there has ever been such a German-Jewish dialogue in any
> genuine sense whatsoever, i.e., as a *historical phenomenon*. It takes two to
> have a dialogue, who listen to each other, who are prepared to perceive the
> other, who are prepared to perceive the other as what he is and represents,
> and to respond to him. Nothing can be more misleading than to apply such
> a concept to the discussions between Germans and Jews during the last
> 200 years. It died when the successors of Moses Mendelssohn – who still
> argued from the perspective of some kind of Jewish totality, even though the
> latter was determined by the concepts of the Enlightenment – acquiesced in
> abandoning the wholeness in order to salvage an existence for pitiful pieces
> of it, whose recently popular designation as German–Jewish symbiosis
> reveals its whole ambiguity.[13]

Scholem's lifelong conviction that Zionism was the only modern alternative by which to preserve his idea of Moses Mendelssohn's Jewish "totality"
led him, with increasing vehemence after 1945, to deny the historical validity either of a blending of German–Christian and German–Jewish cultures
or even of a productive dialogue between them. On the other side of the
argument, historian George Lachmann Mosse, eminent for his own work
on German–Jewish culture, consistently disagreed with Scholem, who was
a personal friend of his as well as a scholarly interlocutor. In books such
as *German Jews Beyond Judaism*, Mosse affirms both the historical existence of a German–Christian – German–Jewish dialogue as well as that of
a "German–Jewish identity." Mosse often stated – though I am not aware
that he ever said so in print – that he used to tell Scholem that Scholem was
himself the finest example of what he denied ever to have existed.[14]

In all discussions of the foundations and definitions of German–
Christian – German–Jewish dialogue or of German–Jewish culture,
the figure of Moses Mendelssohn looms largest. Scholarship on Felix
Mendelssohn has tended to devote little attention to the thought and legacy
of his grandfather. Mercer-Taylor's discussion (see fn. 5) is a distinct exception. In all discussions of the Mendelssohns, Moses figured as both the point
of origin and the historical referent.

For Scholem, Moses Mendelssohn is the guarantor of a "totality of Jewish
life" for German modernity, a statement that goes unelaborated. For Mosse,
Moses Mendelssohn signifies as the interlocutor and friend of Gotthold
Ephraim Lessing, who elevated their friendship into a model of Christian –
Jewish dialogue and elevated dialogue into the principle of moral and aes-
thetic education that he and others began to refer to as *Bildung*. For Eric

Werner, Moses Mendelssohn's Judaism is consistent with a general humanism, and it is as humanism that it is transmitted to and preserved by his
grandson Felix. For Werner, Felix Mendelssohn is a humanist and therefore a defender of the Jews. Through this somewhat imprecise gloss of
"humanism," Werner argues for the "European" ideals of Felix and states
that "in his case the conflict between Germanism and Judaism came as close
to a solution as the German nation would permit."[15]

Bildung encodes the principle, indeed the cult, that forges the common
German–Christian and German–Jewish project in the period 1815–48. It is a
bourgeois project and a civic one, locating both intellectual and commercial
life in patterns of exchange available in cities such as Berlin, Hamburg, and
Leipzig, and deliberately differentiating the patterns and politics of such
urban life from the styles and claims of imperial centers such as Vienna.
Until 1848, the reactionary gaze of Metternich's Austria still fell on German
cities, and the livelihoods within those cities that many historians have called
"unpolitical" were in fact carefully elaborated political, indeed even radical,
practices.

In a more tempered vein, Scholem said the following about the relations
between Christians and Jews in Germany:

> The first half of the nineteenth century was a period in which Jews and
> Germans drew remarkably close. During this time an extraordinary amount
> of help came from the German side, with many individual Jews receiving
> cooperation in their stormy struggle for culture. There was certainly no
> lack of good will then; reading the biographies of the Jewish elite of the
> period, one again and again finds evidence of the understanding they
> encountered.[16]

As always, Scholem insisted here on the polarity of Germans and
Jews, thereby reifying the nationalist essentialism that grew dominant later
in the nineteenth century. Scholem pursued this categorical polarization
deliberately; most historical scholarship has inherited it more passively.
Scholem refused consistently to use the categories "German Christian" and
"German Jewish," and thus refused to acknowledge the Germanness of the
German Jews, which they of course themselves proclaimed with the shared
work of *Bildung* and civic consciousness as their measures.

In correcting Scholem's nationalist counter-history, one must assert the
historical fact that modern literary German was invented in the century
to which Scholem refers as the most remarkable for the German – Jewish
encounter. "Germany" as an idea was produced by Christians and Jews. In
this quite literal "production of Germany," the Mendelssohn family in its
multigenerational, multicultural, and multiprofessional eminence plays a
key role.

Felix's cultural and religious sensibilities can be understood according to (at least) three issues: his relationship to Judaism and to Jewish assimilation, his growing devotion to Protestant music, and the social taboo of the discussion of Jewish matters among the assimilated, largely converted Berlin intelligentsia. Abraham Mendelssohn's famous letter to his son of 8 July 1829 is a stern charge that his son adopt exclusively the name Bartholdy and drop the name Mendelssohn. Only thus could Felix reap the benefits of the Lutheran identity to which the family conversion entitled him. The letter bears quoting:

> My father felt that the name Moses Ben Mendel Dessau would handicap him in gaining the needed access to those who had the better education at their disposal. Without any fear that his own father would take offense, my father assumed the name Mendelssohn. The change, though a small one, was decisive. As Mendelssohn, he became irrevocably detached from an entire class, the best of whom he raised to his own level. By that name he identified himself with a different group. Through the influence which, ever growing, persists to this day, the name Mendelssohn acquired great authority and a significance which defies extinction. This, considering that you were reared a Christian, you can hardly understand. A Christian Mendelssohn is an impossibility. A Christian Mendelssohn the world would never recognize. Nor should there be a Christian Mendelssohn, for my father himself did not want to be a Christian. "Mendelssohn" does and always will stand for a Judaism in transition, when Judaism, just because it is seeking to transmute itself spiritually, clings to its ancient form all the more stubbornly and tenaciously; by way of protest against the novel form that so arrogantly and tyrannically declared itself to be the one and only path to the good.[17]

This passage is a profound reflection of and on Jewish assimilation in Prussia in the first half of the nineteenth century. The historical logic is Hegelian: assimilation represents historical development and the maturation of spiritual life. Abraham did not see his conversion and name change as a rejection of his father's path, but precisely as a continuation of it. Moses had changed his name in accordance with the social changes of German Jewry; Abraham took the process one significant step further and expected his own son to respect this historical trajectory. Felix's rebellion must therefore be seen in terms of his general rejection of a Hegelian historical linearity. Felix thus recomplicated the cultural identity in relation to which his father and grandfather had sought harmony and resolution.

With regard to this spirit of complication, Felix's determination to remain a Mendelssohn must be understood in conjunction with the growing devotion to Protestant music – as a mark of his increasing insistence on a critical and self-forming cultural identity. The 1829 revival of the *St. Matthew Passion* is the strongest example. One might argue that Mendelssohn's relation to Protestantism and the integrity of its aesthetic representations foreshadows Mahler's attachment, two generations later (however more conflicted the latter's may be), to Catholicism and Catholic theatricality. Mahler roamed the contours of the German world, holding positions in Prague, Budapest, and Hamburg, and carved the return to the center, which meant the cultural, musical, and symbolic world of Vienna. His own conversation to Catholicism must therefore be understood as a dimension of a desire to participate in the majority culture of the Austrian Catholic Baroque.[18] Similarly, Mendelssohn's itinerary had taken him from Hamburg, Düsseldorf, and Leipzig to the new cultural center of Berlin, and his Protestant devotion represented also a devotion to cultural traditions of northern Germany, with Bach as cultural as well as musical hero.

Nevertheless, the confidence and mastery Mendelssohn showed in 1829 were not free of Jewish self-consciousness, as noted in the memoirs of Eduard Devrient. Devrient, an actor (Haemon in the 1841 *Antigone*) and close friend of Mendelssohn's, recalled Mendelssohn's remarks on the success of the *St. Matthew Passion*: "To think that a comedian and a Jew must revive the greatest Christian music for the world."[19] The fact that the performance took place in the Singakademie generated the recurring disapproval, in the nineteenth-century literature, of the alleged secularization of Bach.[20] Such uncertainties persisted.

The difficult episode of the Singakademie's rejection of Mendelssohn's candidacy for the directorship in 1833 reaches to the core of the culture of *Bildung*, Christian–Jewish relations, and civic life.[21] In his 1991 essay "Mendelssohn and the Berlin Singakademie: The Composer at the Crossroads," William A. Little takes issue with the view, advocated by Werner, that anti-Jewishness was involved in the rejection of Mendelssohn for the directorship. Little writes: "Eric Werner, by reading selectively and falling back on polemics, sees the entire episode in terms of a Judeo-Christian conflict, and more specifically as one more example of Judeo-Christian enmity. Such a reduction falters however, on both the facts and nuances of the case."[22] But it is Little's argument that falters, in my view, on precisely that border between fact and nuance. His solid circumstantial argument awakens the scholar's most frustrating anxiety: does one read the lines, or does one read between the lines? In Little's account, the election of Carl Rungenhagen over Mendelssohn never touched the question of religious origins, but rather swayed in favor of reliability and experience over youth and unreliability. Mendelssohn, in Little's summary of the Singakademie's attitude, was "urbane, and his outlook, fashioned by wide experience, was broadly cosmopolitan."[23] It is the cultural and ideological loadedness of precisely these terms that must be considered: the virtue of cosmopolitanism and urbanity become faults and they begin to signify rootlessness and insincerity, and they do so in nineteenth-century discourses precisely as they are attached to Jews. Increasingly at the midpoint of the nineteenth century, the civic is caught between the international and local, with the common denominator of national language no longer able to hold the center.

As early as 1833, one can therefore suggest, the Jewish-Protestant symbiosis that Mendelssohn had internalized was in jeopardy on the outside as well. If Eric Werner believed this to be the case, he was right. If he bent the nails more readily to receive his hammer, he was at fault for doing so – and for doing so unnecessarily.

Another example of the inner symbiosis of Jewish memory and Protestant culture, but increasingly embattled from without, appears in Werner's perceptive reading of the Jewish subtext in a January 1831 letter disparaging the frivolity of the New Year's celebrations. The days around the turning of the year, wrote Mendelssohn, are "real days of atonement." Werner attributes these thoughts to "his parental home, where the very serious attitude towards the New Year had simply been transposed from Jewish to Christian practice."[24] The same sensibility is revealed in the words to the concluding hymn of Goethe's "Erste Walpurgisnacht" (1831), which Mendelssohn set:

> Und raubt man uns den alten Brauch,
> Dein Licht, wer kann es rauben?

> And if we are robbed of our old customs,
> Who can rob us of thy light?[25]

The Sophoclean theme of the robbing of custom must have been evident, perhaps even disturbing, to Mendelssohn. How can a Jewish reference not be inferred from his appropriation of such words?

This question intensifies in the context of Mendelssohn's two oratorios: *St. Paul* (1836) and *Elijah* (1846). (Werner, it should be noted, defends *Elijah* and is condescending with reference to *St. Paul*, which he criticized it for its waste of dramatic potential. It is possible, although I am not aware of his ever having said so, that he scorned it, relative to *Elijah*, for its clear statement of Protestant devotion.) As a final example, I would offer a comment on *St. Paul* that emphasizes the complicatedness of its cultural, devotional, and emotional references.

I would argue that *St. Paul* can be understood in terms of a series of dialogues between fathers and sons, as voiced by the bass and tenor parts. The bass part is consistently inhabited by the dramatic role of Paul. The tenor part shifts between the Handelian anonymity and the role of Barnabas. The shift is itself fascinating in its nomadism, its shifting position possibly allegorical of the difficulty of a son in finding a secure position of self-identification.

St. Paul was written in the aftermath of Abraham Mendelssohn's death and as a tribute to his memory. It transmits Abraham's belief in a linear realization of history through synthesis and, *a fortiori*, conversion. This work's narrative of the conversion of Paul tells this story in a transparent way. And yet it does not do so without representing as well the inner conflict required – and required of Felix – in telling and advocating his father's story. The father/son inscriptions are multiple, as the Abraham/Felix axis is doubled by the Bach/Mendelssohn one and the division of male voices into bass (Paul) and tenor.

In the first half of *St. Paul*, the tenor and bass have two duets. The first is a duet for Paul and Barnabas to the words (II Corinthians 5: 20): "So sind wir nun Botschafter an Christi statt / Now we are ambassadors for Christ." The second duet carries a similar statement. Finally, the tenor has a last cavatina, with cello obbligato, to the words, "Sei getreu bis in den Tod, so will ich dir die Krone des Lebens geben! Fürchte dich nicht, ich bin bei dir! / Be faithful unto death, and I will give you the crown of life. Do not fear, I am with you." Dramatically, it is unclear who is speaking here and to whom. But the tenor voice and rhetoric resonate with the consolation offered by a son to a father – a situation awkward and indeed unrealized in the relationship of father and son but possibly invoked with commemorative affection of a son for a dead father.

If this last statement for the tenor closes the musical as well as the much less certain dramatic relation between tenor and bass, we can ask what may have been achieved, or at least portrayed, by their joint trajectory. If the bass/tenor duets in the second half of *St. Paul* can be understood as projections of harmony between father and son, then they act out in musical terms the alliance between Abraham and Felix that the composition of this oratorio explicitly expressed. The oratorio, named for the father, is concluded musically and dramatically by the son. In a way, Felix anoints himself the successor in Christian music that his father wanted. But the duet form that is so prominent speaks in a different direction. The duet form is Felix Mendelssohn's musicalization of G. E. Lessing's principle of *Nebeneinander*, an aesthetic principle that is also a cultural one with important resonances to the concerns of his friend Moses Mendelssohn.

Lessing's most famous treatise on aesthetics is his essay on the Roman sculpture *Laocoön* (1766). In it he argues for the necessary difference between textual and visual respresentational practice. The sculpture under discussion portrays a father and his two sons being devoured by a serpent. (Obviously, this "plot" resonates as well in my treatment.) But whereas the dramatic

description of this event in Virgil's *Aeneid* describes the horrible suffering
of the victims, the sculptor, at least according to Lessing, portrays the scene
with a reserve of pathos. For Lessing, narrative and its rules of sequence
(*Nacheinander*) can be more literal than an image, with its rule of simultaneity (*Nebeneinander*).

Abraham Mendelssohn's understanding of history and cultural development, as voiced in his understanding of religious conversion through
three generations of his family, follows a code of *Nacheinander*. His son
Felix returns to a Lessingian code of *Nebeneinander*, although he is able to
explore both options in music. In *St. Paul*, these explorations play themselves
out with enormous subtlety. In its most general plan, this oratorio works
in and through the dialectic of sequence and simultaneity; historical evolution and historical dialectics; and a scenario of Judaism into Christianity
(Abraham's scenario) and a scenario of Judaism with Christianity (Felix's
scenario).

If the tension between Judaism and Christianity duplicated the tension
between generations – between fathers and sons – then its resolution would
be more elusive than ever. But a generous culture would allow or even
encourage the negotiation of such resolution as a protected space where
subjectivity might survive.

Eric Werner did not question the profundity of Mendelssohn's Protestant
conviction. He did insist on the profundity of his relation to Judaism. He
insisted on that in a post-Holocaust context in which Jewish and German
Jewish integrity required rescuing. His distortions may have been caused
by such ideological pressure. No matter their motivation, they cannot be
condoned. Moreover, it is possible that Werner had neither the conceptual
nor the historical subtlety to argue the character of that relationship or the
subtlety of the confluence of Jewish and Protestant attachments. It goes
without saying that Werner's factual errors should not be repeated. The
same is true for his conceptual inadequacies, although he cannot be blamed
for these in the same way.

Conceptual and critical adequacy have been at the center of debates
and innovation in the humanities in the decades since Werner's biography was first published. New trends in argumentation, often pooled under
the rubric "post-modernism" and often accused of assuming – or promot-
ing – the "death of the subject" and the "death of the author," are in fact
modes of human understanding that argue against the presumption of the
simple subject or the *simple* author. They are, moreover, grounded in the
modernist positions of Marx and Freud, both of whom understood secular modernity according to a new configuration of misleading surfaces and
submerged truths. Thus the biographical subject or the historical text can

be understood as complicated, over-determined and indeed contradictory formations, contingent on culture, history, and language and possessed of dignity and greatness precisely for their continued confrontations with conflict and complication.

One principle at the core of recent work in cultural studies is that of the hybridity or multiple cultural consciousness of modern identities and positions. The term "double consciousness," first used by W. E. B. DuBois to name what has now become the commonplace of "African–American" culture, has been taken up recently by Paul Gilroy in his studies of modernist Caribbean culture from the standpoint of its multiple legacies and ambitions: black, local, European, cosmopolitan. According to Gilroy, any authenticity that is to be discovered or asserted must be done on the basis of multiplicity.[26]

If we look through these lenses, as I believe we should, onto Mendelssohn and his world, we can begin to understand the subtlety with which it speaks. Toward that goal, we must take at their value corrections in the accumulation of scholarly evidence. But we cannot confuse such corrections with self-appointed new interpretations.

Alternatively, we should ask ourselves, to what extent we late twentieth-century scholars seem driven to do to Mendelssohn what our nineteenth-century predecessors did to Mozart – elevate him to prodigy status so that we can draw circles around him by treating him as a child. In the case of Mozart, this wish to maintain him as a precious child meant soaking him in the eighteenth-century courtliness his music consistently undermined. In the case of Mendelssohn, it means to insist on the shallowness of the bourgeois composer, the opportunist, the spoiled child, devoid of ambition, complication, or conflict. To understand Mendelssohn as a thinking adult requires negotiation with a psychological and cultural composite of great complexity. We should ponder carefully the stakes in attacking Eric Werner, and ponder the hold on historical reality that might be lost with the dismissal of his arguments – which do not live or die by his faulty practices. Does this anti-Wernerian zeal not also allow a certain return of a repressed anti-Mendelssohnianism in its forbearance of a renewed two-dimensionality, if now the two-dimensionality of the "typical *Neuchrist*" rather than the "self-identified Jew"? Contrary to both of these labels, rather, I would suggest that Mendelssohn's life and music are both more productively to be understood according to the subtle negotiation between Jewish and Christian spheres of culture and memory during the formation of the modern German world – and that much at a cultural historical moment, moreover, when the boundaries of all three of these were evolving and unpredictable.

Postscript

Early in 1996 I was contacted by a gifted student of German Jewish history who had developed a business in the used academic book trade. Knowing of my interest in Felix Mendelssohn, he informed me that he had obtained some volumes from Eric Werner's personal library. I subsequently purchased one of these books: Werner's heavily annotated copy of Dahlhaus' 1974 collected volume *Das Problem Mendelssohn*. Werner's signature appears together with the date 1975. He clearly read the book often; margin and other notes appear in various and multicolored pen and pencil markings, often on the same page. The study of marginalia occupies an arcane but delightful corner of intellectual history. As a whole, the quantity and character of Werner's margin notes reveal rigorous and passionate reading. The commonest interjections are exclamation points and question marks. The question mark usually reacts to an error, as it does for example to the statement that Felix Mendelssohn was born in Berlin.[27] Thus the question mark appears to be an abbreviation of "What?" The intensification of the interjection combines the question mark with the exclamation point, often doubling one or the other. An unusually large duo of question mark and exclamation point appears in the margin next to Dahlhaus's oblique reference, cited at the opening of this essay, to the stereotyping that dogs generations of Mendelssohn reception. There is an economy, indeed a poignancy in these markings that survives the devaluation of Werner's scholarship. These qualities reside in the way Werner's wit, bite, silence, and innuendo resemble the same qualities as evinced by Mendelssohn himself, in a discourse of gesture and generosity that Dahlhaus and many of his fellow Mendelssohn scholars seem to have been hard pressed to understand.

3 Felix and Fanny: gender, biography, and history

MARIAN WILSON KIMBER

One must thank God when people who actually belong together stick together and don't part from each other unless separated by death. And, if I remember correctly, it is this then I actually want to mention – and to tell you again once more how your life and activities please me, and how happy I am that we happen to be siblings. FANNY HENSEL TO FELIX MENDELSSOHN, 28 SEPTEMBER 1840[1]

You can well imagine, however, how it is for me – to whom she was present at all times, in every piece of music, and in everything that I could experience, good or evil – and so it is for all of us. FELIX MENDELSSOHN, WRITING TO CHARLOTTE MOSCHELES AFTER THE DEATH OF FANNY HENSEL, JUNE 1847[2]

With the exception of Robert and Clara Schumann, no relationship between two European musicians of different genders is as famous as that of Fanny Hensel and Felix Mendelssohn Bartholdy, siblings who have always been linked in biographical depictions. Many of Felix's first published letters, appearing in the two decades after his death, were to Fanny, and the memoirs of friends such as Ferdinand Hiller, Eduard Devrient, and Ignaz Moscheles, who knew him from childhood, all mention his talented sister. Awareness of Fanny's musical abilities spread well outside the family circle during her lifetime; as early as 1830, John Thomson, writing in *The Harmonicon*, declared that Fanny composed "with the freedom of a master."[3] After her death, but even before the family history by her son, Sebastian Hensel, was published in 1879, recognition of "Mendelssohn's sister" began to appear in wide-ranging sources. The biographical dictionaries of Carl von Ledebur and François Joseph Fétis, both from the 1860s, contained entries on Fanny.[4] In his 1869 inventory, *Hereditary Genius*, British scientist Francis Galton listed both Mendelssohn and his "very musical" sister, described as "of high genius."[5]

After the publication of Sebastian Hensel's *Die Familie Mendelssohn*, over one-third of which is devoted to Fanny's life and letters, the amount of writing about her increased dramatically. Reviewers recognized that Mendelssohn came from a unique family and sometimes spent more of their reviews discussing Fanny than Felix, praising her letters as "spirited" and "full of vivacity and vigorous description."[6] *The Musical Times* stated that Fanny's letters formed "the most interesting portions of the book," calling them "full of shrewdness, humour and perceptiveness."[7] Because Fanny's description of her 1839–40 Italian journey fell into a long tradition of women's literary travel writing, she was readily accepted as an intellectual figure, if not a composer. She appeared in a wide range of published writings dating from between the years 1880 and 1920, including articles, biographical dictionaries, publications about women composers, collective biographies of famous women, and one full-length book published in France in 1888.[8] Although the bulk of her compositions remained unpublished, the biography of Mendelssohn's sister, transmitted through *Die Familie Mendelssohn*, received wide circulation.

The circumstances of the siblings' unusual childhoods reported in these publications are by now well known. Born four years apart, Fanny and Felix were raised in a highly cultured, rarified atmosphere in a wealthy Jewish family and had unusual access to musical training. The *Sonntagsmusik*, or Sunday salon concerts, held in their home at 3 Leipzigerstraße, and their participation in Berlin's Singakademie afforded them frequent opportunities to hear and perform music. Both children were child prodigies: Fanny performed the entire first book of Bach's *Das wohltemperirte Clavier* at the age of twelve, and thirteen-year-old Felix reportedly stood on a stool to conduct his compositions.[9] Both children began composing early, though whether through personal inclination or larger cultural influences, Fanny was more attracted to genres deemed appropriate for women, such as Lieder and piano music, while early on Felix produced larger instrumental forms.[10]

By all accounts, the two were unusually close, in large part owing to their common musical experiences, but they shared other personality traits as well. Sebastian Hensel's description of his mother also brings to mind his uncle: both siblings had decided opinions, little patience with dull, shallow persons or ideas, and a fundamental need for "intercourse with cultured and intelligent people in a small circle, and the pleasures of art."[11] The siblings' upbringings left them both with highly self-critical streaks and a strong-minded sense of their personal and artistic beliefs. Even the slightly hagiographic memoirs of Mendelssohn's friends demonstrate his intense criticism of music which did not meet his artistic standards; Ferdinand Hiller recalled that when he "liked a thing, he liked it with his whole heart; things that did not please him would occasion from him the most singular language."[12] Fanny also had, by contemporary accounts, a strong character; her letters reveal a formidable intellect, a sometimes brutally sarcastic sense of humor, and an intolerance for people and ideas she found not to her liking. William Sterndale Bennett, recalling a visit to the Hensel home in 1842, wrote that he "was never so frightened to play to anyone before, and to think that this terrible person should be a lady. However, she would frighten many people with her cleverness."[13] The year after Fanny's death, Sarah Austin recalled "a woman of strong sense, strong feeling . . . she did not lay herself out to please indifferent persons . . . She was too proud, independent, and upright for the smallest affectation."[14] Given Felix and Fanny's personal temperaments, it is not surprising that they had occasional disputes. Recalling her visit to Leipzig in 1838, Fanny wrote, "We are all very absolute in our opinions, Felix cannot stand any contradiction at all, and thus we came down hard on each other a couple of times."[15] Felix's highly sensitive, self-critical streak sometimes made his sister uncomfortable: "one must be so careful with him in order not to injure him."[16] Nonetheless, her letters to him demonstrate a forthrightness about musical matters unsurpassed among his correspondence.

Throughout their lives the siblings exchanged compositions on birthdays and holidays, but more often for no other reason than mutual interest. In their early years, Felix affectionately called his older sister "the cantor," an indication of her influence in his musical life. In 1822 she wrote, "He has no musical adviser other than me, also he never puts a thought on paper without first having submitted it to me for examination."[17] Felix, known for his severe criticism of some of the leading musicians of his age, demonstrated immense respect for Fanny's abilities. He ranked his sister's pianistic abilities above that of leading virtuosi: "She really plays all of the little fellows . . . into the ground."[18] Mendelssohn showered some of his highest praise on Fanny's compositions: "But truly there is music which seems to have distilled the very quintessence of music, as if it were the soul of music itself – such as these songs. By Jesus! I know of nothing better."[19] In calming his sister's doubts, he wrote, "But you know how I love all your things and especially those that have grown so close to my heart."[20]

For many years Felix relied on Fanny as his foremost musical confidante and, in Marcia Citron's words, his "mail-order critic," who provided extensive comments on his *Melusine* overture op. 32, and the oratorio *St. Paul* op. 36.[21] Fanny, in turn, once described her brother's influence as "demonic" in Goethe's sense of the word.[22] Neither sibling spared the other their true opinions, even on the smallest details of each other's compositional efforts: for example, Fanny complained when Felix removed grace-notes in the Andante of his "Italian" Symphony,[23] and Felix pointed out the weaknesses in his sister's orchestration for her *Choleramusik*.[24] Underlying their various artistic disagreements was a common goal, to make good music. While their treatment of each other has sometimes been construed as overly harsh, it must been seen in the light of their upbringing; their parents stressed a strong work ethic and continuous striving for self-improvement.[25]

Despite their inevitable differences, the supreme importance of the relationship to both of the siblings is revealed through the sheer quantity of their correspondence. Their artistic interchange seems to have lessened somewhat in the last decade of the siblings' lives. As his international stature and circle of musical acquaintances grew, Felix was less in need of his sister's commentary – indeed, his professional commitments were frequently so all-consuming that he hardly had time for the somewhat indulgent correspondence of his youth. In 1837, his sister complained that she knew nothing of her brother's newly published works, in sharp contrast to their youth, when she "knew your things by heart even before you wrote them down."[26] Fanny, in turn, found encouragement for her compositional efforts from young Charles Gounod during her months in Rome in 1839–40, and from Robert von Keudell back in Berlin. Nonetheless, Fanny's early death plunged her brother into a deep depression, ended only by his own death the same year.

Mendelssohn's relationship with his sister granted him an unusual acceptance of women's creative abilities. As a young man he admired Henrietta Herz's efforts on behalf of the education of young women.[27] He later encouraged the compositional efforts of young Emily Moscheles and Josephine Lang. Mendelssohn was greatly amused at Joseph Joachim's surprise at Clara Schumann's ability to write a fugato because Joachim "would not believe a woman could have composed something so sound and serious."[28] Mendelssohn could certainly critique women's compositions as strongly as those of men.[29] However, his own sister's ability to orchestrate music, a skill unheard of in a woman, had been described by an astounded witness in *The Harmonicon* in 1830. With such a musician in his life, Mendelssohn was less likely than most of his male contemporaries to belittle feminine efforts and more likely to judge music on its merits rather than on the gender of the composer.

Nonetheless, it was the gender and class restrictions of the early nineteenth century that shaped the musical paths of both siblings: Felix, as a male, could undertake the dubious career of a musician, in spite of the skepticism of his family.[30] By itself, Fanny's gender would have made it difficult for her to have a career as a professional musician; her father wrote to her that the only calling of a young woman was that of a housewife.[31] But class was equally important in shaping Fanny Hensel's life; Nancy B. Reich has pointed out that her inability to have a professional career as a musician was due to her upper-class status.[32] "Had Madame Hensel been a poor man's daughter," wrote critic Henry Chorley in 1865, "she must have become known to the world as a female pianist of the very highest class."[33] For an upper-class nineteenth-century woman, receiving money for musical activities meant compromising her social position, and both siblings' positions were made more precarious by their status as converted Jews. So instead, Fanny continued the Sunday concerts at the family home, making significant contributions to the musical life of Berlin. Her compositional style, only now emerging through publications and performances of her oeuvre, has numerous resemblances to that of her brother Felix; indeed, R. Larry Todd has suggested that there were not one but two composers in the "Mendelssohnian" style.[34] In spite of an ambivalence about publishing, which she began to do only shortly before her death, Hensel produced over four hundred compositions. Not surprisingly, publishing as well as performing was subject to contemporary beliefs about gender. As late as 1888, an article in *The Musical Times* found it laudable that Fanny Hensel did not undertake a "descent" into the arena of publishing.[35]

Historical reinterpretations: the gendered "other" in biography

Nonetheless Felix and Fanny's relationship has not fared well in history, as biographical treatments of it are heavily influenced by cultural assumptions about the nature of genius, gender, and familial relationships. Biographers have generally felt it necessary to "choose sides," or to present the siblings as a dichotomy. Obviously, Felix's musical output and public career made him the more famous of the two, and many biographies of him only minimally recognize the major role Fanny had in his life. However, late nineteenth-century writings often claim a negative, "feminizing" influence for Fanny on her younger brother. A century later the gender roles are reversed. The "recovery" of Fanny Mendelssohn which has taken place during the past decades of increased scholarship on women composers has resulted in the frequent lament that she remained "in the shadow" of her brother, who is often cast as the sole reason she did not have a professional career. Such exaggerations typically occur without specific discussion of either sibling's music; instead, they reveal how cultural understandings of gender shape biography, a literary genre which is still influenced by nineteenth-century emphasis on the individual (male) genius. This Romantic ideal leaves little room for a biographical model of two persons, particularly of different genders, intertwined in their artistic activities. Nineteenth-century hagiography of the "great man" rarely acknowledges familial support – his genius springs forth, seemingly of its own accord – much less any notion of creative interplay between siblings.[36] Whitney Chadwick and Isabelle de Courtivron have asked the questions which plague the Mendelssohns' biographies: "For if the myth of solitariness prevails, can only one be a genius? And if the reality of community prevails, how is genius to define itself?"[37]

Women who play roles in the lives of "great composers" – for after all, the "great composer" is traditionally assumed to be male – stereotypically either serve the role of muse or of devoted wife supporting their husband's cause: Harriet Smithson and Hector Berlioz, or Cosima and Richard Wagner come to mind. Clara Schumann manages to fulfill both roles nicely, wife and muse to Robert Schumann and then muse to Johannes Brahms, if one overlooks her own efforts at composition. Fanny, sometimes Felix's toughest musical critic, was often portrayed as mystical muse in nineteenth-century writings, without whom he and his music could not survive. In Elise Polko's excessively sentimental analogy, "Versunkene Sterne," from 1852, Felix and Fanny are compared to a willow tree and a babbling brook, who make music together in a seemingly magical fashion: "neither could exist without the other, and both, though apparently separated, seemed to be harmonically one."[38] The tree, Felix, withers without the brook, but the musical partners are united in heaven after death. That Mendelssohn died only six months after his sister is typically portrayed as proof of the mysterious, unbreakable bond inherent in the relationship. Julius Benedict's 1850 description of Mendelssohn's reaction to his sister's death, "With a loud, fearful shriek, he fell senseless to the ground,"[39] apparently excited the more fanciful imaginations of other contemporary writers. In William Alger's 1868 Gothic tale, Felix, at the moment of Fanny's death, "suddenly aware of some terrible calamity, from the disturbance of equilibrium and dread sinking of his soul, rushed to the piano, and poured out his anguish in an improvisation of wailing and mysterious strains, which held the assembly spell-bound and in tears."[40] While such romanticized renderings may seem humorous now, similar ideas persist in somewhat diluted forms: Gloria Kamen's 1996 children's biography of Hensel describes Felix as Fanny's "twin," implying a connection stronger than mere siblinghood.[41]

The more modern approach, perhaps a reaction to such overblown accounts, is to assume that the intense nature of the relationship was in some way psychologically unhealthy. Fanny, whose emotional letters preceding her wedding to the Berlin court painter Wilhelm Hensel (1794–1861) were filled with an exaggerated adoration, is portrayed as having some unnatural attachment to Felix: "[I] get up from the piano, stand in front of your picture, and kiss it, and immerse myself so completely in your presence that I – must now write you. But I am infinitely well, and you are infinitely dear to me. Infinitely dear."[42] Eric Werner claims that the siblings' "consanguinity evoked almost physical impulses and instincts in Fanny," citing her "outbursts of possessiveness and jealousy." Werner cannot allow Fanny's influence in Felix's life, and exaggerates, "she wanted to possess him, body and soul."[43] Felix is the emotionally healthy one, who was "carefully guarding himself against a darker, less normal attachment." Werner, like many other writers, overlooks that Felix, too, took part in this Romantic charade, for example, comparing Fanny favorably to Delphine Schauroth (1813–87), the young pianist with whom he was flirting in Munich in 1830. He wrote to his sister,

> Listen, I want you to be very happy and merry this moment, because I am just thinking of you; and if you were so every moment I think of you, you would never become vexed or out of sorts. But you are a perfect dear, that is for sure, and know a lot about music . . . and if you need a greater admirer than me, then you can paint him or let him paint you.[44]

The exaggerated tone of the siblings' correspondence from around 1828–29 has even led one writer to investigate the possibility that their relationship involved incest.[45] However, these writings stemmed from their involvement with the Romantic literature of the period. As an adult, rereading letters from Felix's European travels ten years later, Fanny commented that "it amused me that all of us expressed ourselves like Jean Paul around the time you left here."[46] Thus, the Romantic role-playing should probably not be taken too literally, and was not uncommon for the period.

Even without such extreme interpretations, Felix and Fanny's respective marriages are frequently overlooked in biographical treatments of the siblings: Cécile Jeanrenaud is a silent onlooker in many biographies of her husband; in Kamen's biography of Fanny, Wilhelm Hensel almost completely disappears from the narrative. Cécile's treatment is perhaps not surprising, given that she had no musical abilities and her destruction of her husband's letters prevented biographers' access to detailed evidence regarding their relationship.[47] It is harder to account for the absence of Wilhelm, who was both professionally artistic and personally supportive, in narratives of his wife's life.

Modern biographer Werner's approach to Fanny has its roots in earlier, nineteenth-century treatments, in which her musical influence on her brother was, because of her gender, considered feminizing and ultimately detrimental. Felix's reported closeness to his female relatives, combined with the association of his *Lieder* and small lyrical piano genres such as *Lieder ohne Worte* with music-making in the domestic sphere, helped create the image of Mendelssohn as "feminine," and thus a failure as a composer.[48] Mendelssohn's friend, the theorist Adolf Bernhard Marx (with whom he later had a falling out), claimed that in the composer's youth the "constant company of his sister's young female friends," and his "dallying in this diminutive and sweetly feminine sphere" resulted in the "sweet, flirtatious, tender" *Lied ohne Worte*, a genre that did not require much musical ability.[49] Marx's student Hermann Zopff also blamed Mendelssohn's supposed musical shortcomings on women, writing that his artistry was

narrowed by that coterie of Berlin ladies, who were in raptures with his
every motion, with his every naive or roguish trick or word; who each of
them was eager to possess another original little song, with or without
words, written by himself and dedicated to herself or the pen with which he
wrote or whatever else he used . . . That was the insidious poison that was
more and more to strangle the high aspiration for which Nature had
endowed him . . . ![50]

In 1886, George Upton wrote, "The influences of mother, sister, and wife,
all led Mendelssohn in the same direction of beauty and grace of style,
rather than of great strength."[51] An 1895 article stated that Felix feared his
sister, who exerted a restraining influence on his Romantic musical style.[52]
Chadwick and De Courtivron find this a common treatment of creative
women in men's biographies: "if only one can be Genius, and if in our
culture that role is usually assigned to men, all attempts at competition
(actual or imagined) by women . . . are considered potential threats to 'his'
productivity."[53]

In contrast, the modern "reinterpretation" treats Fanny's brother as the
villain in the story of her life, preventing her from embarking on a professional career and suppressing her attempts to publish her music.[54] Instead,
Felix allowed Fanny's music to appear under his name, thus dooming it to
oblivion.[55] This story, sometimes presented as a new feminist interpretation,
actually originated in nineteenth-century publications and their associated
ideology. It can be traced to an 1837 letter by Felix first published by his
brother and son in the second volume of his letters in 1863.[56] In the frequently quoted letter, Mendelssohn declined his mother's request that he
encourage his sister to publish her music. Fanny's dilemma regarding publishing was also presented by her son Sebastian Hensel in his 1879 family
history, *Die Familie Mendelssohn*.

Sebastian Hensel and his uncle, Paul Mendelssohn Bartholdy, felt obliged
to present socially acceptable images of the lives of their relatives, images
which conformed to the gender ideology of their day, not accurate portrayals
for twenty-first-century biographers. Paul Mendelssohn Bartholdy believed
that he could draw a book of moral instruction from his brother's letters; he
wrote that "alone the work could become, in my opinion, a guiding star for
many, many people."[57] Sebastian Hensel's apologist approach to his unusual
mother was necessary for his "chronicle of a good middle-class family in
Germany."[58] His book continually emphasizes Fanny's role as a "typical"
daughter, wife, and mother, conforming to contemporary gender roles for
women, in spite of her remarkable musical abilities. It assures readers that
she had no desire to leave the domestic sphere, and the resulting emphasis
on her reluctance to publish, as well as Paul's inclusion of the letter that
documents Felix's "disapproval," reflect the family's task of making sure

that the images of both Felix and Fanny conformed to nineteenth-century bourgeois gender roles. The family's Jewish heritage and the era's rising anti-Semitism meant that any deviation from cultural norms endangered their social status. As a result of these publications, both Felix and Fanny came to be regarded as conforming to moral ideals; in his 1882 review of Sebastian's book, Edward Dowden wrote, "Goodness in a group of persons, and in an eminent degree, is rare; goodness with genius, one and indivisible, is still rarer."[59]

For over a century Sebastian Hensel's and Paul Mendelssohn Bartholdy's publications served as the basis for our knowledge of Felix and Fanny's relationship. Thus biographers who have identified Felix's behavior as the sole source of Fanny's supposed musical frustrations have transmitted a story shaped by the agendas of nineteenth-century men. Even if Felix Mendelssohn did not fully support his sister's publishing endeavors, one must still consider the reasons for such emphasis on the issue. Criticism of the Mendelssohn family has centered entirely on Fanny's restriction to the domestic sphere; however, Sebastian and Paul's portrayal of Felix's involvement in his sister's life is also shaped by gender ideology, demonstrating his appropriate patriarchal behavior.

While Mendelssohn's letter to his mother of 24 June 1837[60] certainly demonstrates a typical nineteenth-century German bourgeois attitude that Fanny Hensel's priorities should be her roles as wife and mother, it also reveals that Mendelssohn felt it was not his place to advise Fanny regarding publication. He wrote that should she decide to publish, he would *support her* in whatever she undertook. Felix's specific request that his mother not mention his opinion to Fanny or her husband, omitted from the original published version of the letter, demonstrates him endeavoring to stay out of the discussion, not attempting to influence his sister's actions.[61]

For Mendelssohn, the issue was not composition but publishing; modern interpretations err in assuming that he found publishing wholly desirable. On the contrary, he considered it a necessary activity for a professional composer, but burdensome in that it required continuous production of musical works, rather than their sporadic appearance.[62] Mendelssohn's letters to German and English publishers reveal his numerous frustrations with publishing, and that he left numerous compositions unpublished, including such major works as the "Reformation" and "Italian" Symphonies, further demonstrates his ambivalence.[63]

Even when she did decide to publish, Fanny Hensel did not view it in the same light, but wrote to her friend Angelica von Woringen that it was an experiment that she could give up if it was not successful.

I'm glad that you, dear Angela, are interested in the publication of my
Lieder. I was always afraid of being disparaged by my dearest friends, since
I've expressed myself against it my whole life and right up to the present
years. In addition, I can truthfully say that I let it happen more than made it
happen, and it is this in particular that cheers me . . . If they want more
from me, it should act as stimulus to achieve, if possible, more. If the matter
comes to an end then, I also won't grieve, for I'm not ambitious, and so I
haven't yet had the occasion to regret my decision.[64]

For Fanny, publishing seems to have been merely a source of personal motivation. Her oft-reported longing for a professional musical career is not
supported by her recently published diaries, which are somewhat surprising for how little they reveal about her musical life. Indeed, Fanny was more
likely to record the recent artistic projects of her painter husband than her
own compositional endeavors.

The rest of Mendelssohn's letter to his mother, expressing his concern
over his sister's health, was not published in the nineteenth century owing to
its private nature. Phyllis Benjamin and Peter Ward Jones have documented
that Fanny had a stillbirth or miscarriage in November of 1832 and again in
March of 1837.[65] Mendelssohn wrote to his mother during his honeymoon
journey; his wife was already pregnant in June of 1837,[66] so it is likely
that the physical dangers associated with pregnancy and childbirth were
newly apparent to him. Thus Mendelssohn's refusal to encourage his sister
to publish was partly a desire to save her from any stresses which might
negatively affect her health, a justifiable concern given her early death from
stroke at the age of forty-one.

Often cited as the strongest evidence for Felix's "repression" of Fanny's
musical voice was the publication of six of her songs in his opp. 8 and 9 in
1827 and 1830.[67] The scant available evidence suggests, however, that the
inclusion of Fanny's songs along with Felix's was not done at her expense.
In a letter to Felix from 1830, referring to her songs in op. 9, Fanny wrote,
"I shoved them down Schlesinger's throat,"[68] implying an active role on
her part (and perhaps suggesting the level of disinterest or opposition a
woman attempting to publish her music faced). Felix himself appears to
have been completely forthcoming about Fanny's contributions to opp. 8
and 9. Writing about his visit to Queen Victoria in 1842, when the monarch
chose one of Fanny's Lieder to sing for him, Mendelssohn recalled good-
humoredly, "Then I was obliged to confess that *Fanny* had written the song
(which I found very hard, but pride must have a fall) . . ."[69] Additional
evidence suggests a wider public knowledge of Fanny's authorship of the
songs in opp. 8 and 9. As early as 1830 the *Harmonicon* informed English
readers that three of Mendelssohn's best songs were actually by his sister.[70]

Sebastian Hensel reported that people believed more of Felix Mendelssohn's published compositions were by Fanny than actually were, and in memoirs published late in his life, Max Müller (1823–1900) maintained that everyone knew which songs were hers, rather than Felix's.[71]

The tale of Fanny, the "suppressed" composer, has so readily found a place in biographies of the siblings, because of its resemblance to prevailing models for the life of a "Great Composer," models based in Romantic ideology about male artists. In her lack of a public career, Hensel fits neatly into a traditional narrative of the suffering artistic genius, the same narrative as male artists who suffer from misunderstanding and neglect during their lifetime, only to receive widespread acclaim after their deaths. As Linda Nochlin writes, "The artist, in the nineteenth-century Saint's Legend, struggles against the most determined parental and social opposition, suffering the slings and arrows of social opprobrium . . . and ultimately succeeds against all odds – generally, alas, after his death . . ."[72] Fanny's unfortunate fate is a familiar story with a modern twist: the feminine gender of its main character.

Thus two talented human beings with deep affection for one another are, in biographical representations, forced to bear the weight of two centuries of gender ideology. Felix's musical output is somehow soiled through his association with the feminine sphere of his sister; when she serves as his muse, her death destroys him. Fanny's creative abilities are repressed by her patriarchal brother who usurped her well-deserved fame, and so fulfills the previously male role of suffering genius. These characters, biographical constructions, would not have written the statements found at the beginning of this chapter. To relinquish the "either/or" approach to the Mendelssohn siblings is to see them as deeply linked, personally and creatively, in one of the most important musical relationships of the nineteenth century.

PART TWO

Situating the compositions

4 Mendelssohn and the rise of musical historicism

JAMES GARRATT

The relation between Mendelssohn's works and the music of the past has preoccupied musicians, critics, and scholars since their first performances. During his lifetime, the view emerged that Mendelssohn's engagement with early music was a defining aspect of his creativity, and confronting this facet of his activities remains central to understanding his works and their significance. Successive generations have, of course, responded in different ways to Mendelssohn's compositional historicism, yet for much of the period from the 1840s to the 1960s it provided a focus for negative assessments of his output: even today, some scholars – disconcerted by the sheer extent of the composer's investment in the past – represent his responses to earlier music as fabricated musical kitsch.[1] In general, however, our post-modern sensibilities are more sympathetic to Mendelssohn's achievement. There is, after all, an essential kinship between his concerns and our own (ironically, the current enthusiasm for his choral works was stimulated by a distinctively postmodern form of historicism, historically informed performance). Indeed, it could be claimed that, in this regard, Mendelssohn was the first composer of modernity: the first musician to wrestle with the dilemma of being dispossessed of a *lingua franca*.

In recent years, several musicologists have reappraised Mendelssohn's compositional historicism: the final section of this chapter outlines different interpretive strategies and reconsiders some of the issues involved. My principal focus, however, is on reconstructing the development of Mendelssohn's historical consciousness and exploring how his shifting conception of history shaped his engagement with earlier works and styles. While scholars have devoted much attention to stylistic pluralism in his music, it is imperative to acknowledge that the matrix of ideas underpinning Mendelssohn's historicism was similarly eclectic. In exploring these aspects of the composer's relation to the past, it is also essential to locate his music and ideas within the broader discourses of contemporary historicism. While his predilection for the past may appear deviant when viewed alongside, say, the music of Chopin and Berlioz, it reflects broader trends in music and the other arts.

Historicism and modernity

It should not be supposed that the term historicism is used here, as in musicological writings of the 1960s and 1970s, to refer to an excessive veneration of the past or dependence on earlier styles. Few, if any, of Mendelssohn's works fit in with Carl Dahlhaus' notion of historicism as a "twilight zone between the dead past and the denied present," or with Walter Wiora's view that it involves the imitation of the old outweighing the invention of the new.[2] To equate historicism with the literal replication of earlier styles not only renders it peripheral to nineteenth-century music, but also diverges substantially from the current use of the concept in other disciplines.[3] Neither should it be assumed – in relation to broader cultural and intellectual developments – that it indicates solely the emergence of historical relativism, and thus stands opposed to the elevation of classical norms or suprahistorical truths.[4] Rather, historicism encompasses a constellation of competing tendencies, a circle of problems generated by the birth of a new form of historical consciousness. In describing the upheaval that occurred at the beginning of the nineteenth century, Michel Foucault argues that as a result of the awareness of the historicity of nature, language and human products, Western civilization was "dehistoricized": a hitherto uniform and essentially unchanging inheritance shattered into a thousand alien pasts; artifacts came to symbolize fragmentation and transience rather than the unity and permanence of a natural order.[5] In Mendelssohn's Germany, the ramifications of this epistemic break were particularly acute. Indeed, this shift is mirrored in microcosm within the composer's own artistic and intellectual development, and was largely responsible for his compositional crisis of the early 1830s.

Even at the time of its emergence, in the final decades of the eighteenth century, historicism comprised a variety of conflicting stances. One strand was the impulse to retrieve and repossess something believed to have been lost by modern civilization: to counter the alienation of the modern subject by reassimilating the past within the present. Another was the desire to challenge contemporary norms, through asserting the validity of the art of a plurality of peoples and periods. A further dimension to historicism, the impulse to elevate monuments from the past as models for the present, interacted uneasily with this burgeoning relativism. Indeed, the conflict between these stances – the realization that time-honored norms were no longer sustainable, and the attempt to compensate for this by constructing new absolutes – is fundamental to historicism and differentiates it from earlier, classicizing tendencies. A clear example of this tension can be seen in Johann Joachim Winckelmann's *Geschichte der Kunst des Altertums* (*History of Ancient Art*, 1764) and in critical reactions to it.[6] While Winckelmann sought to reconcile his historical methodology with the elevation of Greek art as a universal model, others regarded these perspectives as antithetical. The increasing attention paid to the historical study of art generated the conviction that every work and style is the unique product of its particular social, religious, and political context; in addition, the plurality of historical models available to the modern artist rendered the notion of a return to origins difficult to sustain. As a consequence, Herder dismissed Winckelmann's doctrine of classical imitation as a vain delusion, considering the time of the "beloved sweet simplicity" of ancient art to be irretrievably lost.[7] And while Goethe's revelatory encounter with Strasbourg Minster enabled him to disregard the precepts of his age, he did not elevate Gothic architecture as a source for modern artistic renewal: instead, he argued that it is a false tendency to seek to revivify cherished aspects of the past, since they developed under "completely different conditions."[8]

While the enthusiasm of Goethe and Herder for neglected periods and styles was tempered by relativism, other commentators turned to them as a means of revivifying modern art. In the years around 1800, this trend is particularly apparent in relation to Gothic architecture, medieval poetry and early Italian painting. Famously, the poet Heinrich Heine contended that the work of the Romantic circle – Friedrich and August Wilhelm Schlegel, Ludwig Tieck, Wilhelm Heinrich Wackenroder, and Novalis – amounted to "nothing other than the revival of the poetry of the Middle Ages, as it manifested itself in song, sculpture, in art and life."[9] While Heine's polemic provides an oversimplified view of the output of the Romantic circle, he does not exaggerate the enthusiasm with which they exhorted contemporaries to emulate the techniques and spiritual fervor of medieval art. In championing early Italian painting, the Romantic circle, like Herder and Goethe, proceeded from a critique of neo-classicism. Yet in seeking to free art from prescriptions and proscriptions abstracted from antiquity, they represent the art of Raphael and his predecessors as a universally valid ideal. The historical strategies adopted by Schlegel demand attention, since they epitomize a paradox fundamental to nineteenth-century historicism. Although Schlegel admitted that he was responsive only to old paintings, his idealization of early Italian art cannot be understood as an indiscriminate or ahistorical *Schwärmerei* for the past.[10] Rather, he appropriated the concepts and methodology that Winckelmann had applied to ancient Greek art in order to construct a golden age of medieval painting: for Schlegel, as for Winckelmann, it is clear that only through a historical approach could a suprahistorical ideal emerge.[11]

For Schlegel (who converted to Catholicism in 1808), the revival of the techniques and spirituality of early Catholic painting provided the sole source for renewing modern art. This stance found a practical application in the work of the Brotherhood of St. Luke or "Nazarenes," a group of German painters, led by Friedrich Overbeck and Franz Pforr, who settled in Rome in 1809. Inspired by the writings of Schlegel and Wackenroder, the Nazarenes sought to challenge neo-classical principles by returning to the unreflective spirituality, subject matter and fresco techniques of Italian painting up to Raphael. While Heine dismissed the paintings of the Nazarenes – "the long-haired Christian new German school" – as mere parodies of old Italian art, others regarded them as its rebirth.[12] Even Goethe praised drawings by Overbeck and Peter Cornelius as "stupendous things," contending that "this is the first time in the history of art that significant talents have shaped themselves backwards, by returning into the mother's womb in order to initiate a new artistic epoch."[13] Schlegel laid a similar stress on the "living freshness" of the Nazarenes' achievement, arguing that it was a preparatory step on the path to a new golden age of religious art: only through modeling their works on those of Raphael and his school – and being "completely filled and penetrated by their spirit" – can artists progress toward a "truly modern art for the modern age."[14]

Not all commentators shared Schlegel's conviction that the rebirth of art required the revival of the techniques and spirituality of the fifteenth century. Still less were they willing to tolerate the degree of archaism that he considered permissible in the pursuit of this ideal. Crucial in this regard was the view that every style is the unique embodiment of its age and context: a corollary to this was the notion that, to be of value, a modern work must be the authentic expression of its author's convictions and world-view, requiring the use of contemporary materials and forms. This position received its most influential formulation in Hegel's *Lectures on Aesthetics* (given at the University of Berlin in the 1820s and published posthumously in 1835). For Hegel, the perfection and ideal of art was located in the distant past, since the absolute identity of spiritual content and sensory form was attained only in ancient Greek art. Arguing that the Christian era charts an ever-increasing disintegration of this relation, he claimed that the final stage of this process had been initiated by his contemporaries, in whose art can be seen "the severance of the sides whose complete identity affords the proper essence of art, and therefore the decay and dissolution of art itself."[15] Hegel concedes that modern artists are no longer tied to a particular material or mode of representation, and in choosing their forms are not restricted to the styles and resources of the present. He insists, nonetheless, that the external forms adopted must be the authentic expression of the spirit of the age and the product of the artist's personal conviction: "the content must constitute the substance, the innermost truth of his consciousness" and must "shine clearly and thoroughly through the external material in which it has enshrined itself."[16] Modern artists cannot take on a mentality from the past in order to gain a spiritual foundation for their productions; with Schlegel in mind, Hegel stresses that those who convert to Catholicism for the sake of their art can gain no sustenance from a world-view foreign to the present.[17] Neither can the artist make use of forms that are ineluctably linked to a superseded mentality; while the study of older techniques and styles may be beneficial, they cannot be replicated in modern art:

> No Homer, Sophocles, etc., no Dante, Ariosto or Shakespeare can appear in our day; what was so magnificently sung, what was so freely expressed, has been expressed; these are materials, ways of looking at them and treating them which have been sung once and for all. Only the present is fresh, the rest is dull and stale.[18]

This conclusion is hardly surprising, given that Hegel's philosophy of history is grounded on the principle of non-repetition. Yet even though Hegel is hostile to artistic historicism, his insistence that the stylistic freedom of the modern artist is part of the "effect and progress of art itself" tends to mitigate the force of his strictures.[19] Indeed, his demand that the use of older forms must exhibit tangible signs of the modern spirit could be interpreted as a charter for eclecticism. Moreover, it is evident that Hegel viewed the broadening of interest in earlier styles as having benefited modern painting, and he does not question the advantages gained by German culture through its exposure to diverse forms of art.[20]

The latter theme was of fundamental importance to German thought in the first half of the nineteenth century, often accompanied by the notion that it was Germany's destiny to appropriate and unite the artistic products of every nation and age. The idea that Germany had a historical mission to create a *Weltliteratur* resonates through many discussions of the appropriation of earlier styles.[21] The music critic Franz Brendel, for example, claimed – in portentous Hegelian language – that it was "the world-historical task of Germany to assemble the spirits of all other peoples around the throne of its universal monarchy."[22] Not only had German philosophy and literature forged a great whole from "the entirety of the world's previous development," but a "world music" (*Weltmusik*) had been created from the fusion of diverse styles.[23]

From the second decade of the nineteenth century, composers increasingly experimented with the replication and combination of a range of earlier styles. Composers even emulated the didactic programs of historical concerts, in which pieces from a variety of periods were performed in chronological order: Louis Spohr's Symphony No. 6 in G (1839) bore the subtitle "Historical Symphony in the Style and Taste of Four Different Periods," while in the previous year Otto Nicolai had planned a historical concert consisting of his own works in a range of earlier styles.[24] While such eclecticism was by no means the norm in music of this period, composers were subject to the same stylistic anxieties as their counterparts in the other arts. The problems generated by the awareness of a multiplicity of earlier styles are especially evident in architectural debates of this period, in which the question "in what style should we build?" (the title of an 1828 pamphlet by Heinrich Hübsch) centered on choosing an orientation from among competing historical ideals.[25] One solution was to regard each style as equally valid, an option evident in the artistic ventures of Ludwig I of Bavaria:

> Whoever strolls around Munich . . . has the best opportunity to become acquainted with the entire history of architecture from the present back to Egyptian art. This stone artistic atlas remains constantly in view. Beginning with the style of the Renaissance, the models range from the Germanic, Romanesque, Byzantine, Roman and Greek styles, and will culminate – in all probability – in the imitation of oriental buildings.[26]

Different solutions to the crisis of architecture are evident in the work of Karl Friedrich Schinkel, whose buildings and designs reflect shifting conceptions of how the past could be used in the present. In 1810, Schinkel produced two contrasting plans (one a Doric temple, the other a vaulted Gothic hall) for a mausoleum for Queen Luise of Prussia, in order to demonstrate the suitability of the Gothic style for national monuments.[27] If these designs constitute a manifesto in favor of Gothic architecture, Schinkel's later approach was less dogmatic. His eclecticism is apparent in four different designs – two classical and two medieval – for the Friedrich-Werdersche church in Berlin, and especially in his plans (1815–16) for a Befreiungsdom (a memorial cathedral to the wars of liberation).[28] Here, Schinkel's solution to the problem of choosing from among the ancient Egyptian, Greek, and Gothic styles was to combine all three, thus unifying in one design the three forms of art – Symbolic, Classical, and Romantic – that Hegel identified in his lectures on aesthetics. In the 1820s and 1830s, Schinkel increasingly advocated the Greek style as the unique paradigm of architecture; his chief challenge, therefore, was to reconcile this ideal with the demand for contemporaneity, while also acknowledging the merits of intervening styles: "We might draw nearer a solution if we could remain true to ancient Greek architecture in its intellectual principle all the while expanding it to accommodate the conditions of our new epoch and undertaking the harmonic admixture of the best of all in between periods."[29]

Reconstructing Mendelssohn's historical consciousness

Of all the composers active in the first half of the nineteenth century, it is Mendelssohn whose output provides the closest musical analogue to that of his fellow Berliner, Schinkel. Like Schinkel, Mendelssohn experimented with a variety of earlier styles, yet regarded only one – that of Bach – as an ideal valid in a range of different genres. In addition, it is vital to acknowledge that, as with Schinkel, Mendelssohn's historical orientation shifted significantly over the course of his life. This must be borne in mind in interpreting his works: conceptions that are applicable to the *Sieben Charakterstücke* (*Seven Characteristic Pieces*) op. 7 (1827) or the early choral music may have little relevance to *St. Paul* (1836) or the Six Preludes and Fugues op. 35 (1837). Providing a detailed reconstruction of how Mendelssohn's historical consciousness emerged and changed goes beyond the scope of the present essay. It is necessary, however, to outline the key phases of this development, not least because the applicability of historicism to Mendelssohn's earlier output is questionable.[30]

In his childhood and early youth, Mendelssohn's exposure to earlier music stemmed primarily from two sources: the regular cultivation of Baroque music in his home, and his participation in the performances of the Berlin Singakademie and Freitagskollegium. He was first introduced to the music of Bach by his mother Lea; her interest in the *Well-Tempered Clavier* does not suggest antiquarianism, but rather testifies to an enduring family tradition stemming from contact with Bach's pupil Johann Philipp Kirnberger. A similar perpetuation of tradition is evident in Mendelssohn's composition teacher Carl Friedrich Zelter, whose work and ideas were fundamental in shaping his historical orientation. In his numerous memoranda to the Prussian government from the first decade of the nineteenth century, Zelter repeatedly stressed that his activities were the last remnant of Berlin's musical heyday under Frederick the Great, arguing that the value of the Singakademie lay in its preservation of this tradition.[31] A similar appeal to tradition is apparent in a letter to Goethe following Mendelssohn's celebrated performance of the *St. Matthew Passion*, in which Zelter represented himself as Berlin's true guardian of Bach's legacy: "For fifty years I have venerated Bachian genius. Friedemann [Bach] died here, Emanuel Bach was a chamber musician at the court here, Kirnberger and Agricola were pupils of the elder Bach . . . I myself have taught for thirty years in this tradition."[32]

This sense of continuity with the past was clearly communicated to Mendelssohn, whose own contrapuntal studies with Zelter were oriented around this Bachian genealogy.[33] Also important for Mendelssohn's historical orientation was Zelter's endeavor to preserve traditional generic distinctions, and thus to provide a counterweight to the degeneracy he perceived in modern musical culture.[34] In Zelter's view, composers no longer heeded the dividing lines between the "grand, serious church style," the theatrical style, and the chamber style, with the result that "the genres of the beautiful are nullified"; a key role for his Singakademie was therefore to restore musical taste through the performance of Classical works that exemplified the true nature of the church and oratorio styles.[35] Throughout his life, Mendelssohn's compositional engagement with the past was conditioned by a similar conception of genre: this is apparent in his mature orchestral music – in which he was reluctant to depart from the structural norms established by Haydn and Mozart – as well as in his religious works.[36] As for Zelter, the works of Bach and Handel provided models of the possibilities and restrictions of the oratorio style, while Palestrina epitomized liturgical music in its purest form. The impact of Zelter's musical and aesthetic conservatism is apparent in the young Mendelssohn's letters, which present outspoken critiques of contemporary taste and a rigid conception of the church style. Such views were reinforced by his reading of Anton Friedrich Justus Thibaut's *Über Reinheit der Tonkunst* (*On Purity in Music*, 1824) and by his acquaintance with its author, whom he met in September 1827. While even Zelter regarded Thibaut's antiquarianism as one-sided, Mendelssohn acclaimed him for enabling him to appreciate old Italian music.[37] It is significant for the composer's later development that he attributed this revelation not to Thibaut's historical or technical insight but to his enthusiasm and instinctual understanding; no less important is Mendelssohn's insistence that, in spite of the value of other religious music, "everything is gathered together" in that of Bach.[38]

The nature of the teenage Mendelssohn's devotion to Bach requires clarification, since it has sometimes been misunderstood as the product of priggish religiosity or a yearning for the past. These perspectives ignore the unique nature of Mendelssohn's musical upbringing, in which the music of the past formed a "living present"; indeed, in several letters from this period, Mendelssohn pairs Bach with Beethoven, representing him as a vital part of modern German culture.[39] The coupling of Bach and Beethoven is strikingly apparent in Mendelssohn's output from this period. While his Piano Sonata in E major and String Quartet in A minor evidence a creative agon with some of the most idiosyncratic of Beethoven's late works, other pieces testify that Bach's music also represented – as Wulf Konold's argues – a "current compositional challenge," a living yardstick against which Mendelssohn measured his achievements.[40] The latter stimulus is clearest, perhaps, in the Fugue in A major from the *Sieben Charakterstücke*, in which the young composer ventured to surpass the scale and grandeur of his models (the ricercare fugues of the *Well-Tempered Clavier*). While the impact of Bach also resonates in movements from the String Sinfonias (1821–24), their primary models are from the mid-eighteenth century, more specifically, the court of Frederick the Great. These works, described by Lea Mendelssohn as having been composed "in the manner of the ancients," do not suggest an impulse to revive a dead idiom but rather testify to the conservative taste of Zelter and the musical institutions of Berlin.[41] Similarly, in Mendelssohn's choral music from these years, his engagement with German Baroque music and the eighteenth-century Italian *stile antico* should not be understood as a self-conscious archaizing. His quasi-liturgical pieces, such as the Te Deum (1826) and *Tu es Petrus* (1827), reflect an impulse to master idioms that he was continually exposed to via the Singakademie, and thus to demonstrate his fluency in every sphere of modern musical life.

The historical orientation reflected in Mendelssohn's output from the mid 1820s is different from that embodied in his later works. Rather than consciously engaging with diverse historical styles, these pieces represent the assimilation of the music that surrounded him in his youth. In this period, as Susanna Großmann-Vendrey aptly comments, Mendelssohn's conception of music history resembled a "colorful kaleidoscope"; in the absence of a developed historical awareness, he approached the works of the past in terms of their aesthetic impression and of the generic criteria passed on by Zelter. Accordingly, his compositional responses to earlier music cannot be understood in terms of historicism, but rather constitute the forging of a means of expression from generic models. Aspects of this approach, to be sure, continued to inform his composing. Yet it became difficult for him to reconcile the essentially ahistorical nature of his youthful engagement with the past with his mature intellectual outlook: even the conviction that Bach represented a unique, timeless ideal was to be challenged. As a result of his exposure to the views of Hegel and Goethe, his deepening knowledge of music history, and his contact with an extraordinary range of art during his travels between 1829 and 1833, Mendelssohn increasingly regarded works and styles as historically contingent: the exemplars of the church and oratorio styles receded into a foreign past, becoming ideals estranged from the present.

One factor contributing to this development was Mendelssohn's revival of the *St. Matthew Passion* in 1829, an event normally regarded as emblematic of the absorption of the past into nineteenth-century musical life. Such assimilation, however, was complicated by the awareness of cultural change, as is evident from Mendelssohn's conviction that the work required drastic cuts in order to be reclaimed for a modern audience. While Mendelssohn did not share Zelter's belief that that Bach's choral music required wholesale adaptation, his experience of directing the Passion led him to concur with his teacher's view that "Bach, in spite of all his originality, was a child of his milieu and his age."[42] Moreover, as the indignant comments of Zelter and various Leipzig musicians – who thought of themselves as having long sustained a living tradition – attest, the revival of the *St. Matthew Passion* was widely represented as marking the rediscovery of Bach: the notion of a living Bach tradition was increasingly displaced by the view of his works as monuments disinterred from the past.[43] Thus, while Mendelssohn's performance of the Passion catapulted him into the position of a leader of the early music revival, it weakened his sense that Bach formed a part of the living present: this development served to problematize the issue of how modern composers should respond to his works (Mendelssohn's chorale cantatas from these years provide a variety of responses to this question).

Another factor that shaped Mendelssohn's historical consciousness was his exposure to Hegel's lectures on aesthetics, which he attended in the winter of 1828–29. There is little evidence to suggest that he immersed himself deeply in Hegel's thought (indeed, it is clear that he shared something of Zelter's antipathy toward the philosopher), yet he was sufficiently well acquainted with his aesthetics to be able to recount Hegel's ideas to Goethe.[44] In addition, as letters from the early 1830s testify, Mendelssohn was both exasperated and troubled by Hegel's prognostication of the death of art.[45] A further formative experience was the composer's final visit to Goethe in 1830. During his fortnight's stay in Weimar, Mendelssohn gave what Goethe described as "historical exhibitions" on the piano, in order to illustrate the evolution of music: "Every morning, for about an hour, I have to play works by a variety of great composers in chronological order, and must explain to him how they contributed to the advance of music."[46] While Mendelssohn already had some familiarity with the historical development of styles, his conversations with Goethe helped to shape his mature view of music history as a continuum governed by the laws of natural growth. As will become evident, Mendelssohn himself found it difficult to reconcile his compositional inclinations with this linear conception of stylistic development.

Mendelssohn's conception of history as a continuum was strengthened by his exposure to a wealth of earlier art during his travels between 1829 and 1833. This is particularly evident in the letters from his first journey to Italy, in which fragmentary reflections on the task of the modern artist occur in tandem with his responses to the monuments of the past. Two decisions, whether conscious or unconscious, emerged from Mendelssohn's contemplation of the relation between past and present. The first was a rejection of what he viewed as a one-sided focus on one particular historical period or composer: later, he was to note that "it is a constant source of annoyance that one person can see good only in Beethoven and another only in Palestrina and a third only in Mozart or Bach: either all four or none of them."[47] It is for this reason that he rejected the art of the Nazarenes, since their devotion to Raphael and his predecessors led them to scorn Titian and more recent masters.[48] Mendelssohn's second decision was to ground his conception of history on an instinctual, empathetic identification with the great masters and, so far as it was possible, to cut himself off from more critical modes of apprehending the past. His impulse to become absorbed in artworks and make them his own – a notion that has much in common with Romantic hermeneutics – is evident in a remark about Goethe's *Alexis und Dora*: "as with all masterpieces, I often suddenly and instinctively feel that it could have been mine if a similar opportunity had befallen me, and that it was merely by chance that he expressed it first."[49] But Mendelssohn's notion of empathetic appropriation did not entirely resolve his (re)creative dilemmas: it represents a form of denial, an attempt to retrieve the unreflective and secure relation to the past that he had enjoyed in his youth. In a letter to Zelter defending his compositional historicism, Mendelssohn inveighed against "aestheticians and scholars of the arts [who] torment themselves by wanting to prove from external criteria why this is beautiful and that less so, through epochs, style, and whatever else their pigeon-holes might be called."[50] Here, Mendelssohn seeks to externalize his mature historical consciousness, to project the factors impeding his engagement with the past onto aestheticians and scholars, in order to represent himself as an unreflective artist. But only by confronting this problem directly – through composition – was Mendelssohn able to attempt a reconciliation between his competing artistic impulses and ideas.

Back to the future: the problem of religious music

The emergence of Mendelssohn's mature historical consciousness coincided with the publication (between 1828 and 1834) of several pioneering historical studies of early music. Mendelssohn was acquainted with three of the authors of these texts, Giuseppe Baini, François-Joseph Fétis and Raphael Georg Kiesewetter; a fourth, Carl von Winterfeld, was not known to the composer, who singled out his *Johannes Pierluigi von Palestrina* (1832) as an example of the misuse of history:

> Even if such people feel an aversion to the present, they can provide no
> alternative to it and should be left well alone . . . The men have yet to come
> who will show the way again: they will lead others back to the old and
> correct path (which should really be called the forward path), but not as a
> result of writing books.[51]

Given the debates on church music that raged in this period, it is understandable that Mendelssohn mistook Winterfeld's dryly objective study for a polemical tract. More significant is his contention that musical renewal through the past was the responsibility solely of practicing artists: while here, Mendelssohn resembles John the Baptist awaiting a musical Messiah, in the ensuing years he increasingly took on the latter role himself. Mendelssohn's works from 1832 to 1837 testify to his desire not only to resolve his own central compositional dilemma, but to provide exemplars of the true use of history in the present. His dogged pursuit of this goal is the factor responsible for the extraordinary gulf between much of his music from this period and the dominant genres, styles, and ethos of the time.[52] Yet it was his historically orientated works – in particular, *St. Paul* – that led to him being acclaimed as the most important German composer of his day; moreover, these works served subsequently as focal points for assessments of his significance.

Before exploring the broader interpretive issues raised by historicism in this music, it is necessary to discuss how the composer himself justified its eclecticism. In a letter from 1835, Abraham Mendelssohn affirmed his confidence that his son's first oratorio would successfully solve the problem of "combining old ways of thinking [*alten Sinns*] with new materials," avoiding the mistakes of the Nazarenes, whose attempts to regain the religiosity of earlier art resulted in mannerism.[53] Such certainty was not shared by all of Mendelssohn's confidants, some of who believed that the sphere of religious music was inherently dangerous for a composer so devoted to the music of the past. In line with his increasing distrust of aesthetic and historical speculation, Mendelssohn gave no substantive account of the relation between *St. Paul* and its Baroque models. The sole significant discussions of this matter – in letters to Zelter and Mendelssohn's friend Eduard Devrient – come from earlier in the 1830s; it should be borne in mind, therefore, that they reflect a different stage in the composer's intellectual development. Nonetheless, these remarks, responding to criticisms that some of the church music he had written in Italy showed too great a dependency on Bach, reveal at least a part of the foundations of his mature historical thinking. In a letter to Devrient from 1831, Mendelssohn initially affects a disarming naivety and nonchalance: "If it has similarity to Seb. Bach, again, I cannot do anything about it, for I wrote it just according to the mood I was in . . . I am sure you do not think that I would merely copy his forms, without the content; if it were so, I should feel such distaste, and such emptiness, that I could never finish a piece."[54] A more substantial exploration of the matter occurs in a letter to Zelter from 1830:

> Nothing is valid except that which has flowed in deepest sincerity [*Ernst*] from the innermost soul . . . If the object alone has not given rise to the work, it will never "pass from heart to heart" [*"Herz zu Herz schaffen"*] and consequently imitation is the same as the most superficial appearance of the most foreign thoughts. Certainly, no one can prevent me from enjoying and continuing to work at what the great masters have bequeathed to me, because not everyone should start from scratch, but it should be a continued working from one's own powers, not a lifeless repetition of what already exists.[55]

These passages present a conglomerate of ideas drawn from a variety of sources. On one level, they reflect Hegel's influence: Mendelssohn's concern that his music might exhibit a disunity of form and content shows an awareness of Hegel's requirement that the external appearance of a work embodies the substance of the artist's consciousness. Mendelssohn's concern with demonstrating that his church music originated in "deepest sincerity from the innermost soul" is an attempt to show that similarities to older works present in his music are the product of a comparable religious spirit. He implicitly distances his activities from those of the Nazarenes, arguing that his compositions are the product of conviction (Hegel's *Ernst*) and spontaneity ("according to the mood I was in") rather than of a reflective impulse to appropriate old forms. Just as evident in the second passage, however, is a reliance on the ideas of Goethe, to an extent that renders it of limited value as a testimony of Mendelssohn's compositional intentions. As Thomas Schmidt has noted, the phrase "Herz zu Herz[en] schaffen" is a quotation from Part I of Goethe's *Faust*; in addition, Mendelssohn appears to share Goethe's contempt for originality and "creation out-of-oneself" (*Aus-sich-Schöpfen*).[56] It is in the last sentence of this extract, in which Mendelssohn represents repetition as contrary to the processes of history, that his dependence on Goethe becomes fully evident. Not only is the idea of creatively building on the past fundamental to Goethe's outlook, but what at first appears to be a confessional artistic credo on the part of Mendelssohn is in fact a paraphrase of a passage from Goethe's *Italienische Reise*.[57] The extent to which Mendelssohn's letters from Italy constitute literary exercises in Goethe's manner is well known; even so, it seems extraordinary that in repudiating imitation, Mendelssohn should simultaneously resort to it.

Perhaps the most telling remark on Mendelssohn's compositional historicism comes not from these letters, but from a plea to the program committee in Düsseldorf regarding the first performance of *St. Paul*. Here, he reveals his apprehension concerning the reception of the work, an anxiety centering on its relation to the great models of the genre: "I confess that it would displease me if the entire second day [of the festival] were to be filled with classical pieces from the past, and that I would prefer it if at least one modern piece be included alongside them, in order that my oratorio should not come into too direct comparison with the works of the great masters."[58] Mendelssohn's comments might be viewed simply as modesty, were it not for his remark about modern pieces: he appears assured that *St. Paul* solved the problems of composing religious music as well as the works of any of his contemporaries, yet convinced that failure was inevitable in a comparison with the masterpieces of Bach or Handel. Mendelssohn did not share the views of those, such as the aesthetician Eduard Krüger, who were convinced that the modern age was "incapable of the representation of sacred forms"; such a perspective was inimical to his project for the renewal of musical culture, a salvage operation grounded on an engagement with earlier styles.[59] But he evidently regarded the possibility of success in this field as limited and relative, and dependent on "continuing to work at" the forms of his generic models.

Reinterpreting Mendelssohn's historicism

Given the delicate balancing act of attempting to salvage religious music while satisfying the demands of modernity, it is hardly surprising that *St. Paul* stimulated critical controversy in the decades following its premiere. This debate coincided with the strengthening of anti-historicist polemics in relation to the other arts: in the late 1830s and 1840s, Young Hegelian critics and aestheticians (such as Friedrich Theodor Vischer) and more seasoned campaigners (such as Heine) waged war against the Nazarenes and against retrospective tendencies in sculpture and architecture. Mendelssohn provided a musical focus for such debates. Indeed, as the most prominent compositional encounters with the past, *St. Paul* and the music for Sophocles' *Antigone* had a symbolic function in contemporary musical discourse, serving as emblems of a broader artistic problem.[60] As a result, many of these discussions pursue comparisons with activities in the other arts, albeit often at the expense of a detailed consideration of the nature of the stylistic pluralism in Mendelssohn's music. These texts (many of which have still not been submitted to detailed scholarly analysis) are of crucial significance, since the assumptions and terminology that emerged in the 1840s were to pervade discussions of this topic for much of the nineteenth and twentieth centuries. Two contrasting gambits, which continue to obscure the nature and function of Mendelssohn's historicism, emerged in this period. On the one hand, critics hostile to the composer promulgated the notion that his relation to earlier music was a matter of passive dependency, a parasitical reliance on historical styles as a means of manufacturing a religious idiom (the best-known examples of this tactic are the discussions in Heine's *Lutezia*).[61] On the other hand, those critics more favorable to Mendelssohn's achievement – such as Eduard Hanslick and, to a lesser extent, Brendel – stressed that in spite of their eclecticism, his works present a seamless welding together of old and new (it is astonishing how often one encounters the verb *verschmelzen* in German discussions of this matter).[62]

In spite of the persistence of these ideas, they are strangely at odds with the music of *St. Paul*. Very few passages of this or indeed any other work by

Mendelssohn suggest an impulse to replicate earlier idioms, or resemble – in Heine's phrase – "slavish copies" of Bach and Handel.[63] Yet conversely, the nature of the stylistic pluralism present in *St. Paul* palpably contradicts the notion of a seamless organic unity: Baroque and modern elements, forms and techniques collide and coincide in virtually every movement, while the premise shaping the work – the notion that the future of the genre lay in the synthesis of the Handelian epic oratorio with the Bachian church oratorio – elevates eclecticism to a structural principle. How, then, might we interpret the stylistic pluralism of this and other works, and the function of historicism in Mendelssohn's output? Several promising alternative strategies are hinted at in criticism from the composer's own lifetime. One option is to resist viewing *St. Paul* as an autonomous work and instead to regard it as a more complex entity, resembling the single-authored historical concerts of Spohr and Nicolai: a related idea was articulated by the critic Gottfried Wilhelm Fink, who regarded *St. Paul* as "so deliberately Handelian-Bachian-Mendelssohnian" that its primary purpose was to provide listeners with an accessible introduction to the Baroque oratorio.[64] Another perspective – whose formalism, however, is at odds with Mendelssohn's representations of his intentions – is to view his appropriation of earlier styles as a kind of linguistic game: this notion, too, can be traced back to contemporary perceptions of *St. Paul*, since Schumann commented on its "masterly play with every manner of composition."[65]

An alternative approach is to explore how Mendelssohn's engagement with earlier styles and models enacts a critique either of them or of his own compositional premises. This is not to suggest that he set out to parody the works of Bach or Handel, or that he sought – in a manner comparable to that of Heine's poetry – to make the impossibility of modern religious music the subject matter of his own compositions.[66] But while Mendelssohn's procedures do not suggest a polemical confrontation with his models, they nonetheless present – whether through affirmation, omission or reworking – interpretations of earlier music; moreover, in spite of the composer's impulse to represent his appropriations as unreflective, the works themselves arguably contradict this. Both Friedhelm Krummacher and Peter Mercer-Taylor have explored the ways in which the chorale accompaniments in *St. Paul* function as an internalized commentary: for the latter, *St. Paul* thus provides a critical reflection on stylistic pluralism as much as an embodiment of it.[67] Alternatively, one can view Mendelssohn's engagement with the music of the past as akin to the activities of the translator: elsewhere, I have explored how theories of translation can help us understand the dialogic nature of his works and their attempted recovery and adaptation of the spiritual content of other works.[68] No single critical interpretation, of course, can satisfactorily explain either the functions that Mendelssohn assigned to historicism or the stylistic processes involved. But while there is still much work to be accomplished in this field, one breakthrough has been achieved: Mendelssohn's historicism – until recently a source of embarrassed bewilderment for his devotees – is increasingly viewed as one of the most significant and valuable aspects of his creativity.

5 Mendelssohn as progressive

GREG VITERCIK

[N]o one loves his predecessors more deeply, more fervently, more respectfully, than the artist who gives us something truly new; for respect is awareness of one's station and love is a sense of community. Does anyone have to be reminded that Mendelssohn – even he was once new – unearthed Bach, that Schumann discovered Schubert, and that Wagner, with work, word, and deed, awakened the first real understanding of Beethoven?[1]   ARNOLD SCHOENBERG

He [Mendelssohn] is the Mozart of the nineteenth century, the most brilliant musician, the one who most clearly sees through the contradictions of the age and for the first time reconciles them.[2]   ROBERT SCHUMANN

Schoenberg's appreciation, characteristically as generous as it is backhanded, brings the difficulties inherent in the notion of "Mendelssohn as progressive" into clear focus. On the one hand, it can be difficult to remember that his music was ever in any significant way "new." "Progressive" more readily conjures up Wagnerian forays into the uncharted realms of the music of the future than the cultivation of the familiar, if daunting, confines of the past. Mendelssohn, however – alone among composers between Beethoven and Brahms – achieved his most characteristic and personal expression in sonata-form works, while, as Charles Rosen has observed, some of his more intimate lyric utterances may "charm, but they neither provoke nor astonish."[3]

Mendelssohn's music only rarely aspires to provoke, but if his larger forms fail to astonish, it is too often likely that we simply are not paying attention; and this brings us to the second problem. As Schumann's characterization suggests, Mendelssohn contrived to resolve the conflicts of his age by assimilating almost everything that was "truly new" in his style into a tonal, thematic, and formal language of seamless cohesion and Mozartean refinement. As a result, it is often difficult to catch him in the act of doing much of anything at all, much less something out of the ordinary. His most striking achievements tend to elude detection, duping us into a satisfied assumption of condescending comprehension. Even Tovey often mistook Mendelssohn's formal strategies for schoolboy pranks and "easy shortcuts to effect."[4]

The problems to which Mendelssohn's strategies represent solutions were engendered by two fundamental "contradictions" inherent in the early nineteenth century's confrontation with sonata forms. First, the richly expressive harmonic and gestural vocabulary of Romantic music tends to undercut the significance of the large-scale tonal processes that animate the sonata forms of the Classical era. In turn, as the opposition of tonic and secondary key as well as the function of the thematic design as an articulation of that opposition dissolve into the moment-by-moment flux of the expressive surface, the rationale for tonal resolution through formal recapitulation loses much of its dramatic urgency. There was, as Viktor Urbantschitsch put it, a "recapitulation problem"; a suspicion that the recapitulation was simply an "obligatory symmetrical analogy to the first part [the exposition]" that offered composer and listener alike nothing more than "the inflexible repetition of that which has already been said."[5]

This unsavory prospect was rendered even less palatable by the second "contradiction" – the Romantic tendency to place the climax near the end of a piece. Not only would that climax be forestalled by wearisome recapitulatory pedantries for which a rousing, if often formally inexplicable, coda might or might not offer adequate compensation, but the structurally crucial – and always dramatically calculated – effects achieved by Haydn, Mozart, or Beethoven at the opening of the recapitulation, marking the initiation of the movement's formal process of resolution, resist easy assimilation into an end-oriented dramatic trajectory. Berlioz's progressive transformations of the *idée fixe* in the first movement of his *Symphonie fantastique* represent a particularly radical response to these problems; a response, however, that threatens to put every other constituent element of the form into question. Mendelssohn's strategies, characteristically, lean more toward formal insight than hallucinatory mania.

These "problems" mark the fault lines of a fundamental shift in formal meaning from tonal process to thematic expression – in Dahlhaus' characterization, the replacement of "the idea of a balance of parts distinguished by their functions . . . by the principle of developing ideas, the concept of musical form as something which presented the history of a theme."[6] The most convincing formal procedures in Mendelssohn's early works typically emerge in his negotiation of these fault lines – specifically in the reconciliation of his highly individual lyric impulse with the imperatives of sonata-form processes. If that reconciliation at times tamps down the dramatic impact and provocative intensity of his music, it offers in compensation a reevaluation of musical relations that often proves as logically inevitable as it is intensely beautiful and "truly new."

One example from Mendelssohn's preposterously masterful early output, the Piano Quartet in F minor op. 2, completed in 1823 when the composer was fourteen, offers a sense of the depth and delicacy with which that reconciliation could be accomplished. The first movement is one of the beautifully crafted, but stiffly compartmentalized and verbosely articulated sonata forms that seem to have been the pedagogical ideal of Carl Friedrich Zelter's schooling and the epitome of classicist formal thought. The

Example 5.1 Piano Quartet in F minor op. 2, movement 2
(a) first theme, mm. 1–9

(b) second theme, mm. 25–33

Example 5.2 Piano Quartet in F minor op. 2, movement 2, opening of recapitulation, mm. 68–76

second movement, an Adagio in D♭ major, draws us into a more distinctly Mendelssohnian realm.

The Adagio is not, strictly speaking, monothematic, but the first and second themes are obviously very closely related; both derive, in turn, from the opening theme of the first movement (Example 5.1).

The first-theme version exhibits a restrained but affecting lyricism. The radically simplified outline of the second-theme version weaves through canonic overlappings in the strings, floating high over the piano's barely audible tremolos, achieving a kind of ecstatic placidity. The development verges on lyric recklessness, simply repeating these intertwinings over and over as they drift through a shimmering modulatory field.

Eventually, the harmony begins to slide back toward the tonic. But at the double return, the tonic teeters on its second inversion, pointing toward, rather than accomplishing, resolution (Example 5.2). The main theme returns as though it were the second theme, floating high in the violin, continuing to occupy the registral space maintained throughout the development and even tracing a path through the same pitches as its simplified second-theme outline in the exposition. The piano, which had originally introduced the main theme in the opening bars of the movement, simply continues the rippling sextuplets it has played throughout the development section.

Everything returns, but nothing is quite as it was; obligatory symmetry dissolves into ethereal transformations, and repetition gives way to that which had been only hinted at before. The earlier stages of the story fall away. The main theme never returns in its original form, and the second theme never returns at all, replaced by a murmuring coda of veiled allusions to transitional passages in the exposition. The thematic and tonal dialectic set out in the exposition resolves in a synthesis that simultaneously realizes and recasts the processive shape of sonata form, subsuming tone color, register, and texture not as ornamental accompaniments to the musical idea, but as the vehicles through which that idea, the lyrically unidirectional story of the theme, is told. In this most delicate of climaxes recapitulation becomes transformation and culmination.

Slow movements are, of course, the natural habitat of lyricism in sonata-form works; but Mendelssohn's genius lay less in the intensity of expression that flowers here – it remains distinctly Mendelssohnian in its restraint – than in a mutual accommodation of formal process and expressive design that carries the movement's lyric impulse far beyond its modest origins.

The disjointed verbosity that weighs down the first movement of op. 2, on the other hand, is typical of the classicist dilemma the young Mendelssohn, like most of his contemporaries, faced. Even confined to the expressive realm of the "contrasting second-theme group," outbreaks of lyricism posed severe problems of pacing and function, dissipating forward momentum in the breadth of their leisurely unfolding, and subverting harmonic tension in a wash of expressive detail.[7]

Mendelssohn developed various responses to these problems in the great works of his early maturity, ranging from the coiled spring that briefly masquerades as the lyric second theme in the first movement of the Octet op. 20 (1825, revised and published 1830), to the magnificent seascape second theme of the *Hebrides Overture* op. 26 (1829–35).[8] But his most intriguing synthesis of lyricism and formal process shapes the first movement of the least appreciated of these early masterpieces, the String Quintet in A major op. 18 (first version, 1826, revised and published 1832) – a touchingly individual assimilation of the influences of his predecessors through which the composer fashioned one of his most personal and progressive utterances. It is a music grounded in the past that is truly new, pointing unobtrusively to the future.

As always, the composer's design is enveloped in a luminous sheen that tends to mask the originality and implications of his strategies. The premises of that design rest on a distinctly Mozartean balance of parts clearly – at first glance, perhaps, all too clearly – "distinguished by their functions." Exposition, development, recapitulation, and coda follow one another in orderly succession, seeming to fulfill their functions like cogs in a sleek neo-classical machine. But in contrast to the slackly elastic outlines of the first movements of Mendelssohn's earlier pedagogically classicist chamber works, with their inevitable diffusion of dutiful first-theme bustle into indulgent lyric inflation, the exposition in the first movement of op. 18 spins out an infectiously energetic trajectory from its lyric, gently formal main theme.[9]

The exposition recalls the structural design of Mozart's G major and A major quartets K. 387 and 464; works in which Mozart, in one of his periodic confrontations with Haydn, was working out his own reformulation of the relation of formal process and motivic impulse. In both Mozart's and Mendelssohn's designs, lyricism is not simply accommodated as the contrasting, and usually disruptive, structural "other"; it is posited as the primary topic – the "main theme" – of the music, engendering rather than derailing the structural process. All of the primary thematic material – indeed it seems almost every note – of the first movement of op. 18 can be traced back to the lyrically unfolded first-inversion tonic triad that initiates the main theme.

This motivic impulse manifests itself in a web of thematic relations as clearly articulated as the structural succession of the work's formal design. Less obviously, it is deployed over – and, indeed, manifests – a trajectory of increasing pace, expanding sonorous palette, linear fragmentation, and harmonic destabilization that almost surreptitiously fractures both the lyric continuity and the orderly sequence of the formal design through which it is realized.

The main theme, for all its Classical balance, exhibits a curious reticence, self-absorbed in its hesitant pauses, oddly mulling fragmentation and repetitions, and increasingly meandering melodic and harmonic course. These traits are intensified in the compressed juxtapositions of the transition and spill over into the second theme, which, thrown slightly off balance metrically, harmonically, and even texturally from the first, never quite succeeds in establishing the secondary key, E major, with any authority. Even as the second theme does finally begin to gather itself into a cadence (mm. 102ff.),

Example 5.3 String Quintet in A major op. 18, movement 1, cadence theme, mm. 102–17

it gets caught up in itself; dangling from the first violin's repeated a″–g♯″ neighbor-note figure, it takes only a gentle nudge from the cello to suddenly lift the passage from E major to F♯ minor (Example 5.3).

At first this might seem to be some sort of Mozartean "purple passage," delaying and intensifying the inevitable cadential affirmation of the dominant. But the exposition never returns to E major; it closes, quietly but unambiguously, in F♯ minor. This is not really a purple passage, then, or a "three-key exposition" in any normal sense of the term, or a modulatory design moving from I to vi along the lines of the first movement of Beethoven's String Quintet op. 29; the exposition simply closes in the wrong key. But the delicate flash of harmonic color this entails is only part of the story.

The end of the second group became entangled in one of the seemingly inescapable half-step neighbor-note figures that are woven through the exposition (the first 4-3 pairing throbs momentarily in mm. 5–6 of the main theme). At the end of the exposition, however, the figure's inflectional tendencies are reversed: g♯″ suddenly resolves up to a″ instead of a″ resolving down to g♯″ (and, secondarily, c♯″ is no longer drawn down toward b′). These are of course simple inflectional facts of tonal life that would barely

draw attention on their own. But this reorientation lifts the melodic framework of the cadential theme up from the E major triad (laid out melodically
in second inversion, b'–e''–g♯'') to an F♯ minor triad (c♯''–f♯''–a''), reestab-
lishing the inflectionally stable elements of the melodic line in almost exactly
the disposition that frames the opening of the main theme (e''–c♯''–a'').

At the same time, while locally this reorientation of the thematic topology
introduces a fairly severe harmonic disruption, on a larger scale, it turns the
end of the exposition into a transition back toward the tonic. In this sense,
the intrusion of F♯ minor might register as a truly deceptive cadence carried
out on a structural level. The instability of the second group as a whole
might then be heard as a manifestation of an episode-like function, passing
through, rather than confirming, the dominant key; the peculiar weakening
of the local tonic pitch, E, throughout this passage certainly suggests that
this is the case. The resulting double meaning of the passage, simultaneously
intensifying and reducing tension, is characteristic of Mendelssohn's almost
wistfully ephemeral reformulation of the past in his finest works.

The head of the main theme returns at the end of the development
section, poised over a first-inversion tonic chord (m. 250). We are almost
home, but the decisive cadence is once again nudged out of place by the
cadential theme, this time pulling the music into the thoroughly implau-
sible key of G minor (m. 254). This startling intrusion negates the leading tone itself, introducing in its place a new cluster of chromatic upper
neighbors – b♭'' and d'' – gravitating toward the triadic corner posts of main
theme – a'' and c♯''. At this point, it becomes clear that tonally functional
harmonic hierarchies are being subordinated to a purely inflectional play
around the pitches of the tonic triad, deployed in the thematic gestalt of the
main theme. That gestalt might best be thought of as the movement's *pôle
harmonique*, the stable sonorous configuration around which its harmony,
form, and thematic articulations revolve, deviate, and converge.[10] As the
end of the development section gradually works its way back to the tonic,
the motivic frame is drawn back to its "polar" home configuration (m. 278).

The cadence theme functions, then, primarily to derail V–I cadential
resolutions at crucial junctures of the movement's lucidly Mozartean formal
design. Tonal process is superseded, if not quite countermanded, by the
pervasive snares of the motivic web spun from the unassuming triadic wisps
of the lyric main theme. Although the movement stakes out conventional
harmonic realms and formal articulations, these are exploited less as the
agents of large-scale tonal processes – the traditional polarity of structural
dissonance and resolution – than as the boundaries of shifting fields of
harmonic gravity that reorient the inflectional relations established by the
tonic configuration, the *pôle harmonique*, of that motivic web.[11] Tonality,
that is to say, has become a function of thematic configuration, and form is

Example 5.4 String Quintet in A major op. 18, movement 1, mm. 261–69

becoming the story of that thematic configuration and its vicissitudes over time.

Indeed, neither the establishment of large-scale harmonic tension nor its resolution is accomplished in any normal sense within the confines of exposition and recapitulation; it is the function of the coda to synthesize the resolution and closure of the music's motivic and harmonic impulses.[12] The displacement of the movement's structural climax to the coda is, of course, a hallmark of the Romantic style; but here, for once, it seems to emerge naturally from the mutual interplay of form and content that has shaped the movement from the beginning.

After a last intrusion of the cadence theme at the end of the recapitulation (m. 237), this time only slipping to the tonic minor (leaving a″ and e″ in place, with c♮″ pressing back toward c♯″), the main theme returns, *espressivo*, to open the coda (Example 5.4). Its expressivity is focused in a touching simplification of the accompanying texture and harmony that draws the theme into a flowing I–II^7–V^7–(I) four-bar cadence that encapsulates dominant and tonic, tension and resolution, expression and articulation, in purely lyric terms and proportions. The movement, which has flowed over every formal articulation in the course of its sprawling progress, simply rounds back into its transformed self, closing its lyric circle.[13]

The rest of the coda is concerned primarily with tying up an important registral thread, gradually climbing to an ecstatic c♯‴ (m. 305) that reaches back to the intrusion of the cadential theme at the end of the recapitulation (m. 237), where c♯‴ had been displaced to c♮‴. Oddly enough, this fails to lead to a conclusive cadence or upper-voice descent to the tonic pitch, A. Even the first violin's ascent to a‴ in the last two bars of the movement registers less as resolution than as a lingering recollection of the main theme; its point is not finality but incompleteness – a reluctance to let go.

A wonderfully "poetic" gesture, this close offers striking evidence of Mendelssohn's detailed control of the large-scale structural imperatives of a multi-movement sonata-form work. The first movement never steps beyond its melodically conceived design; formal process seems little more than a nostalgic recollection, and closure is really none of its business. The tonally defined structural process of the Quintet is only completed when the upper voice settles onto the tonic pitch in the last bar of the finale, a movement in which large-scale tonal relations fulfill their structural functions in a more straightforward way, and the thematic design functions to articulate rather than interfere with those relations.

In hailing Mendelssohn as the Mozart of the nineteenth century, Schumann also observed, in his own left-handed way, that "after Mozart came Beethoven; this new Mozart will also be followed by a Beethoven – perhaps he is already born."[14] By 1840, when he wrote this, Brahms – the Beethoven who would follow Mendelssohn's Mozart – was seven years old, and the future toward which the first movement of op. 18 discreetly points dawns in his early chamber works. Mendelssohn's influence is almost palpable in the two String Sextets opp. 18 and 36, from the 1860s; the two Serenades opp. 11 and 16, and the Symphony no. 2 (1877), especially the first and third movements, belong to this family of works as well. All stand somewhat to the side of Brahms' development, infused with an uncharacteristic directness of expression and gesture framed in the formal certainties of the past. They share strikingly similar thematic profiles – simple triadic outlines like the main theme of Mendelssohn's op. 18 – marked by an inward-turning self-absorption manifested most clearly in lingering repetitions within phrases – an unhurried mode of thematic generation that might be termed *Zurückspinnung*. Most striking, perhaps, is Brahms' adoption of Mendelssohn's almost obsessive concentration on oscillating half-step figures that spawn new themes and from which unprepared, and – in purely local harmonic terms – distinctly far-fetched, modulations hinging on the reversal of neighbor-note inflectional relations are hung (op. 18, first movement, mm. 60ff.; op. 36, first movement, mm. 32ff.). On the other hand, it is striking that although Brahms' harmonic language is far richer than Mendelssohn's, he is considerably more circumspect about the structural role of these modulations, deploying them as colorful, but somewhat isolated, way stations along the course of Schubertian "three-key" expositions rather than following Mendelssohn's more structurally subversive lead.[15] By the 1860s form has become more expansive, but at the same time less flexible.

This blend of melodicism, formal breadth, and barely disguised schematic inflexibility might seem a recipe for neo-classicism, but it was in Brahms' op. 18 that Tovey found "in a mature form the expression of a deliberate reaction towards classical sonata style and procedure."[16] As always, he is elusive about how that reaction manifests itself, but Kofi Agawu suggests a productive critical orientation in his overview of the symphonies.[17] In approaching these later works, Agawu urges the adoption of a dual perspective that takes into account two "fundamentally opposed compositional impulses": the imperatives of a "pre-compositional" architectural design – sonata form, for example; and those of a "logical form" that "dispenses with the outer design of architects [sic] and assumes a form prescribed by the nature, will and destination of the musical ideas themselves."[18] If in the first movement of Mendelssohn's op. 18 the claims of form and content – architecture and idea – are balanced with seemingly effortless elegance, in the Brahms Sextets there is an undercurrent of uncertainty, a sense of lyricism already shading into withdrawal and loss. The neo-classicism Walter Frisch ascribes to these works is, perhaps, itself a vehicle of expression, a token of the composer's regret over what Charles Rosen characterized as "the sense of an irrecoverable past" that will haunt his entire output.[19] Even the way thematic content maintains only a precarious equilibrium between technical sophistication and at least the pretence of an expressive directness that the composer only rarely indulged so unrestrainedly in later works seems to express that sense of loss. By 1860, the poise of the high Classical style had already slipped beyond Brahms' reach, even through the mediation of Schubert and the young Mendelssohn.

In a number of works that follow op. 18, Mendelssohn continued to explore his own reactions to the Classical heritage in a series of confrontations with Beethoven. The String Quartet in A minor op. 13 (1827), is a valiant – if unsettlingly obsessive – foray into the world of the late quartets, in particular, the Quartet in A minor op. 132, which the young composer must have studied in manuscript.[20] In the slightly later Quartet in E♭ major op. 12 (1829), perhaps the most satisfying, if not the most outwardly provocative, of these works, Mendelssohn retreats to the more congenial lyricism of the "Harp" Quartet op. 74.[21]

Once again, the structure of the first movement might seem almost too clearly delineated: the main theme reappears to mark each of the principal junctures in the "external form" of the first movement – the opening of the exposition, development, and recapitulation, and finally at the climax of the coda – but each time except the last in guises that momentarily weaken rather than reinforce the listener's sense of formal articulation. The alterations are subtle – nothing like the Romantic frenzy expressed in the increasingly hysterical transformations of the *idée fixe* in the first movement of the *Symphonie fantastique* – but their purpose is the same: to assimilate the dynamic trajectory of "external form" to the "logical" unfolding of the story of the theme.

The story in op. 12 hinges on the theme's gently elusive relation to the tonic key. The first violin traces its way through the framework of the tonic triad, but beneath it, details of voice-leading blur the boundary between Eb major and its submediant, C minor. The effect is fleeting, but it is not simply coloristic; the tonic is less the structural given of the movement than the goal toward which that structure is moving – or at least drifting. The effect is heightened at the opening of the recapitulation, where Mendelssohn contrives to make the return of the main theme over an Eb major triad firmly planted on a tonic pedal in the cello sound unstable – a dissonance rather than a resolution.

As in the first movement of op. 18, it is left for the coda to draw the theme through a subtle harmonic reorientation into a cadential formulation that assimilates tonal process to the confines of a thematic impulse that straddles the boundary between the articulative, "architectural," functionality of form and a lyricism that, as Mercer-Taylor has aptly put it, "would have seemed daringly pervasive even to Schubert".[22] The movement closes in a dying fall of genuine poetic inspiration that Brahms seems to have recalled at the end of the first movement of his Third Symphony; he even follows Mendelssohn's lead in bringing back the first-movement coda at the end of the finale.

In both works, the return of music from one movement in another obviously implies an overarching expressive design – a logical form – that could not be contained within the formal processes of the individual movements. Mendelssohn's influence lies lightly on Brahms' shoulders; not surprisingly, the challenge of maintaining the formal and expressive intensity his Beethovenian aspirations engender in the latter stages of op. 13 weighed far more heavily on Mendelssohn's. As Mercer-Taylor observes, the "jagged juxtapositions and sudden changes of direction" that buffet the Finale seem to lack any "palpable sense of emotional motivation."[23]

The perplexing trajectory of the finale wavers uneasily between mannerism and convention, but its compositional logic is nearly impeccable. Its overheated outbursts mark the fissures where previously unsuspected cyclic processes break into the self-contained architectural form of the movement with a vehemence rarely encountered in Mendelssohn's expressive world.

The third movement, a brief but eloquent Andante espressivo in Bb major, closes in a tonic cadence strongly colored by its subdominant, which is, of course, Eb major, the tonic of the work as a whole. The pull toward Eb major is so strong, in fact, that the final bar of the Andante, marked *attacca*, registers unmistakably as V of Eb major and retrospectively seems to transform the entire slow movement into a lyrically impassioned anticipation of the return to the tonic at the opening of the finale.

But the first bar of the finale erupts in an agitated fanfare on V of vi (C minor in place of Eb major once again!) that eventually leads us into a full-blown sonata-form exposition in C minor, moving to G minor as its secondary key area (the use of the minor dominant is yet another foreshadowing of formal procedures usually associated with Brahms). This is not a movement that begins in the wrong key, but one that simply *is* in the wrong key. The jagged juxtapositions that fracture the finale mark lines of stress where harmonic/thematic detail and tonal/formal structure – logical and architectural form – collide. This is perhaps most striking in a cluster of otherwise almost inexplicable changes of direction in the exposition – the intrusions of a secondary exposition articulated by its own network of themes, gravitating around the work's "real" tonic: Eb major within the C minor of the first group and its dominant, Bb major, in the second group. A fleeting ambiguity that had colored the lyric opening of the first movement's main theme has become the structural framework of the quartet's roiling conclusion.

The return of the coda from the first movement seems to emerge naturally from the web of thematic resemblances and quotations that span op. 12, drawing the entire work back into the unassuming dimensions of its lyric beginning. But the sense of inevitability with which the coda returns – closing the work's somewhat misshapen circle with the reestablishment of the commensurability of tension and resolution, elaboration and closure – arises from the integration of the cyclic design across every stratum of the work's musical substance; motive and theme, harmonic detail and tonal structure, register, dynamics, and voice leading are all subsumed in its dying fall.[24]

Cyclic procedures represent the most sweeping manifestation of logical form, breaking down the structural integrity – the closed architectural forms – of the individual movements of a work in order to fully realize what Agawu calls the "nature, will and destination of the musical ideas themselves."[25] The four movements of op. 12 have grown together in ways that overwhelm the finale, its meaning rendered inexplicable except in the narrative context of the whole. That growth, from barely perceptible detail to the largest dimensions of tonal form, manifesting itself in subtly new forms at each stage of its development is, I believe, one of Mendelssohn's most impressive achievements, one that seems to demand consideration in the exuberantly organic terms of Romantic creative theory. Indeed, Mendelssohn's transformative methods are perhaps best understood in terms of the conception of botanical metamorphosis propounded by Goethe in his *Versuch, die Metamorphose der Pflanzen zu erklären* (1790).[26] "Everything is leaf," Goethe had written. The plant develops itself – both in form and function – through alternating stages of expansion and contraction of the embryonic leaf-forms already present in the germinated seed. In the whole as in the smallest detail, the plant manifests itself as transformed realizations of the

leaf that is its origin and its defining characteristic. The aesthetic corre-
late had already been expressed in Carl Philipp Moritz's *Über die bildende
Nachahmung des Schönen* (1788): "a work is not *put together* from *without,*
it is *unfolded* from *within. One* thought embodied in several forms."[27] The
seeds of the E♭ major/C minor confrontation that colors all of op. 12 lie,
nearly concealed, in the opening measures of the first movement but come
to thoroughly unexpected, but logically grounded fruition in the formal
and expressive turmoil of the finale. A letter written in 1828 indicates how
central this idea was to Mendelssohn's musical thinking at this time (the
work under discussion is Beethoven's recently published String Quartet in
C♯ minor op. 131):

> You see, that is one of my points! The relation of all 4 or 3 or 2 or 1
> movements of a sonata to the others and to the parts, so that from the very
> beginning, and throughout the work, one knows its secret (so when the
> unadorned D major reappears, the 2 notes go straight to my heart); it must
> be so in music.[28]

The final page of op. 12, too, goes straight to the heart, although the plot –
the dynamic sequence of events – through which the composer leads
us there may seem unpersuasive and overwrought, its secret, intimated from
the very beginning and woven through all four movements, never quite
measuring up to its emotional aspirations.[29] The problem is not unique to
op. 12, and the inability of his most sympathetic listeners to recognize the
"one thought" embodied over the whole course of each of his extended
works vexed the composer greatly. In the same letter to his friend Adolf
Lindblad, Mendelssohn wrote of his own op. 13 that

> many people have already heard it, but has it ever occurred to any of them
> (my sister excepted, along with Rietz and also Marx) to see a whole in it?
> One praises the Intermezzo, another this, another that. Pfui to all of them![30]

In a roughly contemporary letter, Mendelssohn puts up an oddly half-
hearted defense of the work against his father's breathtakingly heavy-handed
criticism:

> You seem to mock me about my A minor Quartet, when you say that you
> have had to rack your brain trying to figure out what the composer was
> thinking about in some works, and it turned out that he hadn't been
> thinking about anything at all. I must defend the work, since it is very dear
> to me; its effect depends too much on the performance, though.[31]

This almost universal lack of comprehension – which surely could not
be solely a product of inadequate performance – clearly troubled the young
composer. The appeals to religious sentiment that begin to crop up in his

works around this time – the Fugue in E minor (1827; published in 1837 as op. 35) or, staked out in grandiose biographical and historical dimensions in the ambitious cyclic and programmatic design of the "Reformation" Symphony (1831), and later in the finale of the Piano Trio in C minor op. 66 (1845), or the evocations of civic ritual – in the last pages of the Overture, *Meeresstille und glückliche Fahrt* op. 27 (1828), or the "Scottish" Symphony (begun in 1829; published in 1843) – might well be understood as attempts both to render the untranslatable force with which musical facts go straight to the heart manifest and comprehensible – especially to the growing nineteenth-century lay audience – and at the same time to endow a work's expressive "secret" with an unimpeachable emotional authority that would render questions of motivation moot.

Those questions, which invariably become more pressing as the emotional stakes are raised, tend to cluster around issues of closure on the largest scale. If the high-Classical progression from complexity in the first movement to a relatively lower level of intensity in the finale – the design achieved so brilliantly in Mendelssohn's op. 18 – had come to seem stiffly academic and overly architectural, formal patterns merely "put together from without," the thrilling, explicitly cyclic and implicitly narrative trajectories of Beethoven's most characteristically "Beethovenian" works – the Fifth and Ninth Symphonies, for example – offered models as seductively attractive as they were fundamentally unrepeatable. It is at once one of Mendelssohn's signal accomplishments and one of the more unsettling characteristics of his style that his greatest cyclic designs effect a compromise between the Classical progression of loosely related movements and Beethoven's epically expressive plots; the return of the Scherzo in the Finale of the Octet, for example, owes at least some of its brilliant and magical wit to the fact that it operates at an exuberant but unabashedly lower level of expressive intensity than its obvious model, the high drama of Beethoven's Fifth Symphony.

It is not surprising, then, that one of the most successful of these compromises shapes one of Mendelssohn's most effervescent conceptions, the Piano Concerto in G minor op. 25 (1831). Mercer-Taylor has written perceptively of the first movement's most striking deviations from Classical concerto procedures: the elimination of the double exposition and the page of skittish virtuosity that stands in its place; and later, the drastically foreshortened recapitulation, where the orchestra barely has a chance to mention the main theme before the soloist interrupts with the lyric second theme. In particular, he is struck by the cumulative effect these maneuvers produce – an impression that the soloist "refuses to be bothered by any sense of responsibility to the principal theme around which the whole musical structure was to be organized" – suggesting that this might

reflect the composer's own "very serious anxieties concerning the insidious (as he saw it) impact of empty virtuosity on contemporary concert
life."[32]

I would suggest that the work's "secret" – its single thought – does, indeed,
concern the relation of soloist and orchestra, and the principal theme of the
first movement stands at its core. But the dynamic sequence through which
it discloses itself is not completed within the first movement; it is a story that
takes three explicitly interconnected movements to tell, and its organization
represents one of the composer's most satisfying cyclic designs. It will prove
to be less about overcoming virtuosity than about justifying virtuosity as
the agent of resolution in that design.

The gist of the story is simple enough: it involves the eminently Classical
confrontation of the minor and major modes of the tonic, pivoting, of
course, on the relation between B♭ and B♮, and played out in a sequence
moving from the instability and gestural expressivity of the first movement's
G minor to the unbuttoned exuberance of the finale's G major. What is new
and uniquely Mendelssohnian is the unexpectedly rich – yet clearly delineated – harmonic language in which that confrontation takes place, the
delicate play of inflectional relations it entails, and the masterful thematic
and expressive design through which the story is articulated. All of the work's
themes can be traced back more or less directly to the upward rush of the
orchestra's brief introduction, which already in its second bar juxtaposes
the minor and major thirds, B♭ and B♮. The downward plunge of the first
movement's principal theme is simply an inversion of this ascent, draped
over a rhythmic diminution of mm. 1–3. The lyric second theme, first heard
in the piano in B♭ major, combines versions of these ascending and descending motions in an expressive line – littered with performance directions –
that can only maintain the major mode for four bars before falling into B♭
minor in what might appear to be an example of what Tovey took to be the
composer's inability to tell major from minor (the same instability within
the second theme is central to the cyclic design of the contemporaneous
"Reformation" Symphony).[33] A few moments later the harmony drifts even
farther afield, drawn to B♭'s own minor third for an idyllic episode in the
thoroughly unlikely – and implausibly un-Mendelssohnian – realm of D♭
major, the major mode of the key a tritone from G minor, the overall tonic
(mm. 79ff.).

The premature intrusion of this almost schizophrenically expressive lyric
second theme just after the opening of the recapitulation does, indeed,
suggest that the soloist has little use for the orchestra's grimly forthright
main theme and its virtuoso bluster; but even the second theme is severely
curtailed, its *espressivo* musings drifting quickly into "virtuoso ambling"
that never manages to escape G minor.

Example 5.5 Piano Concerto in G minor op. 25, movement 3
(a) mm. 40–47

(b) mm. 71–77

In fact, G major doesn't make an appearance until the transition leading into the second movement, where its major third, B♮, is immediately taken as V of E major, the key of the Andante. This movement, lying somewhere between extended song, rondo, and a loose set of variations on a theme that is itself a variant of the second theme of the first movement, achieves a lyric climax of rapturous textural refinement, *piano* and *tranquillo*, in B major – an ecstatic celebration of B♮ in a context equally visionary and ephemeral.

The soloist reverts to flashing outbursts of virtuosity in the transition that storms in on the final cadence of the second movement, but this time its goal proves to be emphatically thematic and structurally central: the passage culminates in the long anticipated establishment of G major, marked by an exuberant, fully (indeed, elaborately) formed theme beginning on the major third, B♮ (Example 5.5a).

This new theme is, in fact, simply a G major version of the principal theme of the first movement: the piano's initial b♮''' emphatically trumps the b♭'' proposed by the orchestra in the first movement; the line also reworks the gestures of the second theme of the first movement. The piano, having at last established the "real" version of the principal theme – the secret only fleetingly glimpsed in the opening bars of the first movement, seems reluctant to relinquish its new-found form-creating power, moving on to another new theme which will dominate the finale, manically expounding that secret – the resolution of B♭ to B♮ (now heard in a neighbor-note motion, B–A♯–B) – in its swirling figuration (Example 5.5b).

Tovey claimed that in the suppression of the double exposition "Mendelssohn may truthfully be said to have destroyed the classical concerto form." But he admitted that, at least in the case of the Violin Concerto, the composer was "not so much evading a classical problem as producing a new if distinctly lighter art-form."[34] In its modest and distinctly accessible way op. 25 had already established that new form with much of the rigor and energy that marks his finest early works.

In op. 25 Mendelssohn reconstitutes what Tovey called "the primary fact . . . of concerto style . . . that the form is adapted to render the best effect expressible by opposed and unequal masses of instruments or voices."[35] In op. 25, tonal resolution, realized in terms of a delicate but surprisingly rich network of chromatic inflectional transformations, motivic process, and the dramatic form-defining role of the soloist in its confrontation with the massed forces of the orchestra are all expanded beyond the formal processes of the first movement, coordinated within a multi-movement cyclic process spinning out a single, immediately comprehensible expressive trajectory from the abrupt juxtapositions of the opening of the first movement to the joyous exuberance of the Finale.

That this new art form remains true both to its heritage and to its present – with neither condescension nor provocation – is, of course, the signal attribute of Mendelssohn's often elusive progressivism. Like Mozart writing to his father about his own piano concertos, Mendelssohn could say of op. 25, as of all his finest works, that it struck

> a happy medium between what is too easy and too difficult; they are very brilliant, pleasing to the ear, and natural, without being vapid. There are passages here and there from which connoisseurs alone can derive satisfaction; but these passages are written in such a way that the less learned cannot fail to be pleased though without knowing why.[36]

Even today, we continue, learned connoisseurs and general audience alike, to be pleased by Mendelssohn's finest works, all too often without quite knowing why.

PART THREE

Profiles of the music

6 Symphony and overture

DOUGLASS SEATON

Orchestral music in Mendelssohn's career

The symphony occupies a remarkably limited place in Mendelssohn's oeuvre. Because he published just two symphonies – one a work of his sixteenth year and the other only after a fourteen-year incubation – one might well imagine that the anxiety of Beethoven's influence overwhelmed him. Certainly, Mendelssohn's history with the symphony demonstrates his intense self-criticism and even self-doubt. It also reflects other factors, however, including his schedule of professional activities and his restless compositional imagination.

Mendelssohn was the most influential and widely admired orchestral composer of his generation. His experience with the orchestral repertoire of both eighteenth-century masters and his contemporaries gave him an unerring sense for original and imaginative structures. His gift for musical characterization, manifest in his concert overtures, captured an aspect of Romanticism in a way that appealed equally to unsophisticated listeners and to critics, whether progressive or conservative. And in a few works he explored the possibilities of complex narrative in music.[1]

The apprentice sinfonias to Symphony no. 1 (1821–1824)

Mendelssohn gained his orchestral mastery through rigorous study. Karl Friedrich Zelter's tutelage brooked no shirking of assignments in harmonization, elementary forms, and rigorous counterpoint in a tradition extending back to J. S. Bach.[2] After about two years of these studies Mendelssohn began to work in full-scale compositions in more complex forms.

Among his first experiments with fully developed multi-movement works are the twelve sinfonias that he composed in 1821–23. It is not clear to what extent these belong to Mendelssohn's studies or whether they should be regarded as independent artistic works. As study pieces, they go beyond mere exercises in writing for the string choir, developed beyond what purely pedagogical intention would require – indeed, the time consumed in writing movements and passages that did not represent any systematic compositional problem would simply stall didactic progress. On the other hand, as independent compositions – either as domestic chamber music, with one player per part, or with a larger, orchestral group – they obviously bear the marks of exploring technical challenges, especially in counterpoint, and their style, at least at first, derives from the eighteenth-century models that formed the basis of Mendelssohn's studies up to this time. Regarded from either viewpoint, the sinfonias must have demonstrated in performances within the Mendelssohn family home how the youthful composer was moving toward independent artistry.

The sinfonias trace a developmental trajectory through several phases, suggesting both progress through a chronological succession of models and Mendelssohn's increasing imagination.[3] The first model seems to have been the Italianate sinfonia of the early eighteenth century, converted from operatic to concert performance in the generation of Sammartini and spread throughout the German-speaking regions in the middle of the century. The first five sinfonias, composed between May and December 1821, feature motoric rhythms, both imitative and free fifth-species counterpoint, chains of suspensions, opening and pre-cadential *unisono* passages, quasi-trio sonata texture (the slow movement of Sinfonia 2), limited and terraced dynamic indications, Baroque dance rhythms (e.g., siciliano in the second movement of Sinfonia 1 and gigue in the finale of Sinfonia 2), cadential hemiola, and the absence of clear thematic material associated with the secondary keys in rounded binary opening movements (see Example 6.1). They also have only three movements each, and in Sinfonias 3 and 4 the slow movements do not conclude with full cadences but lead directly to the finales. We might describe this group as representing a sort of "neo-pre-Classicism."

The next group of sinfonias approach the High Classical style of the Enlightenment. There are moments of Haydnesque wit, as in the three-measure pauses that interrupt the finale of Sinfonia 6, and increasing interest in the "conversational" texture perfected by Haydn and Mozart from about 1780 onward. With Sinfonia 6 the three-movement plan continues, but the interior movement is a minuet with two trios. Thereafter the four-movement plan becomes standard: opening allegro (in Sinfonias 8 and 9 preceded by a slow introduction), slow movement, minuet or scherzo (the latter in Sinfonia 9), and fast finale. Sinfonias 7 and 8 could be characterized as "post-Classical" symphonies, while in Sinfonia 9 the use of a Scherzo instead of a minuet, together with the inclusion of a Swiss folk tune (see Example 6.2) for its Trio, might bring the piece into the range of early Romanticism.[4]

Sinfonia 10, a single movement in the form of a substantial adagio introduction and an allegro sonata form, resembles an overture more than a symphony. Expanding the Classical/early Romantic model, Sinfonia 11 has five movements. The second movement is a Scherzo, again based on a Swiss

Example 6.1 Early 18th-century traits in Mendelssohn's sinfonias
(a) Sinfonia 5, mvt. 3, mm. 24–40. Fugal imitation

(b) Sinfonia 4, mvt. 3, mm. 6–9. Chain of suspensions

folksong, this time – astonishingly – joined by a "Janissary band" of timpani, triangle, and cymbals. After the central slow movement there follows
a "Minuet," which, however, employs 6/8 rather than 3/4 meter. The last
sinfonia, no. 12, has just three movements, but it does not belong to the
pre-Classical style like the first several. Its first movement consists of a slow
introduction and a double fugue; the andante second movement perhaps

Example 6.1 *(cont.)*
(c) Sinfonia 2, mvt. 1, mm. 1–2. Opening unison

(d) Sinfonia 2, mvt. 1, mm. 68–73. Cadential unison

suggests a nocturne or, even better, an aubade; and the last movement combines sonata form with a double fugue. The fugal writing demonstrates the influence of Bach both in the highly characteristic subjects and in the working out, but it is embedded in frameworks that include passages of post-Classical and Romantic styles.

Mendelssohn was well aware of more up-to-date styles, too. We encounter hints of the influence of Rossini's exuberant overtures, and some moments suggest the atmospheric style of Weber, starting with the

Example 6.2 Sinfonia 9, mvt. 3, mm. 41–50. Swiss folk tune

nocturne-like slow movements of Sinfonias 4 and 5. Notably, little of this music suggests any influence from Beethoven (although the principal theme of the first movement in Sinfonia 4 somewhat resembles the trio subject in the scherzo of Beethoven's Fifth Symphony). One clear foreshadowing of a distinctively Mendelssohnian device occurs in the minuet of Sinfonia 6. In the second trio comes the unexpected effect of a chorale-like (but apparently original) melody in whole-measure note values set against counter-melodic material in quarter and eighth notes (see Example 6.3). This anticipates the use of such texture in, for example, the "Reformation" and "Italian" symphonies and the second part of the orchestral opening of the *Lobgesang*.

One clear trend among the sinfonias is Mendelssohn's increasing interest in fuller scoring. Beginning in Sinfonia 9 he regularly divided the violas into two sections, producing five-part rather than four-part texture. In the second

Example 6.3 Sinfonia 6, mvt. 3, mm. 60–83. Chorale-like style

movement of that same piece the violins play in four parts, the violas in two, and the cello and bass parts split, creating both high and low four-part string choirs and then, at the very end, eight parts. We have already noted that in the Scherzo of Sinfonia 11 percussion instruments join the strings. This tendency toward enriching and experimenting with scoring culminated in Sinfonia 8, which Mendelssohn composed first for strings but immediately re-scored for full orchestra.

Overall, these sinfonias give the impression of a highly precocious and energetic youngster. While imagination and exuberance emerge everywhere in this music, ambition now and then gets the better of formal sensibility. In the later pieces, for example, Mendelssohn does not seem to have realized that the attempt to integrate a grand double fugue with a sonata form would inevitably overload the capacity of the structure.

The work conceived as Sinfonia 13 ultimately became Mendelssohn's first published work in the genre, the Symphony no. 1 in C minor op. 11. After performances in Berlin (1824) and Leipzig (1827), this work was featured

Example 6.4 Symphony no. 1 op. 11, mvt. 1, mm. 1–8, violin 1. Principal theme in "overture" style

Example 6.5 Symphony no. 1 op. 11, mvt. 2. Theme in principal and secondary key areas
(a) mm. 1–8

(b) mm. 33–48

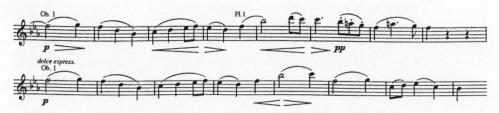

in Mendelssohn's London concert on 25 May 1829, during the composer's first visit to England. Mendelssohn presented the autograph manuscript to the Philharmonic Society and dedicated the work to the Society when it was published in 1831.[5]

The Symphony turns sharply away from the heavily contrapuntal and chromatic style of its immediate predecessors and toward a more modern, even operatic style. The fast movements include a number of overture-like gestures: the opening theme of the first movement (see Example 6.4), which Thomas Grey has compared to a number of themes from opera overtures by Cherubini, Weber, and Marschner;[6] the theatrical crescendo in the closing section; and the effective suspension of the rhythm at the beginning of the coda; as well as the "curtain-raising" style of the coda to the finale. Both outer movements exhibit a Mozartean profusion of thematic ideas.

The inner movements offer interesting takes on conventional models. The second movement assumes an unusual sonata deformation. The theme that establishes the principal key (E♭) is a song-like, eight-bar phrase. This returns in the dominant area, this time ending as an antecedent phrase, to which the transposed original phrase responds as consequent (see Example 6.5). An extended transition leads to a reprise that again uses the full antecedent–consequent pairing.

The "Menuetto" is really a scherzo, "Allegro molto" in 6/4 meter. The trio sounds almost hymn-like, with its melody in long notes in the woodwinds over a flowing, triadic accompaniment from the strings. As in several of the earlier sinfonias, this ends in a transition that introduces the da capo.[7]

The symphony as a whole demonstrates that Mendelssohn had acquired a thorough familiarity with the symphonic style of late Mozart and Haydn and the early symphonies of Beethoven. It stands as the final foundation stone in Mendelssohn's preparation for a career as an orchestral composer in the mature Romantic style.

The "characteristic" – literary inspirations

From symphonies Mendelssohn turned to a new kind of orchestral project, which inspired him to something more original and personal: musical interpretations of two literary works. The programmatic concert overture, despite some notable operatic and non-programmatic predecessors, really constituted a new genre.[8]

The first concert overture demonstrates unarguable genius: the Overture to *A Midsummer Night's Dream* (1826). The piece works something like an operatic medley overture, in the manner of Weber's overture to *Der Freischütz*. In this case, however, no preexisting operatic numbers were available to be mined for material, so Mendelssohn constructed themes as representations of the characters or images in the play. Because he had the opportunity to compose the incidental music for a performance of the play seventeen years later, and the overture's themes return as underscoring, we do not need to guess at their intention. The opening chord progression accompanies the application of the love potion to the eyes of the young mortals and Titania. With its "reversed" order of chords and major-minor ambiguity (I–V–iv–I), it also serves in the overture to lead the listener into a "looking-glass world" of magic and mystery. The principal theme proper is one of the great examples of the Mendelssohnian elfin style, and it comes as no surprise that it accompanies Puck in the incidental music. The bold, Weberian transition theme turns out to be associated with Theseus, while the lyrical secondary theme, with its long descending lines, evokes the lovers. A particularly felicitous touch is the abandonment of decorum in the closing theme, in order to depict the "hempen homespuns."[9] Not just the obvious braying sound here to represent Bottom in his ass's head but also the simple, formulaic melody creates this effect.

The design is not programmatic in the sense that the overture follows the action of the play. Rather, it adopts a relatively straightforward sonata form, the themes clearly functional in terms of the conventional tonal plan. Framing and articulating this are the ritornello-like returns of the opening chords at the reprise and the very end of the overture. The coda

presents an interesting effect, reinterpreting the transition theme, associated with the character of Duke Theseus, in a slow, sleepy style. The passage
thus suggests that the overture as a whole might be heard as Theseus's
dream.[10]

Mendelssohn next turned to Goethe, with the overture *Meeresstille und
glückliche Fahrt* (Calm Sea and Prosperous Voyage). Zelter had introduced
Mendelssohn to Goethe several years earlier, and the old poet and boy
composer had taken to each other immediately.[11]

Goethe's poems describe the terror of a sailing ship becalmed at sea,
followed by the coming of wind and the joy of returning to land. The first
poem captures the motionlessness of the ship in eight lines of trochaic
tetrameter and long vowels:

Tiefe Stille herrscht im Wasser,	Deep stillness rules over the water,
Ohne Regung ruht das Meer,	The sea rests motionless,
Und bekümmert sieht der Schiffer	And the sailor looks troubled
Glatte Fläche rings umher.	At the smooth surface all around.
Keine Luft von keiner Seite!	Not a breeze from any direction!
Todesstille fürchterlich!	Terrifying deathly stillness!
In der ungeheuren Weite	And in the uncanny distance
Reget keine Welle sich.	Not a wave moves.

The second poem features ten short lines of amphibrachic dimeter, with a
pattern of lines and rhymes that rushes ahead by forcing two "extra" lines
into what it sets up as a second quatrain.

Die Nebel zerreißen,	The mists are rent apart,
Der Himmel ist helle,	The sky is bright,
Und Aeolus löset	And Aeolus releases
Das ängstliche Band.	The fearful bond.
Es säuseln die Winde,	The winds rustle,
Es rührt sich der Schiffer.	The sailor rouses himself,
Geschwinde! Geschwinde!	Quickly! Quickly!
Es teilt sich die Welle,	The waves divide,
Es naht sich die Ferne,	The distance approaches,
Schon seh' ich das Land!	Already I see the land.

At this time in his life Mendelssohn had never undertaken a sea voyage.
Beyond Goethe's poetry, he may have learned something of the horrors of
being becalmed at sea from the popular literature of nautical disasters that
circulated at the time. And, of course, it is the artist's ability to construct
both a world and an experience in the imagination that finally determines a
successful work. Mendelssohn expressed Goethe's two-part design through
an overture with slow introduction. The work is unified by a recurring

motive, first introduced by the bass in the opening measures and developed though a variety of permutations in both slow and fast tempos. In this case, the introduction expands to unusual dimensions in order to allow time to establish the seemingly unending calm. A transition leads into the fast, compact, sonata form that represents the ship's swift sailing into port.

The Adagio tempo, repressed dynamic level, and lack of forward-directed activity in the *Meeresstille* section effectively express both the sea's flatness and the ominousness of the situation. The transition creates a remarkably realistic impression of rising breeze and sea, beginning with the slightest gust from the flute, then gradually growing and accelerating, as it builds up harmonic anticipation. The *glückliche Fahrt* becomes a lively, rollicking trip, with plenty of motion but never confronting any threat from wind and waves. By way of coda the overture brings celebratory brass fanfares and even some cannon shots from the timpani.[12] Perhaps most striking from a programmatic point of view, Mendelssohn departed from the end of Goethe's poem, so that at the very end of the work the slow tempo and flatness of the first part return, closing the overture with a plagal cadence. R. Larry Todd considers this to represent "ultimately a circular, self-renewing act of discovery," and Grey takes it to "recall the calm sea of the beginning, now recollected in a new tranquillity."[13] One might consider an alternate interpretation, however, in which the entire happy voyage is framed as only the hallucination of the dying mariner, and the conclusion, yielding to the reality of the calm sea, represents his death.

What makes these two first concert overtures particularly important in Mendelssohn's development as a composer is the remarkable nature of their melodic material. The thematic ideas in these works no longer suggest Classical (or Baroque) models, for the themes owe more to expressive content than to the functional requirements of their forms. In this way the music appeals to the aesthetic that Friedrich Schlegel identified as the "characteristic,"[14] moving Mendelssohn decisively from a post-Classical style to a Romantic one.

The "characteristic" – music and place

Mendelssohn's travels in the years 1829–32, then a common practice for well-to-do young men as a means of developing cultural literacy and taste, produced orchestral works that reflected his experience. Such a Grand Tour generally included the major European capitals, especially Paris and Vienna – for the sake of the great museums, concert halls, and opera houses – and Italy as the garden bed of culture for both classical antiquity and the Renaissance. There were various ways to capture the experiences of one's

Grand Tour. One obvious means was by writing a journal or a series of letters to one's family at home, letters that the family would keep or return to the writer for later reminiscing.[15] Another was through drawings in pen or pencil, or paintings in watercolor, at which Mendelssohn was highly skilled. For Mendelssohn not only letters and pictures filled this function, but also music. Here we shall consider one overture, *The Hebrides*, and one symphony, the so-called "Italian" Symphony in A major.

Mendelssohn's visit to Britain in 1829 – not necessarily a standard part of the Grand Tour for young Germans – brought both professional success and personal adventure. He made a very positive impression in London through his musical appearances, which led to nine later visits to England. More important from the viewpoint of compositional creativity, he undertook a walking tour of Scotland with his friend Carl Klingemann. At the historic palace of Holyroodhouse in Edinburgh he conceived the opening of an A minor symphony. We shall discuss the work itself later; for the moment, however, it is noteworthy that he seems to have deliberately sought such inspirations from his Scottish adventure. Writing to his family, he says, "I believe I found today in that old chapel the beginning of my Scotch symphony,"[16] as if he had been expecting to find it. The ruined palace chapel, and the story of Mary Queen of Scots that it inevitably represents, triggered the musical idea.

Similarly, when Klingemann and Mendelssohn arrived at the west coast of Scotland, Mendelssohn found the opening of the *Hebrides* overture. In this case, again, inspiration seems to have arisen from intention. The composer notated the beginning of the overture, in remarkable detail and nearly in its final form, before actually visiting the famous cave associated with the story of Fingal. Indeed, Mendelssohn's reading of James Macpherson's invented "translations" of poems by the legendary third-century Gaelic bard Ossian colored his view of the physical setting. The work is part seascape and part evocation of bardic poetry; hence the variety of titles that Mendelssohn attached to it: *Overture to the Lonely Island*, *The Hebrides*, *Overture to the Isles of Fingal*, *Overture to the Hebrides*, and *Fingal's Cave*.[17]

Like the *Midsummer Night's Dream* overture, *The Hebrides* is not narrative but "characteristic." Its first theme unfolds as six repetitions of an ornamented descending triad, twice on B minor, twice on D major, and twice on F♯ minor. The use of A rather than A♯ (the leading tone does not appear until m. 12) gives a modal character that implies both the ancient and the exotic. The static, repetitive appearances of the motive belong to the conventions of the pastoral, though here the waves of the sea, rather than fields, are evoked. The sequential, non-functional harmonies open up a sense of distance. The theme associated with the secondary key (D major) is a wide-ranging melody featuring the cellos (with woodwind assistance).

Its song-like lyricism is romanticized by asymmetrical phrasing, and, like the first theme, it manifests a tendency to shift phrases to different pitch levels. The closing area employs martial fanfares derived from the rhythm of the first motive. The development proceeds in an episodic rather than a dramatic fashion, not unlike Macpherson's epic tales. A compact reprise of the two main themes leads to an extensive coda that climaxes in a wild storm scene. The very end brings the descending opening motive and the rising gesture of the lyrical theme simultaneously in contrary motion, as the music fades to silence.

The compositional process of *The Hebrides* is quite revealing. Todd has demonstrated that in revising the overture Mendelssohn worked to eliminate the impression of a lurking contrapuntism, striving, as he himself put it, to evoke more of "train oil, sea gulls, and salt fish."[18] At the same time, he found ways to impose the rhythm and contour of the opening motive on a number of formerly rather featureless passages. The work thus not only lost any trace of the "learned" but gained far greater organic unity than its original version.

The other important work to come from Mendelssohn's Grand Tour was the Symphony in A major, known as the "Italian." Because this piece has become one of his best known, it is difficult to keep in mind that not only did he never publish it, he thoroughly revised the second, third, and fourth movements and believed that the first needed fundamental revisions, as well.[19] Thus the version familiar to audiences today does not represent even his latest conception, much less a definitive one.

Thomas Grey has suggested that the four movements of the symphony might be understood as a series of *tableaux vivants*. There is no plot line across the entire symphony but rather a quartet of scenes around the topic of Italian life – seen, of course, through German eyes.[20]

The composer spent much of his Italian sojourn in Rome, where he experienced the brilliant, lively carnival season, which he described in colorful letters. It is easy to hear the festive activity in the acrobatic, Harlequinesque opening theme of the symphony's first movement. The second theme maintains the overall spirit, superimposing on it just enough lyric relaxation to provide contrast. One distinctive aspect of this form, the entrance of a jaunty new theme in A minor early in the development, seems to have resulted from Mendelssohn's revisions to the work; the theme had actually appeared in the exposition, in a passage that the composer excised. The effect in the symphony as we know it is that this intrusion, soon juxtaposed with the movement's opening motive, helps to launch the development. The concise reprise incorporates the jaunty theme, again in the tonic minor, after the lyric theme, and integrates it into the coda.[21]

The second movement belongs to the processional *topos*, also famously illustrated in the second movement of Beethoven's Seventh Symphony and the pilgrims' march in Berlioz's *Harold en Italie*. The movement opens with a unison invocative recitation. A "walking bass," part of Mendelssohn's background from his training in Baroque styles, accompanies a hymn-like melody in D minor, with counter-melodic material in the flutes added to the repetitions of the two strains. After this reflective tune comes a brief interlude, its first half based on the movement's opening formula and the second half consisting of some new material that seems to stand apart from the style up to this point. A. W. Ambros, writing in 1856, suggested that in this movement "the eye of the poet also smiles sadly through,"[22] aptly capturing the impression of this Germanic-sounding intermezzo. The second half of the movement begins at the dominant but returns quickly to D minor by means of a striking, modal B♭ at the end of the first phrase. Here, as in the first movement, "foreign" material introduced in the middle of the movement is integrated into the return. The second movement concludes with the intonation, the return of the walking bass, and fragments of the hymn melody fading to *pianissimo*. In another context this might serve as a symbol for tragedy, but probably here it merely represents the singing procession receding into the distance.

Rather than either a stately minuet or a boisterous (or elfin) scherzo, the next movement takes the form of a gliding, weaving dance. At the same time, by means of a quiet signal-call rhythm in horns and bassoons, the Trio also evokes the German forest and hunting, arguably adducing a mood of nostalgia for Germany in the midst of the Italian setting. After the return of the gliding dance motion the two styles unite in the coda – perhaps once again suggesting the integration of a foreign element.

The carnivalesque first movement having approached so close to what in another work might have been a finale style, the finale of this symphony must perforce become truly wild. Mendelssohn titled the movement "Saltarello," but it comes closer to the popular dance style that would now be referred to as a tarantella.[23] The folk dance is suggested not only by the break-neck tempo and compound meter but also by the scoring, which from the beginning sets up the jangling sound of tambourines and *tamburo-*drumming, together with a piping flute duet. In addition, the use of the tonic minor for the finale of a major-key symphony suggests a shift in the direction of folk-based modality. The movement treats sonata form rather loosely, with an attenuated reprise that fades into the distance in a manner that suggests the pictorial and spatial, so that formal conventions seem to yield to programmatic considerations.

Criticism must not reduce the "Italian" Symphony (or *The Hebrides*, for that matter) to simplistic program music in the sense of underscoring for a travelogue. Nevertheless, the aesthetic of the "characteristic" extends here to one of Romantic local color. Despite Mendelssohn's not having left much in the way of specific interpretive indications, the symphony clearly does not manifest post-Classical epigonism. How far one wishes to carry hermeneutic interpretation depends on each critic or listener. It seems at least safe to identify the thematic styles as more "characteristic" than conventional, and their manner can reasonably be taken as Italian rather than German, except for the German in both the "symphonic intermezzo" of the second movement and the nostalgic sylvan music of the Trio. Structurally, the idea of something foreign introduced into the scene after the midpoint and then integrated into the picture forms a recurrent trope in the first three movements. At the same time, the sense of spatial separation from a scene is evident, especially in the second and fourth movements, in closing passages where the music seems to recede. In short, while we should not read the work as autobiography, we need not contrive any other explanatory model for the symphony than that of a set of Italian vignettes seen through the eyes of a German observer. The "Italian" Symphony thus constitutes a sophisticated manifestation of Romanticism in which the persona or aesthetic subject is made evident.

Toward the narrative – historical inspiration

Shortly after his return to Berlin from his Grand Tour, Mendelssohn's Symphony in D, the "Reformation" Symphony, received what appears to have been its only performance during his lifetime. He had composed the work in 1829–30, responding to the celebration of the three hundredth anniversary of the Augsburg Confession. He had failed to get the work played in Berlin during the festival in 1830,[24] and possible performances in other German cities at the start of his travels had come to naught. On the return leg, swinging through Paris, the piece got as far as rehearsal, but the musicians rejected it as too learned and unmelodious – perhaps this amounted to saying that the work seemed too "German" for Parisian tastes.[25] Several passages manifest a seriousness of style and content that belongs to German history, Lutheran tradition, and Germanic identity; Paris seems a highly unlikely place to have introduced it. Mendelssohn himself had doubts about the work, though. Having at last heard it in Berlin in 1832, he set it aside; it was published only posthumously, as op. 107.[26]

The aesthetic and style of the "Reformation" Symphony occupy a somewhat peculiar position in Mendelssohn's oeuvre. Conceived after the first two concert overtures, at the time of the inspiration for the *Hebrides* and the A minor Symphony, it tends toward the historical in its approach to the "characteristic" and might appear a bit pedantic. While it does not have the studied contrapuntism of the late sinfonias, it still leans backward toward the post-Classical style. These qualities suit the intention of the occasion of its composition, but they did not suit audience tastes in a time when historicism in concerts had not yet replaced novelty and virtuosity as the guiding principles, and it must already have seemed *veraltet* to Mendelssohn himself. Nevertheless, the work is both imaginative and well constructed, far beyond merely occasional value.[27]

The symphony opens with a slow introduction in D major, not of the stately, ceremonial type but suggesting a sort of awakening. After the first few measures[28] the focus is entirely on the woodwinds; although the lower strings give some support, the violins are held in reserve, and the block-like scoring resembles organ registrations. A declamatory fanfare crescendos to a *fortissimo* from the winds. This is then followed by the strings, with the first appearance of the violins, in a "celestial" *pianissimo* statement of the "Dresden Amen," a liturgical formula more associated with Catholicism than Protestantism at the time.[29]

The first movement proper is in D minor, reversing the more conventional Classical prototype of a minor-key introduction progressing to a main movement in the parallel major. The sonata-form body of the movement is devoted to a militant theme and energetic activity, interrupted momentarily by a quieter, more lyrical secondary theme. The relation of this latter idea to the surrounding belligerence is not immediately clear – it certainly does not fit some of the obvious possibilities for a contrasting theme in such a context, such as the fearful prayers of the wives and families left at home, or the pleas of the vanquished. In the development, the dotted rhythm of the principal theme evolves into the fanfare motive of the introduction. At the end of the development the Dresden Amen leads into the reprise, which now starts softly and soberly, quickly dispatching the thematic returns in order to resume an aggressive, martial style for the coda.

The second movement is in B♭, the expected key (submediant) for a slow movement in a D minor symphony but not for one in D major, in which this symphony begins and ends, and in any case this is not the slow movement but the scherzo, headed "Allegro vivace." Its homorhythmic texture and dotted rhythms, combined with the 3/4 meter, make it something between a dance and a march. The Trio, in G major (unusually distant from B♭ but subdominant to D major) has a more lilting rhythm and comes across as a folksy Ländler.

The very brief slow movement in G minor, an arioso full of sighing figures, injects a personal voice into the symphony. Critics have described this as a lament,[30] but it is difficult to identify whose lament this might be, or what its cause. One might hear it as expressing nostalgia, a voice from outside the main action of the symphony that tends to turn the symphonic plot into narrative rather than direct dramatic action.[31] In this case, the slow movement embodies the "modern" or "present" narrative persona, and the other movements act in the narrative past. The Andante concludes by citing the secondary theme of the first movement, which retrospectively could itself be considered a narrative interruption in or observation of the action rather than an otherwise inexplicable part of it.

Out of the closing unison G of the slow movement come the flutes, playing the Lutheran Reformation chorale "Ein' feste Burg ist unser Gott." Like the opening of the symphony, this introduction to the finale proper is scored only for winds and the lower strings, with groups of instruments added in stages, again producing the organistic effect of adding registration. This gives way to a preparatory crescendo that brings in the body of the Allegro maestoso, a rather pastiche-like succession of ideas ranging from overture-like flamboyance, to contrapuntal seriousness, to military-band-like ceremony, to cantus firmus quotations of the phrases of the chorale. The coda somewhat recalls the ship's arrival in the *Meeresstille und glückliche Fahrt* overture but ultimately gives way to a triumphal, homorhythmic setting of the first two chorale phrases.

Although critics have expressed skepticism about the symphony for its obvious use of quotation and the apparent primacy of plot over musical form in the finale, even these presumed weaknesses deserve reconsideration. The citations of the chorale theme in particular work interestingly into the texture and form. Semantically, musical ideas extend over a spectrum, from the "abstract," to references to *topoi*, to actual quotation, and in recent decades we have learned the impossibility of ignoring the semantic even in the most seemingly "absolute" music of the Classical/Romantic period. In the case of the "Reformation" Symphony, the variety of contrasting materials, including learned and antique fugue, military style, and chorale quotations, demonstrates how relative the specificity of meaning can be. If we hear the bulk of the symphony as framed within a narrative level of discourse, that would also justify the eclecticism of the materials. At the very least, if the symphony fails, it does so as a remarkably sophisticated experiment and not as naive programmaticism or epigonism.

Returns to legend and history – developing the narrative

In his maturity Mendelssohn returned to inspiration from legend and history, but with a new and more evidently narrative approach. From this period come two overtures and a symphony.

The first of these, the overture *Die schöne Melusine*, was composed in 1834. It seems to have been partly a response to a production of Conradin Kreutzer's opera on the subject, which Mendelssohn had seen and found displeasing.[32] He took up the fairy tale of the ill-fated water sprite who adopts human form when she falls in love with a mortal, a story well known from La Motte Fouqué's *Undine* (1811) but most likely familiar to the composer in Tieck's version (1800).

The thematic material reflects the images and characters in the story. The opening motive, a waving melody introduced by clarinets, suggests the water from which Melusine emanates and which sustains her. This F major material diminuendos peacefully, after which a galloping theme intrudes in F minor, representing the character of the knight Reymund. The contrasting key then turns out to be Ab, the relative major of F minor, expressed in a passionate, lyrical song theme – or rather a duet, since the cello is repeatedly seduced into joining the first violins.

The piece employs a version of sonata form, and it might therefore seem primarily concerned with the characters of the themes, as in the *Midsummer Night's Dream* and *Hebrides* overtures. Certain aspects of this sonata deformation, however, might derive from the plot. After the exposition – Melusine introduced in her natural habitat, the arrival of Reymund, the lovers together – the development proceeds to work up the conflict. The undine is seen bathing, with a longing oboe theme, then the Reymund music intrudes again, followed by the love theme, intensified into conflict. The water music reemerges, now with a sad countermelody in the clarinet, leading into the considerably varied reprise, in which the love music returns directly, and surprisingly in Db. When the galloping theme arrives, it is punctuated by wailing slurs in the winds. The coda once again brings the water theme, the key of F major, and a rather tenderly sad diminuendo to the end.

The composer's sense of humor, and his aversion to excessive programmaticizing, can be found in an anecdote that Schumann tells in a footnote to his review of the piece: "Someone once asked Mendelssohn what the overture *Die schöne Melusine* was actually about. He promptly answered, 'Hmm . . . a *mésalliance.*'"[33] One should not attempt to describe the details of the story too closely in the form of the music. After all, sonata form fundamentally follows the basic outline of a plot in any literary genre, and Mendelssohn reminds us that words express less precisely than music. As with every story, the details make the retelling both unique and worthwhile. There is no such thing as *merely* presenting the characters of a story in a sonata deformation, since plot is inevitable. Mendelssohn neither replicates another narrator's plot nor offers a textbook form. The Melusine *Märchen* here is his own.

In 1839, initially quite in spite of himself, Mendelssohn found himself composing an overture to Victor Hugo's play *Ruy Blas*. He held a very low opinion of the play and originally declined the commission from the Leipzig theater for the occasion of a benefit performance for their theater fund, pleading that the time was too short. When the delegation returned to apologize for such short notice and request an overture for the next season, Mendelssohn's pride got the better of him, and he composed the overture more or less overnight. The piece succeeded so well that he used it a few days later for a concert with the Gewandhaus Orchestra, joking in a letter to his mother that, while he did not like the play, he was rather pleased with himself about the brilliant, rousing overture, though he would call it not the Overture to *Ruy Blas* but the Overture to the Theater Pension Fund.[34] The work was published only posthumously.

The overture opens with a solemn call to arms from the brass and winds, based on a descending minor (or Phrygian) tetrachord in the bass. This motto returns at several points, variously harmonized. As William Pelto and Siegwart Reichwald have shown, in several ways the motto generates contours of the thematic material in the remainder of the piece.[35] After a couple of "false starts" the first theme is launched, a breathless, rushing melody introduced over agitated syncopations. The motto establishes E♭ for the second theme, a rather corny tune that first tiptoes in with the strings and is then sung by clarinets, bassoons, and cellos as a sort of congenial university song. The closing theme is a rollicking, tonally simple idea based on arpeggiated figures. The development works with all the themes. The reprise of the principal theme leads to a return of the motto, in the form in which it appeared at the very opening of the overture, and then the secondary and closing themes, now in C major. The coda, which features a crescendo to *fortissimo*, combines the principal and closing materials for a rousing finish.

Commentators have usually emphasized that the Overture to *Ruy Blas* is basically a potboiler and have turned up their noses at it, taking their cue from Mendelssohn's attitude toward Hugo's play. At the least, however, the work should receive its due as an extremely effective and skillful potboiler, as well as demonstrating the composer's astonishing facility. More important, though, it may have provided a breakthrough for Mendelssohn. As Reichwald points out, Mendelssohn had seemingly come to a sort of barrier in his career, as far as orchestral composition is concerned, and the revival of Schubert's Great C major Symphony, with its own noble beginning, spurred his imagination in this overture. Further, the innovations in form here – the uses and variants of the motto – helped to launch a new interest in composing large-scale forms for Mendelssohn. Shortly after this, of course, he took on the *Lobgesang* project, again using motto material to open the work and integrating it into the structure; this became op. 52. His return to the abandoned *Die erste Walpurgisnacht* of 1831–32, which develops material out of its introduction in an organic fashion, led to its publication as op. 60 (1844). Between the two, and again employing such a cyclic approach, the A minor Symphony, first conceived in Scotland in 1829, at last reached completion and publication as op. 56 in 1842.

Mendelssohn's Symphony in A minor, as noted earlier, stems from an inspiration during his visit to Edinburgh with Klingemann. The immediate situation was the Palace of Holyroodhouse, though neither the edifice itself nor even the picturesque ruin of the royal chapel there suggested the idea, but rather the romantic history of Mary Queen of Scots and David Rizzio. Thus the work belongs not with the scenic *Hebrides* overture and "Italian" Symphony, but to the class of pieces based on history and legend. Although Mendelssohn suppressed the fact that this was his "Scottish" Symphony, when it was performed and published, the tone and form clearly suggest the epic-historical, and there is enough in the content to identify the locale.[36]

The symphony opens with a slow introduction in 3/4 that presents the contour that will come to dominate the thematic material, rising from e′ to a′, then on up to b′ and c″. At the tempo change to Allegro un poco agitato this is transmuted into a 6/8 galloping theme. An approaching crescendo and increase in instrumentation lead to the battle-like transition theme. The material of the secondary area (E minor) combines the principal theme with a new clarinet countermelody, and the battle soon returns. The closing theme might suggest the melody of Schubert's Lied "Gute Ruh" from *Die schöne Müllerin*. The development employs all of the thematic material of the exposition, working through a number of key shifts to reach E to set up the recapitulation. Here the principal and secondary themes are combined before the entry of the transition material, then the closing theme fades away. A second development ensues, bringing roaring chromatic swells that clearly suggest a wild storm. The transition theme interrupts, more or less forcing a conclusion. Before the movement ends, however, the slow opening returns.

Mendelssohn indicated that the movements should follow each other without pauses. The first movement declines to a couple of pizzicato, *pianissimo* chords, and the second begins immediately with a measured tremolo and some distant pipe and horn calls. The main idea here is a lively, quasi-pentatonic melody with a "snap" rhythm at its phrase endings, the most explicitly "Scottish" moment in the work; the second theme exploits a dotted rhythm. The overall character is military, an important *topos* for the symphony. This movement, like the first, ends in pizzicato chords.

The third movement begins in a lyrical style in an A major heavily shaded toward the minor side. The contrasting material evokes a funeral march clearly in the manner of the *Marcia funebre* from Beethoven's Third Symphony, though the form of the movement resembles more the double-variation structure in the slow movement of Beethoven's Fifth. The ending is tragic, however, with a diminuendo, fragmentation of the thematic identity, and emphasis on the minor mode.

The fourth movement, marked Allegro vivacissimo in the score but also described by the composer as Allegro guerriero, is full of rhythmic energy and brilliant orchestration, with horn signals and timpani like cannon shots. The relief theme, softer but still undergirded by agitation, seems more at home in the *fortissimo* in which it later appears. The development actually features a fugal section, recalling the Mendelssohn of the sinfonias but only within the context of the ongoing battle. At the end of the sonata form the secondary theme sounds in the distance, fading away in clarinet and bassoon.

The symphony ends in an independent coda to the work as a whole, derived from the opening of the first movement but here treated in A major as a hymn of triumph. The melody sounds three times, in the manner of a strophic song. The expansion of the scoring at each repetition suggests a gathering of people joining to welcome the victors.

As a whole, the symphony's gestures repeatedly evoke two impressions that bring it into the world of historical epic. The first of these is, of course, the battle music that appears in the first, second, and fourth movements, along with the funeral march in the third. The succession of conflicts, variously leading to tragedy and victory, implies a series of episodes in history. The second important device is the suggestion of the past and of distance. The slow opening of the symphony famously has this effect; Grey attributes to it "the feeling of a narrative frame" and mentions that writers have found in it a "ballad tone."[37] But a number of other soft passages give the feeling of distance – physical or temporal. The crescendos often create a palpable sense of approaching forces. Together the interplay of the signs of the distant and the obvious reporting of events across the cyclic composite work make this Mendelssohn's grandest instrumental narrative.

Conclusion – from the post-Classical to the "characteristic" and narrative

What, then, is Mendelssohn's place in the history of the Romantic symphony and overture? Beginning as a prodigious technician with an unparalleled grasp of the eighteenth-century styles of the symphony, Mendelssohn worked his way through a dozen apprentice and journeyman sinfonias to a Beethovenian *Habilitationsschrift* in the Symphony no. 1. He then turned surprisingly quickly into a Romantic with the "characteristic" music of the first overtures, responding initially to literature and then to the scenes of his travels, inventing themes and scorings that could not possibly belong to Classicism. The "Reformation" Symphony demonstrates that he could find individual responses to events and to historical moments. The A minor Symphony brought him fully into the world of Romantic narrativity, though always in the most authentically musical terms, without the slightest suggestion of trivial programmaticizing. Far from merely a Classicistic symphonist operating in the shadow of Beethoven, one more at home in the lyricism of the song without words than in symphonic struggle, Mendelssohn holds a striking and individual place in the orchestral music of the nineteenth century.

7 The works for solo instrument(s) and orchestra

STEVE LINDEMAN

Sir Donald Francis Tovey declared,

> The best works of Mendelssohn have all in their respective ways been the
> starting-points of some musical revolution. Mendelssohn may truthfully be
> said to have destroyed the classical concerto.[1]

Felix Mendelssohn Bartholdy completed eleven works in the genre of solo instrument(s) and orchestra.[2] Spanning more than two decades, they range from the thirteen-year-old's little-known Concerto for Piano and Strings in A minor, composed in 1822,[3] to one of Mendelssohn's most popular works, the Concerto for Violin and Orchestra in E minor op. 64 (1845).[4] Examined together as a group, they reveal a fascinating trajectory, manifesting a terrific growth in imagination and inventiveness. These works run the gamut from rather insecure and uneven student pieces to a great, confident masterpiece, through light-hearted, quickly dashed off virtuosic showpieces, to deeply introspective, rarified musical statements.

In only one other specific genre, that of the string quartet, did the composer work as consistently throughout his life as he did at the compositions of concertos. And this was not an easy task. As R. Larry Todd notes,

> throughout his career, Mendelssohn found the writing of concertos an
> especially arduous task and confessed to friends his struggle to reconcile the
> competing demands of virtuosity and the integrity of the compositions as
> works of art.[5]

The eleven concerted works reveal Mendelssohn's successive attempts and sometimes tedious revisions over the course of his life, and provide ample evidence of this struggle between these "competing demands." Moreover, the mature composer's experiments with the form of the concerto manifest, as Tovey noted, some of the most radical, progressive, and ultimately highly influential tendencies of the early Romantic movement – attributes not typically associated with Mendelssohn.

On the other hand, critics such as Thomas Grey have noted Mendelssohn's somewhat paradoxical role as one of the principal figure of opposition to the type of modern instrumental virtuoso that had emerged in the first decades of the nineteenth century . . . diametrically opposed to the kinds of gaudy, exhibitionistic display that seemed to have invaded concert and operatic life by the 1820s and 1830s.[6]

Indeed, as in this oft-cited letter where Mendelssohn's expresses his disdain for the fashionable Parisian virtuoso Henri Herz, he complains to Moscheles:

> But why should I hear those Variations by Herz for the thirtieth time? They give me as little pleasure as rope dancers or acrobats: for with them at least there is the barbarous attraction that one is in constant dread of seeing them break their necks . . . I only wish it were not my lot to be constantly told that the public demand that kind of thing. I, too, am one of the public, and demand the very reverse.[7]

Mendelssohn expressed similar reservations about nearly all of the great virtuosi of his day, including Franz Liszt, Friedrich Kalkbrenner, Sigismond Thalberg, Theodor Döhler, and even, on occasion, Frédéric Chopin.[8]

Only three of Mendelssohn's eleven concerted works – the Piano Concertos nos. 1 and 2, opp. 25 and 40, and the op. 64 Violin Concerto – have been more or less consistent staples of the concert repertoire since their respective premieres. Most of Mendelssohn's works in the genre, however, are not well known: his first five concertos were composed during his adolescence, and not published in his lifetime; three lesser-known Romantic concert works for piano and orchestra stem from Mendelssohn's maturity (1831–38). These works – the *Capriccio brillant* op. 22, the *Rondo brillant* op. 29, and the *Serenade und Allegro giojoso* op. 43 – are, in comparison to the mature concertos, more light-hearted, composed to display the composer's prowess as piano soloist.

The early concertos

Mendelssohn is known for his novel and highly influential treatment of concerto form in the Piano Concertos nos. 1 and 2, opp. 25 and 40, and the E minor Violin Concerto op. 64. The five lesser-known adolescent concertos, however, are cast in a rather typical – and, for the time, archaic – late eighteenth-century concerto style. Historically, the form of the important first movement was developed by C. P. E. and J. C. Bach, and codified by Mozart in his works in the genre, described by some theorists as "double exposition" form.[9] This almost pervasively adopted paradigm consists of seven parts, including three (sometimes four) orchestral ritornellos (tuttis) which frame three sections that feature the soloist. An improvised cadenza is typically inserted at the end of the final solo section, leading to the closing tutti.[10]

The young Mendelssohn also discerned this Mozart model in the concertos of older contemporaries such as Weber, Field, Cramer, Dussek, and Moscheles (a number of which were in his repertoire). Beethoven published seven essays in the genre (the five piano concertos, the Violin Concerto, and the "Triple" Concerto op. 56), and their respective first movements are all cast in the Mozart paradigm. However, in works such as the Third, Fourth, and Fifth Piano Concertos opp. 37, 58, and 73, and the Violin Concerto op. 61, Beethoven begins to exert pressure on the Mozart model. The C minor Piano Concerto (no. 3, op. 37) contains a hint of connection (the lingering last tone of the second movement becomes the upbeat to the Finale) between the last two movements. The Fourth, in G major, op. 58, begins with the piano soloist "intruding" into the domain of the tutti's first ritornello, as does the "Emperor" (no. 5, in Eb major op. 73), the latter featuring a written cadenza. Moreover, the "Emperor's" slow second movement, in the distant, chromatic-mediant related key of B major (enharmonic Cb major), is linked to the Finale by a transition. Mendelssohn, who frequently performed all three of these works, was listening.

Mendelssohn's five early concertos date from what Karl-Heinz Köhler has described as a phase of ripening maturity in the composer's youthful evolution, beginning in the wake of the twelve-year-old Mendelssohn's visit with Goethe in Weimar for the first time in November of 1821.[11] Shortly after completing preliminary study with Zelter, Mendelssohn began a series of compositions in the larger forms, including the twelve string sinfonias, and the five early concertos (composed 1822–24).

The first of these, a piano concerto in A minor, most likely received its premiere at one of the Mendelssohn family's Sunday *musicales* in their Berlin home at 3 Leipzigerstraße, as did most of the young composer's works. The Concerto was first performed on 5 December 1822.[12] Like the twelve early *sinfonias*, the Piano Concerto in A minor is scored for strings alone. The young composer closely modeled his work on the A minor Piano Concerto op. 89 of Johann Nepomuk Hummel.[13] In addition, the strong influence of Carl Maria von Weber's Piano Concerto no. 2 in Eb major is revealed in Mendelssohn's unusual placement of improvised cadenzas before the secondary theme.

Mendelssohn's sense of harmony in the development of the first movement reveals a fascination with Romantic color, particularly in the juxtaposition of chromatic third-related keys. The Adagio second movement, in E major, contains a melodic design prefiguring Mendelssohn's later *Lieder ohne Worte*-type works. The third-movement Finale in A minor is a sonata rondo.

Mendelssohn wrote the D minor Violin Concerto for, and dedicated it to, his friend and violin teacher, Eduard Rietz, a member of the Berlin court orchestra (Mendelssohn would also compose the Double Concerto for Violin and Piano for him, as well as the Violin Sonata op. 4). Rietz had been a student of the Parisian violin virtuoso Pierre Rode, who most likely introduced him to the concertos of the late eighteenth to early nineteenth-century French violin school that included such composers as Viotti, Kreutzer, and himself.[14] Mendelssohn briefly studied with Pierre Baillot, another pupil of Rode, in Paris in 1816.[15] Through the association with these figures, we may assume that Mendelssohn was very familiar with the formal conceits of the late eighteenth-century French violin school. Indeed, as Todd has noted, Mendelssohn's study with Zelter in the early 1820s focused primarily on musical practices and forms of the eighteenth century.[16] The form of the first movement is modeled on the Baroque ritornello concerto design of alternating tuttis (in this case, five) framing four solo sections. However, the highly virtuosic violin sections seem heavily indebted to the popular French violin school of the early nineteenth century.

Mendelssohn's third completed attempt in the genre is a double concerto, and his only concerted work for violin and piano. The fourteen-year-old composer dated the completed score, for soloists and strings, 6 May 1823. Shortly thereafter, he chose to augment this manuscript with a separate four-page score, containing a supplemental orchestration for twelve wind instruments and timpani.[17] The Concerto received its premiere on 25 May 1823 at one of the family's Sunday *musicales*, with the composer and violinist Eduard Rietz as soloists, and was shelved shortly thereafter.

Recalling the D minor Violin Concerto, the opening movement of the Double Concerto is cast in a Baroque ritornello concerto design. Incongruously, however, as in the A minor Piano Concerto, Mendelssohn exploits colorful chromatic mediant relationships, and inserts fermatas and improvisatory scalar passages preceding the statements of the secondary theme. The middle Adagio movement in A major has a song-like quality that strongly resembles the melody and rhythm of the earlier A minor Piano Concerto.

The last two of the five early concertos – the E major and A♭ major Double Piano Concertos from 1823 and 1824 – are considerably more ambitious in scope than their three predecessors. Todd describes Beethoven as a "major new influence" at this time on the young Mendelssohn.[18] Commensurate with this influence, and with what Friedhelm Krummacher described as the "new kind of composition"[19] discernible in these works, is the enriched scoring in the Double Concertos, including winds, brass, and timpani in addition to the strings.

Both the E and Ab major Double Piano Concertos were written as birthday presents for Felix's sister Fanny (born 14 November 1805), and were first performed as part of the Mendelssohn family's Sunday *musicales*, with the two siblings as soloists.[20] The E major Concerto received its premiere on 3 December 1823.[21] The composer seems to have thought highly of the work, for he performed it with Moscheles five and a half years later during his debut visit to England (July 1829).

The Concerto has come down to us in two sources: the composer's heavily revised autograph score and a manuscript copy of the original version in Moscheles' hand. The work is particularly interesting because it is the most heavily revised of the early concertos. Moscheles' copy was made before Mendelssohn made the most significant revisions to the score and therefore helps to clarify many heavily crossed-out passages in the autograph. It is not clear when Mendelssohn revised the work – perhaps for his 1829 London debut. A comparison of the original and revised versions of the first movement permits us to observe the changes that the mature Mendelssohn made to the adolescent work.[22] The first movement is in Mozartean double-exposition concerto form, the second movement in the chromatic mediant-related key of C major, in typical ternary (ABA') design. The Finale is a rondo. The extensive revisions – primarily concerning concision, the removal of excess virtuosity, and the reworking of the assignment of thematic material – bear witness to Mendelssohn's desire to mold the adolescent work into a cohesive, organically conceived mature statement. In an 1839 *Neue Zeitschrift* essay titled "Das Clavier-Concert," Robert Schumann summarized the current state of the genre at the end of the 1830s.[23] He derided the current wave of fashionable Parisian virtuoso concertos wherein the pianist displayed brilliant soloistic passages while the orchestra merely "looked on." Mendelssohn's revisions in the E major Double Concerto seem to manifest his own desire to recast the work from a similar aesthetic perspective.

That the revisions were probably undertaken just before the composition of the G minor Piano Concerto perhaps provides a clue as to why Mendelssohn abandoned his revision efforts on the E major Concerto. As we shall see, the G minor work pointed up a new direction in his approach to the genre, one that he was to follow in each subsequent concerto. Perhaps Mendelssohn sensed that the E major Concerto was too bogged down with an archaic approach to the genre.

The fifteen-year-old Mendelssohn composed the last of the five early concertos in the fall of 1824, about one year after the E major companion piece. The autograph of the Concerto for Two Pianos in Ab major is noteworthy for the apparent ease and assurance with which Mendelssohn created the concerto, in comparison to the heavily revised manuscript for the preceding

E major work. The A♭ Concerto was premiered 26 December 1824. Only one other performance of the concerto is documented, on 20 February 1827 in Stettin, with Mendelssohn and Carl Löwe at the keyboards.[24]

In this work, there are echoes of the then-popular Piano Concerto no. 2 in A♭ major (1811) by John Field. At over 600 measures, Mendelssohn's first movement is massive in scope, the longest of the five early concertos. The middle-movement Andante is set in the distant, chromatic-mediant key of E major, with a rather unusual blend of sonata and variation. Stylistically, R. Larry Todd notes that Mendelssohn, in the Finale, may have been taking his cue from Beethoven's Piano Concerto no. 3, as is evidenced by Mendelssohn's inverted order of themes, and the pervasive employment of fugue.[25] It is in rondo form, with cyclic relationship between the themes of the first and third movements.[26]

After completing the A♭ major Double Concerto, Mendelssohn never returned to traditional late eighteenth-century ("double exposition") concerto form. Curiously, after so much activity in the early 1820s, he completely abandoned the genre for seven years.

Clearly, Mendelssohn had reservations about the quality of all five of the early concertos. His decision not to publish these works may well indicate ambivalence regarding the efficacy of double-exposition concerto form for his purposes (although perhaps in combination with other aesthetic concerns). Indeed, the composer completely dismissed the five early concertos, as his titles for the mature piano concertos, opp. 25 and 40 – "no. 1" and "no. 2" – reveal.

The mature works

The influence of Carl Maria von Weber's 1821 *Konzertstück* in F minor for Piano and Orchestra op. 79 most readily appears when, after a seven-year hiatus, Mendelssohn resumed his work in 1831 with the G minor Piano Concerto "no. 1" op. 25 and the *Capriccio brillant* op. 22. The Weber work, which Mendelssohn knew intimately, was a favored performance vehicle for the younger composer on numerous occasions throughout his career. Other works of Mendelssohn's reveal Weber's imprint, such as the *Perpetuum mobile* in C major of 1826 (published posthumously in 1873 as op. 119), modeled on the finale of Weber's C major Piano Sonata op. 24.[27]

The Weber *Konzertstück* consists of three inter-connected movements, with the first featuring a radically new approach to the composition of a concerto. It is constructed, not with two distinct expositions, as in the Mozartean design, but with a unified solo and tutti exposition, very brief development, a highly abridged recapitulation, and no cadenza.[28] We will witness the profound effect this work had on all of Mendelssohn's subsequent essays in the concerto genre.

Both the *Capriccio brilliant* for Piano and Orchestra in B major/minor op. 22, and the Piano Concerto no. 1 in G minor op. 25 were composed during the course of Mendelssohn's tour of the European Continent and the British Isles during the years 1830–32. Op. 25 is dedicated to Munich pianist Delphine von Schauroth, with whom Mendelssohn seems to have become romantically involved while he was in that city. The composer performed as soloist at the premiere of the Concerto in Munich, in October 1831. Subsequently, Mendelssohn substantially revised the work before it was published two years later, in 1833.[29]

We may identify five principal features of the G minor Concerto. These include

(1) the cyclical treatment of thematic material,
(2) unified tutti and solo exposition in the first movement,
(3) transitions between movements,
(4) the elision of the punctuating ritornello (following the solo exposition of the first movement) with the beginning of the development.

Perhaps the most radical aspect of Mendelssohn's design for op. 25 is the combined tutti/solo exposition of the first movement. In the structure of this movement, it is as if Mendelssohn suddenly saw, from Weber's cue, a solution to the problem of *redundancy*, one of late eighteenth century concerto form's most critical issues in the early nineteenth century. Previous to Mendelssohn, all composers in the genre had typically run over the same ground twice, as it were, with discrete statements of the movement's thematic material by both the tutti and the soloist in their respective expositions. Mendelssohn's solution dramatically casts aside the redundant aspect of double exposition form, providing a cogent, closely argued, single presentation of unified solo/tutti thematic material.

Unlike Weber's *Konzertstück*, however, the first movement of Mendelssohn's op. 25 contains a nearly complete recapitulation of all thematic material introduced in the combined solo/tutti exposition. The result amounts to a *fusion* of the two single-movement paradigms, sonata and double-exposition concerto form, into one unified whole (Mozart's double-exposition form may be seen as *grafting* of single-movement sonata form onto Baroque ritornello form). In combination with the highly charged drama of the unified exposition in op. 25, the full recapitulation creates the sense of a balanced structure.

Other aspects of the first movement of op. 25 manifest Mendelssohn's concern for balancing original ideas with the genre's more conservative traditions. For example, in the second group of the exposition, we sense that the soloist, after stating the secondary theme two times in the remote key of D♭ major (mm. 83–102) and then adding another theme to this rarified atmosphere (mm. 102–13), suddenly realizes that they have exceeded the boundaries of "proper behavior" in a concerto and so abruptly returns to the "correct" orbit of the mediant, B♭ major. This dose of reality is confirmed by the statement of the primary theme (mm. 113–21) in the "right" key, B♭. By framing these bold thematic statements in a distant key with a statement in the "right" key, Mendelssohn provides a sense of perspective that firmly anchors the fanciful or whimsical nature of this section to the "correct" goal of harmonic motion.

The use of such a distant key in the secondary group suggests a metaphor of a separate world for the soloist/individual quite removed from the traditional confines of the orchestra/society. The statements of the secondary group in D♭ major are scored almost exclusively for the soloist, the orchestra providing only accompanimental background, thereby creating a separate realm for the soloist (one of the goals of the revisions to the E major Double Concerto as well). In the second movement, the composer's exploitation of the distant key of E major to create a dreamy and lyrical world contributes to the same goal. This key of four sharps, so remote from the two-flat world of the first movement, contributes greatly to this effect.

At the close of the exposition of the first movement, Mendelssohn obscures wonderfully the formal demarcation of three areas: the end of the exposition, the beginning of the second ritornello, and the development section. Here, at one of the most traditional (and perhaps, to Mendelssohn, cliché-ridden) junctures of the form, we normally expect the soloist's trills, accompanied by the tutti's dominant sonorities, to climax in a definitive cadence in the new key, signaling the end of the exposition, and the beginning of the second ritornello; this, subsequently, will lead to the development section. Instead, however, during the soloist's climactic trills, the orchestra mysteriously enters too early, as it were, with statements of the primary theme. The definitive cadence in the new key is jettisoned altogether. Only in hindsight, several measures later, we realize that we are in the midst of the development section, and that Mendelssohn has, in fact, elided the end of the exposition with what would have been the "second" ritornello, together with the beginning of the development. Nevertheless, the brief hint of a tutti in the midst of the soloist's trills effectively provides the punctuation necessary to signify the end of the exposition, and the beginning of the development. Mendelssohn thereby achieves a highly effective balance of progressive, even radical ideas in perfect harmony with the traditional gestures of the form.

Mendelssohn, taking his cue from the *Konzertstück* (Weber, and Mendelssohn, too, probably following the lead of Beethoven, in the "Emperor" Concerto), weaves transitions between the three movements. This creates a seamless whole; Mendelssohn directs the movements to be played without a break. The subsequent second movement's song-like Andante is in ternary form, the A section consisting of an aaba' pattern, the B section in the dominant largely constituting an elegant, improvisatory solo figuration. The ensuing Finale is a rondo. Here, the treatment of themes is cyclical, with a return of the primary theme of the first movement in the latter portion of the Finale. Mendelssohn had begun his experimentation with cyclic techniques around 1823: not only – as we have witnessed – in the Finale of the A♭ major Double Piano Concerto, but also in the Piano Sonata in B♭ major (1827, but published posthumously in 1868 as op. 106), and in the finales of the Octet, op. 20, and the Sextet op. 110.[30]

At roughly the time of the composition of the G minor Piano Concerto, Mendelssohn was also working on the *Capriccio brillant* op. 22, a piece that shares several of the concerto's important features. The bulk of the work on op. 22 occurred before September 1831 (Mendelssohn's date of the manuscript version for solo piano), with most of the orchestration completed eight months later (18 May 1832, the date of the completion of the orchestral autograph). Curiously, Mendelssohn's correspondence refers to the work not as a *Capriccio*, but as a *Rondo brillant* (and this is not the work known by that name published as op. 29, composed three years later). The composer premiered the *Capriccio brillant* in London in July 1832.

The *Capriccio* is Mendelssohn's first attempt at a single-movement concerted work, consisting of a fast movement preceded by a slow introductory section. There is an interesting parallel to this conception with that of his concert overture, *Calm Sea and Prosperous Voyage* (*Meeresstille und glückliche Fahrt* op. 27, 1829–35). In the overture, Mendelssohn took pains to make clear that he regarded the Adagio, representing the *Calm Sea*, as the first of two distinct *tableaux*, rather than as an introduction, leading to the subsequent fast section.[31] This overture may thereby be seen as standing in a relationship to the symphony vaguely analogous to the *Capriccio brillant*'s relationship to the concerto. A parallel also exists with a roughly contemporaneous work, the *Rondo capriccioso*. This work was conceived in 1828 as an étude, and reworked in 1830 as a present for Delphine von Schauroth, the dedicatee of the G minor Concerto. The *Rondo capriccioso* also consists of a lyrical Andante introduction, linked by a transition to the subsequent Presto. Todd notes the similarity between this design, "not unlike the condensed second and third movements of a concerto," and adumbrating similar procedures in the two piano concertos, the *Capriccio brillant*, and the *Serenade und Allegro giojoso*.[32]

The influence of the Weber *Konzertstück*, again, is felt in the *Capriccio*. Mendelssohn replicates almost exactly Weber's distinctively halting articulation of the *Konzertstück's* introduction. Moreover, following a huge transition to the dominant of the relative major, the march-like second theme (mm. 99ff.) is set off much more dramatically than in a typical concerto-form movement.[33] This creates the feeling that the music from this section (in D major) almost belongs to another movement.

This delineation is further emphasized by the fact that Mendelssohn initially scores the second theme for the orchestra alone (until m. 116), just as Weber had orchestrated the march in the *Konzertstück*. This underscores the orchestra's distinct personality, far removed from that of the soloist, whose exclusive domain is the primary theme; the orchestra never formally states the primary theme, but merely accompanies the soloist's statements of it. This segregated disposition calls to mind the respective treatments of the secondary theme in both the Molto Allegro con fuoco of the G minor Concerto op. 25, and the revisions to the first movement of the E major Concerto for Two Pianos.

Peter Mercer-Taylor notes that the strong connection with Weber may have been apparent to the London audience, but that

> as a second subject, this march makes no sense whatever . . . [however] we may discern here an act of musical self-mythologizing. Mendelssohn seems to make reference to the furthest extreme of virtuoso piano music with which he had associated himself – the *Konzertstück* – only in order to cast its jolliest moment in the form of a musical problem. He, in the persona of the pianist, swaggers in at the eleventh hour to regularize this wayward impulse, to bring it into the fold of classical normalcy . . . the piece emerges as little short of an aesthetic manifesto.[34]

As in the first movement of op. 25, the passage following the exposition (mm. 166ff.) admirably merges the qualities of the exposition-concluding ritornello and the subsequent development. The development itself is fairly brief, consisting of alternating tutti and soloist statements of the march theme in various keys, with the soloist later adding statements of a theme from the primary group (mm. 177ff.). This section climaxes with a return to the transitional passage that originally preceded the area of the second theme from the exposition, which prolongs vii°/V (mm. 195ff.). When the recapitulation commences (mm. 206ff.), Mendelssohn artfully enmeshes the return of a theme from the primary group, and the end of the development.

The design of the recapitulation further evidences the composer's desire to balance the radical innovations of op. 22 with a more traditional approach to the genre. At issue is the disposition of the two statements of the march (secondary) theme. In the exposition, this theme is heard in the scoring for the orchestra alone, first in the relative major, and then a whole step lower in colorfully juxtaposed C major, ♭VII/III, or ♭II/i. While Mendelssohn, as a precocious teenager, might have allowed this challenge to the hegemony of the tonic to remain unchecked in the recapitulation of one of the five early concertos, the mature composer apparently would not allow it in the *Capriccio*. In the recapitulation of op. 22, the second statement of the march occurs in the harmonically pallid subdominant key of E major, not A major, as it would have if Mendelssohn had followed the pattern established in the exposition.

After all of this discussion about the contrasting roles of the soloist and orchestra in the *Capriccio*, it is of particular interest that the *Capriccio* was, in fact, originally conceived for solo piano.[35] This fact raises at least two questions: was Mendelssohn's decision to orchestrate the work merely a pragmatic expedient to provide a concerted vehicle that he could play during the English tour in the spring of 1832? Or did Mendelssohn realize, following the example of the first movement of op. 25, that a highly effective structure could be created by the fusion of a concerto- and sonata-form movement? Perhaps both of these reasons hit the mark.

As we shall see, all of Mendelssohn's subsequent works in the concerto genre follow the lessons learned in the G minor Concerto and the *Capriccio brillant*: the two subsequent concertos – in D minor (for piano, op. 40) and E minor (for violin, op. 64) – employ single- (combined tutti/solo) exposition concerto form in their first movements, transitions between movements, and either written-out cadenzas, or no cadenzas at all. The remaining pair of single-movement works – the *Rondo brillant* and the *Serenade und Allegro giojoso* – also contain unified solo/tutti statements of thematic material. Moreover, all of these works, in varying degrees, continue to challenge and stretch the traditional approaches to the genre. Discrete lines of formal demarcation are artfully blurred: punctuating tuttis, which recall exposition-closing "second" ritornellos, frequently begin in unexpected keys, and elide with the subsequent development section. Secondary themes are stated in distant (often chromatic third-related) keys, before finding their "correct" location. Recapitulations ensue from dominant pedals before the "end" of the development, blurring the line dividing the two. We now examine these subsequent works in turn.

In the year following the publication of the *Capriccio brillant* and the First Piano Concerto, the 24-year-old Mendelssohn began work on a light, one-movement work, entitled *Rondo brillant*. The work was premiered in London by Moscheles, its dedicatee, in a version for solo piano, on 11 May 1834, and first published for solo piano in London later that year. Subsequently, however, the composer subjected the work to substantial revision, resulting in an edition for piano and orchestra issued the following year in Leipzig.[36]

In performances of the *Rondo brillant*, Mendelssohn occasionally improvised a slow solo piano introduction, creating a format something like the *Capriccio brillant*, and the subsequent *Serenade und Allegro giojoso*.[37]

Mendelssohn was apparently frustrated with the work, as a letter to Moscheles reveals:

> My own poverty in shaping new forms for the pianoforte once more struck me most forcibly whilst writing the Rondo. It is there I get into difficulties and have to toil and labor, and I am afraid you will notice that such was the case.[38]

Nevertheless, the fruit of this labor produced a distinct balance between the opposing forces of solo and tutti, with the latter entrusted with quite a bit of material, as opposed to fulfilling a merely accompanimental role. Moreover, the extensively revised digressional passages, and the elaborate development section, reveal laborious thought and effort.

The form of the *Rondo brillant* is that of a seven-part sonata-rondo, but with some interesting formal twists. For example, the A section contains two distinct themes. The second of these (beginning m. 37) is reutilized as part of the B thematic group (mm. 157ff.), so that this theme creates a tangible thread of organic continuity between the two sections. Next, at the completion of this theme in the B section, a rather lengthy digression ensues (mm. 164–77). The B section is finally capped by a new, closing theme (mm. 177ff.).

The subsequent development (C) section is extensive, with rigorous treatment of the rondo, and other thematic material, in fugal and sequential fashion (as is typical in a sonata–rondo). Using a favorite Mozartean trick, Mendelssohn begins the recapitulation (m. 383) with the B theme, omitting the A (rondo theme). But, as the B group contains one theme from the A section, Mendelssohn's ploy creates an effect that is fresh and convincing.

Nevertheless, perhaps because of Mendelssohn's ambivalence expressed in this letter to Moscheles cited above, there would be a three-year gap before the restless composer began work on his next essay in the genre.

Op. 40 was composed as a wedding gift by the 28-year-old Mendelssohn for his wife, Cécile, during their honeymoon journey of the summer of 1837. He premiered the work later that fall, on 21 September 1837, at the Birmingham Music Festival, where it was received with great acclaim. A reviewer in the *Neue Zeitschrift für Musik* described the Concerto as "striking and fresh as his other in G, but more mature and sweeter."[39]

More autograph sources survive for the D minor Concerto, op. 40, than for any other of Mendelssohn's concerted works.[40] In speaking of the work, Todd notes:

> One is struck by the care with which Mendelssohn thought out his solo passages – instead of relying solely upon virtuosic filigrees, he has taken pains to relate the pianistic figuration to the essential thematic structure, to integrate the solo part into the structure of the whole.[41]

The first movement is cast in the same form as that of the G minor Concerto op. 25, with in a single, unified tutti/solo exposition. Also echoing op. 25, the D minor Concerto contains elided formal demarcations, an abridged recapitulation in the first movement, and transitions between movements. The second movement Adagio in B♭ major, a *Lieder ohne Worte*-type melody, is in compound ternary design (the A section itself a small rounded binary form, mm. 6–25). The third movement Finale in D major begins with a transition leading to a sonata-rondo design, with much virtuosic piano writing.

This pyrotechnical passagework features the fashionable "three-hand" technique of virtuoso Sigismond Thalberg (1812–71), whom Mendelssohn cited as one of the greatest virtuosi of the early nineteenth century. In this technique, the melody is stated in the inner voice, usually by the right (or sometimes in combination with the left) thumb(s), ornamented with florid figuration above and below (for example, in the first movement, the soloist's statement of the second theme in the exposition, mm. 151ff.). Mendelssohn also employed this technique in the Six Preludes and Fugues, op. 35, the Prelude in E minor (1842, without opus number), and the Etude in B♭ minor op. 104b no. 1.[42] And while there are a number of challenging passages within op. 40, virtuosity for its own sake is certainly not the primary focus of the work. Robert Schumann's review addresses this issue, and reveals a certain ambivalence about the work:

> Virtuosos will find it difficult to display their astonishing proficiency in this concerto, for it gives them almost nothing to do which they have not done and played a hundred times before. We have often heard this complaint from their lips. There is some justice to it; opportunities for displaying *bravura* through the novelty and brilliancy of passagework should not be missing in a concerto. But *music* should be the prime consideration, and the composer who always gives us this in the richest measure will ever deserve our greatest homage.[43]

Schumann was also not convinced that the D minor Concerto was at the front rank of Mendelssohn's efforts in the genre, as this other passage from his review reveals:

> This concerto belongs to his most casual products. If I am not mistaken, he must have written it in a few days, perhaps in a few hours . . . So let us enjoy this bright, unpretentious gift; it is like one of those works we know from the old masters done when they are resting from their more important labours.[44]

Schumann's perception of the D minor Concerto seems to mirror contemporary reception of the work: as pleasant and interesting, but by no means Mendelssohn's greatest effort in the genre.

The *Allegro giojoso* op. 43 is probably the least known of Mendelssohn's concerted works composed during his maturity. Completed in 1838, approximately eighteen months after the D minor Piano Concerto, the *Allegro giojoso* shares the same tonality as the earlier work, with some thematic elements in common as well.[45] It is also the last work for piano and orchestra that Mendelssohn completed.[46]

The *Serenade und Allegro giojoso* is a curious piece, in that it reveals a side of the composer seen much less frequently than in this other works in the concerto genre. This is a tendency towards the open display of virtuosity, seemingly for its own sake. And this tendency is in sharp contrast and runs contrary to the aesthetic criteria that Mendelssohn so passionately espoused concerning his distaste for this fashionable issue.

Moreover, and also in contrast to almost every other Mendelssohn work, the *Serenade und Allegro giojoso* was composed extremely rapidly, as the composer indicates in a letter to his family of 2 April 1838, apparently as a point of pride:

> This evening Madame Botgorschenck's concert takes place, – an excellent contralto singer, who persecuted me so much to play, that I agreed to so, and I realized only afterward that I had nothing either short or suitable to play. So I resolved to compose a rondo, not a single note of which was written the day before yesterday, but which I am to perform this evening with the whole orchestra and rehearsed this morning.[47]

Mercer-Taylor, describing the work as "rightly forgotten," notes the composer's "obvious delight" in having completed it in a mere forty-eight hours.[48] However, Thomas Grey hears the work differently:

> Like the *Rondo brillant*, [the *Serenade und Allegro giojoso*] aspires to nothing more than providing cultivated entertainment. In their jovial directness, both works make a nice foil to the quasi-pathetic rhetorical posturings of

some of the other concerted works . . . Here we seem to witness the quick-witted, humorous side of the composer so often manifested in the correspondence – a biographical point that likewise serves as an appropriate foil to the familiar, but one-sided, notion of Mendelssohn as a primly decorous exemplar of bourgeois piety. In music like this we hear Mendelssohn conversing musically, as it were, with professional friends such as Moscheles or Hiller, unconcerned, for the moment, with any of those imposed figures from the past or present.[49]

At the premiere, op. 48 was entitled *Adagio and Rondo*, and the *Neue Zeitschrift für Musik* described the event: "Mendelssohn's masterful playing of a new Adagio and Rondo, full of singing and brilliance, crowned the whole."[50] The *Allgemeine musikalische Zeitung* described the public's response:

> Herr Doctor Mendelssohn performed, to the great joy of the audience, an Adagio and Rondo for piano with orchestral accompaniment composed by himself, to which was granted, after each movement, the usual thunderous applause of a strongly roused pleasure.[51]

Formally, the *Serenade und Allegro giojoso* consists of an opening 73-measure *Serenade* (Andante), a wistful tune in B minor, cast in compound ternary (ABA) design. The first A is a 16-measure rounded binary form, with parallel construction throughout. The B section modulates to several nearly related keys, and then returns to an abridged restatement of the A theme. Following m. 73, double bar lines and a meter and tempo change to 2/4, Allegro giojoso announce the beginning of this section. The music modulates to D major, first attained with the statement of the "giojoso" theme by the piano in m. 91. This theme mirrors the *Serenade* theme, also cast in rounded binary form, with parallel construction.

The design of the "giojoso" section is quite similar to the *Capriccio brillant*, with a combined solo/tutti exposition, brief development, and abridged recapitulation. Mendelssohn does not appear to have performed the work many times after its composition, and the *Serenade* is not a common staple of the modern concert repertoire.

It is fitting that we conclude our examination of Mendelssohn's concerted works with a discussion of the concerto that is the capstone to his lifelong work in the genre. Op. 64 is not only his last concerto (and last completed large orchestral work), but also the only one regarded by both scholars and performers as "standing quite apart" from all of the others. As Thomas Grey writes, "more than any other of Mendelssohn's works (the "Wedding March" excepted), it seems almost to have dissociated itself from its composer and to lead an autonomous existence, like some product of nature."[52] The work has been heralded for its many novel features, including: (1) the soloist's "elegiac" theme stated at the beginning of the unified solo/tutti exposition; (2) the written-out cadenza that bridges (quite unusually) the development and recapitulation; and (3) the transitions between movements. Perhaps more importantly, the beauty of the work as a whole is profound.

Mendelssohn seems to have initially conceived the work as early as 1838, only a year after the completion of the D minor Piano Concerto op. 40. From its inception, he intended the work for his concertmaster at the Leipzig Gewandhaus, Ferdinand David (1810–73), as a letter of 30 July 1838 indicates:

> I'd like to do a violin concerto for you for next winter [season]; one in
> E minor is running through my head, and the opening of it will not leave
> me in peace.[53]

It would be a full six years before he would, in fact, be left in peace. During this period, Mendelssohn frequently enlisted the aid of David, regarded as one of the great virtuosi of the nineteenth century, for technical advice. The composer finally completed the score while on a recuperative holiday in Soden, near Frankfurt am Main, in September of 1844. The concerto received its premiere on 13 March 1845, in the Gewandhaus.

As we would perhaps expect, several pages of sketches, revealing considerable revisions and corrections for op. 64, survive. Todd sees this as clear evidence that

> Mendelssohn came to regard the concerto more and more as a serious art
> form, just as he regarded the modern theme and variation as part of a great
> Classical tradition . . . in an age when variation and concerto form all too
> often were represented by fatuous examples of mass-produced virtuosity.
> Mendelssohn continued to remain aloof from such commercialism.[54]

While we may perhaps quibble that the composer did not remain entirely unaffected by that commercialism, as his three one-movement concerted works may reveal for some, unquestionably, the E minor Concerto is one of the greatest works in the genre, standing shoulder to shoulder with the violin concertos of Beethoven, Brahms, and Tchaikovsky.

Like the previous two Piano Concertos, opp. 25 and 40, the opening movement of the E minor Violin Concerto is cast in combined tutti/soloist "single-exposition" concerto form. Mendelssohn therefore dispenses with the opening orchestral ritornello, and begins almost immediately with the haunting primary theme stated by the soloist. The orchestra continues this theme, leading to a distinctive transition theme that will reappear in the development, and coda. Joseph Kerman describes the second theme (beginning m. 138) as

Mendelssohn's brilliant gloss . . . on the Beethoven Violin Concerto. In both composers' opening movement, the exposition of the second theme begins in the woodwinds, Beethoven's violin meanwhile holding on to a superior pedal, a long trilled E above the staff . . . Yet a bravura element, the violin's first trill, is also on display and refuses to register as mere accompaniment. Mendelssohn gives *his* violin nothing but a low, open-string G, marked *pp*; instead of bravura, the very lowest common denominator of violinsitic virtu. Even here, as he knew, the solo will refuse to be grounded. (Mendelssohn uses a long plunge to highlight his low G, too; an uncharacteristically brazen move. Later Prokofiev, in a feature of defiant humility, would gloss Mendelssohn by starting his Violin Concerto No. 2 with open-string G played by the solo mezzo piano, the orchestra silent.)[55]

Concerning this theme, Friedhelm Krummacher notes that it (like that of the "Scottish" Symphony's first movement) is "introduced in such a way that the main theme sounds as a counterpoint to it – no different than in the theme combinations of the *St. Paul* choruses."[56]

The famous written-out cadenza (a feature not present in any other Mendelssohn concerto) is stated not in the usual way, in between the end of the recapitulation and the beginning of the final tutti, but instead at the end of the development. Grey notes that the cadenza thereby functions as a "retransition," preparing for the recapitulation, making this the dramatic high point of the movement.

The lyrical, cavatina-like second movement Andante in C major is wedded to the opening movement with a transition. Moreover, the transition connecting this second movement with the Finale contains allusions to the opening theme. The E major Finale is a loose sonata-rondo, and its effective orchestration and has been compared with the *Midsummer Night's Dream* music. There are thematic links between all three movements.

As Thomas Grey notes,

It seems fitting, if fortuitous, that [the E minor Concerto] should combine one of his most serious and personal orchestral movements (the opening Allegro) with a nostalgic return to the world of *A Midsummer Night's Dream* in the finale – the world of Mendelssohn's "enchanted youth" and the music that, more than any other, epitomizes his contribution to the history of music.[57]

Conclusion

Much more remains to be done in our study of Mendelssohn's concertos. For example, efforts toward the analysis of the relationship between the composer's progressive approaches to form in relation to the thematic content – which Friedhelm Krummacher has discussed in regard to the string quartets – would yield many insights.[58] Further work in the area of reception history would prove telling as well.

Finally, as the reexamination of the life and works of Felix Mendelssohn Bartholdy that began in the late twentieth century continues with increasing activity in the early years of the twenty-first, all students of this special composer will continue to be greatly enriched.

8 Mendelssohn's chamber music

THOMAS SCHMIDT-BESTE

In the case of a composer like Mendelssohn, it is not easy to claim that a certain part of his oeuvre is more important than another: it was his avowed goal to be active and successful in as many different musical genres as possible, and – with the single exception of opera – he achieved just this. Nevertheless, it can be said that the mature chamber works of Mendelssohn rank not only among the finest works of the composer, but among those achievements of his that were of lasting importance for the entire century. The techniques of motivic combination, derivation, juxtaposition, and interplay that characterize his mature chamber style, which arose from Mendelssohn's fascination with the music of both Johann Sebastian Bach and Ludwig Beethoven, exercised a considerable influence on nineteenth-century instrumental music in general; it is hardly an exaggeration to claim that the technique of "developing variation" has its roots precisely here. Furthermore, their sheer beauty and highly idiomatic writing for all instruments have secured a place in the performance repertoire and the recording market for at least some of these works – particularly the two piano trios and some of the string quartets.

The chamber music can be divided up – roughly as Mendelssohn's work as a whole can be – into three phases of differing length and importance: a number of youthful works ranging from the first attempts at the age of eleven (in 1820) up to the first publications in 1824; the works of the "first maturity," beginning with the third Piano Quartet op. 3 and the Octet op. 20 (both 1825) and ending around 1830; after a rather long period in which no chamber music was written (with the exception of a few occasional works, like the two *Konzertstücke* for basset-horn composed in 1832/33 for the clarinettist Carl Bärmann) comes the period of full maturity, bringing forth works like the Quartets op. 44 (1837–38) and the two Piano Trios opp. 49 (1839) and 66 (1845).

Early works

Among Mendelssohn's first attempts at composition, transmitted in the exercise book he prepared under the supervision of Carl Friedrich Zelter in or around 1820, a small number of chamber works are already extant among counterpoint exercises, chorale settings, and piano pieces. All of them are scored for violin and piano, reflecting the practical situation in which Felix would play the top part on the violin and Zelter would accompany on the piano.[1] Some are three-part fugues in the style of Johann Sebastian Bach; we also find two sets of variations reminiscent of Haydn, although, characteristically, with rather more contrapuntal writing than would be considered typical for the older master. The two short monothematic movements (also in imitative counterpoint) that round off the small group of "chamber music" pieces in the exercise book are in fact more reminiscent – in form as well as in texture – of bipartite movements in the Baroque trio sonata tradition than of "monothematic sonata form" as R. Larry Todd rather generously classifies them.[2]

A number of fully developed multi-movement chamber works were also written for Zelter's lessons. The earliest, of May 1820, is a piano trio in C minor, with the unusual scoring of viola instead of violoncello (possibly because of the lack of a cello player in the family: the youngest son of the family, Paul – who was to fill that position in later years – had only been born in 1813 and could hardly have been expected to participate just yet). Over the course of the next months, two sonatas followed, again for violin and piano; after that, the production of chamber music largely ceased. As in all other genres, Zelter did not hold his pupil to abstract "rules," but encouraged him to practice certain textures and styles through the repeated composition of pieces;[3] later, in the "lessons" Mendelssohn himself held as teacher of the Conservatory of Music in Leipzig, he used the same method.[4] Hence, the "practice works" of the early 1820s usually come in tight groups and in a certain style; the "chamber music phase" of 1820 is followed by string symphonies and sacred vocal music in 1821–22. Only a set of twelve fugues for string quartet and a piano quartet in D minor is extant from 1821, only the Piano Quartet op. 1 in C minor from October of 1822.

With the three Piano Quartets opp. 1–3 and the Violin Sonata op. 4, Mendelssohn reached a new stage in his creative output. This manifests itself externally in the fact that the ever self-critical composer and his equally critical mentors – his father Abraham and, of course, Zelter – now felt that the time had come to step outside the self-contained world of private study and semi-public performance in the family-owned *Gartenhaus* and to introduce himself to the general public through carefully planned series of works in important genres. It is certainly no accident that this first step was taken in the form of chamber works; nor is it accidental that, before op. 10 (the opera *The Marriage of Camacho*), all published works were not for the truly "public" venues of church, stage and concert hall, but for smaller contexts: after the four chamber works, opp. 5 to 7 are for piano solo, opp. 8 and 9 are songs.

Chamber music, then, would have been considered a prudent and time-tested choice for an "opus 1." But why piano quartets? In fact, the genre could be considered the ideal point of departure for the career of a young composer-pianist. Its piano part – exacting, but not too extroverted – gave Mendelssohn the opportunity to prove himself as a performer without lowering himself to the status of a mere virtuoso; at the same time, the quartet genre appealed to the tradition of "serious" chamber music with all its compositional rigor, and the added possibility of showing one's ability as a contrapuntist. And this particular genre, having as its only famous predecessors the two works by Mozart (K. 478 and K. 493), was not as overburdened with tradition as was the string quartet (which might otherwise have appeared to be the more natural starting point) where Beethoven loomed as the seemingly insuperable precursor.

Not surprisingly, the three piano quartets could be called "conservative," with formal and thematic structures clearly delineated, the piano and the three string instruments forming separate entities treated in an "antiphonal" manner. Particularly the first two quartets (finished in October of 1822 and May of 1823) point back to the late eighteenth century with their light texture and *galant* piano figurations. All three quartets are in four movements and, somewhat unusually, all in minor keys (C minor, F minor, and B minor). But even at this early stage, individual traits begin to emerge, in op. 1 most strikingly in the "elfin" *perpetuum mobile* piano figurations of the Scherzo. In the Finale of op. 2, this penchant for continuous motion leads to an early manifestation of what was to become one of Mendelssohn's trademarks: the superimposition of a new theme over one introduced earlier. The restless eighth-note theme of the first group is reused as accompaniment (in the violin) for the *cantabile* second-group theme in the viola (see Example 8.1); in the recapitulation, the same combination even appears in double counterpoint with the *cantabile* tune sounding below the first theme. This method of combining two seemingly independent lines (originating in the counterpoint lessons with Zelter)[5] demonstrates Mendelssohn's predilection for contrapuntal devices that are at once simple and complex: simple on the surface, in the sense that they are clearly audible and comprehensible; complex in the sense that the two parts fit together in a fashion that is not at all apparent when hearing them independently. Another innovation of op. 2 is the substitution of the Scherzo movement with an "Intermezzo" of suitably light character, but without the standard structural and rhythmical features of the traditional tripartite form in triple meter based on the minuet.

The Third Quartet op. 3, of January 1825, shows richer sonorities and a better integration of the piano and string parts, while raising the integration

Example 8.1 Piano Quartet op. 2 in F minor, finale, mm. 59–68

of form and textures to a new level. In the first movement, the theme of the second group (mm. 111–17) is derived from a countersubject in the piano to the continuation of the first theme in the strings (mm. 24ff.); at first a simple, sequentially repeated chordal figure, it develops into a chorale-like melody. The first themes of all four movements are related in motivic substance through the opening gesture of a rising second followed by two or more falling seconds. The *perpetuum mobile* Scherzo is given more pronounced contours than in op. 1; Goethe himself, for whom Mendelssohn had played it during his second visit to Weimar on 25 May 1825, noted the "elfin" poetic association:

> The Allegro, on the other hand, had character. This eternal whirling and
> turning brought to my imagination the witches' dances on the Blocksberg,
> and thus I had a concept after all to associate with this wondrous music.[6]

One last work among the youthful compositions deserves mention: the Piano Sextet in D major, finished in May of 1824 and published posthumously in 1868 as op. 110. The unusual addition of a double bass was apparently intended to add sonority to the established piano quintet texture.[7]

Werner's classification of the work as "a little piano concerto"[8] seems somewhat exaggerated; the piano part demonstrates considerable, but by no means excessive, virtuosity – no more than the later piano quartets and trios. At the same time, there is too much thematic dialogue between piano and strings, and independence in the voice-leading of the string instruments, for the work to be classified as anything but chamber music. Formally the sextet is the first composition to introduce a device which was to become almost standard for Mendelssohn's instrumental music of the later 1820s: the theme of the "Minuetto" (really more a Scherzo) is quoted verbatim over a length of thirty-one bars in the coda of the finale, including a change of time signature from common time to 6/8. The intention to unify the four-movement cycle through thematic references into a "poetic" whole is as obvious here as is the model of Beethoven.

First maturity

The Third Piano Quartet, with its development of a number of techniques that were to become standard procedure in Mendelssohn's later chamber music, could be perceived as a logical stage in his development as a composer. The String Octet (op. 20) of the same year is anything but logical. At first sight, it appears to be in almost all aspects – character, texture, formal planning, sheer size – a radical departure from anything the composer (or, for that matter, anybody else) had attempted in chamber music. Its texture is not – as in earlier works for eight strings – that of a polychoral "double quartet," but a true eight-voice composition in which the sixteen-year-old composer explored all possible constellations. Frequently the first violin part (written for Mendelssohn's friend Eduard Rietz, the violinist whose career was cut short by his premature death at the age of twenty-nine in 1832) has *concertante* passages of staggering virtuosity, with varying accompaniment; but virtually no other possible combination of instruments is left unexplored, in solo texture, parallel movement in thirds, sixths and octaves, imitative counterpoint, antiphonal treatment of high against low voices, and so forth.

The strategies of thematic and formal unity found in the piano quartets are apparent in the octet as well, though superseded by the heightened possibilities of contrast and variation in the eight-voice medium. The texture varies between full orchestral treatment (as in the very first bars) and intricate counterpoint; the thematic development in particular, although embedded in a process outwardly full of drama and contrast, abounds with motivic relationships and derivations. In the exposition of the first movement alone, the following elements can be listed:[9]

m. 1: arpeggiated theme 1 in the top voice

m. 9: new motive in the violins, accompanied by theme 1 in the two cellos, followed by a falling eighth-note figure in the violins

m. 16: prolongation of the falling eighth-note figure

m. 21: "new" sixteenth-note motive (but really an extension of the rising arpeggiations of theme 1, answered by falling quarter-note figure, derived from the eighth-note figure in mm. 16ff.)

m. 25: development of a segment of the sixteenth-note motive

m. 37: re-entry of theme 1

m. 45: like m. 9, but with theme 1 in inversion

m. 52: like m. 25, followed by prolongation of theme 1

m. 68: "second theme" derived from the quarter-note figure in m. 22 (in inversion) with interspersed segements from theme 1

m. 75: "new" motive derived from the last four eighth-notes of "second theme"

m. 77: like m. 68

m. 84: like m. 75, with prolongation

m. 88: sixteenth-note motive from m. 21 in inversion – which at the same time turns out to be a rhythmic extension of the falling eighth-note motive derived from the "second theme" in mm. 75 and 84! The arpeggiated eighth-note accompaniment is derived from theme 1

m. 96: "second theme" accompanied by sixteenth-note scales

m. 102: scales derived from inverted sixteenth-note motive (m. 88), segment of theme 1.

After so much working and reworking of the thematic material, there does not seem much left for the composer to do in the development – a general trait in Mendelssohn's chamber music which was to become even more pronounced in the later works. Hence, the development is more concerned with texture and dynamics than with themes: The head motive of the first theme is juxtaposed with itself in four texturally separated groups (violin 1/ violins 2, 3, 4/violas/cellos); the sixteenth-note motive is heard in *fortissimo* instead of *piano*; the second theme is augmented and reduced dynamically and texturally to create a sense of almost complete stasis, which in turn makes it possible for the composer to engineer one of the most impressive – although totally unthematic – climaxes in all of chamber music, from two practically silent, immobile voices (viola 1 and cello 2) in m. 200 to virtuosic, *sempre ff* sixteenth-note scales in eight-voice unison in m. 218.

The slow movement can be analyzed in two different ways: first, as a modified sonata form with a development based exclusively on the second (transitory) theme, an abridged recapitulation – missing the entire first group – and a balancing coda reintroducing precisely that first theme;

second, as a binary form with two sections of almost the same length, the first (mm. 1–53) moving from the tonic C minor to the parallel key E♭ major and the second (mm. 54–102) modulating back to C minor, the thematic groups being rearranged from A–B–C in the first section to B–C–A in the second.

After the ethereal sonority of the slow movement, the Scherzo is even more innovative in terms of atmosphere. The first attempts to create the famous Mendelssohnian "elfin" sound had been through piano figurations in the early chamber music; in the eight-voice, all-string setting, the texture comes entirely into its own, in rapid eighth- and sixteenth-note motion, *pianissimo* almost throughout. Unlike almost every other composition by Mendelssohn, the movement appears in the autograph score without any corrections; obviously, it was written in a moment of complete inspiration. According to Mendelssohn's sister Fanny, the music was inspired by the four closing lines from the *Walpurgis Night's Dream* of Goethe's *Faust*:

> Cloud and mist drift off with speed,
> Aloft 'tis brighter growing.
> Breeze in leaves and wind in reed,
> And all away is blowing.[10]

Fanny elaborates further on her brother's intentions concerning the movement:

> The whole piece is to be played staccato and pianissimo, the tremulandos
> entering every now and then, the trills passing away with the quickness
> of lightning; everything is new and strange and at the same time most
> insinuating and pleasing. One feels near the world of spirits, carried away
> in the air, half inclined to snatch up a broomstick and follow the aerial
> procession. At the end the first violin takes a flight with a feather-like
> lightness – and all away is blowing.[11]

The finale takes the *perpetuum mobile* idea and turns it around completely. The movement opens with an eight-voice fugato of a theme entirely in eighth notes – and the eighth-note motion reigns, with few exceptions, throughout. The idea of a *perpetuum mobile* fugue is once again inspired by Beethoven, in this case by the finale of the String Quartet op. 59 no. 3, but taken to further extremes and made more powerful through the participation of twice as many instruments. It could be said that the *perpetuum mobile* not only is the driving force of the movement, but supersedes all other aspects. Even the form – a modified rondo – is subordinate to it, as the otherwise typical elements (change of pace and thematic contrast) are lacking. What themes there are in addition to the eighth-note motion do not replace it, but are superimposed onto it; from m. 321 onwards (little more than three quarters through the movement), E♭ major is reached incontro-vertibly, and the rest functions as one gigantic coda. As in the sextet, the main theme of the Scherzo is restated in the Finale (mm. 273–313), although this time integrated into the texture of the movement.

The one genre, however, that Mendelssohn had largely eschewed up to this point – or, to put it more bluntly, avoided – was the string quartet.[12] Since the works of Haydn and Mozart, the string quartet had been considered the pinnacle of achievement in chamber music; contemporary music the-ory considered the four-voice texture the ideal and perfection of "learned" polyphonic writing. The fact that all four instruments were equal in tim-bre – at least in principle – resulted in the commonplace most famously expressed by Goethe, that in the string quartet "one could hear four rea-sonable people in conversation."[13] A number of Mendelssohn's predeces-sors and contemporaries (including Ignaz Pleyel and Franz Krommer) had introduced themselves to the public with a string quartet or group of string quartets precisely to stake their claim as composers of "serious" music. Mendelssohn's personal route toward string quartets, however, was full of detours. A set of fugues for string quartet is extant from the spring of 1821 – another instance of the "learnedness" of the four-voice texture – and in 1823, we find a complete four-movement quartet in E♭ major. This work, however, has all the qualities of a "study composition," lacking the thematic and textural innovations introduced in the piano quartets.

Even after the composition of the octet, Mendelssohn's approach to the quartet was an indirect one: the first chamber composition to follow was the String Quintet op. 18 written in the spring of 1826. Its scoring, with two violas, is that of Mozart, but Mozart does not appear to be the main model. The textural juxtaposition of two violins versus two violas so com-mon in Mozart is largely absent; on the contrary, many different textures are used, as in the octet, with a clear predominance of the first violin as solo instrument. The influence of Beethoven is not directly obvious, par-ticularly as his C major String Quintet (op. 29 of 1801) is very different in character and level of sophistication, with its almost divertimento-like tone and its predominantly homophonic textures. Mendelssohn, on the other hand, attempts to write a chamber work with all the sophistication of a quartet. In its first version, the quintet consisted of four fast move-ments (the *Intermezzo*, written on occasion of the death of Eduard Rietz on 22 January 1832, replaced an original Allegretto as second movement), and the Scherzo is a highly unusual "elfin fugue."

With the two quartets op. 12 in E♭ major and op. 13 in A minor (the first written in 1829, the second in 1827, but both published in 1830 in reverse order of composition), the compositional and artistic progress of the preceding years – manifested most of all in the octet – is incorporated

into the quintessential chamber music genre. Both works very clearly
show the influence of Beethoven; indeed, they are modeled on the most
"progressive" works of the older master, the very last quartets. Mendelssohn's
father Abraham did not think much of Beethoven, but was broad-minded
enough to acquire all current works for his children directly after they were
published, and both Felix and his sister Fanny were thrilled with what they
found. Particularly telling is a letter Felix wrote to his friend, the Swedish
composer Adolf Fredrik Lindblad, in February of 1828, shortly after finishing
his own Eb major quartet, a work clearly modeled upon Beethoven's op. 132
(which Schlesinger in Berlin had brought out barely a month previously!):

> Have you seen his new quartet in Bb major [op. 130]? And that in C♯ minor
> [op. 131]? Get to know them, please. The piece in Bb contains a cavatina in
> Eb where the first violin sings the whole time, and the world sings along . . .
> The piece in C♯ has another one of these transitions, the introduction is a
> fugue!! It closes very scarily in C♯ major, all instruments play C♯; and the
> next entry is in such a sweet D major (the next movement, that is), and such
> little ornamentation! You see, this is one of my points! The relationship of
> all 4 or 3 or 2 or 1 movements of one sonata to another and their parts,
> whose secret one can recognize at the very beginning through the simple
> existence of such a piece (because the mere beginning in D major, those two
> notes, make me tender-hearted), that must go into the music. Help me put
> it there![14]

As in other "Beethovenian" works, such as the two Piano Sonatas op. 6 (1826)
and op. 106 (1827), Mendelssohn paid homage in three different ways. First,
all works begin with a direct quotation or allusion to a recent work of the
older composer. The A minor Quartet begins like Beethoven's op. 132, the
Eb major Quartet like the op. 74 Quartet of 1809. Second, the linking of
all four movement through motivic references becomes even more pronounced. This technique is of course present in a number of earlier compositions by Beethoven, but increases in importance in the late works, most
prominently in op. 131, which was specifically mentioned by Mendelssohn
in that context. In his own quartets, op. 12 is remarkable primarily through
the recurrence of the second theme from the first movement not once but
twice in the finale, with a complete break in texture and rhythm both times.

The A minor Quartet combines this quest for motivic unity with the third
device taken from Beethoven: the introduction of "poetic meaning" into
the string quartet. Extramusical elements like tone painting, poetic titles,
or programmes had so far been almost completely absent from the string
quartet, embodying as it did "pure," "absolute" music; only Beethoven's
"Heiliger Dankgesang" from op. 132, or "Der schwer gefasste Entschluss"
from op. 135, had broken with this tradition. Mendelssohn obviously took

these works as his inspiration, but went a step further and placed an entire song of his own composition at the beginning of op. 13, with the title "Ist es wahr?" ("Is it true?") and the designation "Thema." The opening motive of that song alludes directly to Beethoven's "Der schwer gefasste Entschluss" ("Muss es sein") in rhythmical and melodic contour (Example 8.2a). It is introduced towards the end of the introduction to the first movement; an extended quotation from the song closes out the finale, thus giving the answer to the question posed at the beginning: "Was ich fühle, das begreift nur, die es mitfühlt, und die treu mir ewig bleibt" ("What I am feeling is only understood by her who feels with me and who always remains true to me"). Thus, the technique of motivic unity simultaneously becomes a device of poetic unity. Moreover, the motive reoccurs in the main theme of the first movement (Example 8.2b), a variant thereof and later its inversion in movement 2 (8.2c and 8.2d); this inversion becomes the first theme of the Intermezzo (8.2e) and a fugato theme in the development of the Finale (8.2f).

The only area in which Mendelssohn remains on the conservative side of Beethoven is in his treatment of harmony. Where Beethoven pushed tonality to its outer limits, particularly in the C♯ minor Quartet op. 131, Mendelssohn remains firmly grounded in dominant–tonic relationships, daring as individual chord progressions may sound. At the same time, both works are unmistakably "Mendelssohnian." They retain the vigor of motion familiar from octet and quintet, most noticeably in the *perpetuum mobile* finale of op. 12 and in the dramatic opening movement of op. 13. The formal patterns are manifold, as always, from the sonata-rondo first movement of op. 12 to the *Canzonetta* of op. 12 and the *Intermezzo* of op. 13, both modifying the traditional Scherzo type considerably; their middle sections also modify the by now familiar "elfin Scherzo." Both finale movements are highly original variants of sonata form combined with recitative-like and cyclical elements as mentioned above; they sum up the entire four-movement cycle. The technique of thematic superimposition recurs in the first movement of op. 13, where two seemingly separate motives are presented in mm. 19 and 24 respectively, then synchronized in m. 42. Perhaps most importantly, however, the two quartets are pure specimens of Mendelssohn's ability to write "melodic counterpoint." The polyphonic ideal manifests itself in innumerable imitative passages and contrapuntal inner voices – the entire first movement of op. 13 has few passages that are not imitative in two or more parts. Particularly Mendelssohnian are combinations of imitative counterpoint with lyrical passages resembling some of his later *Songs without Words*, as in the slow movement of the same work, or with "elfin Scherzo" music, as in the *Intermezzo*.

The two "early" quartets opp. 12 and 13 have always been grouped among Mendelssohn's uncontested masterpieces; their clear indebtedness to the late

Example 8.2 String Quartet op. 13 in A minor
(a) first movement, mm. 13–15 (violin 1)

(b) first movement, mm. 26–28 (violin 1)

(c) second movement, mm. 1–3 (violin 1)

(d) second movement, mm. 20–22 (viola)

(e) third movement, mm. 1–4 (violin 1)

(f) fourth movement, mm. 164–68 (viola)

Beethoven quartets place them on the cutting edge of chamber music writing, and their – sometimes barely controlled – temperament, their novelty of texture and form, and their allusions to extra-musical content made it easy for music historians to integrate them into an over-arching concept of musical progress and into a Romantic ideal of "poetic" instrumental writing. Eric Werner concludes: "Indeed, had Mendelssohn been able to maintain the level of this quartet [the A minor], his name would stand in close proximity to that of a Mozart or Beethoven!"[15]

Mature works

After a long hiatus in chamber music production in the early 1830s – coinciding with a general creative crisis – the years after 1836 show Mendelssohn newly invigorated. And it is perhaps no accident that among the first important works to appear after 1836, a disproportionately large number are in chamber genres: the three String Quartets op. 44 (1837–38), the Cello Sonata op. 45 (1838), the unpublished Violin Sonata in F major (1838) and the Piano Trio op. 49 (1839). By now Mendelssohn shows the poise and self-assurance of the mature artist, and rather than taking detours through string quintet, octet, and piano quartet, he tackles the main traditions head on: string quartet, piano trio, accompanied solo sonata.

The first and greatest achievements of this period are the three String Quartets op. 44, written between summer of 1837 and summer of 1838, published in 1839. Though enthusiastically received by critics and audience alike on Mendelssohn's time, they have not fared as well in the eyes of modern commentators. Eric Werner, who diagnoses an "artistic slump" in Mendelssohn's creative output in the years between 1838 and 1844, states: "he becomes somewhat too smooth, and only his inborn taste and his technical mastery save him, in the following years, from sheer mediocrity."[16] For Werner, the String Quartets op. 44 are prime exemplars for the "tranquil years" between 1837 and 1841. With Beethoven's late works as his yardstick, Werner looks for contrast, struggle, strong emotions; and when he finds the quartets lacking in these, he states regretfully: "[a]s the Second Piano Concerto is far inferior to the First, so these quartets, as a whole, do not reach the heights of originality and inspiration of their forerunners opp. 12 and 13."[17]

However, Werner's preoccupation with drama and contrast, as well as his entirely speculative assertion that it was his happy marriage with Cécile and the resulting "bourgeois" lifestyle that deflected Mendelssohn from the path of a "truly Romantic" composer,[18] tell us more about our modern views of what music history should be like than about the music and its composer. It is too simple to view the Quartets op. 44 as failures merely because they do not maintain the Beethovenian tradition of chamber music. Already in 1835, Fanny had written to her brother that

> we were young precisely in the time of Beethoven's last years, and it was
> only to be expected that we completely assimilated his manner, as it is so
> moving and impressive. But you have lived through it and written yourself
> through it.[19]

According to Fanny, then, Felix had attained maturity precisely by having transcended Beethoven and having created something of his own. In fact,

Mendelssohn was pursuing very specific – and very individual – goals in his mature quartets, goals that owe as much to his interpretation of the idea of a "conversation of four reasonable persons" as to his general ideas on thematic, formal, and poetic unity. Indeed gone are the direct references to Beethoven, gone are the extroverted exuberance and the formal experiments of the early quartets and the Octet. But as Friedhelm Krummacher puts it, "only from op. 44 onwards does Mendelssohn attain a completely individual model of sonata form. It is characterized not by drama and dialectic, but on the contrary by balance and reconciliation. Thematic contrasts are rounded off and subsumed in homogeneous situations, and latent connections of the thematic substance support a specific mediation between quasi-stationary sections."[20]

Indeed, thematic (and poetic) unity reach a new level in the quartets of op. 44 precisely by way of the composer's decision to forgo the dramaturgy of contrast that is a supposed precondition of sonata form. This is best exemplified in the first movement of the E minor Quartet op. 44 no. 2, the earliest of the three works. Its first and second theme are both *cantabile* lines, similar in rhythm and phrasing if not in melody. A sixteenth-note motive that dominates most of the bridge passage between first and second group appears to form a sharp contrast; but it turns out that it is the accompaniment to a falling eighth-note figure which appears to be a variant of the continuation of the first theme, but really is the inverted diminution of that theme itself (see Examples 8.3a and 8.3b). Towards the end of the exposition, this diminution even serves as accompaniment to the theme itself (Example 8.3c). In the development, the possible permutations and combinations of the different related motives are explored further, the sixteenth notes now accompanying the first theme in its original form, the eighth-note version appearing in canon, serving as accompaniment to the recapitulation and subtly reverting back from the arpeggiated to the scalar form in which it first appeared in the exposition.

Besides the "poetic unity" of the mature quartets thus attained through motivic relations, another aesthetic goal of the composer becomes apparent in op. 44. Almost without exception, the movements begin homophonically, usually in basic melody-plus-accompaniment texture with the first violin carrying the theme. In the first movements of op. 44 no. 1, the resulting texture is almost orchestral in character, with all accompanying voices in sixteenth-note tremolo. In op. 44 no. 2 as well, the themes are introduced in the same fashion before entering in the motivic interplay described above. This is in vivid contrast to the earlier chamber music where, especially in the fast movements, the themes are often treated contrapuntally right from the beginning. The reason for this changed manner of presentation is, in all likelihood, bound up with a contemporaneous change

Example 8.3 String Quartet op. 44/2 in E minor, first movement

(a) mm. 1–5: first theme

(b) mm. 32–35

(c) mm. 83–89

in Mendelssohn's aesthetics. The composer had always been very keen on *Bestimmtheit* – clarity – in his instrumental music, in the sense that the ideal listener immediately understood the "meaning" of his music without requiring verbal explanations.[21] Over the course of his creative life, Mendelssohn had tried different methods to achieve such clarity, including literary or topographical references in the early orchestral works. In chamber music, where such "extra-musical" references were not part of the genre history, the "intra-musical" strategies of meaning described above (thematic quotes or cyclical construction) were to serve the same purpose.

Beginning in the mid-1830s, Mendelssohn began to place more importance on the presentation of the thematic material as such: "I want the ideas to be expressed more simply and more naturally, but to be conceived in a more complex and individual fashion," he writes to Wilhelm von Boguslawski in 1834;[22] a good composer has to be able primarily "to clearly present his ideas and what he wants to express."[23] Mendelssohn criticizes Bernhard Schüler's overture *Gnomen und Elfen* primarily "because in many places, particularly in the beginning, but now and then elsewhere as well, I miss a marked musical shape, whose contours . . . I can clearly recognize, grasp and enjoy."[24] Fundamentally, Mendelssohn's concept of the "musical idea" (i.e. the "theme") can be traced back to Hegel's idealism – the idea is the carrier of all meaning, and for that meaning to be "clear" and communicable, it has to become "concrete" in an adequate fashion.[25] Although Hegel himself never considered music to be able to communicate such concrete meaning, and never used the term "idea" in a context referring to music, Mendelssohn – like many of his contemporaries – sought in music an "ideal" art. After having become disenchanted with the potential of "extramusical" representation as attempted in the picturesque concert overtures of the late 1820s and early 1830s, the frequent selection of self-contained, song-like "musical ideas" as well as their clear presentation were steps in that direction.[26]

Next to the concentrated motivic work apparent in the string quartets, the two Piano Trios opp. 49 (1839) and 66 (1845) seem more relaxed – almost exuberant in op. 49 – which no doubt contributed to their comparatively larger appeal to the public. It was in the review of the first trio that Robert Schumann called Mendelssohn "the Mozart of the nineteenth century," and the work itself "the trio masterpiece of the present time . . . which grand- and great-grandchildren will enjoy in years to come."[27] The techniques of motivic development and combination are of course retained, but with the added interest of the two different textures and timbres. Mendelssohn makes use of this "added layer" not only through much motivic permutation and counterpoint, but also by reintroducing the idea of a superimposed theme familiar from the earlier works. The recapitulation in the first movement of op. 49 is enriched by a new countermelody first in the violin, then in the cello. The sheer expansive beauty of the melodic writing – particularly in the first two movements – is enhanced through the typical repetition of the material with exchanges of piano and string texture, at times also between the two individual string instruments; the works gain considerable length this way besides (the first movement of op. 49 is 616 bars long!). Mendelssohn's unpretentious but effective style of piano writing lends itself perfectly to chamber music: it is motivically, but not texturally dense, and abounds with arpeggios and other figurations that can function thematically or as accompaniment. The composer himself was very self-conscious about what he perceived to be the limit of his piano style – his "poverty of new figures for the piano";[28] but its integration into the trio texture can be considered a success surpassing that of his solo piano music, particularly when – as often happens – a new figuration adds an entirely novel character to a familiar theme.

The more concentrated – and hence more typically "Mendelssohnian" – work is the less popular later composition in C minor. Here the thematic material of the entire cycle is interconnected through the common substance of the rising second-inversion chord (see Example 8.4). Moreover, the Finale reintroduces an element of "extra-musical" meaning: in one of the most enchanting moments in all of chamber music, the restless 6/8 motion dies down, and out of nowhere, the piano softly plays a chorale tune in chordal homophony. The composer alludes to at least two traditional hymns – "Gelobet seist du Jesu Christ" and "Herr Gott dich alle loben wir" – in addition to an organ chorale and a psalm setting of his own composition, *Lord hear the voice of my complaint* of 1839.[29] But he does not actually quote more than a few notes from each; without being too specific, he lends a general air of sacred celebration to the movement which culminates in a grand apotheosis of the chorale.

Whereas the octet, the string quartets and the trios are obviously at the centre of Mendelssohn's activity as a composer, and rank among the finest specimens of their genre in the nineteenth century, neither the composer nor his audience paid as much attention to the sonata for solo instrument and piano. As mentioned above, a number of youthful compositions fall into this category, but only the Violin Sonata in F minor of 1823 had appeared in print, as op. 4 in 1824. It is in the old-fashioned three-movement format, but looks forward to the string quartets through the use of instrumental recitative in the introduction to the first movement. The violin sonata of 1838 was never considered worthy of publication. The two Cello Sonatas opp. 45 and 58 were indeed published in 1839 and 1843 respectively; they make full use of the cantabile qualities of the cello, but lack the spark that make the contemporary trios so successful. The earlier work, written for the composer's brother Paul, even returns to the "old-fashioned"

Example 8.4 Piano Trio op. 66 in C minor
(a) first movement, first theme

(b) first movement, second theme, mm. 23–26

(c) first movement, third theme, mm. 63–66

(d) second movement, B section, mm. 39–43

(e) finale, first theme, mm. 1–5

(f) finale, second theme, mm. 20–26

(g) finale, third ('chorale') theme, mm. 129–137

three-movement scheme. The most interesting feature of the later one is the slow (third) movement which is another experiment in instrumental chorale: this time, the chorale appears from the beginning in the piano, alternating with recitative-like passages in the cello before the two different spheres of expression are united.

The problem of the late works

When speaking of Mendelssohn's "late works," it is important to note that all compositions with opus numbers higher than 72 were published after the composer's death. They do not reflect the chronology of composition; more importantly, they refer to works that Mendelssohn himself refused or failed to publish. Among the chamber works in this category, it is easy to disregard the so-called "String Quartet" op. 81, a haphazard combination of an Andante in E major, a Scherzo in A minor, a Capriccio in E minor, and a fugue in Eb major, composed in the years 1847, 1847, 1843, and 1827 respectively. The String Quintet "op. 87" of 1845, on the other hand, was never cleared for publication, but it is a finished four-movement cycle. It continues the tradition of the mature quartets in its presentation of the thematic material in a clear manner in the top voice; the tendency toward orchestral writing becomes even more pronounced. Although contrapuntal writing and "developing variation" are by no means absent from the work, Mendelssohn's interest often turns away from motivic development and toward sound and texture as such, with long passages dominated by a single rhythm or figuration. The first movement with its extensive use of tremolo and unison is an example of this new trend, even more so the darkly intense Adagio e lento reminiscent of the late Schubert. The limits of this style become apparent in the Finale, an almost completely monothematic sonata-rondo. The simple sixteenth-note figuration that is the theme lacks the potential to sustain a prolonged structure, and it is no surprise that this movement was the reason for the withdrawal of the work.[30]

The last finished chamber work is similar to the quintet in some ways, radically different in others. During the summer of 1847, while on holiday in Switzerland, Mendelssohn wrote his F minor Quartet op. 80. Although it is hazardous to link certain works to certain biographical events, the tone of this work – which might well be described as desperate – bears an obvious relationship to the composer's state of mind after Fanny's sudden death on 17 May 1847. "I feel entirely void and without form, when I try to think about music", the composer wrote on 24 May.[31] Eric Werner calls the quartet "the cry of grief . . . of the suffering creature";[32] in any case, the new trend in chamber composition already apparent in op. 87 is put to a much more emotional use. The orchestral texture, the tremoli, the lack of self-contained melodies, the sudden harmonic shifts, the emphasis on sound and rhythm as such – all these are used to transport emotions of unprecedented negative force. Three of the four movements are in F minor; the presentation of material is reduced to scalar passages and occasional snippets of motivic development in the first movement, to unusual rhythmic gestures (see the hemiolic cross-rhythms in the first bars) in the Scherzo, to restless figurations in the finale. As Friedhelm Krummacher has shown, Mendelssohn almost certainly considered the quartet to be a "finished" composition destined for publication; the autograph displays the large number of corrections typical for Mendelssohn when revising on of his works either for performance of for publication.[33] Hence, unlike in the Quintet op. 87 (and unlike the "Italian" Symphony, for that matter), the lack of authorization was not a conscious withdrawal of a work considered unsuccessful, but a result simply of the composer's death only a few months after completion.

Whatever its biographical implications might be, the work stands as a milestone in Mendelssohn's creative development as a composer. It renounces all the techniques of motivic manipulation and interplay, looking forward instead to the compositions of Smetana and Hugo Wolf. All in all, however, Mendelssohn's main legacy to nineteenth-century chamber music was in fact not the "new style" of the last works, but the integration of melodic counterpoint into chamber music, from Schumann to Brahms, Dvořák, and beyond.

9 The music for keyboard

GLENN STANLEY

Felix Mendelssohn was, like Brahms a generation later, one of the great pianists of his time, without having striven for a virtuoso career. On the organ he had no peer; virtually alone he popularized – in the best sense of the word – Bach's organ music, and his compositions for organ are a cornerstone of the post-Baroque repertory for the instrument. But his music for piano does not enjoy this status. Unlike Brahms, unlike his contemporaries Schumann, Chopin, Liszt, and unlike revered past masters such as J. S. Bach, Mozart, and Beethoven, Mendelssohn did not regard the piano as a preferred medium for his most significant artistic statements, and this attitude expresses itself in his choice of keyboard genres and in the dimensions and character of individual works. It is a question not of their quality – most of the keyboard music is of the highest order – but of how he weighed the importance of the genres that he cultivated. Nonetheless, his music for piano and for organ constitutes one of the more significant keyboard repertories of his century,[1] and his contributions to the cultivation of serious keyboard music in public performance were, in their time, unsurpassed.

Beginnings: counterpoint, sonatas, and Romantic character pieces

Mendelssohn learned to play and compose at an astonishingly early age – the probable earliest extant keyboard work, a three-movement sonata for two pianos, was composed by the ten-year-old c. October 1819. He began to study the organ in 1822, and his interest in the instrument intensified during his travels in England (where he met Samuel Wesley), Switzerland, and Italy in 1829–30. His mentors in Berlin exposed him to Bach, the primary early influence, and he learned music by Scarlatti, Frescobaldi, and the French clavecinists. He was, of course, also exposed to contemporary keyboard music by Clementi, John Field, and Weber, and also the Classical works by Haydn, Mozart, and Beethoven. R. Larry Todd characterizes the "student compositions" (up to roughly 1823–24) as "conservative": they display diverse stylistic and genre influences, consisting of sonatas, variation movements, dances, fantasias, etudes, fugues, and other common forms.[2]

His engagement with Beethoven began somewhat later and, not unexpectedly, stimulated the composition of several piano sonatas in the early 1820s, after which Mendelssohn abandoned the sonata as a compositional genre. The Sonata, op. 6 in E major (1826), is the only piano sonata published by Mendelssohn,[3] and it is the most mature. The first movement virtually cites the beginning of Beethoven's op. 101, and the return of the first theme at the close of the non-fugal Finale (op. 101 concludes with a fugue) also harks back to the model, while the third-movement "Recitative" can be linked to op. 110. Yet we should not overestimate the extent to which the still young Mendelssohn was able (or even desired) to penetrate Beethoven's sonata thinking. He limited himself to surface allusions; he applied neither Beethoven's formal-harmonic nor his developmental procedures, and he certainly did not attempt to create movements and works with the weight and scope of Beethoven's most substantial sonatas. The latter point is most apparent in Mendelssohn's Sonata in B♭ of 1827, published in 1868 under the opus number 106. (Would that have pleased the modest composer?) The first theme of the first movement evokes that of the "Hammmerklavier" Sonata (Beethoven's op. 106), but the brief movement and the brief complete sonata do not realize the expectations raised by their own first idea, let alone the monumental model.

After op. 106 Mendelssohn cultivated the sonata only as a pianist; as a composer he concentrated on one-movement character pieces, publishing them either as single works or, more typically, in collections. Perhaps he felt more confident in this area, or focused on it because he knew that such pieces were more marketable in the music culture of his day. In the first published character piece, the Capriccio in F♯ minor op. 5 (1825), the fusion of contemporary and Baroque styles in a genre with a long history foreshadows a life-long interest in such syntheses. The first part of the loosely constructed ternary form paraphrases the opening theme of Bach's D minor Concerto for Harpsichord BWV 1052, and the texture of the middle part resembles a two-part invention, although the slower moving part is harmonically conceived. But even in the A sections the style is contemporary; there is little strict counterpoint, the harmonic language is of its time, and the virtually perpetuo-moto rhythms characterize many of Mendelssohn's fast movements.

Until his death, Mendelssohn produced a steady, if not prolific, stream of characteristic pieces as single works or as groups. In the late 1820s and thereafter, with the exception of the historical pieces for piano and organ, he depended less on recent and more distant past models (but continued to make allusions) and found his own pianistic style. It is marked by clear forms and phrasing, uncomplicated textures, a modern harmonic language that largely eschews the chromatic advances of Chopin, Liszt, and even Schubert, and a level of virtuosity that challenges skilled amateurs but usually does not overwhelm them. Some of the most attractive fast pieces are either designated "Scherzo" (e.g. the second of the *Three Fantasies or Caprices* op. 16) or possess that inimitable scherzo character best known from the Incidental Music to *A Midsummer Night's Dream*. Slow pieces display Mendelssohn's skill as a composer of beautiful "bel canto" melodies.

One of the more interesting and curious of these pieces (though not a masterpiece in any way) has escaped critical attention. While traveling in Ireland in 1829 Mendelssohn wrote a derisive letter to his brother-in-law pleading, "But please, no national music!" and lamenting the "harper . . . in every inn" playing "infamous, common, faked so-called folk melodies."[4] A year later he began to compose a "Fantasy on 'The Last Rose of Summer'" (op. 15, pub. 1831), an extremely popular Irish song of the time. While there is no dedicatee, it seems likely that Mendelssohn wrote it only to satisfy a request or as an act of friendship or gratitude. An introduction evokes a minstrel's harp or guitar, then the song (Adagio) is presented over a simple chordal accompaniment. It ends on a full close under a fermata; a sudden Presto agitato in E minor begins the actual *Fantasy*, which presents several ideas beginning with a dialogue between the hands on a two-note motive strongly reminiscent of the first movement of Beethoven's Piano Sonata in E major op. 109. This long and fiery music is interrupted by two short recitatives and a fragmentary recall of the song, which is otherwise quite overwhelmed by the Fantasy. (Was this a purposeful destructive act stemming from his dislike of the pseudo-folk style?) But song prevails, in the extensive concluding apotheosis, which returns to E major and evokes folksong before a Schumannesque postlude. The Fantasy is a problematic and intriguing work, and a departure from the usual well-mannered restraint that characterizes Mendelssohn's keyboard music.

What's in a name? The *Songs without Words*

Through their sheer number, their attractive melodic writing, and their "playability," the forty-eight *Songs without Words* (issued in eight volumes of six pieces) are the most familiar and enduring piano works by Mendelssohn. Their prominence might not work to the composer's best advantage, however, because, although "much loved by the cultivated daughters," they became "a synonym for the stuffy middle-class salon, with embroidered table cloths and ladies' circle."[5] Is this judgment fair? It resembles deprecatory remarks by Mendelssohn himself (that do not reflect well on him); his friend the theorist and Leipzig St. Thomas Cantor Moritz Hauptmann related Mendelssohn's response when asked to play some of the songs:

"At first he did not want to play the songs without words (Lieder ohne Texte) and said, they are only for women . . ."[6] Or does it also arise from an incomplete knowledge of the repertory, in which the (in)famous sixth song of op. 62 in A major (untitled by Mendelssohn but popularized as "Spring Song" and a favorite concert piece of Clara Schumann) and a handful of others may indeed seem clichéd and overly precious? There is much fine music among the songs, and Mendelssohn took them seriously indeed, making numerous revisions to individual songs and their arrangement into volumes – they were not lightly tossed off.[7] His actions, which also include his own public performances of some of the songs, speak more accurately than his occasional words.

Despite the modest initial sales of the first several volumes, they soon became widely imitated, which annoyed the family and also provoked some critical commentary in musical journals.[8] Schumann and other critics admired Mendelssohn's pieces and some found them to be an important artistic innovation, but this favorable reception was soon countered by negative views toward the idea of the genre (not the music itself) that began to emerge in the 1840s. Mendelssohn had his own reservations about the songs; after preparing the third volume for publication in 1837 he wrote to Fanny: "I won't publish any more very soon; I would rather write bigger things." In the next sentence he mentions finishing one string quartet and his plans to begin another.[9]

The genre name – cleverly oxymoronic – generated some confusion and controversy about their aesthetic basis and propriety that has continued to this day.[10] Felix, and Fanny too, who helped invent them in the late 1820s, remembered their origin more as a game than a problem. They were, as she wrote to him in 1838, "jokes that we, as mere children, contrived to pass the time."[11] But serious aesthetic goals developed from their play: in addition to the successful experiment of transferring vocal idioms to the keyboard, Mendelssohn chose the songs to advocate absolute music. (He surely saw them in this way – only a handful have characteristic names). This emerges in the most famous remark Mendelssohn ever made about music (see Chapter 11, p. 190), which came as a reply to a question about the meaning of the generic title and the works it describes and argues for the definiteness of instrumental music as opposed to the multiple meanings in verbal statements.

What makes these pieces wordless songs? As stated above, only a few were published with descriptive titles; Mendelssohn did delete several titles of several songs inscribed in the manuscript versions. There are three Venetian boat songs ("Gondellieder"), two of which provide charmingly quiet and melancholy conclusions to volumes one and two; there is one "Volkslied" (vol. IV no. 5), an Allegro con fuoco that (purposefully?) defies expectations of idyllic simplicity or sentimentality in this artificial genre; and there is one "Duetto in A♭ major," which presents the etude-like problem of voicing out a higher and most of a lower voice in the right hand that also plays a continual lively accompaniment figure.[12] Several other songs contain etude-like features, for example vol. II no. 5, Andante grazioso, in which the pianist must learn to play "Il Basso sempre piano e leggierissimo." Here the idiomatic pianistic style is integrated into a lyrical conception; in some other songs, notably several long virtuosic pieces in fast tempos that provide effective contrasts to the slow lyrical ones (e.g. vol. II no. 4, vol. III no. 5), the texture is so tailored to the keyboard and the lyrical elements so de-emphasized that any close relationship to a song form is difficult to discern.

The material of many untitled songs does, however, betray its origins in texted music: for example the horn calls and homophonic textures of the hunting songs; the continuous triplet rhythms in fast 6/8 songs suggestive of the romantic ballade. The primary accompaniment figure of vol. VI no. 4, nicknamed "Spinning Song," alludes quite clearly to Schubert's "Gretchen am Spinnrade". Many of the songs are cast in a three-part texture: an upper-voice melody, which may be doubled at the third or sixth, is supported by a harmonically conceived bass line and a middle "voice" that adds chords to the bass line or arpeggiations or more complex figurations in quicker rhythms. Another typical texture also presents the primary line in the upper voice, but it moves in homorhythms with the other parts, often in a texture that offsets a one-voice bass line against a multi-voice chordal right hand. These have been compared to Biedermeier part songs.[13]

Most of the songs are in either a ternary or a modified rondo form lacking distinct thematic contrasts. There are no strophic pieces, even in the music suggestive of folk songs. Several pieces begin and end with identical or similar music that is clearly set off from the "song" itself and functions as introduction and postlude. The songs in this subgroup are unified by more than their structural design: their textures mix melody and block-chordal accompaniment with homorhythms in all the voices; the latter texture predominates. They also possess a "once upon a time" narrative quality.[14] The fast songs in the group, the folk song in A minor mentioned above, and vol. V no. 4, a G major Allegro con anima, are dramatic in a way comparable to the fast texted romance/ballade, although they lack typical ballade features such as compound meter and a pervasive accompanying figure.

Three of the slow pieces in this group are in the bright keys of A major (vol. I no. 4; vol. III no. 4; there is also an Allegretto in A major in vol. VII no. 5) and one in E major (vol. II no. 3), which helps establish an idyllic quality to the evocation of a past suggested by the style. (Vol. VI no. 5 in B minor is a melancholy Moderato movement suggestive of a *cavatina*.) Both

A major pieces are linked to A-tonality neighbors. Vol. I no. 4 follows a fast A major song evocative of the hunt or a fast horse-ride (which in turn follows a slow melody-and-accompaniment piece in A minor), and the beginning of the "solo part" cites the characteristic horn call material of its predecessor, as if the thrill of the experience of the former song is distilled through the filter of its memory in the latter and becomes sentimental. Vol. III no. 4 precedes an A-minor "Agitato" song in ballade style evocative of a horse-ride that is one of the longest and stormiest pieces in the entire set. In this case action follows contemplation. A less obvious but more pervasive relationship than that in the A-major pair in vol. I consists of several common elements: two-measure phrase lengths beginning with an upbeat eighth note and pitch repetitions. The latter song emphasizes them from the outset at the beginning of phrases; in the former they emerge gradually; at first they are presented at the end of phrases (m. 6), and by mm. 16/17 they also initiate them, thus anticipating their prominence in the next piece.

The shared tonalities and motivic links between these songs are not indicative of a systematic tonal plan to organize a volume. A major and E major are preferred keys throughout all the volumes. On the other hand it seems that Mendelssohn took pains to achieve something of a balance between major and minor tonalities and also slower and faster tempos, whereby the faster pieces are usually in the middle of a set. A slow movement concludes every volume save no. IV, which closes with a long, thickly scored, and brilliant A major Molto allegro vivace that "overcomes" the equally brilliant Allegro con fuoco A minor "Folk Song" (and creates a third A-tonality pair of movements).

Can we determine an evolution or progress (however problematic we may now find these concepts) in Mendelssohn's piano style during the many years of *Songs without Words*? Let us consider vol. V no. 4 in G major. It cannot be dated definitively, but three of the songs in this volume originated in the mid 1840s. The introduction presents conventional fanfares, but the "song" begins with an gesture that is more individual and intriguing than most principal themes in earlier volumes and which, in my view, owes a debt to Schumann, especially in its rhythmic dynamism (Example 9.1). This idea permeates the entire pieces and exemplifies new qualities that emerge more conspicuously in later volumes: more rhythmic and textural complexity, a more nuanced harmonic language that shares Schumann's penchant for sequences of non-dominant seventh chords, dissonances arising through contrapuntal activity, sometimes over pedal tones, greater interest in gesturally strong motives and motivic development, and, finally, an increased level of virtuosity that avoids surface brilliance (fast scales and arpeggios) more systematically than ever before in Mendelssohn's piano music. All of these contribute to a new tone of expressive subjectivity; despite critical

Example 9.1 Song without Words op. 62 no. 4, mm. 5–9

commentary in the early 1840s by Schumann and others on self-repetition in this repertory, a new voice is heard in the late *Songs without Words*. Hence it was fortunate for posterity that two volumes were arranged from works in the *Nachlass*, and were published soon after his death. With these pieces and with the *Six Pieces for the Piano-forte* (pub. 1847), miniatures as they are, Mendelssohn began to find his way into the pianistic world created by Chopin, Schumann, and the mature Liszt, which Brahms would soon also enter. His untimely death robbed him of the opportunity to consolidate his progress and, perhaps, extend it to pianistic "bigger things" to which he aspired.

Wearing Bach's "wig": preludes and fugues and the organ sonatas

In 1837 Mendelssohn published Six Preludes and Fugues op. 35 for piano and also Three Preludes and Fugues op. 37 for organ. These ambitious works, some of which originated in the late 1820s, are the most prominent keyboard manifestations of his continuing interest in historical styles and strict counterpoint. Some years earlier Mendelssohn had composed two fugues for piano that he made into the third and fifth of the *Characteristic Pieces* op. 7. The decision to compose and publish complete sets of preludes and fugues suggests a more ambitious self-conscious compositional agenda. What were his motivations?

Letters to Devrient and Hiller in the winter of 1837 reveal that the "strict discipline of the fugues, after all the *Songs without Words*, will do him good,"[15] although he fears that "they will not be much played."[16] The letter to Hiller also announces the forthcoming publication of the organ pieces and comments "me voilà perruqué" (behold me in my wig), making use of a slightly mocking metaphor in use at the time (Schumann called galant-style keyboard sonatas "Perückensonaten") that denoted "outdated" historical styles.[17] With it Mendelssohn expresses a distancing self-awareness but also, perhaps, a certain pride: behold – these are my musical values, like them or not.

Without knowing the music to which it refers, a reader of this letter might expect not only a commitment to a historic genre but also an essay in strict historic style. This is not the case; as in the earlier fugues and the string sinfonias, and, in the 1840s, the *Variations sérieuses* and the oratorios, Mendelssohn strove to achieve a synthesis of old and new musical idioms.[18] As Schumann observed in his review of op. 35: "the fugues have much of Sebastian and could fool the sharpest critic, were it not for the song, the fine melting quality [*der feine Schmelz*], in which one perceives the modern time, and here and there those small touches peculiar to Mendelssohn."[19]

With good reason, Mendelssohn and Schumann refer only to the fugues, for there is very little "Sebastian" in the preludes.[20] Only no. 2 displays Baroque idioms: it evokes a trio-sonata with a walking bass line in eighth notes doubled at the octave (implying a pedal part) above which move a middle voice in continuous sixteenths and a slower moving cantilena in the upper voice. The music is more suggestive of Handel than of Bach. Except for no. 3, a very fast compound-meter movement in close to perpetual motion in triplets (here in both hands), the other preludes are lyrically conceived; they come close to *Songs without Words*, the very pieces he wanted to put aside.

Pace Schumann, the fugues of op. 35 owe much more to the nineteenth century than to Bach. The debt lies principally in the choice of genre; the only striking direct stylistic consists in Mendelssohn's skillful assimilation of the way Bach designed fugal subjects, and this distinguishes his fugues from many of his contemporaries – to his advantage. But only a handful of the piano fugues in op. 7 and op. 35 contain anything approaching the thematic concentration typical of Bach's fugues that consists in frequent subject entries, operations on the subject (augmentation, diminution, inversion), stretto, strict part writing retaining the number of voices introduced in the exposition, and episodes that largely maintain the contrapuntal density of the fugal exposition and fugal entries and present material closely derived from the principal subject and countersubject. The last two differences are the most crucial; in de-emphasizing contrapuntal textures, especially in the episodes, Mendelssohn decisively shifts the emphasis from Bach's priorities to his own. All the fugues contain octave doublings and other homophonically conceived expansions of sonorities that pay little heed to principles of *strenger Satz*, and the episodes, while they do not shun the subject (how could they?), develop it in a Classical-Romantic rather than a Baroque manner. Often the counterpoint virtually disappears in favor of melody-accompaniment textures. The juxtapositions of fairly strict contrapuntal textures for a subject entrance and these episodes impart a kind of sectionality that also departs from Baroque (or at least Bach's) fugal principles. The most pronounced instance of this occurs in Fugue no. 5, mm. 115–39, in

Example 9.2 Op. 35, fugue no. 5, mm. 115–139

which the passage preparing the structural return to a tonic statement of the subject resembles the retransition of the development section of a sonata (Example 9.2). These elements, along with the graduated intensifications of tempo and accelerated rhythms (the latter often deriving from the introduction and continuing presence suggestive of a new countersubject) create intensifications that produce a monumental character of a very contemporary nature.

Character is the operative concept for the piano fugues; Mendelssohn's first published fugues appear among the *Characteristic Pieces* of op. 7 and they, too, are not strict. It seems to have been enough that these pieces evoked the spirit of fugue, possessed its character. And it seems also that for Mendelssohn the most crucial aspect of fugue character was monumentality (regardless of the nature of the subject), for a fugue was a great and hoary thing, not a song-without-words trifle for the ladies of the salon. The irony is, as we have seen, that he achieved this character with modern means. The most radical departure from strict fugal form in op. 35 occurs in Fugue no. 1, in which the grand penultimate section introduces a chorale composed by Mendelssohn himself in E minor, the key of the prelude and fugue. The melody appears in the upper voice as a cantus firmus that is supported by tri-adic harmonies in the right hand and a walking bass in, as usual, octaves. The chorale, thoroughly Romantic in tone, gives way to a slow and quiet close in E major that reintroduces the fugue subject but places it in a non-contrapuntal context and seems to reflect on the chorale while shifting the ethos from the chorale's public pageantry to private religious contemplation – *Andacht*. Surely it is the problematic but strangely appealing nature of this piece that motivated Charles Rosen to view it as the "invention of religious kitsch" (he uses the attribute with sympathy toward Mendelssohn's religious aesthetics) and a "masterpiece" virtually in the same breath.[21]

The organ music of op. 37 might cause us to wonder whether Schumann simply got his opus numbers wrong. Both the preludes and the fugues, but especially the fugues, are far more retrospective than those of op. 35. There are two main differences. The subject is much more predominant – there are more frequent subject entries (although, as in op. 35, there are few operations on the subject, e.g., inversion etc.), and the episodes concentrate more on material derived from the subject. The texture is much more strictly contrapuntal in both the subject entries and the episodes. Moreover, both of these elements produce formal designs that do not have the sectionality of the op. 35 fugues and thus are closer to Baroque models. Their most Bachian element is the much higher concentration of chromaticism than is found in the fugues of op. 35, which largely avoid nineteenth-century harmonic practices. The subject of Fugue no. 2 in G major is itself already highly inflected, but even in the other fugues the chromaticism is well integrated into the course of events. Neither the fugues nor the preludes are particularly virtuosic, and the pedal parts are less demanding than those for the hands. (Even into the late 1830s Mendelssohn found it necessary to improve his organ technique and he remarked several times on his difficulties with the pedals.) The only true challenges for the feet are found in Fugue no. 1, a *Con moto* Gigue, in which the pedal part contains several extended passages in triplets.

On the whole Mendelssohn viewed the tasks of composing preludes and fugues for the piano and the organ very differently. The modern elements of the op. 35 fugues may be understood as compromises on the behalf of the player of the modern piano, which compromises were not necessary for the organist, whose knowledge of and respect for tradition he assumed. If this hypothesis convinces, the next large set of organ pieces surprises all the more.

After completing op. 37, seven years passed before Mendelssohn began another large project for the organ.[22] At the request of the English publisher Coventry, who had printed his edition of Bach *Chorale Preludes* in 1844, Mendelssohn composed twenty-four independent one-movement organ pieces (July 1844 – Janaury 1845), which he assembled into six "Sonatas" op. 65. They constitute one of the most extreme cases of stylistic synthesis in all his music, so much so that one sympathetic modern writer has acknowledged their "stylistic disunity."[23] Baroque-style movements, notably fugues and German chorale settings, alternate with movements in contemporary idioms. Sonata no. 3, for example, consists of only two movements: a double fugue that enfolds a chorale cantus firmus on "Aus tiefer Not," followed by an Andante that is nothing less than a Mazurka in disguise!

Coventry had asked for "Voluntaries," the most popular contemporary organ genre in England. Mendelssohn called them "Sonatas," most likely in view of their planned publication in Germany, but the title does not denote works along the lines of multi-movement piano sonatas. Sonata no. 4 comes closest by virtue of the movement tempos and their order: Allegro con brio, Andante religioso, Allegretto (6/8), and Allegro maestoso e vivace, but the first movement is not a sonata form and the third is not suggestive of a Scherzo. The idea of a Baroque church sonata – a genre undoubtedly known to Mendelssohn – seems to hover behind the sonatas, in part because they include so many chorale settings and fugues. Indeed chorales are the basis for cyclical design in several sonatas, in which all the movements contain material derived from a chorale that is presented in its entirety in the first movement. Sonata no. 1 begins with a church-style setting of "Was mein Gott will" with an introduction, interludes and conclusion, in which the contemporary chromatic harmonies contrast with the chorale phrases. The weighty first movement of Sonata no. 6 contains variations on the chorale "Vater unser in Himmelreich," which are as substantial as the *Variations sérieuses*. The chorale settings, the meditative character of several slow movements, and the direct paraphrase of mvt. 25 from Bach's *St. Matthew Passion* in Sonata no. 1 mvt. 1 all reinforce the religious (but not liturgical) character of the opus and also emphasize its Germanness.

Mendelssohn must have recognized the eclectic nature of the collection; indeed, he meant it to represent his "own peculiar style of performance on the organ," as an announcement of the work by Coventry explained. English critics understood them in this way, pointing out new elements and comparing them to Mendelssohn's improvisations, which had been overwhelmingly positively received in his second home country.[24] Mendelssohn never performed them publicly, and his failure to do so may be suggestive of some ambivalence on his part about them.

Variations sérieuses: a Bachian homage to Beethoven

In March 1841 Mendelssohn was asked by the Viennese publisher Pietro Mechetti to contribute to an "Album-Beethoven," which was conceived to raise money toward the erection of a monument to the composer in Bonn. Mendelssohn first declined, but was soon persuaded by the musical journalist Karl Kunt, whom he asked for details about the contributors (Chopin, Liszt, and other prominent pianists) and their pieces and queried if he could give Mechetti a "short song" rather than a "long instrumental piece such as a fantasy."[25] We do not have Kunt's reply, but by July 1841 Mendelssohn was busy working on a set of variations for the album that he called "Variations sérieuses." Christa Jost notes that the variations are the only contribution in a strict Classical form in sharp distinction to the impromptus, nocturnes, and other Romantic genres that dominate the collection, which appeared in winter 1842. Early reviews in the *Allgemeine musikalische Zeitung* (vol. 44, 1842, col. 447) and *Neue Zeitschrift für Musik* (vol. 16, 1842, p. 57) note that the variations are the most substantial piece in the album, and the choice of genre, along with the gravity of the work, must certainly have influenced its reception.[26]

Why did Mendelssohn, who wrote a handful of piano variations in the 1820s, but had then left the genre untouched, choose them now? They would be an appropriate tribute to Beethoven, a master of the piano variations. The alternative would have been a piano sonata, but that would have been too long for the album. So it was variations, but only *serious* ones on a severe Andante sostenuto theme in a chromatically rich and dissonant D minor. A letter to Rebecka (31 July 1841) reveals that he had already devised the title; Mendelssohn wanted to make it clear that he did not plan to compose variations *à la mode*; he would countenance neither superficial virtuosity nor Biedermeier *Gemütlichkeit* at the expense of thematic invention and development in the tradition of Beethoven and Bach.[27]

After a Beethovenian compositional effort that included (1) the addition of new variations to an original smaller group, (2) the deletion of some of the original variations, (3) re-orderings of the original sequence, and (4) re-workings of numerous individual variations, Mendelssohn completed a cycle consisting of seventeen variations and an extensive coda. As Jost has shown,[28] some of these revisions are very significant. Several direct allusions to Beethoven's music were eliminated when the original variations 10–14 were discarded, and the first new variation (no. 14 in the final version) became the only one in tonic major. "Maggiore" and "Minore" variations were often used as formal articulations that also provided the opportunity for strong expressive contrast. Variation 14 is an Adagio (Example 9.3a) that refers quite clearly back to the theme itself (Example 9.3b).

Example 9.3 *Variations sérieuses* op. 54

(a) Var. 14

(b) Theme

Example 9.4 *Variations sérieuses* op. 54
(a) Var. 16, mm. 1–5

(b) Var. 17, mm. 1–5

It concludes with a *ritardando* leading to a fermata over the cadential chord, which together create a strong sense of closure, thus emphasizing the modal change. The thematic recollection, modal change, and cadence mark the formal function of this variation, which directly precedes the final three variations and coda. This music constitutes the last of several groups of variations that are linked together by elisions (e.g., variations 1–4), and by common motivic material and textures (e.g., the perpetual-motion variations 8 and 9 that share triplet sixteenth notes). Each of the last three variations flows into the next: the *poco a poco più agitato* of no. 15 leads to the more motivically intense *Allegro vivace* variations of nos. 16 and 17 that are related to each other by inversion (Example 9.4). Variation 17 spills over into the coda, which boils along until a *ritenuto* allusion to the theme over a pedal dominant harks back to Classical variation technique and suspends time in a way similar to no. 14 before the final Presto rushes to a brilliant but grave conclusion. The addition of a "Maggiore" variation was a crucial and happy stroke.

Mendelssohn did *not* adopt a strategy favored by Beethoven in variations on slow themes: fast codas close with paraphrases of the theme in the Finales of opp. 109 and 111, so that the sonatas end quietly and contemplatively. Mendelssohn decided on a bravura ending, whose virtuosic style is legitimized by the presence of many brilliant numbered variations. These are counterposed against variations that retain much of the character of the theme, thus creating an intensifying contrast to the theme and to

Example 9.5 Beethoven, Thirty-two Variations in C minor WoO 80. Theme

"closely thematic" variations. Nevertheless, none of the brilliant variations parades technical virtuosity as an end in itself; like the coda they all remain serious.

The theme could be considered less than ideal for variations, because it is very highly defined by its voice-leading and harmonic details. (Many of Beethoven's original variation themes, e.g., op. 111 mvt. 2, are rudimentary *tabulae rasae* awaiting exploration and articulation.) But if Mendelssohn created a problem for himself with the theme, he solved it easily, by further developing thematic details, in particular the chromaticisms and the contrapuntal devices, and by introducing the virtuosic elements discussed above. Apart from extending several variations, Mendelssohn took no other liberties, eschewing such Beethovenian techniques as the introduction of non-tonic keys or fragments and transitional passages.

The theme and the variations have been the subject of speculations regarding influences and models. Charles Rosen suggests that Beethoven's C minor Variations (WoO 80) might have been the model;[29] other authors see ties to a Handel keyboard suite,[30] and to Beethoven's *Serious Quartet* in F minor op. 95 and the "Diabelli" Variations op. 120.[31] Todd embraces Rosen's idea and seeks to ground it analytically: Mendelssohn appropriated the chromatic descent of the bass line in the WoO 80 theme (Example 9.5), but used it only for melodic-contrapuntal details in the foreground. Todd also argues that the composition and rejection of a variation (the original no. 13 in the group discussed above) that makes more extensive use of the bass descent betrays Mendelssohn's debt to WoO 80, implying that Mendelssohn did not wish to acknowledge this debt or to honor Beethoven with direct allusions to his music. (Mendelssohn also removed the original variation 11, which paraphrases the final song of "An die ferne Geliebte," an act of discretion in striking contrast to Schumann's endearingly gushing reference to the same song in his piano *Fantasie* op. 17, that was first conceived as a work for Beethoven.) Mendelssohn must have known the C minor Variations; nevertheless we can ask whether the motivic links discovered by Todd are so very specific that Mendelssohn could have "found" them only in Beethoven's variations.

Example 9.6 *Variations sérieuses* op. 54, Var. 10, mm. 1–6

A descending minor-mode chromatic bass line was a Baroque cliché, and one that Mendelssohn had encountered in innumerable works.[32]

I propose a relationship to the cantata *Christ lag in Todesbanden* BWV 4, of which Mendelssohn apparently owned a manuscript copy that is found in his *Nachlaß*. Stylistic elements of Bach's chorale harmonizations for organ are recognizable in the four-part texture and the active inner voices. Moreover, if the rhythms of the upper voice are made regular – beginning with the conversion of the first G♯ to a full quarter note and so on – the theme's proximity to a chorale melody becomes clear. (Let us note that Bach's own chorale cantus firmus lines "regularize" the much less uniform rhythms of the chorales in their original sixteenth- and seventeenth-century forms; and the theme of Mendelssohn's op. 82 Variations also evokes chorale textures and the uppermost voice closely resembles a Baroque chorale cantus firmus.) The relationship between the works is most audible in the fugal beginning of variation 10 (Example 9.6: op. 54, variation 10, mm. 1–6), in which the melodic contour (the lower chromatic neighbor notes [incomplete lower neighbors in Mendelssohn], and the outlining of the tonic–subdominant fourth) and rhythms (quarter notes giving way to eighths) of the subject and the imitations are reminiscent of the beginning of Versus 4 of the cantata. Moreover, in both works lower chromatic neighbor-note motions beginning on the first and fifth degrees saturate the texture of every movement (Jost [p. 60] calls the A–G♯ D–C♯ in the upper voice of the beginning of Mendelssohn's theme a "germ cell"), and their *affect* helps determine the character of both works. Another link resides in the formal structure of the works: *Christ lag in Todesbanden* is a strict chorale cantata: each movement is a variation on the chorale theme. Even Mendelssohn's D minor tonality harks back to the chorale: not to the E minor of Bach's cantata, but rather to the original Dorian modality of the sixteenth-century *Kirchenlied*.[33]

These relationships are as audible and meaningful as any hitherto proposed. If my model is accepted, we can imagine Mendelssohn memorializing Beethoven via Bach *qua* liturgical composer, thus embedding the Catholic Rhineland-Viennese Beethoven in a cultural tradition to which he did not directly belong, but whose spirit both Beethoven and Mendelssohn had absorbed. Mendelssohn said nothing about models or allusions; we simply do not know what exactly he intended. One plausible tie does not exclude another; indeed herein lies the richness of the *Variations sérieuses*, in its wealth of possibilities, its integration of historic and contemporary styles, and, above all, the mastery of thematic invention and variation technique underlying the whole.

Performance

In considering Mendelssohn as a performer on the piano, it may be useful to distinguish between public and private repertories. According to Ferdinand Hiller, his private repertory was broad, centering on Bach, Mozart, Beethoven and, of course, his own music. Hiller also has him playing Chopin, but without enthusiasm;[34] Hiller does not mention Liszt, but we know that Mendelssohn actively disliked Liszt's music and, after some initial enthusiasm, became very wary of the man, especially after Liszt's behavior during his first concert visit to Leipzig in 1840 caused great tensions in the city's musical circles. He always admired certain aspects of Liszt's playing, although he did not like Liszt's free way with music by Beethoven and other historical composers.[35] Apparently Mendelssohn knew very little of Schubert's piano music.[36] Significantly perhaps, there is no document preserving Mendelssohn's opinion about Schumann's piano music; despite the Schumannesque character of some of his late piano music, he had reservations about much of Schumann's music and there is little evidence that he played any on the piano. The public repertory was apparently narrower than the private one, centering on selected works by Bach, several Mozart concertos, Beethoven's Fourth and Fifth Concertos (the Fourth Concerto was his "war horse"), and, on occasion, a late Beethoven piano sonata, in addition to his own music.[37]

Mendelssohn achieved enormous success as a public performer and improviser on both the piano and the organ; on the organ he was the preeminent player of his time (there was more competition on the piano!), enjoying even more success and giving more frequent public recitals in England than in Germany.[38] He was not the first nineteenth-century organist to play works by Bach in public performances, but was the first to give a recital entirely devoted to Bach's organ music (save for an opening improvisation before the "St. Anne" Fugue) in a benefit concert for the erection of a Bach monument in Leipzig, a project that he helped initiate.[39] These concerts were as much didactic as aesthetic experiences; Mendelssohn taught his listeners. Some of the private performances, in salons and for musicians, also can be understood as pedagogical exercises, for example the well-known story that he convinced Goethe to reconsider his view of Beethoven's music by playing the Fifth Symphony at the keyboard for him during a visit to Weimar in 1830, the astonishing fact that he introduced Beethoven's piano music to musical circles in Munich,[40] or private performances of Handel's organ music in London in 1833.

Early in his career he was applauded at a piano recital in the dour Baltic seaport city of Stettin, an unprecedented act of homage according to a local newspaper report. Testimonials to his playing often emphasized his artistry in distinction to his technical prowess, which was simply assumed and considered to be subsumed into his art. Later in the century Clara Schumann recalled that

> It never occurred to me to compare him with virtuosi. Of mere effects of performance he knew nothing – he was always the great musician, and in hearing him one forgot the player, and only reveled in the full enjoyment of the music.[41]

But she also confided to her diary immediately after hearing him play in December 1836:

> Arrival in Leipzig. I dressed immediately and went to the Gewandhaus concert to hear Mendelssohn play the E Flat major Concerto by Beethoven. He could not do any better with it than all the other pianists who have played the piece. He played well, just rushed too much a few times.[42]

Generally sympathetic accounts must be weighed against a disquieting negative one, Franz Brendel's review of Mendelssohn's performance of Beethoven's Piano Sonata in C minor op. 111 in the *NZfM* in 1846 (vol. 24 no. 8 [25 January 1846], pp. 31–32). He found wanting Mendelssohn's lightness of touch in the first movement, because the resulting "milder lighter character" sacrificed its "monumental character," and "painful inner strife." The criticism would be innocent enough, without the historical context in which it appeared. Even before his death, even before the "official" appearance of a New-German School that vehemently opposed Mendelssohn's continuing influence as a pedagogue and composer, an ugly specter hovers: despite his conversion, this "Jewish" musician could not grasp the sublimity of German music at its most lofty heights. But this was a minority opinion. Perhaps Mendelssohn did not consciously seek to "reform" piano music as a composer and performer, as has been suggested, yet his supreme gifts and high standards in both areas invigorated the culture of the piano decades after his untimely death.

10 On Mendelssohn's sacred music, real and imaginary

R. LARRY TODD

Though scholarship is generally agreed about the prominent position in Felix Mendelssohn Bartholdy's oeuvre of sacred music, how to assess its role for his identity as a composer has generated contrasting lines of inquiry. We shall begin by briefly considering the dynamic of religion in the composer's family, and then propose some ways in which the dynamic played out in his sacred choral and chorale-related works.

As the grandson of the leading Jewish philosopher of the *Aufklärung*, Moses Mendelssohn, Felix was of course mindful of his Judaic roots, which encouraged some scholars to search for Jewish influences in his music. As early as 1867, Camille Selden assumed that Felix had frequented a synagogue and was well versed in Hebrew;[1] two years later, Hippolyte Barbedette was able to hear in the composer's music echoes of Jewish psalmody.[2] In 1880, Sir George Grove, whose pioneering encyclopedia article set the foundation for modern Mendelssohn research, assessed his setting of Psalm 114 op. 51 ("When Israel out of Egypt came," 1839) thus: "The Jewish blood of Mendelssohn must surely for once have beat fiercely over this picture of the great triumph of his forefathers, and it is only the plain truth to say that in directness and force his music is a perfect match for the splendid words of the unknown Psalmist."[3] More focused attempts to trace Jewish elements in Mendelssohn's music ensued in the second half of the twentieth century. Jack Werner proposed in 1956 that a cadential figure comprising a descending minor triad, encountered in a variety of works ranging from the oratorio *Elijah* to *Lieder ohne Worte* and the *Variations sérieuses*, alluded to a blessing sung during Passover and other Festivals; Werner even speculated that Felix had visited a synagogue "in search of 'local colour.'"[4] And in 1963, Eric Werner associated the head motive of the chorus "Behold, God the Lord passed by!" (*Elijah*, no. 34; I Kings 19: 11, 12) with a melody "to which the 13 Divine Attributes (Exodus 24: 6, 7) have been sung since the fifteenth century in all German synagogues on the High Holy Days." The source, Werner assumed, "must have impressed itself upon the boy and associated itself with the representation of the Divine. Thus, through the mysterious workings of creative fantasy, this association may have been conjured from the subconscious."[5]

But the search for a Jewish character in Mendelssohn's music is not at all unproblematic. First of all, as Jeffrey Sposato has argued,[6] there is no evidence Felix ever attended a synagogue during his youth; rather, the composer's father, Abraham, intended early on to raise his children as Christians. Felix's name does not appear in a Jewish register of births for Hamburg, where he was born on 3 February 1809;[7] and Carl Friedrich Zelter later even claimed to Goethe that Felix was uncircumcised.[8] On 21 March 1816, Felix and his siblings were baptized as Protestants in Berlin, and received the additional surname Bartholdy – the seven-year-old Felix Mendelssohn became Felix Jacob Ludwig Mendelssohn Bartholdy – evidently on the advice of Jacob Bartholdy (a maternal uncle of Felix who had converted eleven years before) that the family "adopt the name of Mendelssohn Bartholdy as a distinction from the other Mendelssohns."[9] (Whether the composer's parents noted the significance of the day – J. S. Bach's birthday – is not known.) Six years later, in October 1822, Felix's parents were baptized in a clandestine ceremony in Frankfurt, and from this time date the earliest surviving family letters with signatures that incorporate the name Bartholdy. When, two months later, Felix appeared in a concert of the soprano Anna Milder-Hauptmann, an anonymous critic asserted that the "boy was born and raised in our Lutheran religion,"[10] a bit of misinformation presumably disseminated by his parents. Still, though Abraham preferred that in time the family surnames would contract to M. Bartholdy and eventually Bartholdy, the composer signed his name and published his music throughout his career as Felix Mendelssohn Bartholdy, as if, in Rudolf Elvers' phrase, to join the two names in a single breath.[11]

A tension between Felix's Jewish ancestry and his Protestant upbringing might help elucidate the breadth of his sacred music, which of course draws on scriptures from the Old Testament, such as the cantata-like psalm settings and oratorio *Elijah*, and the New, including the oratorios *St. Paul* and the unfinished *Christus*, which also feature such staples of Protestant worship as the chorales *Wachet auf* and *Wie schön leuchtet der Morgenstern*. But Felix's familial life and sense of spiritual identity were in fact more complex than might be explained by Jewish–Protestant ambivalence. Indeed, the Mendelssohns were no strangers to questions of religious tolerance, outside as well as inside the family. Though Moses Mendelssohn, who had argued in *Jerusalem* (1783) that Judaism, as a rational religion based upon universal truths, was not incompatible with the interests of the modern Prussian state, continued to practice his faith, four of his six surviving children did not. Two, including Abraham, became Protestants, and two, Catholics. The eldest, Brendel, managed to experience all three faiths: she married the Jewish banker Simon Veit, had an affair with the young literary critic Friedrich Schlegel, divorced Veit in 1799, converted to Protestantism, assumed the name Dorothea, married Schlegel in 1804, and embraced Catholicism with him in 1808. One generation of the Mendelssohn family thus tested the boundaries of the three principal European faiths.

As Felix Gilbert suggested perceptively in 1975, the fault lines in the family emerged not so much between the Jewish and Protestant branches – Felix Mendelssohn Bartholdy maintained lifelong cordial relations with his uncle Joseph Mendelssohn, and in the 1840s assisted in advocating a new collected edition of Moses Mendelssohn's works[12] – as between those members holding liberal versus conservative religious views.[13] Thus, Felix's grandmother, Bella Salomon, an Orthodox Jew, responded to the apostasy of her son Jacob (Salomon) Bartholdy by cursing and disinheriting him when he accepted baptism into the Protestant faith in 1805. Similarly, when the young painter Wilhelm Hensel, son of a Protestant minister and a suitor for Fanny Mendelssohn Bartholdy's hand, seriously considered becoming a Catholic in 1823, Fanny's mother Lea intervened, for in her view "Catholicism always led to fanaticism and hypocrisy."[14] And when, in 1827, Felix composed the motet *Tu es Petrus* on a fundamental Catholic text (Matthew 16: 18, "Thou art Peter, and upon this rock I will build my church"), Felix's circle wondered, perhaps in jest or perhaps half seriously, whether Felix "might have turned Roman Catholic."[15]

The dynamic of contrasting religious faiths thus played itself out in the Mendelssohn family – not at all surprising, when one considers that in the eighteenth century Moses Mendelssohn himself had argued eloquently for religious tolerance. According to Joseph Mendelssohn, Moses held that "different religious views must not be suppressed among mankind, and that the world would succumb to dreadful barbarism if it were possible to make one religion the only religion."[16] Now when we survey the corpus of Felix's mature sacred music, we find, not surprisingly, a heavy weighting toward German Lutheran music, but also a representation of other faiths. There are, for example, several by no means insignificant Catholic settings – in addition to *Tu es Petrus*, the polychoral motet *Hora est* for sixteen voices and organ (1828), Psalm 115 op. 31 (originally set after the Vulgate version, *Non nobis Domine*), *Responsorium et Hymnus* op. 121 (1833), Three Motets op. 39 composed for the cloistered nuns of Trinità del monte in Rome in 1830, and the unjustly neglected late setting of St. Thomas Aquinas' sequence *Lauda Sion* op. 73 (1846), to cite a few. For Anglican tastes, Mendelssohn composed that favorite of Victorian parlor rooms, the anthem *Hear My Prayer*, on William Bartholomew's paraphrase of Psalm 55, and also several pieces for use in Anglican services. Of these, the most prominent are his final sacred works, the sublime Evensong canticles, Magnificat and Nunc dimittis, and, for the Morning Service, the Jubilate Deo – all three were conceived with English texts and scored for chorus and organ, though published in Germany posthumously (1848) in *a cappella* versions as the *Drei Motetten* op. 69. Of considerably lesser significance is the chorale-like *cantique* of 1846, "Venez chanter," though its purpose – a contribution to the hymnal of the Frankfurt Huguenot Church[17] – underscores the composer's first-hand experience with that faith: in 1837, he had married Cécile Jeanrenaud, daughter of a Huguenot minister, an event attended by the Catholic Dorothea Schlegel.

Evidently only once during his career did Mendelssohn contemplate composing music for a Jewish service, the consecration of the new building of the Hamburg Neues Tempel in 1844. Eric Werner believed that the result was no less than a commissioned setting of Psalm 100 scored for chorus and orchestra (now lost), and eventually published for chorus alone.[18] But the full details of this project are obscured by the passage of time, and the surviving primary sources produce as many questions as answers.[19] Because this work has been neglected in the literature since Werner's research, a brief digression is in order here.

I

The year 1843 marked the twenty-fifth anniversary of the founding of the Temple in Hamburg, when preparations were made to construct a new building, to be consecrated at Pentecost (Shavuot) in 1844. On 14 November 1843, Dr. Maimon Fränkel, *Praeses* of the Temple, invited Felix to compose some Psalm settings for the ceremony. "Your sublime talent," Fränkel wrote, "is too much the common property of the entire Fatherland, and the Mendelssohn name still always too dear to every German Israelite to prevent us from yielding to the pleasant prospect of your undertaking to compose some of these pieces . . ."[20] Though Felix's reply does not survive, it was encouraging enough to prompt Fränkel to forward on 8 January 1844 a copy of the *Gesangbuch* of the Tempelverein, and to propose that Felix set three Psalms deemed appropriate for the consecration, Nos. 24, 84, and 100. Fränkel recommended that Felix arrange the first two as a cantata, and employ the translation of Moses Mendelssohn (1782). Fränkel restricted the instrumental accompaniment to an organ, but noted that the choir could be expanded from its normal complement of sixteen boys to forty, to include "ladies and gentlemen of Jewish and Christian faiths."[21] At this point, Felix evidently began to envision a more ambitious composition, and on 12 January posed the possibility of an expanded setting with orchestral accompaniment; in addition, Felix inquired if the Lutheran version of the Psalms would be acceptable.[22] On 21 January, Fränkel agreed to the stipulation of an orchestra, and added, "we also have nothing against the use of the Lutheran Psalm translations, as long as the severities and errors [*Härten und*

Unrichtigkeiten] of the same are avoided." By 1 February, Felix was apparently willing to commit himself to Psalm 24; near the end of March, Fränkel was still hopeful Felix would also complete Psalms 84 and 100. But on 8 April, Felix wrote he would be unable to take on the additional psalms;[23] on 12 April, Fränkel regretted this decision, but reaffirmed his intention to provide a worthy performance of the new setting of Psalm 24, which he expected to receive no later than mid-May. Here, regrettably, the surviving correspondence ends.

To date, no score of Psalm 24 has come to light, so it is not yet possible to verify whether Mendelssohn ever completed the composition. Compounding the mystery is the survival of one other source – an *a cappella* setting of Psalm 100 finished by Mendelssohn on 1 January 1844, and published posthumously in 1855 in the eighth volume of *Musica sacra*, a compendium of sacred music for the Berlin Cathedral. The autograph, unavailable to Eric Werner but preserved today in Kraków, Poland, shows no link to the Neues Tempel; there is, for example, no evidence that Mendelssohn revised or modified the text, which transmits the Lutheran version (*Jauchzet dem Herrn, alle Welt!*). Then, too, Fränkel's letters establish that Felix declined the invitation to set Psalm 100 for the Temple; as we know, in April 1844 Fränkel was awaiting the delivery of Psalm 24. The preponderance of evidence suggests that Mendelssohn's setting of Psalm 100 was intended for the Berlin Cathedral. Indeed, during this period the composer, newly installed by Friedrich Wilhelm IV as director of sacred music in Berlin, was engaged in composing works for the new Prussian *Agende*, or Protestant liturgy, introduced at the Cathedral on December 10.[24] Among them were the three *a cappella* Motets op. 78 (Psalms 2, 43, and 22), and the larger setting of Psalm 98 op. 91, for double chorus and orchestra. Almost certainly, Psalm 100 belonged to this repertory, and was not a commission of the Hamburg Temple. But whether Mendelssohn finished that project, and, if he did, whether he employed the Lutheran text for Psalm 24 or drew upon his grandfather's translation – whether the commission afforded him an opportunity to reexamine his roots late in his short life – are tantalizing questions that remain unanswered.

II

Despite a willingness to compose sacred music for different faiths, in his personal convictions Mendelssohn adhered to the Protestant creed. By the act of conversion mandated by his parents he had become a *Neuchrist*, and appears to have practiced faithfully his adopted religion. Though Heinrich Heine, who converted in 1825, cynically described baptism as an "admission ticket to European culture," and indeed questioned the motives behind Abraham's urge to assimilate his family,[25] there is little reason to doubt the sincerity of Felix's faith. He remained a devout Protestant, as attested by his confirmation in 1825,[26] by his statement in 1830 that he had become a follower (*Anhänger*) of the Berlin theologian Friedrich Schleiermacher,[27] by Hector Berlioz's recollections of his meetings with the composer in Rome in 1831,[28] and by Felix's correspondence with the pastor Julius Schubring and others, which reveals an intimate knowledge of the New Testament, and, as Martin Staehelin and Jeffrey Sposato have argued, Christological readings of the Old Testament in the oratorio *Elijah*.[29]

Felix's faith might explain a prominent feature not only of his sacred music but his oeuvre as a whole – the prominent use of chorales. Of course, as a student of Zelter the young Felix was steeped in the didactic utility of chorales, a fundamental part of J. S. Bach's own method of instruction, and of his pupils', including the theorist J. P. Kirnberger. Thus in the early 1820s, under Zelter's guidance, Felix harmonized dozens of unembellished and embellished chorales, following a course of instruction derived from Kirnberger's *Kunst des reinen Satzes*,[30] and composed several chorale fugues for string quartet. No doubt, too, Felix's abiding attraction to the music of J. S. Bach encouraged him to draw upon the repertory of familiar Protestant chorales for the foundations of several student compositions, including the organ variations on *Wie groß ist des Allmächt'gen Güte* (1823), and the extended series of chorale cantatas left unpublished by the composer, of which no fewer than nine bespeak a deep study of Bach: *Jesus, meine Zuversicht* (1824), *Christe, Du Lamm Gottes* (1827), *Jesu, meine Freude* (1828), *Wer nur den lieben Gott läßt walten* (1829), *O Haupt voll Blut und Wunden* (1830), *Vom Himmel hoch* (1831), *Verleih' uns Frieden* (1831), *Wir glauben all' an einen Gott* (1831), and *Ach Gott vom Himmel sieh' darein* (1832).[31] It is no coincidence that Felix's concentration on the chorale cantata fell during the period 1824–32, the very years leading up to and immediately following his historical "centenary" revival of J. S. Bach's *St. Matthew Passion*. Performed at the Berlin Singakademie on 11 March and 21 March (Bach's birthday) 1829, before a capacity audience that included the Prussian court and several celebrities (Hegel, Schleiermacher, Heine, Rahel von Varnhagen, Spontini, Zelter, and possibly Paganini), the Passion triggered the modern-day Bach Revival and rescued a foundation stone of musical Protestantism from oblivion.

According to Eduard Devrient, the actor/baritone who sang the part of Christ, Felix captured the significance of the performances by observing, "And to think that it has to be an actor and a young Jew who return to the people the greatest Christian music!"[32] We cannot corroborate the veracity of Devrient's account, but the statement, if uttered by Felix, would suggest an acute awareness of his own relationship to Bach's masterpiece. It is well known that Felix heavily edited the Passion, and cut no fewer than ten arias, four recitatives, and six chorales. The rationale behind these excisions has attracted scholarly attention, and indeed provoked controversy. In 1993 Michael Marissen suggested that the cuts partly reflected Felix's desire to de-emphasize anti-Semitic passages in the text.[33] But more recently, Jeffrey Sposato has argued that Felix acted "as he perceived any other Lutheran conductor would, for he must have been aware that the idea of a Mendelssohn bringing forth this greatest Christian musical work would be viewed with skepticism."[34] Thus, the deletions removed passages he deemed textually or musically redundant, as in Felix's treatment of the Passion chorale *O Haupt voll Blut und Wunden*, the melody of which recurs six times in Bach's Passion, but only three times in Felix's abridgement. Perhaps more telling, though, are two slight modifications Felix made to the chorale text. In the third phrase of *O Haupt voll Blut und Wunden* (no. 63 of the Passion) – "O Haupt sonst schön gezieret" – Felix altered the reference to Christ's "adorned" (*gezieret*) head to "crowned" (*gekrönet*), and in the fifth – "jetzt aber hoch schimpfieret" – replaced the word "insulted" (*schimpfieret*) with "mocked" (*verhöhnet*). By so doing, Felix altered Bach's version to conform textually to the Berlin version.[35] That is to say, Berliners encountering the colossal Passion in March 1829 – and we must remember that the work was publicly then unknown – found a chorale identical to the one they themselves would sing in Good Friday services only weeks later, on 17 April. In one small way, then, Felix seems to have bridged the gulf separating an abstract work of art that had lain dormant for a century and the common reality of Protestant congregational worship in Berlin, heavily dependent, of course, upon chorales.

With the 1836 Düsseldorf premiere of his first oratorio, *St. Paul*, the 27-year-old composer achieved a breakthrough, international recognition. More than any other composition, *St. Paul* – readily embraced throughout Germany and abroad (including England, Denmark, Holland, Poland, Russia, Switzerland, and the United States, where three performances were given in Boston, Baltimore, and New York between 1837 and 1839) – secured Mendelssohn's emergence at the forefront of German music. Early on, the work was viewed as a synthetic effort drawing upon the exemplars of Bach's Passions and Handel's oratorios. For G. W. Fink, *St. Paul* was "so manifestly Handelian, Bachian, and Mendelssohnian that it appears as if it really exists to facilitate our contemporaries' receptivity to the profundities of these recognized tone-heroes."[36] More recently, Friedhelm Krummacher has summarized *St. Paul* as offering a "New Testament narrative as with Bach, but neither Passion nor liturgical music; complete dramatic plot as with Handel but saturated by lyrical moments; primarily Bible text without free poetry but full of text compilations and chorale citations . . ."[37] The prominent role of chorales – Mendelssohn interspersed throughout the forty-odd numbers of *St. Paul* five staples from the sixteenth- and seventeenth-century Protestant repertory – reveals the dependence of the oratorio on the *St. Matthew Passion*, and Mendelssohn's Bachian proclivities, recalling Abraham's assertion that "every room in which Sebastian Bach is sung is transformed into a church."[38]

Though the theorist A. B. Marx argued strenuously against the use of the chorales as an anachronism ("What? Chorales in Paul's time, and in the events that make up his life?"), Felix's friend Karl Klingemann viewed them as "resting points" that, like a Greek chorus, drew the attention "from the individual occurrence to the general law," and diffused "calmness through the whole."[39] The composer carefully coordinated the chorales to reinforce the crescendo-like sense of *Steigerung* that animates the oratorio, as it traces the conversion of Saul of Tarsus to Paul, the missionary of early Christianity. Thus, the overture begins with the wordless intonation of the opening strains of the chorale *Wachet auf* (A major), subsequently redeployed in the adjoining accelerando chorale fugue that constitutes the main body of the movement. After the initial chorus, on verses from Acts 4, we hear a straightforward, homophonic presentation of the Lutheran Gloria, the chorale *Allein Gott in der Höh sei Ehr* (no. 3).[40] Then the narrator introduces the first dramatic segment of the oratorio (Nos. 4–9), culminating in the martyrdom of Stephen, and concluding with another caesura-like chorale, this time an unadorned setting of *Dir, Herr, dir will ich mich ergeben*. But after Saul's epiphany on the road to Damascus, Mendelssohn resorts to a more elaborate, embellished chorale, by reintroducing *Wachet auf* in D major (no. 16), now presented with complete text, and with a brightly lit orchestration that, anticipating Saul's conversion and restoration of sight, features intermittent brass fanfares.

The topic of embellished chorale returns in Part II in no. 29, to demarcate the first phase of the apostle's missionary work, among the Jews. At the conclusion of this chorus ("Ist das nicht der zu Jerusalem") the chorale *O Jesu Christe, wahres Licht* appears, sung in a straightforward chordal style but embellished by delicate arabesques in the clarinets, bassoons, and cellos. Here Felix increases the textural complexity by arranging the accompanying patterns in imitative counterpoint, thus enriching the underlying homophony of the chorale. The final stage in his chorale treatments is achieved in no. 36, where, after Paul's and Barnabas's proselytizing among the Gentiles, Paul introduces a verse from Psalm 115 ("Aber unser Gott ist im Himmel, er schaffet alles, was er will!"), subsequently taken up by the Gentiles. Rising from the lower register in a sequential pattern above a tonic pedal point, the movement seems calculated to recall the opening chorus of the *St. Matthew Passion*. Felix strengthens the allusion a few bars later, when the added second soprano part begins to intone in sustained pitches against the choral polyphony strains of the Lutheran Credo, the chorale *Wir glauben all' an einen Gott*, recalling Bach's addition of the chorale *O Lamm Gottes unschuldig* to the majestic polyphony of his opening chorus. Felix's chorus sings in imitative counterpoint, so that the appearance of the chorale as an additional contrapuntal strand effectively reorients the movement toward a chorale fugue. The choice of genre here is strategic – the Paulinian assertion of justification by faith completes the series of intensified chorale treatments, ranging, as we have seen, from the text-less, partial chorale of the overture to fully texted, homophonic and embellished chorales, and the culminating treatment in five-part counterpoint.[41] No. 36 also balances the chorale fugue of the overture, where the two competing elements symbolize spiritual awakening and struggle.

In the case of *Elijah* (1846), based largely on the Old Testament account in I Kings, Mendelssohn restrained considerably his reliance on chorales. Only one movement, no. 15 in Part I ("Cast thy burden upon the Lord," for solo quartet and orchestra), offers a free-standing chorale, heard before the prophet prays for fire from heaven to answer the vain implorations of the Baalites. As Felix explained, somewhat cryptically, to his English librettist, William Bartholomew, "I *wanted* to have the *colour* of a Chorale, and I felt that I could not do *without it*, and yet I did not like to have a Chorale."[42] What resulted was an adaptation of the hymn "O Gott, du frommer Gott," from the Meiningen *Gesangbuch* (1693, Examples 10.1 a–b), to which Felix fitted verses from four psalms (55, 16, 108, and 25), and which he described as "the only specimen of a Lutheran Chorale in this old-testamental work."

Though the melody would have sounded familiar to contemporary audiences, it adopted its own shape and text, and approached the status of a freely composed chorale, a middle ground that suggested the *color* of a chorale, without being *a* chorale. Felix took special care to tie his fabricated hymn to the role of Elijah. Thus, no. 15 appears in E♭ major, the key of Elijah's preceding aria (no. 14, "Lord God of Abraham"), the opening phrase of which is cited *pianissimo* by the orchestra in the final cadence of no. 15. What is more, Elijah's subsequent recitative (no. 16, "O Thou who makest thine angels spirits") begins by replicating in the minor mode the initial rising third of the chorale (Example 10.2). These musical manipulations seem to reinforce a Christological reading of Elijah as prefiguring Christ, a common nineteenth-century exegesis of the Old Testament prophet.[43] That is to say, no. 15 – to which we might add two freely composed, hymn-like passages that appear within nos. 5 ("For He, the Lord our God, He is a jealous God") and 16 ("The Lord is God: O Israel

Example 10.1
(a) *Elijah* op. 70, no. 15

(b) "O Gott, du frommer Gott," from the Meiningen *Gesangbuch* (1693)

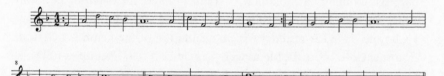

Example 10.2 *Elijah* op. 70, no. 16, beginning, bass

hear!") – interrupts the unfolding drama, as if to interpret the Old Testament story through the lens of Christianity and to relate it to Protestant worship.

There is, of course, another possibility – that Mendelssohn was in effect attempting to bridge the two faiths, and thus reconcile the tension between his Judaic ancestry and identity as a Christian musician by focusing on the extent, as Leon Botstein has proposed, "to which Christianity was a universalization of Judaism."[44] The fragment of what would have been the composer's third oratorio – titled in his posthumous catalogue of works *Christus* op. 97 (1852), though probably intended for the first part of a

Example 10.3 *Christus* [op. 97], excerpt

tripartite oratorio Felix had conceived in 1839 as *Erde, Himmel und Hölle*
(*Earth, Heaven and Hell*)[45] – provides some intriguing evidence in the chorus
"Es wird ein Stern aus Jacob aufgeh'n." Cast in E♭ major, a prominent
tonality in the first part of *Elijah*, the chorus begins with shimmering string
tremolos and a rising triadic figure to depict the star of Jacob (Example 10.3).
The text, from the fourth prophecy of Balaam in Numbers 24 ("There shall
come a star out of Jacob, and a scepter shall rise out of Israel"), is traditionally
interpreted to predict the ascendancy of King David. Now in 1834 Felix had
indirectly encountered the same image when he composed the song "Sun

Example 10.4 "Schlafloser Augen Leuchte" (Byron), beginning

of the Sleepless," to a text by Lord Byron. Nearly twenty years before, the Englishman Isaac Nathan had set Byron's poem and incorporated it into a song anthology based upon cantorial sources, *Hebrew Melodies* (1815–16). Here, Byron's verses of an "estranged lover" became a "Hebrew melody of the long, lonely vigil, waiting for 'the light of other days' to shine again."[46] Felix had borrowed a copy of *Hebrew Melodies* from Charlotte Moscheles in 1833,[47] when he may well have become aware of Nathan's reading linking the poem to Numbers 24. Felix's setting, for which he himself provided the German translation "Schlafloser Augen Leuchte,"[48] begins and ends with a gently repeated high pitch on the fifth scale degree, capturing Byron's couplet, "So gleams the past, the light of other days, which shines but warms not with its powerless rays" (Example 10.4).

In *Christus*, Felix's setting of Numbers 24 ends with a radiant chord, again exposing the fifth scale degree in the soprano register, though now supported with a complete triad, in contrast to the hollow fifths of "Sun of the Sleepless." But more telling is the final portion of the chorus, in which Felix elides the verses from Numbers with a setting of the familiar chorale *Wie schön leuchtet der Morgenstern*, and thus links the Star of David to the Star of Bethlehem (Example 10.5).

The chorale preserves the E♭ major tonic and also reveals a close motivic relationship to the head motive of the chorus; both describe forms of the

Example 10.5 *Christus* [op. 97], excerpt

tonic triad supported by C, neighbor note to the fifth degree, and are musically compatible. Mendelssohn's Christological reading of the Old Testament text seems clear enough, but the music also possibly expresses a symbolic intent to bridge the Old and New Covenants. In this case, the chorale is the agent of that inter-faith connection.

Be that as it may, to contemporary nineteenth-century audiences, the introduction of popular chorales in Felix's music – to the examples adduced we might add the insertion of *Ein' feste Burg* into the finale of the "Reformation" Symphony (1830), and of several chorales in the Organ

Example 10.6 Fugue in E minor op. 35 no. 1, mm. 116–24, melody

Sonatas Op. 65 (1845), not to mention the striking appearance of *Vom Himmel hoch* in *Athalie* (1845)[49] – would have imparted a seemingly clear meaning: like an avowal of faith, they would have symbolized to the general public Felix's musical Protestantism.

Equally significant in this regard is the persistence with which he employed chorales in a variety of genres – vocal *and* instrumental, with *and* without clear ties to liturgical function – and, furthermore, his willingness to create freely composed chorales of his own. These "imaginary," textless chorales, which Mendelssohn insinuated into several instrumental works, including the piano Prelude and Fugue in E minor op. 35 no. 1 (1827), slow movement of the Cello Sonata in D major op. 58 (1843), and finale of the Second Piano Trio op. 66 (1845), form a special group.[50] What was his motivation in these experiments? Injecting an element of spirituality into the concert hall, the pseudo-chorales entice the listener with skillfully designed melodies that have a ring of familiarity and seem to connote collective, congregational worship. Thus the culminating chorale of the Fugue op. 35 no. 1, which Charles Rosen has viewed as a masterpiece but also as the "invention of religious kitsch,"[51] approaches in one of its strains almost note for note a phrase from *Ein' feste Burg* (Example 10.6). Mendelssohn wrote this fugue in 1827 after the death of his friend August Hanstein; the highly dissonant fugue, on a subject rent by tritones, depicted the course of Hanstein's disease; the culminating chorale at the end, in the major mode and distinguished by smooth, stepwise motion, his release through death and spiritual redemption.[52] The unabashedly religious character of the piece thus bore a personal significance for Mendelssohn. We do not know if similar autobiographical elements inform the free chorales in the Second Cello Sonata and Piano Trio, but almost certainly the motivation was the same – to inject spiritual elements into the music, so that works intended for the concert hall began to encroach upon the domain of sacred music for the church.

III

The symphony-cantata "Lobgesang" op. 52 (1840), and the events attending its Leipzig premiere in the Thomaskirche, document in especially compelling fashion this tendency in Mendelssohn's oeuvre. Now generally the least esteemed of Mendelssohn's five mature symphonies – it was severely criticized by his erstwhile friend, A. B. Marx, and others for an "excessive" reliance on Beethoven's Ninth Symphony – the "Lobgesang" raises afresh the question of what Carl Dahlhaus, in discussing *St. Paul*, framed as "imaginary church music."[53] The context in which the symphony was first heard reveals the length to which Mendelssohn endeavored to break down the traditional divisions separating church and concert music. In June 1840 Leipzig commemorated the quadricentennial of Gutenberg's invention of movable type. As the center of the German book trade, Leipzig had long been associated with publishing, and the anniversary was thus an occasion to celebrate the centuries-old trade and its guilds.[54] But the festival honored more than printing: it championed the Gutenberg Bible as the lamp that had disseminated spiritual enlightenment in German realms. And, Gutenberg's technological advance was linked to Luther and the spread of the Reformation; as it happened, the second day of the festival, 25 June, coincided with the commemoration of the Augsburg Confession, one of the signal events in the Lutheran calendar.

On 24 June 1840, the Leipzig Marktplatz became the site of several ceremonies, including a church service, dedication of a new statue of Gutenberg, and speech by the publisher Raimund Härtel, who likened the inventor to the John the Baptist of the Reformation. For this occasion Mendelssohn composed a *Festgesang* for male chorus and double brass band, spatially separated so as to generate echo effects in the square. The text, by an obscure Gymnasium teacher, Adolf Prölz, summarized in some insipid verses the principal metaphors of the festival – Gutenberg as a German hero who had lit a symbolic torch, and the victory of light over darkness through the dissemination of printing. To underscore the quasi-sacred function of his music, Mendelssohn framed the work with two staples of Lutheran worship, the chorales *Sei Lob und Ehr der höchsten Gut* and *Nun danket alle Gott*, to which he fitted Prölz's verses. Today these two settings are forgotten, but one of the internal movements, a part-song that celebrated Gutenberg as a German patriot, enjoyed a curious afterlife never imagined by Mendelssohn: in 1856 the organist William H. Cummings set the words of Charles Wesley's Christmas hymn, "Hark! The herald angels sing," to the melody. By 1861, the new *contrafactum* had appeared in a hymnal, and begun its second life as a Christmas carol.

On the second day of the Gutenberg festival, 25 June 1840, Mendelssohn premiered in the Thomaskirche his "Lobgesang," a hybrid concatenation linking three symphonic movements to a cantata of nine movements. Mendelssohn himself chose the texts from the Bible, chiefly from the Psalms, and calculated to underscore in a general hymn of praise the triumph of light over darkness, of spiritual awareness over ignorance. In

Example 10.7 *Lobgesang* op. 52, mvt. 1, mm. 1–2, trombones

many ways, the textless symphony impresses as an instrumental composition aspiring toward imaginary church music, while the cantata, with
the addition of sacred texts, in turn approaches the condition of liturgical
music.

Thus the symphony begins by imitating responsorial psalmody – the
trombones announce a formulaic intonation answered by the orchestra,
establishing an alternating pattern between the two (Example 10.7, recognizable in the intonation is the psalm formula Mozart used in the
finale of his "Jupiter" Symphony, and Mendelssohn applied in a variety of
works).[55]

But the meaning of this abstract psalmody is unclear – there are of course
no words, and the introduction gives way, with a bit of a jolt, to a fully orchestral movement in sonata form, resonant with echoes of the recent symphonic
tradition of Beethoven and Schubert (in 1839 Mendelssohn had premiered
the latter's "Great" Symphony, D. 944). Now in the second movement, a
lilting scherzo in G minor, comes another allusion to an imaginary sacred
melody: in the Trio Mendelssohn introduces a freely composed chorale –
this one in G major, with phrases that sound at once familiar and unfamiliar.
But again we can only imagine the text of this voiceless chorale. The answer
comes with the introduction of texts in the cantata. First the chorus adds to
the trombone intonation the closing verse of Psalm 150 – "Let everything
that breathes praise the Lord." And a few movements later, after we have
experienced the turn from darkness to light, we encounter the chorale *Nun
danket alle Gott*, first *a cappella*, and thus divorced from the symphonic
context, and then with orchestral accompaniment. The chorale appears in
G major, reviving the key of the textless chorale in the scherzo. What is more,
Nun danket alle Gott is the chorale previously used in the *Festgesang*, and
thus a direct link between the symphony-cantata and the public ceremonies
celebrating the Gutenberg anniversary.

The "Lobgesang" marked Mendelssohn's most ambitious attempt to dissolve the barriers between concert music and functional church music. In
the last years of his life, he attempted a somewhat similar experiment, but
from the different perspective of writing music for actual liturgical use.
The venue now shifted from the Leipzig Gewandhaus and Thomaskirche
to the Protestant Cathedral of Berlin, where in 1842 Friedrich Wilhelm IV
named Mendelssohn Generalmusikdirektor in charge of sacred music. A

new male choir was trained and established at the cathedral, and the king oversaw a reform of the Prussian liturgy; among the changes was the institution of an Introit psalm and verse before the *Alleluia*, both sung by the choir, and the sharing of responses throughout the service by the choir and congregation.[56] The revised liturgy was introduced during Advent, on 10 December 1843; then, for the Christmas service, new music by Mendelssohn was performed, including a setting of Psalm 2 for chorus and organ (op. 78 no. 1),[57] and an *a cappella* verse, "Frohlocket ihr Völker" (op. 79 no. 1). But what the cathedral clergy had not anticipated was Mendelssohn's decision to replace the Gloria patri after the Psalm with the chorus "For unto us a Child is born" from Handel's *Messiah*, for which he hastily prepared an organ accompaniment.[58] And for the service on New Year's Day 1844, Mendelssohn went considerably further. His newly composed Introit psalm, Psalm 98 (op. 91), began, appropriately enough, with an *a cappella* double choir, introduced by an intonation in the bass that strikingly recalls the opening of the "Lobgesang" (Example 10.8). But for the fourth, fifth, and sixth verses – the command to make a joyful noise to the Lord with all manner of instruments – Mendelssohn introduced a harp, trombones, and trumpets, the thin end of an instrumental wedge that eventually materialized fully in the seventh verse as a full orchestra for "Let the sea roar, and all that fills it." The closing verse, "He will judge the world with righteousness and the peoples with equity," unfolded as a Handelian celebratory chorus. And the key of the conclusion, D major, facilitated the final surprise – the use of the "Hallelujah" chorus from *Messiah* in lieu of the Gloria patri. The effect of the whole was thus to begin in a pure *a cappella* style but then to introduce instrumental forces, a crescendo effect that gradually impelled a piece of liturgical music to approach the condition of concert music.

Mendelssohn composed music for two more services in 1844, Passion Sunday and Good Friday, for which he contributed the two introit psalms, nos. 43 and 22 (op. 78 nos. 2 and 3), now joined to compact settings of the lesser doxology, "Ehre sei dem Vater." Conspicuously, all of this music is *a cappella*, probably in response to controversy between Mendelssohn and the cathedral clergy about the role of instruments, with Mendelssohn seeking to increase their scope, and the clergy to limit it. But in the case of Psalm 43, Mendelssohn seized the opportunity to find a new bridge between liturgical and concert music. Noticing that Psalm 43 cites verses from Psalm 42 – notably "Why are you cast down, O my soul, and why are you disquieted within me? Hope in God, for I shall again praise him, my help and my God" – he could not avoid reusing music from his cantata-like setting of Psalm 42 op. 42, for chorus and orchestra (1838), a work composed as concert music and premiered in the Gewandhaus (Examples 10.9 and 10.10). In the end,

Example 10.8 Psalm 98 op. 91, beginning

Example 10.9 Psalm 42 op. 42

Example 10.10 Psalm 43 op. 78, no. 2

self-quotation thus became a way of uniting imaginary and functional church music.

IV

The divide between concert music and music for worship informs also Mendelssohn's Catholic settings, and the principal work conceived during the Italian sojourn of 1830–31, the "Italian" Symphony op. 90. Though Eric Werner proposed that the plaintive opening theme of its slow movement was an *in memoriam* to Zelter,[59] there can be little doubt that Mendelssohn

Example 10.11 *Responsorium et Hymnus* [op. 121]

had in mind a sacred procession of responsorial psalmody reminiscent of his experiences in Rome. Thus the Andante begins with a formulaic intonation that hovers around the fifth scale degree. Against a walking bass, the winds then present a modal melody (with lowered seventh degree), answered by the violins, which establishes the pattern of responsorial chanting. The effect is compellingly close to a passage from Mendelssohn's little-known Vespers setting for the twenty-first Sunday after Trinity, the *Responsorium et Hymnus* op. 121, composed in 1833 but left for posthumous publication in 1873 (Example 10.11). Here again we encounter an initial intonation centered on the fifth scale degree, answered in this case by a male choir in harmony.[60] If the Andante of the "Italian" Symphony transcended generic limitations by alluding to responsorial plainchant, in the case of the *Lauda Sion* op. 73, Mendelssohn composed a substantial work specifically intended for liturgical use. Indeed, when, in 1847, the English choral director John Hullah proposed a performance in London, the composer maintained "it would hardly do to use it without the Catholic Church and its ritual."[61] Commissioned for the six-hundredth anniversary of the Feast of Corpus Christi, the composition was premiered at the Church of St. Martin in Liège on 11 June 1846. Mendelssohn decided to set the complete Latin text of Thomas Aquinas' famous sequence, at the core of which is the doctrine of transubstantiation, the belief that during Communion the eucharistic elements are transformed into the body and blood of Christ. To convey something of the ineffable mystery of the doctrine, Mendelssohn resorted to two stratagems in the three central movements of his composition (nos. 4, 5, and 6). First, he allied the transformation of the consecrated Host, the "dogma" handed down to Christians ("dogma datur christianis"), with applications of solemn, ritualistic counterpoint – canons in no. 4, and a fugue in no. 6 (Example 10.12 a–b). Concerning the latter, on the text "Sub diversis speciebus, signis tantum, et non rebus, latent res eximiae" ("Beneath different types, only in signs, not in real things, do the exceptional realities

Example 10.12 *Lauda Sion* op. 73

(a) no. 4

(b) no. 6

Example 10.13

(a) Sequence, "Lauda Sion"

(b) Mendelssohn, *Lauda Sion* op. 73, no. 5

reside"), Mendelssohn originally had some ambivalence, as he explained to the Belgian musician H.-G.-M.-J.-P. Magis: "I had withdrawn this piece because the words already occur in the preceding section and I was afraid that it could be too long. After a renewed reading of the score with a clear head, I would like again to include this piece in the place where it belongs, *although* it is a bit strict and *although* it is a fugue and *although* it is too long."[62] But despite his decision to retain the movement, the first edition of the score, published posthumously by Schott in 1849, omitted it, and thus concealed its significant role in underscoring the association of high counterpoint with one of the central dogmas of the Church.[63]

Mendelssohn reserved a second stratagem for the culminating fifth movement ("Docti sacris institutis, panem, vinum in salutis consecramus hostiam").[64] Here he unveiled the opening strains of the centuries-old sequence melody as a foreboding cantus firmus, sung three times by the choir in unison, and then once in harmony, with the cantus inverted to the bass. Mendelssohn's source for the chant is not known. In any event, he employed not the original mixolydian setting, with its distinctive closing cadence by whole step, from the *subfinalis* F to *finalis* G, but rather a modified version to make the melody compatible with an aeolian setting centered on A (Example 10.13 a–b).

Furthermore, by raising the seventh degree at the cadences to a G♯, Mendelssohn adapted the modal melody to meet the "modern" tonal requirements of a movement in A minor. The "different" modal/tonal "types" of musical organization were thus allied with the text "sub diversis speciebus," and its message explored further in the subsequent fugue. Here, against the four-part counterpoint, the sequence melody appeared one final time in prolonged values in the trombones and trumpets, transforming that movement into another example of a chorale fugue, now centered not on a familiar Protestant hymn, but on a Catholic sequence.

According to Henry Fothergill Chorley, the Belgian premiere of *Lauda Sion*, attended by Mendelssohn, fell considerably short of his expectations. An under-rehearsed, "scrannel orchestra" and singers "who evidenced their nationality by resolutely holding back every movement," struggled to make their way through the score, among an impressive gathering that including archbishops and bishops, "magnificently vested in scarlet, and purple, and gold, and damask – a group never to be forgotten."[65] But in the final *alla breve* of the last movement ("Ecce panis angelorum," "Behold the bread of the angels"), as the Host was elevated, came a "surprise of a different quality." As the gilt tabernacle turned slowly above the altar, and as incense was swung from censers, "the evening sun, breaking in with a sudden brightness, gave a faery-like effect to curling fumes as they rose; while a very musical bell, that timed the movement twice in a bar, added its charm to the rite." Mendelssohn reportedly whispered to Chorley, "Listen! How pretty that is! It makes me amends for all their bad playing and singing, – and I shall hear the rest better some other time."[66] He never did; within a few weeks, he would turn his attention to final preparations for the Birmingham premiere of *Elijah*, in August 1846, and then consume much of his final year in revising the oratorio. Though *Lauda Sion* was thus consigned to posthumous publication, it did afford Mendelssohn an opportunity to explore an alternate model of sacred music, based upon the *auctoritas* of the chant and its modal incarnation, supported by the rich traditions of ritualistic counterpoint. Here the composer, grandson of Moses Mendelssohn and a *Neuchrist*, momentarily left the collective congregational space of Protestant chorales to ally himself, symbolically, with the priests, those "learned in the sacred institutions." One has the impression that in *Lauda Sion*, as in Mendelssohn's other sacred music, and indeed a fair amount of his music for the concert hall, he explored in manifold ways the elusive boundaries of real and imaginary sacred music. Perhaps this dynamic of Mendelssohn's creative muse will yet be recognized.

11 Mendelssohn's songs

SUSAN YOUENS

Mendelssohn began composing songs as a child – his setting of "Raste Krieger, Krieg ist aus" of 1820 anticipates Schubert's setting of the same text from Sir Walter Scott's *The Lady of the Lake* by five years – and continued to engage the genre throughout his life.[1] One scholar has observed that in the span of twenty-eight years from 1819 to 1847, there was scarcely a single month in which he was not occupied with song composition.[2] He published fifty-four songs with opus numbers (opp. 8, 9, 19[a], 34, 47, 57, and 71) and thirteen without opus numbers during his lifetime; after his death, thirty-one additional songs have been published, with approximately thirty-five either unpublished or available only in facsimile. But the 135 or so songs[3] have often received less than their due, in part because many are apt for performance by amateurs, because they reflect salon culture in *Vormärz* Berlin, and because their composer does not probe Romantic subjectivity after the fashion of Schubert or Schumann. Reappraisal of Mendelssohn's lieder, however, reveals greater variety and depth than some have supposed. There are songs which make few concessions to an amateur musician's limitations, such as "Andres Maienlied" (Another May Song), op. 8, no. 8, or the "Reiselied" (Journeying Song), op. 34, no. 6; there are songs which acknowledge complex poetry in complex ways; there are poetic tastes to be accounted for and an aesthetic of song composition to be defined. This repertory holds riches still to be mined.

How Mendelssohn regarded the role of words in song is a complicated issue. There can have been few composers as suspicious of language as he was, and his mistrust of words' power to say anything definitive had consequences for his song oeuvre. If his famous grandfather believed in the power of reason elucidated in words to bring about emancipation for Germany's Jews, his children and grandchildren were no longer so optimistic. Berlin's Hep-hep riots in 1819, the dissolution of reforms in the wake of Napoleon's downfall, the association of Jews with the "evils" of commerce and modernism, the particular onus placed on the assimilated Jew – all of this conspired to crush the ideals of tolerance in Lessing's drama *Nathan der Weise*, its title character inspired by Moses Mendelssohn. Any thoughtful Jew – and Mendelssohn never denied his Jewish origins – in post-Napoleonic Europe would have known language as an instrument of anti-Semitism and hence might well be wary of words. One thinks of the dirty, villainous Jew in Ludwig Rellstab's novel *1812* about Napoleon's Russian campaign, and realizes once again the virulence of the stereotype. For Mendelssohn, music was more precise in its connotations than words could ever be, as he attempted to demonstrate in his provocatively entitled *Lieder ohne Worte*. When people insisted on seeing these works as "Music Minus One" and supplied the "missing" poetry (the Hamburg tax assessor Eduard Otto[4] and the critic Karl Christern actually asked for Mendelssohn's blessing on their poetic appliqués), Mendelssohn was displeased.[5] In a famous letter of 1842 to a former student named Marc André Souchay, the composer responded to the matter with what is in effect a credo.

> So much is spoken about music and so little is said. For my part I do not believe that words suffice for such a task, and if they did I would no longer make any music. People usually complain that music is too many-sided in its meanings; what they should think when they hear it is so ambiguous, whereas everyone understands words. For me, it is precisely the opposite, not only with entire speeches, but also with individual words. They too seem so ambiguous, so vague, so subject to misunderstanding when compared with true music, which fills the soul with a thousand better things than words. The thoughts that are expressed to me by the music I love are not too indefinite to put into words, but on the contrary, too definite. And I find every effort to express [in words] such thoughts legitimate, but altogether inadequate . . . this, however, is not your fault, but the fault of words, which cannot do better . . . because the same word never means the same thing to different people. Only melody can say the same thing, can arouse the same feelings in one person as in another, a feeling which may not be expressed by the same words . . .
>
> Will you accept this as my answer to your question? It is, in any event, the only one I know how to give, although these too are just ambiguous words.[6]

Resignation to fate, praise of God, melancholy, and a hunting song (these are some of the subjects Souchay had found in the *Lieder ohne Worte*), he continued, could be confused for one another in words, but that is not the case with music.

Mendelssohn had clearly formulated this aesthetic early in his compositional career. He explained the differences between his approach to song composition and that of other composers in another often-quoted letter of 1831 to his aunt Henriette von Arnstein-Pereira. She had suggested that he set to music Johann Christian Zedlitz's "Die nächtliche Heerschau," a ballad famous at the time; despite being censored for its Napoleonic subject matter, it was declaimed in Metternich's own salon. Mendelssohn replied:

> I like to take music very seriously, and I consider it impermissible to compose something that I do not feel through and through. That would be telling a lie, for notes have just as precise a meaning as words – perhaps they

are even more precise. Now to me, it seems completely impossible to set a descriptive poem to music. The majority of such compositions speak not against but for me in this, for I do not know a single successful one among them. One is caught midway between a dramatic interpretation or a merely narrative way of doing it; in the "Erlkönig," one [composer – clearly Schubert] has the meadows rustling, the child crying, the horse galloping, while another one envisions a bard who relates the grisly story altogether calmly, the way one tells a ghost story. The latter is still the more correct (Reichardt almost always did it this way), but it does not appeal to me – the music gets in the way. For me, it would be more imaginative to read such a poem to myself in silence and to think up the rest of these things myself than to have it painted for me or read aloud to me.

Nor will it do to compose the "Nächtliche Heerschau" in narrative fashion because there really is no specific person who speaks, and the poem has nothing of the tone of a ballad. To me, it seems more a clever idea than a poem [Schubert too, one remembers, rejected a proposal that he set this poem to music]; it is as if the poet did not believe in his misty images. Now of course, I would have enjoyed setting the poem in a descriptive manner, as [Sigismund] Neukomm and Fischhof in Vienna have done; I could have introduced a quaint drum-roll in the bass, trumpet calls in the treble, and all sorts of other ghostly apparitions. But again, I like to take my music more seriously than this. To me, such things always seem like a game, rather like the paintings in children's primers in which the roofs are painted bright red so that the children will know that they are roofs.[7]

That this is a rejection of the Schubert, Loewe, Schumann, etc. approaches to song is clear, and some critics recognized the difference. In a largely sympathetic review of Mendelssohn's op. 8 songs, Adolf Bernhard Marx (a fellow student of Zelter's and a friend to Felix) wrote that the composer "always knows how to convey the basic tone of the poem successfully – but in such a fashion that the expression of details is only partially conveyed with the same precision and success as that of the whole."[8] Those who wanted both the nuances and the larger architecture of a song to track the words closely would not find Mendelssohn to their taste. A cautionary note: Mendelssohn's aesthetic of songwriting does not mean disregard of the text. Rather, the composer must realize in music the idea which had given rise to the poem and therefore enable performers and listeners to identify with that idea. Both words and music in song are responses to larger, universal concepts, and the listener must be allowed to participate in his or her own unique way in the conceptualization of that realm. Music that was too specific in its attachment to this or that textual nuance interfered, he believed, with the ability to perceive more important things in poetry.

In a letter to his friend Karl Klingemann, an amateur poet who supplied the words for eight of Mendelssohn's solo songs and the duet "Herbstlied"

(Autumn Song op. 63 no. 4),[9] the composer tells Klingemann that he is a consummate creator of *poesia per musica*: "With your words, I have the singular feeling that I don't need to create any music: it is as if I read it [the music] between the lines [of the poem], as though it already stood before me. And if with other poems, especially Goethe, the words turn away from music and want to stand alone, so your poems cry out for music." Leon Botstein and R. Larry Todd have suggested that Mendelssohn's imagination was visual in nature, that the composer wanted the listener's ear to take in the whole in a manner somewhat analogous to the way in which the eye takes in a drawing or painting virtually all at once.[10] Hence Mendelssohn's preference for strophic song: not only can the ear apprehend a musical strophe as a unit but it has the opportunity to do so several times, reinforcing the sense of the whole. This preference for literal strophic repetition is owing in part to the contemporary fashion for *Volkstümlichkeit* (art song imitating folk song in an artsy way), although one notes with amusement that Mendelssohn was at times exasperated by the fad. Writing to his father from Wales in August 1829, he exclaimed, "May ten thousand devils take all folklore":

> Here I am in Wales, and, oh how lovely, a harpist sits in the lobby of every reputable inn playing so-called folk tunes at you – dreadful, vulgar, fake stuff, and simultaneously a hurdy-gurdy is tootling out melodies. It's enough to drive one crazy; it's even given me a toothache. Scottish bagpipes, Swiss cow's horns, Welsh harps, all playing the Huntsmen's Chorus with ghastly variations or improvisation, not to mention the lovely songs in the lobby – it's the only real music they have! It's beyond understanding. Anyone like myself who can't abide Beethoven's folksongs should come here and hear them howled by shrill nasal voices, accompanied by doltish, bumbling fingers, and then try to hold his tongue.[11]

Mendelssohn asserted that choral song was better than the solo lied for setting folk poetry because "every piano accompaniment smacks both of the drawing room and of the music cabinet [*Notenschrank*]."[12] Piano music was too individual/personal, civilized/bourgeois to convey communal experience.

Mendelssohn's best-known song, "Auf Flügeln des Gesanges" (On Wings of Song), constitutes an interesting case-study in this composer's approach to the genre because it is so often cited as an example of Mendelssohn ignoring aspects of the text.[13] This poem from Heinrich Heine's *Buch der Lieder* was a magnet for composers from the start; even Adolf Bartels, the anti-Semitic literary critic who hated Heine so much that he wrote two books intended to demolish the great poet's reputation, had to concede that this poem was splendid.[14] Mendelssohn's setting of these verses by a man he knew personally and disliked (the antipathy was mutual)[15] has impelled at least one Heine scholar to plead that we *forget* the song in order to restore the poetry to understandings unbiased by the familiar tune.[16] To many, "Auf Flügeln des Gesanges" is the arch-example of the composer's songs: non-virtuosic, without tonal adventurism, warm and sweet, the strophic whole of more import than pictorial details, simpler than Heine's poem. But viewed from another angle, one can argue that the composer understood the poet fully and plays along with Heine's exercise in deception. That both men create beautiful surfaces is intrinsic to the game.

In Heine's words, one finds the notional Orient beloved of Romantic escapists in the 1820s, but the exotic items are sketchy and keep company with Germanic motifs in a patently artificial manner. The persona of this poem invites his sweetheart to fly with him to a fantasy-India, a Schlaraffenland on the Ganges, where lotus flowers are the welcoming committee and synaesthesia makes the fairy stories fragrant.

(from the *Lyrisches Intermezzo*, no. 9)	(from the *Lyrical Intermezzo*, no. 9)
Auf Flügeln des Gesanges,	On wings of song,
Herzliebchen, trag' ich dich fort,	beloved, I carry you off,
Fort nach den Fluren des Ganges,	off to the banks of the Ganges,
Dort weiß ich den schönsten Ort.	there I know the loveliest spot.
Dort liegt ein rotblühender Garten	There a garden of red blossoms
Im stillen Mondenschein;	lies in the quiet moonlight;
Die Lotosblumen erwarten	the lotus flowers await
Ihr trautes Schwesterlein.	their dear sister.
Die Veilchen kichern und kosen,	The violets giggle and gossip
Und schaun nach den Sternen empor;	and look up at the stars,
Heimlich erzählen die Rosen	and the roses tell fragrant fairy tales
Sich duftende Märchen ins Ohr.	secretly in each other's ears.
Es hüpfen herbei und lauschen	The pure, wise gazelles
Die frommen, klugen Gazell'n;	skip by and listen,
Und in der Ferne rauschen	and in the distance rustle
Des heiligen Stromes Well'n.	the waves of the holy stream.
Dort wollen wir niedersinken	There let us sink down
Unter dem Palmenbaum,	under the palm tree,
Und Liebe und Ruhe trinken,	and imbibe love and peace
Und träumen seligen Traum.[17]	and dream blissful dreams.

It looks and sounds the epitome of beauty, but the gazelles, palm trees, roses, violets, lotus blossoms, and India's sacred river, cobbled together in improbable conjunction, are verbal veils for poverty: the sweetheart is invited to a night out in the open, without food or drink. Instead, they will imbibe love – cheaper than wine – and dream unspecified dreams together to the lilting strains of melodious verse, devised free of charge. One thinks of Baudelaire's "L'invitation au voyage" (Invitation to a Journey) from *Les fleurs du mal*, its Dutch canals as unrealistic as Heine's India and its "luxe, calme, et volupté" the twin to Heine's "Liebe und Ruhe." That Heine subverts conventions of all sorts is evident in the anthropomorphized violets, no longer traditional symbols of maidenly modesty but silly coquettes of the sort Heine derides elsewhere in the *Buch der Lieder*; the beloved may be complimented as sister to the exotic lotus, but her kin are more common. If bourgeois society, with its shallow young women and poverty-stricken poets, is an object of subterranean satire in this poem, so too is poetic language. "Ein Bild! Ein Bild! Mein Pferd für'n Bild!" (An image! An image! My horse for an image!), Heine once wrote, in a Shakespearean "send-up" of those writers desperate for new ways to tweak outworn words; here, the persona hopes to create new worlds via language (the Romantic project in a nutshell) that will seduce the sweetheart/the reader. Because he can stitch the borrowed improbabilities together with such skill, perhaps the bourgeois beloved will not notice the touches of the surreal, or if she does, might find them a welcome escape from tea-table conventions. When Heine's sarcasm is obvious, one knows to look for irony, but in poems like this, where we are beguiled by surface loveliness, one might well overlook the strangeness of it all.

Did Mendelssohn not see it? Did he choose to ignore what Heine was up to in this poem? Or is recognition of the poet's purposes encoded some-where in the song? Certainly the music seems to refuse all exoticism, incongruity, or oddity. The piano's broken-chordal figuration in Ab major is the epitome of *Hausmusik* accompaniments with its simulation of harp-playing, and the famous tune is a masterpiece of melodic symmetry, its rising-and-falling contours beautifully balanced. The intervallic leaps of a sixth, ascending to launch the first phrase, then descending in the next bar, are among the most memorable hallmarks of a memorable melody, its larger intervals interspersed with scalewise motion like graceful garlands hung between columns. It is characteristic of Mendelssohn's strophic melodies that the singer avoids the tonic pitch in the vocal line until the end of each musical strophe, the voice hovering above rooted foundations in the piano; one notes too that this melody does not spread its wings very far. The gentle melancholy of dominant minor harmonies in mid-strophe (mm. 10–13) is apropos in a general sense for the muted passion – not eroticism in its wilder manifestations – hymned here. That a slightly more intense outbreak of chromaticism (but nothing radical) happens in the piano interlude between the first and second musical strophes seems perfectly in accord with this composer's belief that pure music could say more than words.

Occasionally, one can point to a text-specific detail in "Auf Flügeln des Gesanges," such as the singer lingering on the verb "erwarten" (await) in mm. 19–20 or the linear descending chromaticism of the "seligen Traum," a hint that these dreams are erotic in nature; his persona even repeats the words "sel'gen Traum" to prolonged, dying-away tones, as if hypnotizing himself into a dream-state. But Mendelssohn does nothing with leaping gazelles or flirtatious violets or pseudo-Hindu melody, and the omissions are significant. Mendelssohn, I would speculate, recognized that the backdrop of this poem was actually a Biedermeier drawing room in which the persona sings to a middle-class German girl whom he wishes to seduce and does so with a parlor song of consummate loveliness, accompanied by a genteel young lady's harp transmogrified as a piano. This music is not a depiction of the persona's subjective inner world in Schubertian fashion but is instead a *performance* by a masked persona who devises bourgeois music calculated to win over the sweetheart/the public. In his words, Heine can hint to the cognoscenti that all is not as it seems, but Mendelssohn refuses to do so in his music. Scholars are right to point out that this composer was suspicious of the "lyric persona" in the songs of his day, and "Auf Flügeln des Gesanges" can be understood on one level as a repudiation of those Romantic lieder which bring subjectivity to sounding life. It is an irony worthy of Heine himself that Mendelssohn has been so often castigated for his supposed failure to "translate" this poem adequately into music (an exercise that would have horrified him) when in fact, he understood it perfectly. He even joined the poet at his own game – after all, each man in his own fashion points out the duplicity of words. One wonders if the composer took added delight in the fact that his song would surely be sung in German parlors for purposes similar to the persona's, whether or not the listeners could grasp the deeper crises of language and identity at work beneath the polished surface of the lied.

This was not the only occasion on which Heine brought out the best in Mendelssohn. Part of this poet's enterprise was to make myth modern, to bring the old gods of antiquity and the fantastic creatures of folklore into the present. For a composer who loved to trip the light fantastic, who mined musical gold from Shakespeare's mixture of supernatural and human worlds in *A Midsummer Night's Dream*, the text of "Neue Liebe" (New Love) was an irresistible magnet. The poem appears both in Heine's *Neue Gedichte* (New Poems) of 1844 and his treatise on *Elementargeister* (Elemental Spirits), in which Heine asks whether it is true that a mortal who sees an elfin queen will die shortly thereafter. He then recites this poem as if such an experience had happened to him, not in the distant past but a short time ago.

In dem Mondenschein im Walde	Lately in the forest, by moonlight,
Sah ich jüngst die Elfen reiten [reuten];	I saw the elves ride by;
Ihre Hörner hört ich klingen,	I heard their horns resounding,
Ihre Glöckchen hört ich läuten;	I heard their bells ringing.
Ihre weißen Rößlein trugen	On their little white horses were
Goldnes Hirschgeweih und flogen	antlers of gold, and they flew
Rasch dahin, wie wilde Schwäne	swiftly through the air,
Kam es durch die Luft gezogen.	like wild swans.
Lächelnd nickte mir die Königin,	Smiling, the queen nodded to me
Lächelnd, im Vorüberreiten	in passing.
[Vorüberreuten].	
Galt das meiner neuen Liebe,	Does this signify my new love
Oder soll es Tod bedeuten?[18]	or does it mean my death?

"Dance," Heine continues, "is characteristic of spirits of the air," and Mendelssohn sets Heine's poem as a specimen of his scherzo style (also familiar from the *Rondo capriccioso* for piano, the third movement of the op. 20 String Octet, and the incidental music to *A Midsummer Night's Dream*, to cite only the best-known examples). The song is in the F♯ minor Mendelssohn would have known from eighteenth-century convention as the tonality associated with death, the afterlife, and the supernatural (Schubert calls on the same tradition in his song "Schwestergruss," or "A Sister's Greeting" from beyond the grave). This song poses more difficulties for the performers than "Auf Flügeln des Gesanges," whose suitability for amateurs is part of the point: the presto accompaniment is demanding, and the broken-chordal contours of the singer's line are difficult to keep in tune. What makes the piano part more of a challenge than most of his songs is the ringing of elfin chimes in the guise of measured trill figures, appearing first in mm. 5–9. These trills sound throughout the entire first beat in 2/4 meter, and the energizing of the downbeat in this manner is delicately diabolical in effect. The fantastic-musical worlds in Mendelssohn are charged with an animistic vitality that conveys a sense of the superhuman, even (perhaps particularly) when the sounds are soft.

The introduction alone is enough to tell us that the elves' music is located in the piano, its simulacrum of fairy horns, horses' hooves, and bells devoid of words. The Other which can deal out death does not traffic in the ratiocination of mortal speech. Consequently, the persona's vocal line is harnessed, helplessly, to the other-worldly music throughout the song; he can only sing to the elfin company's strains and in their rhythms. It is the verb "läuten" (to ring, to resound) in mm. 24–26 that is the catalyst for an outbreak of

Example 11.1 Op. 19[a] no. 4, "Neue Liebe" (Heine), mm. 19–38

extremity, the singer swooping, plunging, and leaping in elemental intervals while the piano punches out a series of *sforzando* chords that look on the printed page for all the world like a passage from early Beethoven (albeit in the treble register). In Mendelssohn's imagination, the persona realizes at this very instant that the sounds he hears are deathly and leaps up an octave in alarm. The realization transforms the vocal line into something extraordinary. Every downbeat is accented in a fashion counter to correct prosody; this is the collision of the supernatural with the mortal, and coercion is implicit in the singer's inability to make the speech accents accurate as mortals measure such matters (Example 11.1). Here, Mendelssohn emphasizes the poet's trochees by prolonging the initial accented syllable of each foot in order to underscore the words which tell of sound and hearing ("Hörner, hört, klingen, Glöcklein, hört, läuten"); Heine repeats words to incantatory effect, and the composer repeats them even more often. The high A in mm. 27 and 31, difficult to execute because the singer has little time before-hand to take a breath, make of the adjective "ihre" something unforgettable: "*their* horns, *their* little bells," the persona sings, his fear palpable. Harmony heightens the menace; from the light, hollow, horn-fanfare figuration in F♯ minor, Mendelssohn jumps to similar fanfare figures on D major, and from there, to G minor harmonies – the flatted supertonic of F♯ minor and, like all Neapolitan chords, an agent of darkness.

Mendelssohn was fond of the varied strophic format in which literal repetition of musical strophes is followed by a final varied strophe, and the third and last stanza of Heine's poem is given special treatment in accord with that particular formal design. The composer's imagination was clearly piqued by the painterly image of the elfin procession riding by, for which he conceived the felicitous juxtaposition of the fairy horses' hoofbeats in the piano part with the words "im Vorüberreiten" set as half-notes in the vocal line, one per measure until the final two syllables, prolonged even more. The passage somehow conveys the sense of the persona watching the elves so intently that he cannot say/sing anything else, the vocal line as if hypnotized; the persona is bound to the sight, and eyes and voice alike swivel to watch the departing company. When he ponders what the vision might mean, whether Eros or Death ("Galt das meiner neuen Liebe? / Oder soll es Tod bedeuten?"), the listener is reminded of Schubert's miller lad in "Pause," who also asks recitative-like questions which temporarily blot out the previous music; even the unharmonized repeated dominant pitches which precede the quasi-recitative phrases are a device familiar from Schubert, who occasionally melts from one section or passage to another in this fashion. The more dreadful of the two possibilities, "Tod," is dramatized by a loud diminished seventh harmony which makes of the tonic pitch F♯ something indeterminate; when we hear another diminished seventh "horror" chord, trilled rather than struck, in the postlude (an abbreviated *pianissimo* return of the introduction – the elves have the last "word"), we are reminded of death. The entire song is brilliantly conceived. Although the horn-call motifs and hoofbeat figures seem to contradict Mendelssohn's stated disdain for pictorialism, the composer might well have noted and approved the persona's inability to define what the apparition means, or in musical terms, what the sounds in the piano signify. Music and the super-natural lie beyond the scope of mere language, even of Heine's witchery with words.

If "Neue Liebe" is a glittering specimen of scherzo-esque virtuosity, it is not as brilliant as "Andres Maienlied" op. 8 no. 8, truly a work-out for the pianist. The young composer was clearly fond both of Johann Heinrich Voss's original poetry and Voss's popular edition of Ludwig Hölty's poetry, the latter being Mendelssohn's source for the text of "Andres Maienlied" (the

title refers to the song immediately preceding it, a "Maienlied" to a poem by
Jacob von der Warte). Voss took considerable liberties with Hölty's verse: the
entire fifth stanza, in which the demonic is made comic ("A fiery dragon flies
around the roof and brings us butter and eggs; the neighbors see the sparks
flying and cross themselves by the fire . . ."), is Voss's invention.[19] There is a
long tradition of making the horrific comic (Schubert's setting of Friedrich
von Matthisson's "Der Geistertanz" is one example), and this poem tells of
a witches' coven celebrating the arrival of spring on the Brocken mountain-
top, where a gallimaufry of creatures swarm to worship Beelzebub. For this
lighthearted exercise in *diablerie*, Mendelssohn devises a piano part bubbling
and boiling over with a succession of brilliant accompanimental patterns, all
couched in the 6/8 meter of folk song. (Given the association between virtuosity and diabolism à la Paganini, one wonders whether Mendelssohn wrote
this song as a humorous "send-up" of the phenomenon.) The mixture of
tonic G minor with G *major* in the introduction and the fact that major mode
comes before minor are clues that we should chuckle, not shudder, at the
supernatural forces unleashed here; the final G major chord of the song, with
B♮ in the topmost voice, is as much a shout of laughter as of Satanic triumph.
Clichés of musical horror are put to gleeful use – for example, the convention of ascending chromaticism that is bone-chilling, awe-inspiring, in the
Schiller-Schubert song "Gruppe aus dem Tartarus" (Group from Hades) is
mock-horrific in "Andres Maienlied" (Example 11.2). Lightning-bolt arpeggios shooting upwards and then back down in a flash, tremolos, drum-
roll patterns, menacing *unisono* figures, grace-noted low bass scalar figures
leading to an accented pitch, octave leaps to high pitches for the singer –
"Did I leave anything out?", one imagines Mendelssohn asking himself,
tongue-in-cheek. That he could indeed be pictorial in song is evident;
that he does so here as a "special event," with humor aforethought, is also
evident.

I have already asserted that there is more variety in this composer's
song oeuvre than some have admitted, and the point can be demonstrated
from within this same opus. The fourth of the twelve songs in op. 8 is the
darkly beautiful "Erntelied" (Harvest Song) with the subtitle "Altes Kirchenlied" (Old Sacred Song) on a poem from *Des Knaben Wunderhorn*. For this
strophic poem about Death the inexorable reaper who mows down all the
lovely flowers/people, no matter what their beauty, Mendelssohn mingles
modal harmonies, imitations of folksong, and chorale features to powerful effect; one need only look at its two printed pages chock-a-block with
chromaticism to realize the complexity of this seemingly simple song. Each
of the first five stanzas, with its catalogue of floral beauties doomed to
extinction, culminates in the warning, "Hüte dich, schöns Blümelein! Hüte
dich!" (Beware, lovely little flower! Beware!), and each time, it is the piano

Example 11.2 Op. 8 no. 8, "Andres Maienlied" (Hölty), mm. 16–32

Example 11.3 Op. 8 no. 4, "Erntelied," conclusion

which must complete the final cadence of the musical strophe. The dread dénouement has not yet happened to us, and we steer clear of Death's tonic pitch, at least with the singer's own breath. The piano goes on to predict the future – and it is not far off. With the final stanza of the poem comes willed, defiant metamorphosis of dread into joy ("Come here, Death, I do not fear you . . . I shall be in the heavenly garden we all await. Rejoice, beautiful little flower, rejoice!"), but Mendelssohn does not convert fear-haunted modal darkness into major mode rejoicing. In his imagining, music gives the sounding lie to the assertion made in words, telling us that the fear of death is not so easily overcome (Example 11.3).

Immediately after the "Erntelied" in op. 8 is another "geistliche Lied" entitled "Pilgerspruch" (Pilgrim's Proverb) to a poem by the Baroque poet Paul Flemming, but this is in a tamer, gentler musical manner, diatonicism adorned with a few secondary dominants of the sort that can at times make nineteenth-century church music a cloying affair. This in turn is followed by a "Frühlingslied" (Spring Song) in Swabian dialect on a poem by the beautiful, talented Friederike Robert (a friend of Mendelssohn and Heine), its vivacity complete with trilled birdsong in the piano. Variety indeed, and yet the opus clearly has an overall design, with spring songs at the beginning and end enclosing a religious core.

Mendelssohn mostly shunned song cycles of the Schubertian or Schumannian kind, except in part-songs, such as the op. 41 *Drei Volkslieder* to

Heine's three linked poems entitled *Tragödie* (Tragedy); one scholar has also proposed what he calls a "shadow cycle" (an original cyclic design which does not subsequently appear in publication) in the first three songs of op. 48, collectively entitled *Der erste Frühlingstag* (The first day of spring).[20] About half of this composer's choral songs were composed for social gatherings, for almanacs, for festivals, for the choral singers who took part in his Leipzig Gewandhaus concerts, and not for publication, but in those works published in Mendelssohn's lifetime or shortly thereafter, one occasionally finds quasi-organization by poetic or literary theme. For example, the op. 59 *Im Grünen* (In the Green Woods) part-songs for mixed voices, on texts by four different poets, are all Nature songs, and the four male chorus songs of op. 75 of 1848 are all wandering songs (a venerable Romantic topos). However, the six male choruses of op. 50 have no such bonds in common, and Mendelssohn evidently did not consider thematic unity necessary in all instances.

We will take leave of Mendelssohn's solo songs with a brief consideration of a prophetic late song, one which anticipates music composed half-a-century after his death. Mendelssohn is so often characterized as a conservative composer that it is useful to be reminded of his originality, his capacity on occasion to see into the future. Perhaps because he spent much of his life in the gray climate of northern Germany, Mendelssohn was particularly attracted to spring songs and composed numerous specimens of the genre to texts by poets medieval (Ulrich von Lichtenstein, Jacob von der Warte) and modern. Most of them are joyous celebrations of spring's arrival; one thinks of the exultant, fanfare-like strains of the "Frühlingslied" op. 34 no. 3 on a poem by Klingemann and the "Frühlingslied" op. 47 no. 3, irresistible in their vitality, or "Im Grünen" op. 8 no. 11, on a poem by Voss. But on 7 October 1847, only a few weeks before his death, Mendelssohn created a spring song in another vein: the "Altdeutsches Frühlingslied" (Old German Spring Song), published posthumously as op. 86 no. 6 (he considered including it in op. 71). Its text is a heavily rewritten segment from the *Trutz-Nachtigall* of Friedrich Spee (1591–1635), a Jesuit mystical poet famous in his own day for his opposition to the burning of witches. In its original form, the poem is entitled "Anders Liebgesang der gespons JESV. Zum Anfang der Sommerzeit" and tells in twelve ten-line stanzas of mystic marriage with Christ as the only source of healing for a wounded spirit. Mendelssohn's song-text uses only verses 1 and 6 and completely alters their meaning.[21] Here, Nature rejoices, but the persona's pain admits no alleviation because "I had to part from you, beloved." There is no mention of anything religious, and one can understand the extract in a wholly secular sense – a means for Mendelssohn to recount the loss he had suffered the previous spring when his beloved sister Fanny died.

In his setting of Spee modernized, Mendelssohn created what present-day listeners can hear as a foreshadowing of Mahler's "Der Einsame im Herbst" (The Lonely Man in Autumn), the second movement of *Das Lied von der Erde*, composed sixty years later. If the two poems hail from different seasons, they are sisters under the skin, both measuring grief against the gauge of the changing seasons – and Mendelssohn too was an "Einsamer im Herbst" that last autumn of his life.[22] Mahler plunges deeply into fin-de-siècle melancholy, while the earlier composer is more reticent, and yet the two compositions are allied by their similar *Bewegung*. Ceaseless rising and falling streams of equal note values (sixteenth notes in Mendelssohn, eighth notes in Mahler) in the same middle register, neither high nor low, flow through both works. Mahler's motion is mostly scalewise in 3/2 meter, Mendelssohn's a complex alternation of scalar, broken-chordal, and inter-vallic motives in 4/4, but the effect is eerily the same, and it is tempting to speculate that the two songs arose from the same conceptual ground. In both songs, time flows in a gently inexorable stream of pitches, bearing the grief-stricken personae to their deaths in the wake of those lost and mourned. In both the large and the small song, the vocal line is often disposed in equal note values of twice the duration of the moving accompanimental figuration (eighth notes in Mendelssohn, quarter notes in Mahler), and this quasi-chant-like syllabic style conveys weary resignation in the face of the inevitable. In both compositions, the texture is translucent, austere in a fashion appropriate to sad knowledge on the brink of the grave, and in both, the instrumental motion seems unpredictable in its twists and turns, not the regulated accompanimental patterns in songs such as "Auf Flügeln des Gesanges" but something serpentine. Mendelssohn might have been invited to do so by the words "wie Schlänglein krumm / gehn lächelnd um / die Bächlein kühl in Wäldern," and the asymmetry is not truly random but rather is held together by the occasional internal sequences (the descending sequence between the two musical strophes is one example) and recurring motivic elements. One is tempted to find metaphysical meanings in both Mahler's and Mendelssohn's recourse to such figuration, with its artfully meandering contours and its ceaselessness: life and Nature go their way nonstop, whatever our weariness or sorrow, so says this figuration.

"Altdeutsches Frühlingslied," like so many of Mendelssohn's songs, is strophic, and it seems evident that the composer took his cue not from the first stanza but from the second, with its quiet statement of grief beyond reparation. The darker minor harmonies in mm. 11–12 accord precisely with the words "Nur ich allein, ich leide Pein" in Mendelssohn's second strophe, not with the words to which they first appear ("Laub allgemach nun schleicht an Tag"), while the tonic minor harmony in m. 15 and the sudden *pianissimo* hush go with the statement of parting ("seit du von mir

Example 11.4 Mendelssohn, "Altdeutsches Frühlingslied" [op. 86 no. 6], beginning

Example 11.5 Gustav Mahler, "Der Einsame im Herbst," beginning

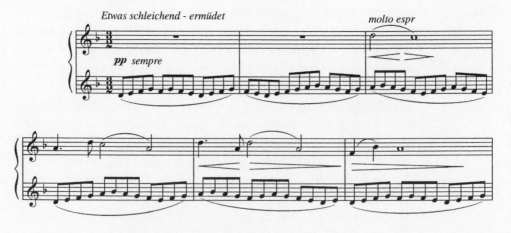

und ich von dir . . .") more than with the winding brooks of stanza 1 (they had their own influence on this music). The prolongation of the verb "mußte" in m. 18 ("o Liebste, *mußte* scheiden") is perhaps the most moving detail of all. This parting, Mendelssohn tells us, was forcibly compelled.

This brief essay barely scratches the surface of Mendelssohn's song oeuvre. Were there room enough and time, one could expound on the fascinating comparison between Schubert's and Mendelssohn's settings of Ludwig Uhland's "Frühlingsglaube" (Faith in Spring); on the merry, folksong-like "Warnung vor dem Rhein"(Beware of the Rhine), with its invocation of the recently invented Loreley myth; on this composer's dabblings in the musical-exotic for his pseudo-Spanish "Romanze" op. 8 no. 10 and the "Todeslied der Bojaren" (Death Song of the Boyars) from the *Nachlaß*; and much more. If his emotional range in lied was narrower than that of Schubert, that is hardly surprising: Schubert composed many more songs than Mendelssohn across a wider spectrum, and the Viennese master announced his intent to modernize the song composition of his day when he was in his early teens. This was not Mendelssohn's mission, but if one understands his idiosyncratic approach to the lied, there is much to be gleaned from this music. There are, after all, reasons – good ones – for the fact that certain songs by Mendelssohn are "chestnuts," beloved of both musicians and the public. Others deserve to become so.[23]

12 Felix Mendelssohn's dramatic compositions: from Liederspiel to *Lorelei*

MONIKA HENNEMANN

For someone who has not entered the pages of history as an opera composer, Mendelssohn's output of dramatic music was remarkable, and the attention attracted by his failure to complete a mature opera is unparalleled. To describe the first and explain the second are the objects of this chapter.

Had Beethoven and Schumann died, like Mendelssohn, at the age of thirty-eight, the lack of *Fidelio* (completed by Beethoven at the age of forty-four in 1814) or *Genoveva* (Schumann was forty at the 1850 premiere) would hardly have affected their final evaluation by posterity. Why is it, then, that Mendelssohn's unfulfilled operatic ambitions were considered such a significant – and suggestive – artistic failure?[1] Two reasons come immediately to mind: first, had Mendelssohn lived only a year longer – as his contemporaries were acutely aware – the world might have witnessed the completion of *Die Lorelei*, an opera that occupied much of his creative energy in the months before his death. Other projects were in the queue, such as a commission for Her Majesty's Theatre in London, which had not reached fruition in time for the 1847 season, but which could well have seen the light of day the following year.

Second, as a child prodigy of exceptional talent, Mendelssohn was compared to Mozart from a very early age, and was expected to match his predecessor's brilliant output in a multiplicity of genres.[2] In Mozart's case, we have nine stage compositions before he turned twenty, including *Bastien und Bastienne* and *La finta semplice* (both 1768) written in his early teens. Mendelssohn created six completed stage works before 1829, but – as opposed to Mozart, who followed through with his development – never delivered a mature opera to the eagerly expectant public. Among his immediate family and closest circle of friends were several people who envisaged him conquering the stages in Berlin, Paris, and London, not least his father and his close friend and supporter, Eduard Devrient. In the latter's influential *Recollections of Mendelssohn*,[3] Mendelssohn's entire career was presented through the lens of his various still-born operatic projects, leaving a malign – and often inaccurate – trail in subsequent biographies. Numerous contemporaries joined in with his demand that Mendelssohn write an opera, including the journalist Eduard Maria Oettinger ("I believe I am the voice of all your admirers when I ask you to turn your beautiful, marvelous talent back to dramatic music. You would celebrate a triumph and give new brilliancy to German opera."[4]) and lawyer friend Julius Becher ("It is absolutely necessary that you write an opera – and it would not have to be the last one – and you will turn every text into something competent".[5]) In addition, the composer himself, as the foremost musical figure in Germany in the 1830s and 1840s, felt strongly obliged to contribute to the genre of opera, particularly after having heard new works by colleagues: "I then feel as if it were a duty for me, too, to lend a hand to the cause, and record my vote in score."[6]

Since for the Romantics the success of a composer was still mainly measured by his accomplishments on the stage – as Berlioz was never allowed to forget – it became clear only in retrospect that Mendelssohn belonged to a new age of specialization (Wagner's experiments with instrumental music were sidelines for similar reasons), as opposed to the popular prodigy role model of Mozart. After all, Mendelssohn's thwarted desire for an operatic triumph finds nineteenth-century parallels in the careers of Schubert, Beethoven, and Schumann, and later also with figures as self-consciously diverse as Brahms and Liszt.[7]

Mendelssohn's operatic initiation began early. His creative activities, and those of his three siblings, were encouraged by the family from a young age, and a spacious home in rich cultural surroundings provided ample opportunity to experiment with various types of *tableaux vivants*, staged dramas, musical performances, and other forms of entertainment, such as a home-produced journal. Owing to the talent and imagination of the children (not to forget the driving ambitions of their parents), these performances soon developed into social occasions, first for family members and close friends only, and later for the Berlin intelligentsia. It was in this protected and supportive environment that Felix's first attempts at dramatic music came into existence.

First dramatic sketches and six early stage compositions

The first evidence of Mendelssohn's dramatic endeavors was a fragmentary scene, consisting of the duet "Quel bonheur pour mon cœur," dated 7 March 1820. In the same year, he supplied an overture – possibly only as an improvisation, since no written score exists – for a performance of the French farce-comedy *L'homme automate*, translated and adapted by his mother Lea. Also from 1820, one (out of a projected three) rudimentary scenes for a "Little Comedy about Family Events" called *Ich J. Mendelssohn – Ich*

A. Mendelssohn survives (the text probably self-assembled), which represents little more than the experiment of a remarkable eleven-year-old running through various standard dramatic styles. Certain passages of this work, in which the two protagonists discuss the disputed merits of Spontini's *Olimpie*, show the family's awareness of Berlin's contemporary opera scene and the polarized reception of the current *Generalmusikdirektor*. Despite the fragmentary state of the piece, Mendelssohn's dramatic talent became so obvious that a systematic approach to further his inclinations was taken.

At the urging of Felix's parents – most strongly his father, who in 1820 expressed the desire that Felix "should dare to compose a work of greater scale than previously"[8] – the composer created five Singspiele and one Liederspiel between 1820 and 1829. All but one were based on texts by family friends and designed for performance on family occasions in the 120-seat concert hall of the Mendelssohn home. Felix's mother had a more practical but equally powerful impact: the manuscript libretti (especially for the first one-act Singspiel, *Die Soldatenliebschaft*) show numerous changes in her hand.

A "house poet" (title by Lea Mendelssohn), who readily supplied texts for Felix's first four operas was found in the family friend Johann Ludwig Casper (1796–1864), a medical student and later professor of forensic medicine. He worked as an editor of medical journals, but had scant experience in more artistic forms of literary production. During a scholarly excursion, Casper had, however, become familiar with light French stage pieces such as the "vaudeville," the character of which (especially in their progressive political undertones) well suited the Mendelssohn family. That his libretti tackled controversial contemporary issues – dealt with extremely maturely by the youthful composer – is best exemplified in his second text, for *Die beiden Pädagogen*, which debates the inadequacy of education as a preparation for the realities of life.

It is important to bear in mind that these stage compositions were in no way part of Mendelssohn's ongoing composition lessons with Carl Friedrich Zelter, but independent achievements by the teenage composer. His parents took precautions that nobody, with the exception of Felix's sister Fanny, was to see a note of these works until the success of the experiment was guaranteed. In order to secure a premiere on his father's birthday, it therefore fell on the young composer in the case of *Die Soldatenliebschaft* to complete the work within nine weeks, to copy out most of the parts by himself, and to conduct the necessary rehearsals. The first performance took place on 11 December 1820 with piano accompaniment only, but an orchestra was hired for a subsequent one on Felix's birthday on 3 February 1821. After his successful operatic initiation Felix was immediately informed that Casper would prepare a second libretto for him, to be composed for his mother's birthday on 15 March. Although presented with the first part of the text for *Die beiden Pädagogen* (a comic operetta in one act, adapted from Scribe's *Les deux précepteurs, ou Asinus asinum fricat*) only on 24 January, the young composer promptly delivered the completed composition on the evening before the scheduled performance.

The third opera, *Die wandernden Komödianten* (a comic opera in one act) was composed in the fall of 1821. Again, Casper's libretto was based on the style of French "vaudevilles" and offered many opportunities for straightforward characterization through protagonists with accentuated personal features and grotesque names, such as Fixfinger, Fröhlich, Hasenfuß, Schwarzauge, and Holzbein.

The musical realization of Casper's fourth libretto bears the title *Die beiden Neffen* on the overture and *Der Onkel aus Boston* on the manuscript score of the opera. It consists of three acts,[9] and was composed between May 1822 and October 1823. Of much broader scope than its predecessors, it includes two ballets and takes about 150 minutes to perform. With this work (the plot of which runs out long before the libretto does), Casper's dramatic talents were stretched to the point of hindering Mendelssohn's musical development, and this would be their last collaboration. *Die beiden Neffen* was premiered in 1824 on Felix's fifteenth birthday, and, as is well known, Zelter – though he himself did not deserve much credit for the opera – afterwards proudly made his student a member of the fraternity of composers "in the name of Mozart, in the name of Haydn, and in the name of the old Bach."[10]

After these four operatic successes in the sheltered environment of their home, Felix's parents soon took steps to turn their son's operatic career into a public affair, still retaining control of the librettist and libretto. Searching for a suitable replacement for the over-taxed Casper, they accepted an offer from the Hanover amateur writer Friedrich Voigts to provide a libretto based on Cervantes' recently translated masterwork *Don Quixote*.[11] By this point, the young composer had developed his own clear prerequisites for a suitable text and was not shy about verbalizing them in his correspondence with Voigts. After a detailed criticism of the libretto draft, the fifteen-year-old concludes: "However, one rarely finds criticism that is totally unjustified. Therefore, I took the liberty to note those passages that do not appeal to me entirely."[12]

Begun in 1824 and completed in August 1825, *Die Hochzeit des Camacho* was submitted to the Königliche Schauspiele in Berlin at the request of Felix's mother, and accepted by Generalintendant Graf Brühl. However, it still needed the approval of Generalmusikdirektor Spontini, who, having requested a score, invited his young colleague into his office. There he supposedly declared: "Mon ami, il vous faut des idées grandes, grandes comme cette coupole,"[13] pointing to the cupola of the adjacent French church. Spontini's patronizing attitude was hardly a surprise – he was generally known to be jealous and unsupportive of other (particularly German) opera composers and had tried to block the Berlin performance of Weber's *Euryanthe* and Marschner's works. Despite this, *Die Hochzeit des Camacho* was finally accepted for performance, and the public premiere took place on 27 April 1827 on the smaller stage of the theater. Although Mendelssohn was so disappointed with the performance that he left before the end, the work earned encouraging, though not euphoric, press reviews: "On the whole, the young composer, whose models appear to be Mozart, Beethoven, and C. M. von Weber, has presented with this first opera a decisive test-piece, even if not a masterpiece, of his outstanding talent which is cultivated in such a well-rounded fashion that it will certainly bear beautiful fruits . . ."[14] When the repeat performance was first postponed owing to the illness of the lead baritone Heinrich Blume (Don Quixote), then completely canceled, Mendelssohn did not seem too unhappy. He had matured greatly in the two years since the completion of the work and had gained a critical distance from his own composition.

Mendelssohn's subsequent failure to complete a mature opera was blamed by many scholars on the disappointment arising from *Die Hochzeit des Camacho*, starting with Schünemann's evaluation that "it offers hardly more than Felix's youthful operas and remains significantly behind the earlier works in terms of inventiveness and humor." This supposedly resulted in a "fateful interruption" of a logical and promising development, which "destroyed all hopes for a dramatic career in young Felix."[15] In reality, Mendelssohn felt an increasing pressure to undertake further operatic attempts, as he wrote to Devrient: "You want me to devote myself to opera, and think it is wrong in me not to have done so long ago."[16] First, though, he chose to return to the home concert hall for his next large vocal work, *Die Heimkehr aus der Fremde*, op. 89 (known in the English-speaking world as *Son and Stranger*), an extended Liederspiel.[17] Mendelssohn's contribution to this dying genre represents a Romanticized extension of the usual chain of simple songs linked by a textual thread; ensemble numbers were added and more sophisticated orchestration is apparent throughout.

Again, there was a specific occasion for this production, namely his parents' silver wedding anniversary on 28 December 1829, as well as a biographical background to the libretto: Mendelssohn had recently returned from an extended trip through England and Scotland, himself "coming home from foreign lands." The text was created by Karl Klingemann (1798–1862), a close friend of the Mendelssohn family who had accompanied Felix on his British sojourn and who provided him with song lyrics, libretto sketches, and

English translations of German texts throughout his career. In *Die Heimkehr aus der Fremde*, Mendelssohn's comic sense found an outlet in the part for a new family member, his thoroughly unmusical brother-in-law Wilhelm Hensel, who had married Fanny on 3 October: Terzetto no. 7 included a role for Hensel, which consisted of only one note. Even this, to general hilarity, he failed to intone properly during the premiere. Other family members and friends, such as student friend Eduard Mantius and Devrient (as director), also participated in this home performance. Felix's youngest brother Paul played the cello and his sisters Fanny and Rebecka had the two female roles. Librettist Klingemann contributed to the music, as well: he composed "Lisbeth's song" (no. 12), and Felix incorporated one of his melodies into the overture. The work became a favorite of the family and the audience, and even Mendelssohn himself only spoke admiringly of it: "It has become one of our most precious memories, and I think it is my best composition."[18] Nevertheless, he vehemently opposed a commercial performance, insisting on the separation between public and private spheres. By public demand, it was finally staged after Mendelssohn's death, the libretto being adapted by Devrient, but the chamber-size instrumentation retained.

Considered as a sequence chronicling the development of one of the most precocious compositional talents in musical history, Mendelssohn's early operas contain much of musical interest, although perhaps only the last two, *Die Hochzeit des Camacho* and *Die Heimkehr aus der Fremde*, can be evaluated without more or less patronizing reference to the youth of the composer. *Die Soldatenliebschaft*, the earliest completed work, shows a deft sureness of touch in its delineation of (still conventional) characters, and a burgeoning facility in imitating the lighter aspects of Mozart's style. The overture is especially successful in its combination of rhythmic energy and slick counterpoint, features vividly shared by the overture of *Die beiden Pädagogen*. Although in this next opera, too, reminiscences of Mozart abound, for example in the Terzetto (no. 7) "Ach, ach, ach, mich so zu kränken," Mendelssohn becomes increasingly bold in his own attempts to increase the impact of the drama through music. At the end of this number, the unexpected and unwelcome entrance of the third character calls forth an equally unexpected move to the mediant, and a sudden change of orchestration and dynamics. The composer had originally intended to follow this shock with a similar one a few bars later, but decided on second thoughts not to overplay his hand (Plate 12.1 a–b).

Particularly striking in *Die beiden Pädagogen* is the assured, and often charming, scoring for brass and woodwind (see, for example, the evocative writing in the "Quartetto e Coro," no. 10). Mendelssohn's interest in orchestral color continued to develop in *Die wandernden Komödianten*, along with a talent for parody (the deliberately wretched mini-overture to the strolling

Plate 12.1a: *Die beiden Pädagogen*, concluding mm. of No.7 (Terzetto), antograph manuscript of the composer. Staatsbibliothek zu Berlin–Preußischer Kulturbesitz, Musikabteilung mit Mendelssohn-Archiv, Mus. ms. autogr. F. Mendelssohn Bartholdy 8, 58–59.

Plate 12.1b

Example 12.1 *Die wandernden Komödianten*, No. 11, mm. 1–15

players' theatrical performance begins with the strings tuning up in open fifths; see Example 12.1)[19] and an ability to sustain larger musical structures than hitherto.   The almost exclusively comic nature of the plot of this opera did, however, thwart any attempt to enlarge the emotional range of the music, although Mendelssohn takes full advantage of the opportunity to write several numbers of remarkable verve and wit. *Die beiden Neffen*, which so impressed Zelter, additionally presented a chance to write ballet music and to assimilate the powerful impact of Weber's *Der Freischütz*, premiered in Berlin in 1821. Ensembles in this work are considerably more extended and worked out with a confidence that makes the evident weakness of the libretto all the more disappointing. It was no surprise that the Mendelssohn family should have chosen another librettist for *Die Hochzeit des Camacho*, but even for this work the flimsy nature of the text excited unfavorable comment from the reviewer in the *Allgemeine musicalische Zeitung* of the first

Example 12.2 *Die Hochzeit des Camacho*, Overture, mm. 1–16

performance ("concerns were raised by the inadequacy of the libretto").[20] The influence of Weber is evident immediately from the vigorous, leaping melody in the strings toward the opening of the overture (Example 12.2). Echoes of Mozart are still to be found in other numbers, and taken as a whole the music is fluent, extensively varied, and effectively orchestrated, even if at times rather long-winded.

Perhaps because, as a Liederspiel, it eschews the too extravagant ambitions of the former piece, *Die Heimkehr aus der Fremde* may well be the most attractive stage work of all. Impressing through the imaginative transparency of its scoring (see, for example, no. 5, "Wenn die Abendglocken läuten") and the precise characterization of each individual number, this skillfully crafted piece with many touches of originality amply justifies Mendelssohn's own admiration of it. The overture, which moves from a beautifully rapt introduction for strings to a nimble allegro foreshadowing the high spirits of the first movement of the "Italian" Symphony, is an extremely engaging orchestral work, and the quality of the rest of the music must surely have raised justified expectations in the Mendelssohn household that the composer was set for a successful stage career.

The premiere of *Die Heimkehr aus der Fremde* marked the last large family festivity before the young composer embarked on a two-year trip through Europe. From that time on, he produced no more stage works for private performance, despite the fact that opera was expected to play a major part in his professional decisions. Why these expectations were not fulfilled is discussed in the next part of this chapter.

Attempting to conquer the European stages: opera projects for Munich, London, Paris, and Berlin

Toward the beginning of his travels – which had the purpose "closely to examine the various countries, and to fix the one where [he] wished to live and work"[21] – the young composer was offered, on a stop in Munich in 1831, his first opera commission, by the stage director Baron von Poissl, which he gladly accepted. He was so optimistic as even to plan subsequent performances for his work in Stuttgart. Full of ambition, he declared his mission: "I am resolved . . . to make the attempt in Germany, and to remain and work there so long as I can continue to do so, and yet maintain myself. I consider this my first duty."[22] He proved his commitment to Germany immediately in the search for a suitable librettist – an unfamiliar challenge that brought to the surface stark differences between his preferences and those of his father, who strongly suggested using a French source. Mendelssohn's choice fell on the German writer Karl Leberecht Immermann, whose acquaintance secured him not only the promise of a suitable libretto (called *Der Zaubermantel in Calibans Händen*, based on Shakespeare's *The Tempest*), but also his first professional employment as music director at the theater in Düsseldorf, where Immermann served as general director. The prospect of Mendelssohn working within the world of opera raised the hopes of his family for a new dramatic composition even more, but he remained in this position only from 1832 to 1834 and departed under less than friendly circumstances. His frustration with the administrative aspects of stage performances led to endless quarrels with Immermann, and he resigned in November 1834 – it was to be his only professional position related to opera. Long before that time, the opera project had been conclusively dropped because Mendelssohn and Immermann had failed to come to an acceptable agreement concerning revisions of the libretto.

Frustrated with the situation in Germany, Mendelssohn eventually turned to England for possible opportunities: in the fall of 1837, he agreed to compose an opera for one of the major London stages on a text by James Robinson Planché, provided he would be equipped with a suitable libretto. Planché, who quickly decided on the story of Edward III as the text source, was familiar with Mendelssohn's compositional strengths and English audience preferences, and his libretto therefore emphasized choral pieces: "In the opening scene you will see that my intention is to give you an opportunity for two distinct choruses . . . To work one against the other – either alternately – or at the same time – ending however with a general burst of welcome to the Queen . . ."[23]

Despite Mendelssohn's initial concern that the libretto would be too similar to Weber's *Oberon*, he was pleasantly surprised by its high quality and was – contrary to his customary preference to wait for the complete libretto – immediately inspired to write down some music (which has never been located). He wrote to Chappell about the libretto: "It suggested to me in several places musical ideas which I noted down while reading, and then found how adapted to music these flowing and expressive verses are."[24] Soon, however, Mendelssohn started to demand extensive changes, notably the inclusion of a comic role for entertainment purposes, and finally declined to accept even a thorough rewriting of the text. As far as he was concerned, the "mistake lay in the whole [libretto], with the exception of the subject matter, which could have been turned into something suitable."[25] Planché was bitterly disappointed by the failure of the project: "His treatment of me caused me the keenest mortification, and inflicted on me the greatest disappointment I have ever endured."[26]

Despite these quarrels, Mendelssohn had not lost interest in the London stages and preliminarily agreed to compose an opera for the 1847 season at Her Majesty's Theatre on a libretto by Scribe, once more Shakespeare's *The Tempest* (which thus became the subject for Mendelssohn's first and last commissions). An added bonus of this project was that Mendelssohn's friend Jenny Lind was contracted as the lead soprano. Long before Mendelssohn had officially accepted the commission, however, all major London newspapers enthusiastically reported this forthcoming major event: "The great feature of the season will be the production of an opera, written expressly for the theatre by no less than Mendelssohn Bartholdy, the intimation of which will unquestionably throw the musical public, both professional and amateur, into ecstasies of delight."[27] When the opera was listed in the official theater program in a clumsy attempt to force Mendelssohn into composing the work, he became rather upset, particularly since there was no official agreement and he was busy completing *Elijah*, as he wrote on 18 February to Klingemann: "I have read it [the libretto] since then frequently and attentively – have almost come to the conclusion that I cannot compose it until some (even if very remote) point in this year's season – have not written a single note of it – isn't that 'much ado about nothing' instead of the Tempest?"[28]

Finally, Mendelssohn saw no other way than to officially resign from the project, threatening to take legal steps, should the announcements about his opera not be withdrawn from the theater program. Lumley – with the brazenly optimistic attitude necessary to survive in his profession – still did not give up and asked whether Mendelssohn would be willing to postpone the opera premiere until the next season, with the option of also having it performed in Paris. Mendelssohn responded: "I hasten to reply that I cannot accept an engagement to produce a work of such importance unless it is either quite finished or the greater part written down and the rest in my head."[29] He might, however, have taken up the project again, had not his untimely death on 4 November 1847 prevented this.

Mendelssohn's eagerness to produce an opera for London is underlined by negotiations he undertook, while still contemplating the *Tempest* project, with T. F. Beale, impresario at Covent Garden, for an opera based on Shakespeare's *A Winter's Tale* (with a libretto by Henry Chorley) in early 1847. He replied to Beale's advances: "Could you get this [the libretto] for me by the time I propose being in England, and if this is good and in accordance to my wishes (be it romantic, or tragic or what it may) then I have no doubt we would immediately be at the end of the business . . ."[30] This project never progressed beyond the initial stages, and – more importantly – the London press never found out about it, which saved Mendelssohn from perhaps even greater press hype.

Another metropolis that could have played a major role in Mendelssohn's dramatic career was Paris. Despite the fact that his youthful works were so closely related to *opéra comique*, however, he repeatedly criticized French operatic style and conventions during his sojourn there. Besides unacceptably rude audience behavior, he disapproved of a perceived lack of passion in the Parisian composers, the superficiality of the plots, and the striving for cheap stage effects. Mendelssohn's most weighty concern was the lack of morality in contemporary French opera, and he declared himself scandalized at scenes featuring young women disrobing, or indeed the famous dead dancing nuns of *Robert le Diable*. In a few instances, these concerns were for a short period overpowered by projects or collaborators promising enough to put moral considerations to one side.

Mendelssohn seemed vaguely interested when in 1840 the Paris opera house offered him a contract in collaboration with the renowned librettist Eugène Scribe, undoubtedly the foremost librettist of his time and author of texts for the most successful contemporary operas. Although Mendelssohn declined for reasons of overwork (thus consciously forgoing the fame that often came with operas in French style), he at least left the doors open for a future possible agreement. In 1842, a second project with Scribe was discussed for the Berlin stage (with plans for subsequent Paris performances), which did not proceed beyond initial deliberations.

More extensively documented are Mendelssohn's negotiations with the French stage writer Charles Duveyrier, whom he had met in France in the early 1830s. Duveyrier and his friend Arlès-Dufour – both Saint-Simonians – were trying hard to choose a subject matter that would both inspire the composer and help publicize their political ideals. After Mendelssohn had rejected the subject of *Mohammed*, superficially on the grounds of its close resemblance to Meyerbeer's *Le Prophète* (which was begun in 1836, but only premiered in 1849, so Mendelssohn's opera could easily have been the first on the subject), Duveyrier offered to adapt Schiller's *Joan of Arc*, this time focusing on the "German" virtues of patriotism, nobility, simplicity, and modesty. Owing to a lukewarm reaction from Mendelssohn, Duveyrier finally suggested a medieval subject. In the long run, however, Mendelssohn decided to refrain from being established in Parisian opera life as a mouthpiece of the Saint-Simonians, whose political agenda took precedence over most artistic considerations.

Even in the face of numerous unpleasant experiences in foreign opera capitals, Mendelssohn never liked the cultural apparatus of his home town Berlin, and his negative experiences with the production of *Die Hochzeit des Camacho* had made him wary of opera productions in the city. Despite his 1841 appointment as Preußischer Kapellmeister in service of the king, he was only once invited to provide an opera for Berlin, the above-mentioned collaboration with Scribe. This was mainly due to the fact that King Friedrich Wilhelm IV had also given Meyerbeer a similar position with responsibility for the opera house. In collaboration with "Hofdichter" Tieck, Mendelssohn's "stage duties" chiefly included producing incidental music for ancient Greek and Shakespearean dramas to be revived on the stages of Sans Souci (the king's "private" theater) and Berlin. These works will be discussed later.

Other stage projects

The above-mentioned endeavors only scratch the surface of Mendelssohn's operatic projects and ideas, which amounted to more than fifty throughout his life.[31] Their high number was unusual even in his day, and his correspondence with the respective librettists provides a fascinating insight into nineteenth-century libretto history.

Countless unsolicited plot suggestions reached Mendelssohn, intended to spark his inspiration and often accompanied by friendly offers to provide the respective libretto, should the suggestion fall on fertile grounds. As he mentioned in a 1838 letter to a would-be collaborator, this was his favored approach to finding a subject: "I beg you to convey to me raw subject matter, and I ask you urgently for that because many failed attempts – all of them trying to fix the subject matter – have proven to me that the subject is most important and a central issue that must be discussed."[32]

A steady provider of ideas was his friend Devrient, who listed a good dozen potential subjects in his *Erinnerungen*. Another over-eager librettist, Carl Gollmick, suggested more than two dozen topics in a single letter[33] in the desperate hope of stimulating Mendelssohn's appetite with at least one of them. In general, many suggestions were related to Mendelssohn's extant compositions. Not surprisingly, subject matters related to the fairy style of the *Midsummer Night's Dream* overture were the most popular (if not the most imaginative), as here suggested by the poet Zuccalmaglio: "For me, the opera ... should hold a middle ground between the Midsummer Night's Dream story and the fairy tale of Melusine. Fairies should appear, as well as water nymphs, for whose language your music seemed perfectly suited."[34]

While *The Tempest* came a close second in the popularity stakes (libretti were offered by Immermann, the writer Wolfgang Robert Griepenkerl, the Austrian stage author Otto Prechtler, and Scribe), other suggestions ran the gamut of well-known literary and historical opera sources and included more of the recently translated Shakespeare (*King Lear* and *Hamlet*), Tasso's *Gerusalemme Liberata*, Goethe's *Faust*, Scott's *Kenilworth*, Victor Hugo's *Ruy Blas* (ironically a play that Mendelssohn detested), Schiller's *Joan of Arc* and *Sappho* (perhaps a non-starter given Mendelssohn's moral views). Most of these subjects were generally in the air at the time – especially resonant with associations of competing contemporaries are *Der Sängerkrieg auf der Wartburg*, *Der Schwanenritter*, *Das Nibelungenlied*, and of course *Genoveva* (rejected by Mendelssohn owing to the protagonist's passivity of character).[35] One wonders how differently Wagner's *Tannhäuser*, *Lohengrin*, or *Der Ring des Nibelungen* would have turned out – or indeed whether they would have appeared at all – with an opera by Mendelssohn on the same subject rolling across the stages of Europe.

A fair number of projects reached the stage at which summary plots in outline format were made available to Mendelssohn – whether requested or not. Among the short scenarios he received were those by the historians Gustav Johann Droysen (*Nausikaa*, based on Homer's *Odyssey*), Gottfried Kinkel ("Die Mauren in Spanien" and "Otto und Adelheid"), and the Victorian journalist Henry F. Chorley (*A Winter's Tale*). Mendelssohn himself created (and abandoned) at least three sketches, for *Pervonte* (a project he pursued in collaboration with Klingemann between 1834 and 1835), *Hamlet*, and *The Tempest*. He claimed in a letter to Devrient, however, that he was not able to turn an idea into a layout: "If you would write out the plot on two pages of a letter, my wishes would be fulfilled! . . . If I have this, I have the opera, for I can recognize and trace it out myself from a few broad strokes; but I cannot make them myself."[36]

Only a very few ideas progressed from suggestions and scenarios to become actual libretti. Prechtler, who later in his career wrote at least thirty-eight opera texts (many of them set by minor composers), was most productive with three completed examples supplied between 1841 and 1843 – in addition to numerous sketches and subject suggestions on historical and literary sources. Other now forgotten libretto drafts include Zuccalmaglio's *Schwanenritter* of 1838, and Lyser's *Isola* (not preserved). The vast majority of finished libretti presented to Mendelssohn were subsequently taken on by other composers (though they did not always result in completed operas). This disproves the popular claim that the foundation of Mendelssohn's operatic problems was the lack of a viable libretto (however poor some of the texts presented to him might have been).

In addition to a number of libretti by minor poets set to music by equally second-rate composers, including Carl Gollmick's adaptation of *El Cid* (offered to both Meyerbeer and Mendelssohn in the early 1840s, and composed in 1843 by Heinrich Neeb), Prechtler's *Die Braut von Venedig* (set by Adolf Reichel in 1843), and Kinkel's *Die Assassinen* (turned into a Liederspiel by his wife Johanna in 1844), the very first libretto Mendelssohn rejected, that for *Hans Heiling* by his friend Devrient (1827), was famously set to music by Heinrich Marschner in 1831–32. Mendelssohn, who found the character of the main protagonist unappealing, had declared that "faith in the subject was the first condition from which a work of art should spring, and that it was a crime to art, and consequently to mankind, to enter upon a work without it."[37] Devrient regarded this as a "beautiful, ideal creed, which however is scarcely fitted to be applied in real life."[38]

Mendelssohn's rejection of Immermann's *Tempest* libretto – happily taken on but never completed by Julius Rietz, his successor at the Düsseldorf theater – also meant breaking his contract with the Munich opera house.[39] A similar breach of contract appeared in the case of Planché's *Edward III and the Siege of Calais*. After Mendelssohn's abandonment of the text, the British composer Henry Smart attempted to set it to music, but was unable to finish owing to a severe eye condition. Halévy was more successful in composing Scribe's *Tempest* adaptation, using a translation by Giannone for his 1850 opera *La Tempesta*. The most sought-after of Mendelssohn's libretti, though often criticized as being more lyrical than dramatic and lacking in action, was Emanuel Geibel's *Lorelei*. By the time of its publication in 1860, Geibel, one of the most renowned poets of the day, had denied at least thirteen composers (among them Marschner) permission to set the text to music. Max Bruch, whose opera on the text was premiered in 1863, only secured the poet's approval after introducing him to an excerpt that he had composed without authorization.

Only one of Mendelssohn's mature opera libretti reached the critical stage of actual musical composition, namely *Die Lorelei*, a result of his collaboration with Geibel, with the indispensable mediation of the theatrically experienced Devrient. The text was based on Clemens Brentano's Romantic pseudo-legend of 1801, a story that had been offered to Mendelssohn at least three times before: as plot suggestions by Devrient (1844) and *Oberon* librettist Helmine von Chézy (1846), and as a scenario by Johann Baptiste Rousseau (1844). As often happened, Mendelssohn was more enthusiastic about the idea than about Geibel's libretto, but instead of abandoning the project after receiving the first sketches and revisions in January 1846, he stepped back from taking an active part and entrusted all negotiations to his friend Devrient: "Everything will be fine for me if it is only truly and genuinely dramatic. Therefore I would like you and Geibel to do whatever is right and good."[40] Despite his dissatisfaction with the results – his main point of criticism being the lack of dramatic characterization – he was able to report to Geibel in August 1847: "I have since been very occupied with the work, and the first act has been put on paper almost completely."[41] The planned meeting with the poet in order to discuss changes in the first act and suggestions for the second never took place owing to Mendelssohn's illness and death in November 1847.

Despite its fragmentary state – or maybe even because of it, given the Romantic preference for torso works carrying the fingerprints of death – *Die Lorelei* has not totally been forgotten. The opera fragments were performed shortly after Mendelssohn's death in numerous countries in the original version and in English, French, Spanish, and Hungarian translations in subsequent decades. From the sketches,[42] it is obvious that the *Lorelei* was conceived as a through-composed opera in three acts, musically more complex than Marschner's works but less advanced than Wagner's music dramas. Mendelssohn was quite aware of the musical challenges, but was still confident as late as 1847 that he could turn into a successful opera composer eventually: "After I have written four or five operas, perhaps I shall make something good. But it is so difficult to find a subject."[43]

In addition to the three completed numbers from the work posthumously published as op. 98 (the Finale of Act 1, an "Ave Maria" for female chorus and a "Winzer-Chor"), Mendelssohn sketched the start of a duet for Act 1 scene 2, and most of the music for scene 7, including a jubilant choral march and a quartet. This quartet ("O unglückselig Wiederseh'n") performs an identical dramatic function, at a similar place in the plot, to the famous "Welch Geheimnis" quartet from Act 1 of Auber's *La muette de Portici*, a model that could not have been far in the back of Geibel's mind (even if Mendelssohn's music contains little or nothing of Auber). Distant echoes of Samiel and the Wolf's Glen from *Der Freischütz* can be heard in the most extensive section of music that Mendelssohn completed (the Finale of Act 1). Its rushing chromatic scales in the flutes and piccolos in the introduction and furious trilled figures in the strings for the chorus of water-spirits ("Auf feuchten Flügeln ziehn wir daher") cannot, however, disguise the essential lack of a demonic shudder in Mendelssohn's music.[44] Leonore's calls for vengeance are nevertheless composed with a fine command of dramatic climax, and an unexpected chromatic tinge in the harmony toward the end ("Rache gelobet ihr mir"; see Example 12.3) makes what would certainly have been a memorable, if static, closing curtain. The two other published numbers from the work, the contemplative "Ave Maria" and the rustic "vintners' chorus," are effective examples of stock types. The inner dominant pedal of the former was a notable feature of "Wenn die Abendglocken

Example 12.3 *Die Lorelei*, final passage of Finale of Act I

läuten" from *Die Heimkehr aus der Fremde*, and the unpublished march intended for Act 3 scene 7, though worked out with greater harmonic subtlety, is reminiscent of the wedding march from *Die Hochzeit des Camacho*. Both are a striking reminder of how little the stylistic elements of Mendelssohn's approach had changed in the previous nearly two decades.

It remains a matter of speculation whether Mendelssohn would have completed *Die Lorelei*, and the lack of concrete performance venues or dates raises doubts. However, in addition to feeling obliged to Geibel, Mendelssohn was well advanced with the composition and had never before abandoned a work on which he had progressed this far. Also, he approved whole-heartedly of the German and folk-like character of the subject matter, though it did not, strictly speaking, adhere to his moral standards. In fact, *Die Lorelei* ironically appears to be just the type of opera that the fastidious Mendelssohn spent two decades refusing to compose: a pseudo-legend with its fair share of magic and horror elements (like the rejected *Hans Heiling*), and without a notable ethical quality to the plot. When, at the climax of the work, the heroine lures the hero to a watery death in the Rhine (a fate shared by at least one other character in an early draft of the libretto), the uplifting morality of the plot is difficult to discern. One might, however, argue that even if hardly admirable, the heroine's actions are at least not "vulgar," like Meyerbeer's offensively disrobing nuns.

Considering the amount of time he devoted to opera projects, Mendelssohn must have had good reasons for being unable to proceed with any idea apart from *Die Lorelei*. One of his complaints, his supposed lack of time, is very telling about his priorities: Mendelssohn often claimed that he postponed working on operas in favor of instrumental or sacred works, an argument that he rarely used with compositions in other genres and that therefore seems to be an excuse. More serious was his concern for the quality of the libretto material. Often, Mendelssohn rejected libretto ideas on the ground that they did not meet his structural expectations, the most frequent criticism being the lack of dramatic interest. He was not alone in deploring these deficiencies, which can be attributed to the catastrophic libretto situation in Germany at the time – a situation generally acknowledged by writers and composers alike. However, if one had, in addition to this obstacle, a strong aversion to the practical difficulties and compromises necessary for a successful theater production, together with ambitions to provide a weighty contribution to German national opera (preferably with a female main protagonist), one was effectively engaged in a search for the impossible: a German historical event or legend of noble, educational, and worthy character with a dramatic plot lending itself to stage performance, but with no superficial stage effects or morally objectionable parts (not even dancing nuns, and certainly no Siegmund and Sieglinde).[45] Mendelssohn eventually found two subjects approaching his ideal libretto, but unfortunately they were neither operatic in nature nor German in origin, namely the biblical story of the prophet Elijah and the Greek tragedy *Antigone*.

Successful dramatic compositions: Mendelssohn's incidental works (and oratorios)

Since oratorio and opera are so closely related in regard to resources, Mendelssohn's contemporaries often seemed to mix these genres, possibly hoping for someone to follow Handel's model in both England and Germany. Many, including the critic Eduard Krüger (in his essay "On Contemporary Opera" in the *Neue Zeitschrift für Musik* 1840), expected Mendelssohn's difficulties with writing opera to abate once his first oratorio had been successfully completed and performed – as if the writing of *St. Paul* had been a compositional exercise in large forms: "May heaven and the muses grant that this wonderful talent [i.e., Mendelssohn's] should be led from the field of oratorio, where it is not completely at home, to opera!"[46] These expectations even increased with *Elijah* – much more dramatic in plot and musical realization – and culminated, for the lack of a "proper" opera, in staged performances of *Elijah* itself after Mendelssohn's death.[47] Even more closely related to the requirements of opera composition were Mendelssohn's achievements in the area of incidental music.

Although Mendelssohn had the opportunity to contribute incidental music during his tenure in Düsseldorf (to Immermann's "Vorspiel" *Kurfürst Wilhelm im Theater* for the inauguration of the theater in 1834,[48] as well as his tragedies *Alexis* and *Andreas Hofer* and Calderon de la Barca's *The Steadfast Prince*) and in Leipzig (for a production of Victor Hugo's *Ruy Blas*), this type of composition remained a side-line of his career until he was summoned to Berlin by the king. Neither the Düsseldorf nor Leipzig musical contributions to staged dramas required any radical thought about their form and function – specific pieces were demanded, and Mendelssohn delivered the requested overtures, choruses, and marches. This was to change in the Prussian capital.

After Friedrich Wilhelm IV had ascended to the throne in 1840, one of his immediate actions was to surround himself with Germany's leading intellectuals and the finest works of culture of both ancient and modern periods. Among his new appointees was the aged poet Ludwig Tieck, who, as the king's resident reader, inspired the idea of restaging some masterpieces of dramatic writing, most prominently Greek and Shakespearean dramas. The king's choice of court composers fell on Wilhelm Taubert, Meyerbeer, and Mendelssohn – the last only hesitantly falling into line. In addition to being put in charge of church music and the creation of a conservatory under rather ambiguous terms, Mendelssohn provided (in collaboration with Tieck) music for performances of Sophocles' *Antigone* (1841), Shakespeare's *A Midsummer Night's Dream* (1843), Sophocles' *Oedipus in Colonos*, and Racine's *Athalie* (1844–45) – all hybrids of opera and spoken drama.

The first of the Berlin staging projects, *Antigone*, was based on Donner's strict translation of 1839 and supervised by the philologist August Boeckh. Having studied Greek himself, Mendelssohn was drawn to creating music for the ancient tragedy that many critics thought came closest to an ideal drama. Among them was the philosopher Hegel, whose university lectures Mendelssohn had attended: "Of all the masterpieces of the classical and modern world – and I know nearly all of them and you should and can – the *Antigone* seems to me to be the most magnificent and satisfying work of art of this kind."[49]

A difficult task awaited Mendelssohn: With the only restriction that a choir of sixteen male singers (as in Sophocles' time) was to be part of the production, he had to decide how exactly to recreate and revive Greek drama musically, since a reconstruction of the ancient music was impossible. Any attempt to imitate ancient Greek instrumentation or layout, to provide strict mimesis of textual prosody in music, etc., was abandoned early in the process. In addition to using a full Romantic orchestra plus harp, Mendelssohn even added – straying far from ancient models – an orchestral introduction in an attempt to "comprehend the spirit of antiquity through modern means of expression."[50] By reflecting the play's emotions in the music (his usual approach to vocal composition), Mendelssohn himself became a commentator on the text, thus fulfilling a function similar to that of the ancient Greek chorus. After having made these principal decisions and adjusting the text to his needs, Mendelssohn completed the composition within eleven days. Despite his initial skepticism about the project and performance context, he was so impressed by the play that he even forgot about the linguistic difficulties:

> The wonderful, natural poem made a deeper, more powerful impression
> than anyone could have dreamt of. It gave me an overwhelming enjoyment
> I will never forget. Although the rather clumsy words cause no end of
> trouble, the moods and verse rhythms are everywhere so genuinely musical
> that you don't have to think of the individual words and only have to
> compose those moods and rhythms; then the chorus is done.[51]

His decision to focus on structural aspects, such as poetic rhythm, declamatory gestures, and the strophic structure of the choir parts instead of experimenting with Greek scales and instruments contributed to a lively, approachable, and tremendously successful work. Some critics went so far as to proclaim: "German music has been enriched by a new genre: The choruses of Greek tragedy have found their composer in Mendelssohn."[52] After the premiere in Sans Souci and before it was given in the Berlin Schauspielhaus, the first publicly accessible production took place in Leipzig on 5 March 1842. It was also staged in Paris and London (forty-five times between 2 January and 21 February 1845) and caused both a vivid discussion among scholars and an "antiquity hype" among the public.

Owing to the success of *Antigone*, Mendelssohn was asked in 1845 to provide music for Aeschylus' *Eumenides*, but was unwilling to comply, as subsequently was Meyerbeer. Mendelssohn's written offer to resign from his post, after his refusal was met with disapproval, reveals another dramatic project that never saw the light of day. Asking the king to acknowledge his achievements, he wrote: "By requesting your Excellency to communicate this to his Majesty, I also ask you to mention three of my compositions that upon order of his Majesty lie ready for similar performances, namely Sophocles' *Oedipus at Colonos*, Racine's *Athalie* and Sophocles' *King Oedipus*."[53] Strangely, no signs are to be found of the music for the last, suggesting that it only existed in Mendelssohn's head.

Mendelssohn's incidental music for Sophocles' *Antigone* and *Oedipus at Colonus* marks a genuinely new departure within his output. His classical education well equipped him to enter into the antique world of Sophocles' dramas by direct acquaintance with the verse rhythms of the original Greek.[54] It is the attempt to imitate these verse rhythms – in both the German translation and the music – that give Mendelssohn's work its unique flavor. One fortunate consequence of this approach is that it tends to demand irregularity of phrase length, and of accent within phrases, thus avoiding the over-reliance on symmetrical four-bar phrases for which Mendelssohn has often been criticized. The rewards of this are strikingly obvious even in the first chorus of *Antigone*, "Strahl des Helios, schönstes Licht," where the opening four-bar phrase is followed by an imaginatively varied sequence of great plasticity in both rhythm and meter. A similar flexibility illuminates the setting of Sophocles' famous hymn to love, "O Eros, Allsieger im Kampf," in which the initial two, non-symmetrical, four-bar phrases are followed by a remarkably limpid five-bar continuation ending with a subtle dissonance at "Wangen webet." In this music Mendelssohn most closely approaches the freedom of declamation of Berlioz, or even the mature Wagner, although he would no doubt have deprecated either comparison.

In the case of the incidental music to Shakespeare's *A Midsummer Night's Dream*, there were no conceptual challenges to be overcome. The composer picked up in 1842 where he had left off in 1826 with his precocious overture, originally conceived as a concert piece, but now handy for this purpose as well. Many of the themes and motives of the overture characterized Shakespeare's protagonists so aptly that they could be used in the incidental music. Mendelssohn composed thirteen new numbers for the play, including four instrumental intermezzi designed to set the mood for upcoming events between acts. The famous and exquisite Nocturne was supposed to function as a premature sleeping song for the characters, just as the wedding march foreshadows the upcoming triple wedding ceremony of the final act. Mendelssohn's original idea to create through his music a continuous play without act divisions was disapproved by Tieck. Instead, Tieck partitioned the work into three acts, with the result that two intermezzi, the Nocturne and the Intermezzo no. 5, had to be played – against the composer's wishes – with the curtain up.

The perhaps excessive fame of the celebrated wedding march should not blind us to the originality of the off-key opening of the melody, which begins as if in E minor before turning to C, but it is when the march reappears in no. 12, as a prelude to the finale, that this harmonic stroke takes its most imaginative turn. As the wedding procession departs and the stage lights darken, Puck reappears on the scene. The score here mirrors perfectly the shift from the human to the fairy world – the wedding march grows ever more quiet, but at the last repeat of the opening phrase the harmony remains in E minor, the key of Mendelssohn's fairyland, as elfin music steals into the upper strings, superimposed over the last two notes of wedding celebration. The transition is as subtle as it is magical. The whole is one of Mendelssohn's masterpieces, and certainly among the finest incidental music ever written. The premiere was given on 14 October 1842 in Sans Souci with performances following on 18–21 October in the Königliches Schauspielhaus in Berlin, both to an enthusiastic audience.

Although *Athalie*, composed in England in 1844, also met with initial audience approval, it did not secure any lasting reputation, possibly owing – in addition to the flowery language – to the lack of true dramatic momentum "of classical French tragedy that knows neither gripping dramatic accents nor deep self-absorption in lyrical moods."[55] The first version for female voices and piano accompaniment was followed by a second version for mixed choir and orchestra in 1845. The work stands mid-way between the bold austerity of Mendelssohn's music to Sophocles' tragedies and the unparalleled charm of his music to *A Midsummer Night's Dream*. Setting a translation of Racine's Alexandrine verse gave Mendelssohn similar metrical constraints to those of the Greek plays, yet the French drama also provided an opportunity for at least one independent and fully developed orchestral movement. This number, the "War March of the Priests," soon became a favorite in nineteenth- and early twentieth-century orchestral concerts and was removed from its original context almost as frequently as the wedding march from *A Midsummer Night's Dream* (although obviously not for similar ceremonial reasons, turbulent priests being rarer than weddings).

Dream versus reality

One might think that as a result of the success and fame of the incidental works, Mendelssohn would have reconsidered his compositional destiny. Quite the contrary was the case, as he wrote to Kinkel in 1843: "Now, a really nice, fresh, lively opera text has been my most eager wish. I think I could set nothing in this world to music half as well as this."[56] Now that he had succeeded on the stage, these ambitions were fostered by the unexpected consequence that he was offered even more opera libretti (including one by Tieck). However, the transition from incidental music to opera was not made easily, maybe because the former had some important advantages: The works were composed on direct orders from the king, who also supplied set performance contexts, strict timelines, experienced colleagues, and concrete requests – a set-up that in its convenience reminds us of Mendelssohn's family home. In addition, since the main emphasis of the performances was on the literary drama, pressure was taken off the composer, who could rely on the unquestionable quality of the texts. Nevertheless, close as these works may have come to the stage success he dreamt of, they were not the operas that he wanted to write and that the public keenly awaited, even if all this stage experience boded well for an eventual operatic success. Had Mendelssohn lived a little longer, that success might well have come with *Die Lorelei*.

PART FOUR

Reception and performance

13 Mendelssohn received

JOHN MICHAEL COOPER

There can be little doubt that Mendelssohn's star, just fifty years ago threat-ened with obscurity, is again on the rise: his works are more prominently rep-resented in musical life than at any time since the mid-nineteenth century, and the scholarly literature concerning him is more voluminous and more diversified than ever. The recrudescence becomes all the more remarkable if we consider the extraordinary difficulties it has faced – for since the 1850s Mendelssohn's critical reception has centered on ideologically extreme positions.[1] For the last decade of his life he stood at the center of European musical culture and was widely hailed as the personification of modernity, but by the mid-twentieth century his music was portrayed as having been archaic and epigonic even in its own time. Some critiques amounted to lit-tle more than ludicrous lionization, portrayals of Mendelssohn as a musical messiah whose death had robbed the musical world of its only real prospect for future salvation from the turmoils of the present; others descended rapidly into equally vapid dismissals, vitriolic tropes on the political con-troversies of the day that found in Mendelssohn the epitome of many issues that cried out for drastic reform. Mendelssohn was granted little role in the great narrative of nineteenth-century music history as it was written by these self-styled progressives, and many musicians and other music-lovers fell prey to that assessment even after the ideological underpinnings from which it originally derived had fallen from favor. In a word, the verdict was retained even though its evidentiary foundations and reasoning had been renounced.

A growing general awareness of the now-questionable sources of the conventional devaluations of Mendelssohn's music and a fascina-tion with the vacillations in his reception history have propelled a resur-gence of research concerning the composer. Despite considerable dif-ficulties, the past few decades have witnessed great strides, identifying the themes and issues that produced the contradictions, exploring their motives, and revisiting the evidence – much of which has become gen-erally accessible only recently – in order to arrive at fresh perspectives.[2] The following remarks offer a historically organized overview of these developments.

Gradus ad Parnassum: 1825–1847

Writings contemporary to Mendelssohn's ascent to the pinnacle of Euro-pean musical life articulated many of the ideas for which he continues to be celebrated today. The earliest known public mention, published in the Leipzig *Allgemeine musikalische Zeitung* in 1818, offered little detail, men-tioning only his age, parentage, and teacher's name[3] – but shortly thereafter he garnered increasing recognition and increasingly impressive reviews as a composer, conductor, and pianist. A performance of the *Midsummer Night's Dream* Overture – the work that Thomas Grey has called "the quintessen-tial Mendelssohnian miracle"[4] – in Stettin on 20 February 1827 attracted some public attention.[5] Besides this, however, the concert is also significant because it featured two works by the prodigy Mendelssohn (the overture and the A♭ major Double Piano Concerto) on the same program with the Ninth Symphony of Beethoven – the first performance in Northern Europe of a controversial masterpiece by the German-speaking countries' undis-puted musical leader. If Mendelssohn's reputation had up to this point been cultivated primarily in private circles, the door was now open for him to step onto the public stage.

Mendelssohn eagerly seized the opportunity to be an active figure in public musical life, and the public overwhelmingly embraced him. Early in 1828 the young composer received a prestigious commission to pro-vide the music for the Berlin festivities commemorating the tricentennial of the death of Albrecht Dürer[6], and in the spring of 1829 his Berlin perfor-mances of Bach's *St. Matthew Passion* again brought him into the interna-tional spotlight.[7] These performances launched the first of Mendelssohn's international public successes as he ventured to England, where he offered London's musical public a vivid glimpse of his talents as both performer and composer, as well as of his personal dynamism.

Although Mendelssohn's bid for the directorship of the Berlin Sing-akademie in 1832–33 was unsuccessful (almost certainly in part for anti-Semitic reasons),[8] he quickly bounced back. During his two-year tenure as Municipal Music Director of Düsseldorf his fame grew to such an extent that early in 1835 he was invited to take the helm of the Gewandhaus Orchestra in Leipzig, one of the continent's finest orchestras. His increasing involvement with ambitious cultural projects over the course of the 1830s and 1840s reflected his growing public acclaim. In addition to directing numerous music festivals around Europe he was appointed General Music Director for the court of the new Prussian king, Friedrich Wilhelm IV, and charged with implementing an ambitious series of liturgical and musical reforms.[9] He also spearheaded the founding of the German-speaking countries' first conservatory of music and served as *de facto* director of that institution.[10]

Clearly, Mendelssohn had established a strong connection with the needs, ideas, and ideals of contemporary Europe.

Contemporary biographies and notices consistently mention the same attributes in Mendelssohn: his high expectations as composer and educator, his extraordinary gifts as a performer, his brilliance as an advocate for the recovered treasures of the musical past, his unstinting artistic and personal integrity, and – perhaps surprisingly, from a latter-day perspective – his modernity, both as composer and as figure in public musical life. A little-known biographical notice published in *The Musical Gem* (London) late in 1833 reflects the hopes the musical world vested in him. Introducing the 24-year-old composer as one "whose claim to be ranked among the few great composers now living is undisputed, and from whose future exertions we may reasonably hope to see the limits of the art extended," the anonymous author summarizes Mendelssohn's education, draws attention to his private musical accomplishments (specifically, the youthful operas), and then discusses some of the events and works on which his already impressive public acclaim is based: the production of *Die Hochzeit des Camacho*, the Stettin performance of the *Midsummer Night's Dream* Overture, the music for the Dürer celebrations, and his London triumphs from 1829 and earlier in 1833.[11] The final paragraph observes that "as a pianoforte player M. Mendelssohn is surpassed by none in command of the instrument, in rapidity and brilliancy of execution: but we dwell less on his abilities in this department of the art . . . because his talents as a composer have placed him in a much more elevated situation than a mere performer can ever hope to attain."[12]

These remarks, drawing on unofficial as well as public sources of information,[13] bespeak a sense of excitement at Mendelssohn's prodigious and multifaceted accomplishments and his meteoric rise to international renown. But the essay is also noteworthy for its evident lack of concern for the composer's religious background and confession. Except for a footnote mentioning that "the name of Bartholdy was added to his patronymic at the request of a relation" and a statement that Felix was the "grandson of the famous Jewish philosopher and elegant writer of the last century, Moses Mendelssohn,"[14] there is no reference to his Jewish background. Indeed, the casualness of the following paragraph's statement that "about the same period [as the premiere of *Die Hochzeit des Camacho*] he also set some of Luther's Hymns, and composed an *Ave*" suggests that the author attached little significance to the composer's religious heritage or his conversion to Christianity.[15]

Another noteworthy contemporary life-and-works account was published by Johann Peter Lyser (1804–70), a member of Schumann's *Davidsbündler*, in the *Allgemeine Wiener Musik-Zeitung* in December 1842.[16]

Like most commentators, Lyser makes much of the composer's dramatic entry onto the European musical stage, emphasizing his brilliance, his youth, and his promise for future greatness. Yet his remarks also articulate two further themes in the contemporary appreciation of Mendelssohn: his proclivities for implicitly challenging generic conventions, and the standards of integrity that enabled him to tower over other contemporary musical celebrities.

Lyser's techniques for making these points are worthy of comment here. After explaining that he knows the composer not only as "the master of his art," but also as a friend who openly shares with him his feelings and thoughts even though the two do not always agree, he asserts that Mendelssohn has taken an artistic path diametrically opposite that chosen by his enormously successful contemporary Meyerbeer. Lyser reports that whereas Meyerbeer's opponents charge that he offers everything for the sake of effect, Meyerbeer's advocates argue that Mendelssohn avoids effect too strenuously.[17] Although Lyser finds both criticisms too strong, he suggests that Mendelssohn's unflinching artistic integrity was what had made *St. Paul* successful in the New World as well as Europe.

Yet Lyser also finds that after an examination of the score of *St. Paul* – particularly the recitatives – it seems to him "as if the work is more a creation born of an enthusiastic will to meet its challenges than a free outpouring of the soul reveling in its art"[18] – and this observation leads him to a discussion of the works that he considers most indicative of that faculty: the *Lieder ohne Worte*. Together with the concert overtures, these "free outpourings" had established Mendelssohn as "head of the new Romantic school."[19] He further emphasizes the importance of Mendelssohn's mastery of sacred as well as secular music. Perhaps most interestingly, Lyser sees this proclivity for stylistic diversity as accountable for Mendelssohn's active engagement of musical styles of the past, and argues that it was precisely this engagement, together with his fluency in modern musical style and his musical integrity, that established Mendelssohn's position at the forefront of Romanticism.

Robert Schumann's criticisms reflect similar views, especially in their emphasis on both Mendelssohn's modernity and his engagement of the musical past.[20] Schumann, too, emphasizes Mendelssohn's integrity by contrasting his works (specifically *St. Paul*) with those of Meyerbeer: the two composers could hardly be more different, Schumann asserts, for he is at pains to find any merit at all in *Les Huguenots* and to find any substantive problems in *St. Paul*; his review closes with the observation that "*his* [Mendelssohn's] road leads to happiness; the other, to evil."[21] Equally useful are Schumann's comments on Mendelssohn's D minor Piano Trio op. 49 – the first important work in that genre since the great trios of Beethoven and Schubert. For Schumann, op. 49 revealed Mendelssohn not only as a composer who had succeeded in tackling the challenges of that genre, but also as the composer who had "risen to such heights that we can indeed say that he is the Mozart of the nineteenth century; the most brilliant among musicians; the one who has most clearly recognized the contradictions of the age, and the first to reconcile them."[22] And in his posthumously published draft for a memoir of Mendelssohn, Schumann celebrated not only his colleague's manifold musical gifts, but also his artistic integrity: "His judgment in musical matters, especially concerning compositions – the finest and most astute that one could ever imagine . . . [His] self-criticism [was] the strictest and most conscientious that I have ever seen in a musician."[23]

Yet Schumann and Lyser go beyond describing Mendelssohn as merely the leading composer of the present; they assign him a lasting position in the history of music. Despite his youth, both observe, he has already contributed immeasurably to the progress of the art – despite (or perhaps because of) his cultivation of forms, genres, and styles from the musical past. Schumann suggests that Mendelssohn's D minor Piano Trio had resuscitated its genre, and that while Mendelssohn was "the Mozart of the nineteenth century," he also would "not be the last artist; this new Mozart will be followed by a new Beethoven, who perhaps has already been born."[24]

It is worth noting that Lyser, Schumann, and other contemporary enthusiasts also offer constructive criticisms for Mendelssohn: his support came from judicious critics, not slavish hangers-on. His fame was hard-won, the product of sustained and diligent efforts to better society through music – a cultural endeavor that Leon Botstein has termed "the Mendelssohnian project"[25] – and an unremitting self-critical faculty that led him to withhold from print the vast majority of his works. Indeed, Mendelssohn's contemporary acclaim becomes all the more remarkable when one considers that the works released in print during the composer's lifetime embrace only seventy-two numbered *opera* and an additional twenty-four minor publications – this out of a corpus of several hundred compositions. Nor did Mendelssohn's extraordinary success rest on the uncritical judgments of the masses, for even his greatest advocates recognized that he, like everyone in those troubled times, faced challenges. Nevertheless, by the end of his life he was the single most influential composer, performer, and pedagogue in European musical life. With his death, those sympathetic to his cause felt they had lost their standard-bearer. They faced a crisis whose dimensions would not become fully evident for nearly a century.

Divergences, 1847–1875

The success of the "Mendelssohnian project" during the composer's lifetime was both a blessing and a curse in the years after his death. Those who viewed him as a bastion of integrity and champion of musical progress increasingly spoke and wrote of him as a fallen hero, bemoaning the loss of their leader. With the exception of Robert Schumann, whose style in the late 1840s and early 1850s is substantively indebted to Mendelssohn,[26] the composer's followers were unable to sustain their hero's cultural project. And at least partly in response to the musical world's clamoring to hear more of the voice of which it had been deprived, his heirs began to publish many of the works left unpublished at his death. Despite the laudable intention of perpetuating the presence of Mendelssohn's voice in cultural discourse, however, the composer probably would have viewed this development with some dismay. After all, the posthumously published compositions included not only late works that he likely would have published had he lived even one more year (masterpieces such as *Lauda Sion* and the F minor String Quartet), but also many that he had withheld from publication (including, for example, all of the *a cappella* sacred music along with the "Reformation" and "Italian" Symphonies). Collectively, these publications infused Mendelssohn's public persona with dimensions that he had elected not to disseminate in print.

On the other hand, the proximity of Mendelssohn's death to the wave of revolutions that swept the continent in 1848, with the explicit goal of overturning the culture in which he had ascended to the pinnacle of success, presented his detractors with a genuine opportunity. Dissenting voices now offered a variety of arguments to diminish his significance for post-revolutionary culture and contravene the growing Mendelssohn cult.[27] The most notorious of these arguments is, of course, the anti-Semitic critique represented in Wagner's 1850 essay on "Jewry in Music."[28] In general, this critique argues that Mendelssohn (like Meyerbeer, with whom Mendelssohn's advocates had contrasted him so adamantly) was incapable of true musical greatness because of his Jewish heritage; that he therefore could not have contributed to musical progress; and that his ascent to power and political prestige had been symptomatic of Restoration culture's intrinsic flaccidity, which had made most of society's institutions and values susceptible to the pernicious superficialities of Jewry.

It is worth noting, however, that this reasoning derived from an understanding of Germanness and Jewishness that was defined primarily neither by political or geographic criteria (for these were necessarily meaningless to German speakers who felt a sense of national unity before 1871) nor by bloodlines, as modern readers might assume. Rather, in the 1850s Jewishness (like Germanness, Italian-ness, and Gypsydom) was defined first of all by language, culture, and religion. Thus Wagner, in explaining "the involuntary repellence that the nature and personality of the Jews possesses for us, so as to vindicate that instinctive dislike which we plainly recognize as stronger and more overpowering than our *conscious* zeal to rid ourselves thereof"[29] and documenting "the be-Jewing of modern art" (*Verjüdung der modernen Kunst*),[30] discusses his Jews' physical appearance briefly but speaks at great length about Jewish speech, song, and religion: "[i]ncomparably more important – yes, decisive – is the significance of the effect that the Jew exerts on us through his *speech* [emphasis Wagner's]."[31] Because Wagner's Jews speak European languages "merely as learned," they are necessarily incapable of expressing themselves "idiomatically, independently, and confortably [sic] to [their] nature."[32] Moreover, because Wagner's community of Jewry "stood outside the pale of any [European] community, stood solitarily with [its] Jehovah in a splintered, soilless stock, to which all self-sprung evolution must stay denied, just as even the peculiar (Hebraïc) language of that stock has been preserved for him merely as a thing defunct,"[33] that community had by definition "taken no part in the development" of European art and was capable only of aping and mimicking the poetic arts of expression.[34] Such self-expression as "the cultured Jew" (*der gebildete Jude*) could muster would, of necessity, be artistically repugnant – for it would express the voice of "the most heartless of all human beings" (*der herzloseste aller Menschen*).[35]

Similar views are pronounced in the book *Sur les Bohémiens et de leur musique en Hongrie*, attributed to Franz Liszt at its first publication in 1859 (before Wagner had publicly acknowledged authorship of "Das Judenthum").[36] Taken as a whole, this monograph is a celebration of the beauties and artistic wonders of the native musical tongue of the Romani Gypsies – an idiom closely associated with Liszt's fame.[37] Yet the treatise also extensively discusses the Jews and their music (as Liszt thought he understood it, of course), attempting to explain why, despite certain obvious parallels between Gypsies and Jews, the music of the Gypsies was noble, pure, and suffused with true artistic beauty, while that of the Jews was utterly incapable of rising to the status of art. Here, too, the blame is assigned to the Jews' culture, religion, and language. The Gypsies, Liszt asserts, were able to express themselves truly and deeply in music because of their language, and because their historical plight had led them to pour their sorrows, joys, and other emotions into a musical idiom that was as much their own as the Magyar language was. The Jews, by contrast, were by nature and at the mandate of their religion a people who shunned self-expression. They had exerted a disconcertingly powerful presence in European culture and had even deceived some into believing that their art – especially their music – was brilliant. Yet the music of Liszt's Jews could never aspire to the status of art, for it was not produced from the inspired impulse of creation; it was only imitation:[38]

> They [the Jews] have also cultivated art to the point of invading it. They have taken possession of all the genres, and have had some brilliant success stories in the realm of execution as in that of composition. As virtuosos and as authors, their successes have been just; for they have handled form marvellously.

Yet

> They have been able to exercise and practice art, but they have never known how to *create* art. Never having been able to break free of the seal of a silence that is religious and respectful for themselves, [these being] all the movements of their hearts, how should they have learned how to confide these to art? . . . The Israelites have not been able to invent new styles, for they have never sung of their own feelings. Their enduring discretion . . . [and] their religion of silence have never permitted them to express anything of the impulses of *their* souls, to sing of the sufferings of *their* hearts, to recount the pulsing of *their* passions, of *their* loves and hates, in that language of the ideal.[39]

These and other writings from the 1850s reveal that the anti-Semitic reception that diminished Mendelssohn's cultural authority in that crucial decade stemmed directly from cultural and aesthetic concerns whose centrality to issues of musical integrity is still largely accepted: the issues of expression, communication, and social identity. In asserting Mendelssohn's Jewishness as a determinant of his artistic character, Liszt, Wagner, and others impugned the very things that his earlier advocates had considered unquestionable: his deeply felt expression and his artistic integrity. Thus in Wagner's view, no matter how fluent Mendelssohn may have become in the musical idioms of "our" society, his music had to take pathetic recourse to the now-sullied "travesty" of the "sense-and-sound-confounding gurgle, yodel, and cackle" of Jewish music.[40] Mendelssohn had

> shown that a Jew may have the amplest store of specific talents, may have the finest and most varied education, the highest and most sensitive sense of honor – yet even with the aid of all these advantages be unable to call forth in us even once that deep effect that takes hold of our heart and soul, an effect which we await from music because we know her capable thereof.[41]

If one accepted this line of reasoning – and many did – then the celebrated depth of expression and experience in Mendelssohn's music must have been an illusion, the product of superficialities and contrivances. His obviously enormous spheres of influence must have reflected the naivety of a pre-revolutionary society that had been willfully duped out of its *Volk*-rooted legitimate institutions. Most importantly, his position in music – the art that, of all arts, was unquestionably rooted in self-expression – was necessarily an ephemeral and marginal one.

Such anti-Semitic ideologies became all the more influential because they went hand in hand with the ascendance of a substantially different view of the nature and mechanisms of historical processes. The first half of the nineteenth century was generally dominated by a historical model that emphasized constant and multidimensional dialectical processes as the agents of progress. Progress (generally construed to mean increased sophistication, complexity, and size) was generated through the historically mandated synthesis of intrinsically antithetical forces, ideas, persons, styles etc. The influence of this view is reflected in Schumann's, Lyser's, and others' emphasis on Mendelssohn's modernity in the context of discussions that emphasize his use of earlier musical forms, genres, and styles. And Mendelssohn's own intellectual pedigree – he was a student of Hegel and Goethe (for whom Hegel's ideas on history were central) – suggests that he would naturally harbor such a view. Moreover, such a proposition certainly would be consistent with Mendelssohn's frequent contraposing of conspicuously archaic and conspicuously modern musical styles – an aspect of his idiom that has generated considerable controversy.[42]

Increasingly after the mid-1840s, however, a view of historical processes which emphasized modernity and granted little role to any reference to the past was manifest in writings on music.[43] For purposes of this discussion, the most important representative of these views was Schumann's successor as editor of the *Neue Zeitschrift*: Franz Brendel. A philosopher and historian who was a disciple of Hegel, Brendel maintained much of Hegel's historical doctrine while taking it one step further in such a fashion as to deeply alter its ramifications.[44] While dialectics remained central to this modern view of historical processes, those processes themselves were now conceived as unilinear and unidirectional – and the compositional cultivation of earlier musical styles countermanded historical progress. As Brendel put it in his influential *Geschichte der Musik in Italien, Deutschland und Frankreich*, first published in 1851, "in the history of the spirit all that is decisive is newness, originality; everything else is of subordinate importance . . . Those composers who unconditionally ally themselves with the old masters do not work for progress, for a further development of the art."[45] In this view, any overt cultivation of forms, genres, or styles associated with the musical past was suspect, and composers who employed those historically retrospective idioms as vigorously as Mendelssohn did were guilty, at the very least, of not having been sufficiently committed to steady and unconditional musical progress.

This view of historical processes, in turn, engendered an increasingly teleological perspective on musical history: the great narrative was to be understood as a series of successive eras, each of which represented progress that, while predicated on the ideas and accomplishments of earlier eras, represented a further evolutionary development (i.e., an improvement) on that era. Here, too, the presence of influences from earlier musical-stylistic eras – in the opinions of Lyser and Schumann, an essential aspect of Mendelssohn's advancement of music – now became a liability rather than an asset. A composer whose works were substantively infused with ideas, styles, forms, genres, or values of the Baroque or Classical eras necessarily was less thoroughly "Romantic" (and hence less influential in the progress of musical history) than were other composers who did not cultivate those elements.

This change in historiographic values is reflected in countless mid-century assessments of Mendelssohn's life, works, and historical significance. Not only were many of the stylistic features that previously had contributed to his historical import now considered liabilities, but the historiographic methodology of musical form and genre was undergoing profound change. The development of Wagner's thought in his criticisms of Mendelssohn reflects precisely this change in values. Wagner was probably in the minority when he sarcastically lamented that "the whole of Germany lays bare its heart to the musical gospel according to Felix Mendelssohn" in 1841,[46] but in post-revolutionary Europe such accounts were more acceptable. In 1851, in constructing a history of music that proceeded from Mozart through Beethoven to himself, he could overtly fault Mendelssohn for the "perfection" of his music and "lift him off his quilted piano-bench."[47] By 1869 he was safely able to blame him for an entire culture of conducting and musical interpretation that possessed "polish" (*Gebildetheit*) but no "culture" (*Bildung*),[48] and another decade later he blamed his icon of polished unculturedness for the proliferation of an entire culture of "cold-blooded recklessness" (*kaltblütige Unbesonnenheit*) in composition "resembling that old general of Frederick the Great who sang whatever was set before him to the tune of the Dessauer March."[49]

The dilemma is clear: Mendelssohn had posthumously become the whipping-boy of his age, a figure who, for post-revolutionary Europe, personified the failings of the *Vormärz*. He suffered because of his cultivation of styles and forms associated with earlier composers. He was criticized because he excelled in the domain of religious music – a domain of composition that was the rightful province of earlier eras. And despite having published but little of his sacred music, he was increasingly known as a composer of church music as his heirs considerably augmented the quantity of works in those genres.[50] His detractors in the 1850s and afterward made much of his failure to complete an opera in his maturity[51] – for Brendel and others of his historical persuasion, applying the classical categorization of poetry to the perceived laws of historical process, now held that the history of music had proceeded from the epic through the lyric to the dramatic, and that the last of these constituted the realm in which the next age of musical progress would be achieved.[52] Most importantly, Mendelssohn now epitomized not only the weaknesses and perversions to which all Jews, because of what Liszt, Wagner, Brendel, and others considered their cultural homelessness, were liable, but also the detrimental effects of Christian Europe's ostensibly gracious but naive attempt to assimilate Jewry.

Mendelssohn's early posthumous critical reception probably was not helped by the publication, in the 1860s and 1870s, of numerous self-serving memoirs and unreliable collections of letters, or by the generally uncritical adoption of material from these texts in numerous secondary studies.[53] After all, to those convinced of the imperative of progress as the new historians conceived it, such writings merely celebrated the failures of Restoration culture. Moreover, the tone and style of presentation of these collections too often smacked of nostalgia – and a supposed music-historical nostalgia was precisely the trait that Mendelssohn's later detractors most vehemently criticized in his music. These writings may have edified those who were generally sympathetic to Mendelssohn's ideals of ethically bound and societally universal music and musical institutions, and they certainly constituted invaluable starting points for later research – but they probably won few converts to their cause.

Between *Wissenschaft* and *Musikwissenschaft*: Mendelssohn's reception between 1875 and 1914

The completion in 1877 of the series of editions of Mendelssohn's collected works, edited by Julius Rietz and published by Breitkopf & Härtel, constituted another landmark in Mendelssohn's posthumous reception. Even though, as some quickly recognized, this series was neither complete nor true to the developing idea of a critical edition, it nevertheless offered a more comprehensive view of Mendelssohn's creative output than previously had been available. If used in tandem with the widely circulated editions of his letters, the numerous memoirs of his friends and colleagues, and the various life-and-works studies that had already appeared, the *Werke* seemed to meet the final prerequisite for a historically viable reassessment of a composer who had posthumously become extremely problematical.

That task, however, turned out to be more complicated than some might have hoped, since Mendelssohn's detractors and apologists now found themselves entrenched in ideological positions that were worlds apart. Now more than ever, analysts, critics, and historians were obsessed with the grand sweep of music history; now more than ever, most viewed that history as a tale of evolutionary progress that culminated in drama; and now more than ever, most were convinced that history was to be drawn as an end-weighted narrative of heroes and epigones: agents of progress who merited inclusion in the canon, and their followers.[54] Moreover, historians (proceeding from selected important late works of Beethoven)[55] now increasingly emphasized the importance of highly individualized and subjective self-expression rather than universalized communication. And perhaps most importantly, the comparatively new science of musicology (*Musikwissenschaft*) increasingly appropriated philosophical and methodological tenets from the natural sciences, formulating its arguments in terms of issues that lay at the core of those disciplines.

Most important among these issues was the supposed interrelationship between evolutionary advancement, race, and gender. The widespread acceptance of Darwin's theory of natural selection as the mechanism for evolutionary change, and of the comparatively new science of Mendelian genetics, together with general acceptance of contemporary scientific findings that white European males, untainted by oriental or other "inferior" blood-stocks, held the key to human progress,[56] seemed to corroborate the judgments of post-1848 critics who had portrayed Mendelssohn as an outsider to the true progressive causes in European music. As Marian Wilson Kimber has documented in a recent essay, long-standing prejudices concerning race and gender, aided by newly formulated scientific arguments, produced a new image of Mendelssohn in the last decades of the nineteenth century.[57]

Most of these changes in values marked a reversal from those of the culture of the *Vormärz*. Mendelssohn's views on the responsibilities of the musician as a public figure, and his emphasis on music's function as an art of universal but consummately subjective communication ran counter to ideologies asserting that music's proper function was to express each composer's individual personality, even at the risk of not being comprehensible to the broader world. In these "modern" music-historical values, the musical ethic of universalized public communication and participation did not belong to Romanticism per se, but was an evolutionary hold-over from the values of the preceding music-historical era. Proximity to one's musical public, once a virtue and a means of shaping one's time, had become a liability.[58]

Thus Mendelssohn came to be almost universally condemned by scientific and musical scholarship in the early twentieth century. To those who sympathized with the views of his detractors, science now offered an explanation for what was already perceived as verity – the notion of his historical inconsequentiality. The criticisms of the *Zukunftsmusiker* who had succeeded Mendelssohn as champions of musical progress were verified by musicological applications of the techniques and findings of cutting-edge science. Consequently, the deprecatory verbiage of contemporary race-and gender-chauvinists began to pervade musicological assessments of Mendelssohn as well: the composer's putative renunciation of the path of progress after the mid-1830s was now explained by the pseudo-scientific assertion that all Jews, while capable of easy brilliance in their early years, were genetically doomed to recidivism later in life. And the mid-nineteenth-century view that Mendelssohn was a consummately "manly" figure began to give way to increasing charges of "effeminacy" and "Semitic softness," which, in a world in which white European men were the agents of progress, automatically placed him outside that progressive mainstream.[59]

Fortunately, not all were persuaded by these questionable verdicts. Between about 1880 and 1914 a dedicated community of scholars managed to pursue the matter of Mendelssohn scholarship with the same sort of rigor that was being devoted to other scholarly issues that were temporally or aesthetically remote from the musical mores of the late nineteenth century. Foremost was the great patron of English musical lexicography, George Grove, who conducted extensive research on the unpublished materials, contributed numerous articles on little-known and unknown compositions to contemporary English periodicals, and authored, in his own *Dictionary of Music and Musicians*, a Mendelssohn article that remains exemplary to this day.[60] By the centennial of Mendelssohn's birth these accomplishments included several other contributions: editions of Mendelssohn's correspondence with three of his closest friends and professional confidants, Ferdinand David, Karl Klingemann, and Ignaz Moscheles;[61] several smaller critical editions of previously unknown correspondence;[62] Alfred Dörffel's chronicle of the history of the Leipzig Gewandhaus Orchestra;[63] and, perhaps most importantly, a full-scale scholarly life-and-works study (based in no small part on Grove's article in the *Dictionary*) in German by Ernst Wolff.[64] These truly scholarly studies drew extensively on previously unpublished material and presented their material in a fashion that, while fundamentally sympathetic to Mendelssohn, was consistent with the developing ideals of source-critical musicological objectivity. They served as the starting point for a handful of devoted scholars during the stormy years of the early twentieth century.

Aus tiefer Not: 1914–1945

Despite some notable bright spots,[65] the early twentieth century was a particularly dismal period in Mendelssohn's already controversy-plagued reception history. With the corpus of regularly performed works reduced to the E minor Violin Concerto, the *Variations sérieuses*, and the *Midsummer Night's Dream* music, the heyday of Wagnerism and the sheer heat of the other ideological debates of early twentieth-century music left little room for scholarship concerning Mendelssohn – and such potential as may have existed was seriously damaged by rampant anti-Semitism, both in Germany and elsewhere. The anti-Semitism of the 1930s and 1940s was particularly destructive, however – for it permitted no discussion of the merit or lack thereof of any of Mendelssohn's music. Distressingly large sectors of the musical public accepted the notion that, as music composed by a Jew, Mendelssohn's works were intrinsically incapable of any merit but more than capable of seducing unsophisticated auditors into a destructive pleasure. And in the so-called Third Reich any recognition of any of this music would at the very least send the politically unacceptable message that Jews could be capable of great art.[66]

The resulting scenario is well known: in Nazi spheres of influence Mendelssohn's music was banned; books concerning him were burned and monuments destroyed; and he was systematically written out of musical history in a chillingly Orwellian fashion. To name but three examples: Julius Alf's chronicle of the early years of the Lower Rhine Music Festival – a festival with which Mendelssohn was involved continually during the last decade of his life – clearly refers to events, works, performances, and developments that stemmed from Mendelssohn, but consistently fails to acknowledge his role in these events.[67] Similarly (and more enduringly damaging for different reasons), Wolfgang Bötticher's seemingly authoritative biography of Robert Schumann, while drawing extensively on unpublished documents and offering much that remains valuable, not only duly identifies Mendelssohn and other composers with a Magen David, but also alters quotations from Mendelssohn and quotations from Schumann about Mendelssohn so as to reflect negatively on the Jewish composer.[68] Most notoriously, the period abounded with musicological treatises that explicitly updated the findings of Wagner, Liszt, and others in order to validate them through Nazi racial science.[69]

The collusion of some sectors of the musicological community in the Nazi anti-Mendelssohn campaign certainly represents a low point in the composer's posthumous reception, but other scholars also have a certain complicity in the mid-twentieth-century nadir of Mendelssohn scholarship, albeit without the anti-Semitic motivations of Nazi ideology. Alfred Einstein, for example, assigned Mendelssohn to an unenviable position in the teleology of musical style. Whereas Schubert was "the romantic classic" (i.e., forward-looking for his day) Mendelssohn was "the romantic classicist" (a historical throwback with Romantic leanings).[70] Moreover,

The romantic is, in Mendelssohn, the better part . . . His classicism was the
product partly of his natural harmonic disposition, partly of his education,
which was more comprehensive than that of the great musicians before him
and of a different kind. He was a master of form.[71] He had no inner forces
to curb, for real conflict was lacking in his life as in his art.[72]

Einstein then offers an assessment that both recalls the suggestions of Wagner
and Liszt on the derivative nature of Mendelssohn's music and anticipates
the claims of later commentators:

He admitted into his music the powerful simplicity and the contrapuntal
style of Handel and Bach – without, it must be said, being able to assimilate
it. He had to suffer it as a foreign element in his musical language, as, too, he
merely adopted Beethoven's sonata form, without replenishing or renewing
it.[73]

Similarly, Paul Henry Lang, in what remains perhaps the most eloquent general history of music in the English language, perpetuates Einstein's tone as
well as his verbiage. For Lang, Mendelssohn's music possessed a superficiality born of a supposedly unconflicted personality; he was a classicist (and
hence historically retrospective) in an age of progressive Romanticism; and
he was an outsider to the values and conflicts of his age. Lang adds that
Mendelssohn benefited from a natural facility that was ill at ease with the
cultivated Romantic image of the struggling artist:[74]

There can be no question that in many of Mendelssohn's works there is
missing that real depth that opens wide perspectives, the mysticism of the
unutterable. A certain sober clarity permeates his music, not the clarity of
mood and conviction, but that of the organizing mind . . . In the romantic
era most of the great musical personalities ceased to live in harmony with
their social environment, espousing revolutionary ideals. Mendelssohn's
personality was opposed to a secession, for to him an artistic understanding
of the prevailing social order was an emotional necessity . . . While we
cannot help noting the limitations in Mendelssohn's music, largely due
to his nature and his social philosophy, his frail figure becomes gigantic if
we glance at the musical world around him. What he created is not
overwhelming, it does not carry us away; he was not one of the very great,
but he was and remains a master, and he has given us much that fills us with
quiet enjoyment and admiration.[75]

There is nothing to suggest that Einstein's and Lang's views of Mendelssohn
were born of any anti-Semitic sentiments on those scholars' parts. At the
same time, however, these critiques clearly perpetuate the assessments of
earlier scholars whose motivations were unabashedly anti-Semitic, in language conspicuously similar to earlier anti-Semitic critiques – without, it
must be admitted, offering any new evidence for corroboration. That such

views evidently derive from the appraisals submitted in the second half of the nineteenth century is hardly surprising, since both Einstein (1880–1952) and Lang (1901–91) were reared in central Europe during the most spirited years of the scholarly redefinition of Mendelssohn's historical position. But the observation is also troubling – for while both scholars' views are rooted in an ideologically charged but academically vacuous period in the history of Mendelssohn research, those portrayals are also troped in many of today's mainstream music-history surveys.[76]

Wachet auf: The revival of Mendelssohn scholarship since 1945

With the end of the Second World War, musicians and scholars gradually became aware of the travesties of the musical and musicological past. This awareness, together with at least some scholars' need for a *Wiedergutmachung* (a corrective compensation for damage wrongfully inflicted) led to a resuscitation of Mendelssohn scholarship. Initially, progress was slow: the most important products of the early post-war years were Bernhard Bartels' 1947 biography of the composer (which, while offering little new material, represents the first German approach since the mid-1930s to shy away from Nazi anti-Semitic ideologies) and a 1951 reprint of George Grove's original Mendelssohn article for his dictionary – an essay whose substance was still able to throw into unflatteringly sharp relief the deficiencies of most of the Mendelssohn scholarship available at the mid-twentieth century.[77] Equally important was Peter Sutermeister's new, critical edition of the composer's letters from 1830 to 1832 – an invaluable body of primary sources that, although poorly edited even in recent editions, constituted most biographers' and other scholars' primary access to Mendelssohn's correspondence.[78]

But if the revival of genuine scholarship concerning the composer was slow in starting, the pace picked up considerably as the sesquicentennial of his birth neared. In addition to a flurry of short articles and documentary studies, the period surrounding the commemorative year witnessed the appearance of the Eric Werner's Mendelssohn article for the first edition of *Die Musik in Geschichte und Gegenwart* and, in 1963, his full-fledged life-and-works study – the first legitimate scholarly studies to consider the significance of Mendelssohn's Jewish heritage for his life and works.[79] Donald Mintz's dissertation not only addressed a crucial lacuna of Mendelssohn research – the systematic study of his compositional process and the manuscript sources for his music – whose scholarly validity had long since been accepted in scholarship concerning other major composers, but also dared, on the basis of that evidence, to contradict directly one of the most enduring of the platitudes and interpretive fallacies in assessments of Mendelssohn's historical significance: the notion that he was a quasi-reactionary figure in musical Romanticism.[80] The 1960s and 1970s also witnessed the growth of the Internationale Felix-Mendelssohn-Gesellschaft (founded in 1958–59); the issuance of critical editions of more than twenty previously unpublished compositions in a new, truly critical and (by its completion) truly complete *Gesamtausgabe* of Mendelssohn's works; a major scholarly symposium on "the Mendelssohn problem";[81] and the founding of a scholarly journal devoted specifically to research on all aspects of the lives, works, and histories of various members of the Mendelssohn family.[82]

Although this proliferation of work on Mendelssohn, most of it sympathetic to the composer, might be considered a modified recapitulation of the state of Mendelssohn research in the late nineteenth century (an observation that would be ominous indeed if it presaged a repeat of the scholarly holocaust that occurred in the early twentieth century), there are at least two healthy differences. First, the currently flourishing Mendelssohn discourse continues to take recourse to primary sources. This methodological buttressing has led to important findings concerning Mendelssohn's musical output as well as his biography. The former category embraces recoveries and new explorations of previously obscure but musically rewarding works,[83] important findings concerning well-known compositions (for example, the string quartets, all of the mature symphonies, the op. 23 *Kirchen-Musik*, the op. 35 Preludes and Fugues for piano, *St. Paul*, and *Die erste Walpurgisnacht*),[84] and even discoveries of compositions that previously were utterly unknown.[85] The biographical findings, drawing on the largely untapped resource of the composer's unpublished correspondence, have managed to identify and explore with unprecedented productivity issues, ideas, and events that shaped his life and compositional personality, but were overlooked or misrepresented in earlier studies. The year 2003 brought two major contributions of this genre: a new documentary biography by Clive Brown and a magisterial full-length life-and-works study by R. Larry Todd.[86]

Most prominent among these issues is the matter of the composer's Jewish heritage and its significance. Although commentaries devoted little public attention to this aspect of Mendelssohn's identity during his lifetime, it quickly became a major issue in his posthumous vilification, and the verbiage of these pseudo-historical assessments continued to pervade general commentaries well into the twentieth century. One factor that contributed to the success of Grove's and Wolff's biographies was their tactful handling of this issue, which at the time was unavoidably charged with both political and music-historical implications. Those studies, however, tend to portray Mendelssohn as largely unaffected by his Jewish heritage. The work of Eric Werner[87] is significant not least of all because it affirmed what Werner considered the inevitable significance of Mendelssohn's Jewishness, drawing extensively on unpublished correspondence and other little-known documents to situate the composer in the context of assimilatory German-Jewish culture as it existed during the years of his development and maturity. At least in part because of these and other scholars' efforts, it is now possible to discuss Mendelssohn as a cultural figure whose public and private life was materially affected by his Jewish heritage, without having to return to the anti-Semitic platitudes and other superficialities that characterized most nineteenth-century references to that heritage.

This observation leads to another healthy trend in today's Mendelssohn discourse: its thorough self-criticism. The matter of the composer's Jewish heritage is but one prominent example of this trend. In his dissertation and an important recent article, Jeffrey Sposato pointed out Werner's repeated and seemingly deliberate misrepresentation of unpublished documents crucial to this issue;[88] these findings initiated a vigorous debate that spanned three issues of *The Musical Quarterly* and involved several other leading scholars. New ideas continue to be advanced on such issues as his compositional development, the significance of individual biographical events and episodes, his relationships with his contemporaries and with the music of the past,[89] political and philosophical influences on his aesthetic,[90] his relationship with his older sister, Fanny Hensel, and more.

Collectively, these studies, together with the ever-increasing presence of Mendelssohn's music in concert life, have offered an impressive new image of the composer – one that enables us to see beyond the false dichotomies constructed by late nineteenth-century polemicists and rediscover the multifaceted phenomenon who dominated the cultural life of mid-nineteenth-century Europe. Finally, it seems, Mendelssohn's artistic voice is regaining its presence in society.

Mendelssohn's identity resists reduction to a single musical and historical phenomenon: this fact, perhaps, is both the most compelling rebuttal of the dismissals of his opponents and the strongest tribute to the multidimensional complexity he cultivated as he rose to the heights of European musical culture in the 1830s and 1840s. He was at once Christian and Jewish, performer and creator, pedagogue and role-model, public icon and private artist. The vacillations in his reception have diminished the luster of his name, but that damage is by no means irreparable. Indeed, there is now more cause for encouragement than perhaps at any point since 1847, for musicians and scholars everywhere are rediscovering the beauty and complexity of the musical and historical challenges and rewards that for so long remained hidden from view – rewards that are offered in a truly unique constellation in the life and works of Felix Mendelssohn Bartholdy.

In memory of W. G. Andrew, 1922–2002:
history enthusiast extraordinaire

14 Wagner as Mendelssohn: reversing habits and reclaiming meaning in the performance of Mendelssohn's music for orchestra and chorus

LEON BOTSTEIN

It is impossible to separate any discussion of approaches to the performance of the music of Felix Mendelssohn (and therefore conducting Mendelssohn) from the thorny and troubled history of the reception of Mendelssohn's music since his death in 1847.[1] The dynamics of listening are such that when a performer is determined to make a case for the music that is at odds with a reigning albeit reductive sense of a composer's aesthetic, audience expectations will offer resistance. Whether a conductor implicitly or explicitly concedes an established construct of Mendelssohn or not, a particular set of prejudices is present, derived from the standard account of Mendelssohn in music history. In that standard view Mendelssohn is distinct, in terms of surface, sound, and meaning, from Wagner and late Romanticism. This assumption of a stark contrast between Wagner and Mendelssohn concedes the Wagnerian version of the development of nineteenth-century music. The consequences are that one should not expect to hear nearly so radical a disjunction in basic performance practices and sound between Mendelssohn and, for example, Beethoven and Schubert. Yet the audience expects such a contrast when it comes to Wagner, vindicating the idea that Wagner's music and aesthetic contain a stark originality. This may apply as well in a subordinate way to Liszt. The self-justifying rhetoric of the "new" German school has been integrated into our approach to performance. Wagner and Liszt have been set apart from their predecessors by succeeding generations in a manner that suggests a fundamental paradigm shift, requiring a different approach to performance.

Indeed, we expect a lush string sound, flexible approaches to phrasing and tempo, greater gravity in the sound of the brass and winds. We date the modern normative orchestral timbre and sonority from Wagner. With this notion of a new and perhaps more intense and grander sound come allied implications about the meaning and profundity of the music. Mendelssohn is further damaged for the listener vis à vis his predecessors, particularly Beethoven and Mozart. We have accepted the Wagnerian reading that the great Classical repertory, including some Mozart, but mostly Beethoven, contains levels of meaning and an emotion comparable to later developments and adequate to Wagnerian and post-Wagnerian (e.g., Mahlerian) expectations. What Wagner succeeded in doing was to set Mendelssohn apart as essentially an epigone, a composer of superficiality, fashion, and virtuosity, whose command of the craft of musical composition, despite many overt claims to the contrary, did not result in music of profundity. In fact Mendelssohn's music, in the wake of the watershed year of 1848, gradually lost stature as powerfully expressive (as opposed to being entertaining and elegant). The sort of emotionally compelling experience associated with hearing Wagner articulated by Nietzsche in the 1870s and Thomas Mann in the twentieth century – the image of a shattering affective interior and personal response – became an ideal that was applied – as in Mann – back to listening to Beethoven, but not Mendelssohn.[2]

No successful revision of this derailing of Mendelssohn from the dominant trajectory of nineteenth-century musical aesthetics has taken place. In a host of versions, a post-Wagnerian privileged notion of the experience of all music, even instrumental music, in terms of its philosophical and psychological power that excludes Mendelssohn has remained with us. No matter how differently Brahms, even Tchaikovsky and Rachmaninov, and certainly Mahler, not to mention Schoenberg and Berg, are viewed, each seems adequate in terms of a late nineteenth- and twentieth-century ideal of musical communication that we implicitly endorse. That ideal permits listeners to sense something extraordinary that privileges the composer as artist. Within this model of musical communication, the listener is able to locate and appropriate some non-quotidian dimension of intensity or gravity in emotion and meaning. This ideal of musical communication has been, as already suggested, transposed backwards, into the works of Bach, Handel, Mozart, and Beethoven and to music by certain contemporaries of Mendelssohn, notably Schumann and Chopin. The less intellectually prized late Romantic composers – notably Dvořák and Tchaikovsky – have also benefited from the idea that the hearing of the music contains an emotionally riveting and even exhausting encounter with the extraordinary, even though their music has suffered (in a way Mendelssohn's has not) from accusations of formal and technical weakness.

Mendelssohn remains synonymous with refined easy listening, or, in the rare case that the sacred music is performed, a well-realized but emotionally distant evocation of historical models of the musical expression of piety. The neo-classical exterior of Mendelssohn's music succeeds in concealing an interiority that we readily ascribe to Schubert. Other composers who have not fit well into the reception pattern and model of listening and musical meaning initiated by the Wagnerian polemic include Haydn and Stravinsky. But no case has remained as resistant as Mendelssohn to revisionism through performance. In no other circumstance is there such a wide gap between the intentionality and formal qualities of the music and the attitudes of modern audiences. Certainly a few of Mendelssohn's works remain popular. However, the terms of approbation refer to a restricted image of concert music as decorative and pleasing – even beautiful and graceful, attributes that easily suggest little more than cultured superficial taste.

The radical reversal in the reputation and fortunes of Mendelssohn's achievement began in earnest after 1850 when Richard Wagner published anonymously his *Das Judentum in der Musik*. Wagner was obsessed with Mendelssohn's early success, talent, and wealth and the extraordinary popularity his music enjoyed in his lifetime. Mendelssohn's music was already central to the repertory of the home, Protestant church, and concert hall when Wagner completed *Das Liebesverbot* in 1840. Mendelssohn was part of the repertoire of professionals – along with the music of Schumann and Chopin. Mendelssohn's music added to the core materials of music instruction. The solo piano music, the songs, the trios, and the quartets – as well as the octet – despite shifting taste, received repeated exposure to succeeding generations of students. For the innumerable choral societies that flourished after 1848, in England and in German-speaking Europe Mendelssohn's choral music, particularly *St. Paul* and *Elijah*, was indispensable. Mendelssohn's persistence in the repertory – apart from the symphonies and the Violin Concerto – has depended unusually on amateurs who have continued to this day to enjoy playing and singing the music.

Wagner, however, was not alone in challenging the meaning and emotional character of Mendelssohn's music. No one during the second half of the nineteenth century doubted that the music was refined and polished, all hallmarks of Mendelssohn's legendary skills and command of the craft of composition. Somehow, however, beneath the brilliant surface, a lack in profundity was perceived. In the aesthetics of mid- and late nineteenth-century musical taste, when placed against the claims of Liszt and Wagner and the Wagnerian approach to the legacy of Beethoven, Mendelssohn – in contrast to Schumann – came to be viewed as a composer of complacent music. Even among staunch anti-Wagnerians, Mendelssohn was more respected and revered than loved. Ultimately Mendelssohn's extraordinary popularity among middle-class amateurs came to be held against him. In the wake of a reaction against mid-nineteenth-century Victorian conceits, Mendelssohn emerged as emblematic of a musical culture of social affirmation, lacking in a necessary dialectical and problematic complexity adequate to modern life. His music therefore attracted little attention among twentieth-century modernists.

Aesthetic tastes, ideologies of culture, and politics have never been quite as independent of one another as sentimental advocates of the art of music have sought to argue. In Mendelssohn's case, the politics of anti-Semitism and nationalism in Europe in the century between Mendelssohn's death and the end of World War II were decisive. Therefore, in the twentieth century periodic efforts (some motivated by political objectives, as in post-1945 West Germany) to rethink Mendelssohn and peel away at the mix of incomprehension and slander have met with only limited success. Even the rediscovery of the early string symphonies and the reinterpretation of Mendelssohn through the medium of period instrument performances since the 1970s have not appreciably helped to recast the image of the composer. The notion of Mendelssohn as an exemplar of early nineteenth-century neo-classicism, allied at one and the same time with visual and literary Romanticism as well as with the anti-Romantic ideology of Goethe (and his friend and musical confidant, Mendelssohn's teacher, Zelter) after 1815, is certainly appropriate. But if we can embrace (as we have done) the architecture and painting of Karl Friedrich Schinkel, a figure whose career intersected with Mendelssohn's and mirrors it, why cannot we do the same for Mendelssohn?[3] Indeed, the constructive revisionism now underway with respect to German painting and sculpture before 1848 offers an initial encouraging parallel.[4] Schinkel, in both his neo-classical and his neo-gothic work, communicates to contemporary audiences the subjective appropriation of the past. His work suggests not slavish imitation but a powerful model of historicism, an obsession with reconciling history and modernity. In contrast, the range of Mendelssohn's historicism still obscures the expressive power of his music. Expanding the active repertoire within the composer's output remains therefore a subordinate challenge to a basic rethinking, in terms of performance, of those key works that still remain part of the concert repertory.

Reductive as this quick summary of the career of Mendelssohn's reputation may seem (after all, he had his strong defenders, particularly among leading late nineteenth-century composers and performers, notably Brahms and Reger), it is tragically all too close to the truth. By the end of the nineteenth century, despite the fin-de-siècle Mozart revival and a distinct reaction against Wagnerism within modernism, only a small fraction of Mendelssohn's music retained wide currency. There was a conservative school of composition centered in Leipzig, under the leadership of Reinecke, that continued to honor the legacy of Mendelssohn. But by 1900 the works most performed on the concert stage were the Violin Concerto, the incidental music to *A Midsummer's Night Dream*, the overtures, the octet, the trios, *Elijah* (which ultimately eclipsed *St. Paul*) the G minor Piano Concerto and two symphonies, the "Scottish" and the "Italian."

The question that faces the conductor vis à vis the orchestra members as well as the audience is whether even a favorable assessment of the standard account is indeed what Mendelssohn's music is about. If it is not, then the task of overcoming the accepted view of Mendelssohn's place in history and his aesthetic ambitions frames the interpretive challenge.[5] Rejecting conventional wisdom with respect to Mendelssohn is justified in terms of history and biography. It was not Mendelssohn's intent to write music as mere entertainment for the privileged. His contemporary admirers, particularly Schumann, agreed with this assessment and placed him, in contrast to the Wagnerian argument, as a worthy heir to Beethoven, the first great Romantic. He did not consciously "step well out of the way of Beethoven's shadow" but sought to take a step beyond Beethoven, just as Wagner would later claim to have done himself uniquely.[6]

All this is well and good, but the quandary still remains. In my experience Mendelssohn sounds distant even to musicians, and perhaps bereft of some dimension of emotional depth and immediacy. The music seems too sentimental, without sufficient subjective complexity. However beautiful it is, when placed on the concert stage we anticipate delight in the deft use of orchestral effects, refinement, lightness, economy, and the sparkle of delicacy. The Mendelssohn audiences and conductors favor conforms neatly to that sensibility. Mendelssohn fails, for example, to convey a sense of the tragic through music. Although he wrote incidental music for *Antigone* and *Oedipus at Colonus*, even the once-popular concert version of *Antigone* has fallen out of the repertory. Subtly crafted, the music appears consistently optimistic, cheerful, and sunny without evidence of the conflict, self-critical reflection and mythic significance adequate to the text. Despite the composer's own deep debt to the dramatic rhetoric of Bach, Handel, Mozart, and Beethoven, drama and power – the ecstatic qualities we seek in the works of his own models – elude us in dealing with Mendelssohn. The irony in this is, of course, that in Mendelssohn's lifetime the music was not only celebrated and revered, it was understood as being dramatic, spiritual, and certainly more than pretty. It was heard as intense, emotional, and profoundly moving, and devotional in a religious sense. It was not only beautiful but, in the language of eighteenth-century aesthetics, sublime and therefore astonishing and deeply affecting. Consider for example the chorus "Mache dich auf, werde Licht" and the subsequent *Wachet auf* chorale in *St. Paul*.

Compare the case of Mendelssohn in terms of reception past and present with a roughly parallel case, chronologically speaking, in literature. There is little doubt that the language, external events, social context, personal ambition, narrative conventions, and interpretive psychological world view of Jane Austen are as different from the later nineteenth-century novel, particularly Thomas Hardy and certainly the fiction of Henry James, Fyodor Dostoevsky, Marcel Proust, Virginia Woolf, and Thomas Mann, as Mendelssohn seems to us when compared to Wagner, Mahler, or even Strauss, who had considerable respect for and affinity to Mendelssohn. Yet the reading public, helped in part by the film medium, has found a way into Austen – a way of reading – that makes a body of work quite foreign and distant germane and engaging. Contemporary readers have lent Austen a gravity in meaning equal to that found in novels from a later, seemingly less restricted, naive, and simple era. The revived taste for Austen is not merely one of misplaced nostalgia and fantasy about a premodern world crafted to obliterate our consciousness of the ugly messiness of contemporary realities. The rage for Austen, even her least successful novel *Mansfield Park*, has sources beyond any cynical version of the consequences of postmodernism. In contrast to Hardy, for example, Austen deals with the privileged world of the landed gentry. This might appeal to readers seeking an alternative to modernism, or fiction that dwells on social marginalization and disenfranchisement. Yet a post-1960s regressive taste in today's politics of culture is not sufficient to account for the current interest in Austen any more than is her status as a woman novelist. A late eighteenth- and early nineteenth-century aesthetic has been successfully reconfigured. It appears congruent with, for example, Freudian and post-Freudian theory. Austen had been a figure like Mendelssohn, one routinely given a proper place of honor in history. The difference is that Austen has once again been embraced with enthusiasm and deemed relevant as more than the object of dutiful respect. No one, for example would suggest a performance of Mendelssohn's Symphony no. 2, the "Lobgesang," as an alternative to Beethoven's Ninth for use in a celebratory or commemorative public event.

Austen is credited, particularly in Ian Watt's account, with bridging the tradition of social critique in the sense of Fielding and other hallmarks of the eighteenth-century novel with the subjectivity and psychological and narrative techniques that would characterize the later nineteenth-century novel. Mendelssohn can be viewed the same way.[7] His music was innovative and integrated eighteenth-century Classical strategies with the subjective emotionality, formal inventiveness, and rhetoric of early Romanticism. Austen found a way to transpose the narrative from the first-person epistolary pattern of the eighteenth century into the third-person story-telling vantage point of the nineteenth. Mendelssohn altered symphonic form to accommodate a Romantic sensibility, that of personal experience. The circularity in form in several symphonies, the linkages of movements, the reconsideration of the relationship between exposition and recapitulation, novelty in thematic construction, and the shifting of weight and balance within traditional forms are present within his neo-classical appropriations, particularly from the Baroque.

A nearly contemporary subjectivity in Mendelssohn is found in his melodic material and in the listener's awareness of a narrator in the sense of literature and painting. Although it has become fashionable to link Caspar David Friedrich as an intense early Romantic exponent of subjectivity with Beethoven, the comparison is more apt with Mendelssohn. Extending well beyond the example of the "Pastoral" Symphony of Beethoven, Mendelssohn forged a vocabulary of musical response to the human experience of time and space, as well as to the experience of reading and imaginative visualization through sound from texts. Landscape and the individual's capacity to contemplate the world – particularly the sense of the divine – dominate Friedrich's canvases. As a painter he permits the viewer to look, so to speak, over the shoulders and around the figures in his paintings whose backs are to us: faceless representations of ourselves looking out into the world. This occurs as well when the viewer is aware only of the absent painter, in landscapes that have no figures. The frame of the painting is like the frame around us. As we peer into the painting we become directly conscious of our own need to fashion a view of the world and define reality not as objective, as autonomous of observation, but as contingent on ourselves as inventors and viewers.

It was Mendelssohn, not Beethoven, who used instrumental music, particularly public instrumental music, to achieve this sensibility in the listener. Consider the overtures and the "Scottish" Symphony. Music, in his hands, becomes a vehicle through which the imposition or creation of meaning can be observed and appropriated by the listener. Even in the great choral works, the "Lobgesang," for example, Mendelssohn rejects a forbidding monumentality in the manner of Beethoven. The symphonic and choral work of Beethoven, in contrast to Mendelssohn, suggests a self-sufficiency and objectivity in the work of art that does not seem to require the listener's presence, much like a painting whose composition implies the illusion of indifference to the active presence of a viewer. The work of art is objectified. This might be said of even the great Velazquez painting *Las Meninas*, in which the figures look out directly from the canvas and where there is a mirror reflection within the painting, highlighting the virtuosity and objectivity of art as observation and representation. But as in Rubens and later in Goya (for example *The 3rd of May in Madrid*), the paintings imply no need to be completed, or entered into by the viewer. They are self-contained and powerful objects in which the awareness of subjective vision is overwhelmed by the virtuosity of the representative power and imagination. But in Mendelssohn the intimate self is placed on stage. One example can be found in his setting of Psalm 114 op. 51. Indeed, the clearly modern adaptation of a historicist choral rhetoric, combined with the transparent simplicity, reveal the composer's subjective hand. The composer, much like the painter Friedrich, reveals reality as his personal mediation of experience. But Mendelssohn achieves this subjectivity, as does Schinkel, through the use of neo-classical models.

Mendelssohn confronted the towering and imposing legacy of Beethoven not by avoiding it, but by adapting it to an intimacy of communication. In this sense, thinking of Mendelssohn's music in terms of its relationship to the visual experience can help performers. Mendelssohn, by inviting the performer and listener into the construction of meaning, challenged the stability and autonomy of the artwork, evident in Beethoven, as a self-sufficient and objective representation. Monumentality in terms of sound (as in *Elijah* and *St. Paul*) is handled in a manner that is not distancing from the listener just as the viewer's relationship to a canvas can be rendered more intimate and direct. The listener is invited by directness in expression, an emphasis on comprehensibility, and the practicality of amateur participation. The listener is also made aware of the composer's subjectivity – the centrality of the individual in creating meaning – much in the way a reader is linked by the narrator to the authorial voice in Austen or by the isolated figures (and indeed their absence) to the painter in the landscapes of Friedrich.

The issue here is not one of locating originality. Mendelssohn, unlike Beethoven, creates the space for the listener to become aware of his or her own need for engagement. The composer becomes, in this sense, less heroic (defined in a manner that applies to late Beethoven as well as the works of the middle period) and the listener more equal to the artist. The position of awestruck observer is replaced by a sense of community. The hearer, playing Mendelssohn or listening, becomes acutely aware of the personal need to follow suit, to reflect on how a sense of truth, the objective world, and external reality are formed only by the expression of subjectivity. This is what happens as viewers look at and beyond Friedrich's figures and readers reflect on Austen's characters. And there is, through art, the assertion of a normative, positive moral order.

The irony explicit in this analysis is that Wagner may have been right for the wrong reasons. Insofar as he and not Mendelssohn was the true heir to Beethoven, it was on account of his embrace of the aesthetic scale and ambition of Beethoven. Wagner, and Liszt before him, extended the Beethovenian theatrical sense of the dramatic in music. Intimacy and subjectivity once again became objects of observation on stage rather than the substance of musical expression; their work did not invite the listener to emulate and participate. Liszt, not Mendelssohn, sought to equal the *Missa Solemnis*'s account of lyrical and dramatic faith in his *Graner Messe*. Wagner, as he himself correctly argued, restored a mythic and unapproachable level of aesthetic transformation derived from the Ninth Symphony that implied the artist's unique access to objectivity and truth. He effectively hid, through a stunning command of the seductive potential of music and myth for the theatre, the transient, arbitrary, and necessarily subjective artificiality of aesthetic creation.

The contrast between Mendelssohn's religious convictions and Wagner's awkward and nearly tone-deaf engagement with Christianity, despite overt attempts to use subject matter with religious content from *Das Liebesmahl der Apostel* to *Tannhäuser* and *Parsifal*, is instructive. It can place the differences between the two composers in a manner that does not result in a judgment that Mendelssohn's music is less profound or relevant. They held divergent notions of how music ought to function in the public sphere. The difference between Wagner and Mendelssohn becomes more under-standable and less pejorative. Wagner, who failed to hide his lifelong and essentially secular and anti-Christian sensibility, sought in art a surrogate for traditional religious spirituality. Art, not faith, could provide the expe-rience of loss of ego, an exit from the fear of death, and the connection to a divine teleology and metaphysical presence. Wagner's moral universe is ambiguous. Mendelssohn, in contrast, understood art as a signal human achievement that revealed the presence of the divine in all humanity. The temporal experience of music, even in a completely secular context, follow-ing Friedrich Schleiermacher, permitted listener, performer, and composer to transcend the limits of ordinary language, shed the illusion of the suf-ficiency of human reason alone, and sense the grace of God. The love of God that was inexpressible in language was rendered communicable and even personal in choral and instrumental music. The clearly artificial aes-thetic and structural requirements of musical form had to be highlighted and shared, so that in the Lutheran sense, music functioned as a universal, democratic medium. Music assumed, for Mendelssohn, a social function through which the individual established his or her own contact with God using a secular, non-sectarian analogue to ritual and prayer. Through music, the transient, the ugly, and the evil were transcended, highlighting the ulti-mate victory of moral truth. The making of music, for Mendelssohn, was an act of personal piety within a traditional Christian world view, not a surrogate for theology or faith that elevated artists into a new priestly class. Mendelssohn sought combine "ancient conceptions with modern means." This informed Mendelssohn's admiration for Bach, the music's "pure, mild and vast power" and the "transparency of its depths."[8]

The accessibility of Mendelssohn's music mirrored an ideal of the aes-thetic and the beautiful as direct and economical, as inviting of personal engagement, just as the teachings of Jesus were susceptible of wide trans-lation. This demanded a balance between historical standards of aesthetic beauty and craft and accessibility, for the listener was faced with an engage-ment with music beyond the role of passive spectator. Mendelssohn would later be accused of pandering to the philistine tastes of a well-to-do cultured middle class. From a Wagnerian perspective, he denied art its true capacity for meaning. That charge inverted Mendelssohn's ambition to engage his public with ease using a clearly personal style imbedded, through learning and knowledge, in the evocation of tradition. Needless difficulty – even gra-tuitous virtuosity – needed to be resisted so that through music, the public might more readily sense the aesthetic in themselves, the power of the subjective and recognize, through music, the universality and rationality of the grace of God in the world.

How does one, in the early twenty-first century, redeem this spiritual project in modern performance? Religious fundamentalism in America has utilized music, much in the best spirit of Mendelssohn but without demanding the acquisition of tradition and learning. Commercial music easily bought and played is adapted. The music linked to faith is popular. It invites participation but it does not seek to use an aesthetic medium to communicate the optimism of faith. But contemporary religious popular music rejects, as did Mendelssohn, the arrogance of the Wagnerian notion of the artist as prophet or representative of a spiritual aristocracy. The non-trivial irony is that the Wagnerian spectacle, precisely in its success in rendering the operatic aesthetic a secular object of mythic and quasi-religious adoration, became a model for fascism and the enthusiastic abandonment, by masses in modernity, of the challenge of realizing both individuality and a common moral purpose through art. Perhaps it is still listening to Mendelssohn rather than to Wagner that demands an active sense of the aesthetic self, and therefore opens up each individual's consciousness of the divine and unique subjectivity each person possesses in the eyes of God. What seems to make Mendelssohn bland and boring to the modern listener may reveal our post-Wagnerian dependence on spectacle, our resistance to intimacy, our passivity, our pessimism, and our collective susceptibility to manipulation through music. The failure to enter empathetically into the act of listening to Mendelssohn and locating his subjectivity may reveal our inability to participate in the task of the non-imitative personal assertion of gratitude, significance, and meaning through musical culture.

Lest this speculative and polemical excursus into the nexus between theology, music, and aesthetics in the nineteenth century seem irrelevant, let us return to the observation that we fail to identify with Mendelssohn's construct of musical meaning and experience. Yet we have succeeded in finding a new means of access to Austen. The declarative monumentality of Beethoven or the mythic grandeur (and perhaps grandiloquence) of Wagner and Mahler seem easier to rehearse and perform. In the case of Mendelssohn conductors concentrate on the task of achieving polish, accuracy of ensemble, and a sense of lightness. Anything suggestive of spirituality is lost. We seem to have few means of communicating interiority, intimacy, and power in Mendelssohn.

How then, in the case of the orchestral and choral music, might the music of Mendelssohn be performed in a manner that confronts the old clichés, defeats the Wagnerian orthodoxy, represents the composer's ambitions and aesthetic justly, and reveals the dramatic, spiritual, and emotional power of the music? One of the notorious strains in the anti-Semitic polemics is the notion that Mendelssohn's music, in contrast to Beethoven, represents the effeminate and graceful (understood as a pejorative). Masculinity, power, and drama are seen as lacking, as are therefore any true originality and genuine creativity. The first task is to highlight intensity in drama and emotion in Mendelssohn. To this weight has to be added the sound: a non-Mozartian, period instrument weight. We need to resist the instinct to render the musical surface antique by modern standards. If spirituality and complexity seem to elude representation and communication in performance, then tempos and articulation need to be reconsidered. If tempos in Beethoven have been de-romanticized, then perhaps tempos in Mendelssohn need, particularly in movements that are not scherzos, to be less frantic in speed and rendered flexible.

An ironic starting point for rethinking Mendelssohn performances is a reconsideration of the normative assumptions we apply routinely in the performances of Mendelssohn's posthumous nemesis, Wagner. Indeed Wagner's debt to Mendelssohn, in terms of compositional strategies, ideas, and sound world was far greater than Wagner and his advocates have ever admitted. Wagner's endless but occasionally ambivalent trashing of Mendelssohn may have been a classic case of an artist covering his tracks, leading future observers astray, and hiding his debts from posterity. Beneath all the contempt heaped on Mendelssohn lies a crucial clue: that Wagner, in his music, owed much to Mendelssohn's influence and example and sought desperately to conceal it. Wagner's critique of Mendelssohn as a conductor suggests this. A decisive deviation on Wagner's part from the most celebrated musician of his day – Mendelssohn – was in performance style as a conductor. A clear distinction in the way Beethoven, for example, was performed helped keep a connection in composition between the two figures from being exposed. What if, then, one performed Mendelssohn as if it were what we think Wagner, as heir to Mendelssohn, should sound like? Wagnerian sonority, to this day, is construed as clearly different if not opposite from a Mendelssohnian sound. Perhaps this is mistaken. If it is, then the notion of contrasts in meaning, profundity, drama, intensity, and emotion is weakened, and in turn a path is opened to find a new way of hearing Mendelssohn. The task is not to make Mendelssohn a pale Wagnerian defined by the way we have become accustomed to hearing Wagner. Rather, the challenge is to restore the Mendelssohnian element to our performances of Wagner, thereby revealing the continuities in musical expression and meaning between two composers who have been traditionally been seen, by defenders of both, as polar opposites. By so doing we actually bring back from Wagner an aesthetic of drama he so masterfully employed in *Lohengrin*, for example, to its origins in Mendelssohn.

Take for example, the locus classicus of Wagnerian originality and aesthetic meaning, the Prelude to *Tristan*. Imagine that it would be performed at a brisker tempo than commonly anticipated. Perhaps the string fingerings would favor lower positions and a thinner sound. Bow use would be lighter, more flautando and vibrato would be sparing. A smaller string section would result in a less thick orchestral texture. Transparency favoring wind sound over string color could lighten the overall balance. If one performed the Prelude as if it were the opening of the "Scottish" Symphony, what insights might emerge? The possible answers to this question are dependent in part on how one construes, in general, connections between Wagner and Mendelssohn in terms of the character of their music, as well as how one understands Mendelssohn's own ambitions when composing for large forces. This latter issue can be usefully explored by reflecting on differences between the first 1833 and second, incomplete 1834 versions of the "Italian" Symphony. This unique window on the composer's workshop is indispensable in developing a convincing approach to conducting Mendelssohn. Mendelssohn found the earlier version too thin.

But by bringing the orchestral performance strategies closer together, making Wagner Mendelssohnian, we can discover shared attributes of musical expression and meaning. On the matter of spirituality and lyricism – the generation of sound that creates the impression of time suspended and the presence of prayer, devotion, and the divine – a key model for Wagner was *St. Paul*. A useful point of comparison is between the prelude to *St. Paul* and the preludes to *Lohengrin* and *Parsifal*. Furthermore, the use of brass and choir, and the dramatic structure of Part I of *St. Paul* have parallels in these two Wagner works. Wagner was overwhelmed by *St. Paul*; his *Liebesmahl* is a failed effort to set Christian material directly using the secular oratorio model. Mendelssohn's adaptation of recitative, his characterization of the figures of St. Paul and Jesus are key influences on Wagner, audible in the *Ring* and the figure of Wotan. If, in performance terms, one rejects the Wagnerian claim of originality, acknowledges his debt to Mendelssohn, and assumes a shared aesthetic, a new set of possibilities may emerge.

It is with respect to how music evokes nature that Wagner owed his greatest debt. *The Hebrides (Fingal's Cave)*, *Calm Sea and Prosperous Voyage*, and *Die schöne Melusine* are necessary precursors to the opening of *Rheingold*, and descriptive nature-related musical rhetoric in the *Ring*, particularly *Siegfried*. Mendelssohn provided Wagner with a model of how the eighteenth-century symphonic experience that sought to characterize experience and external reality, from storms to battles, could be adapted to fit the aesthetic expectations of Romanticism. Wagner's model was not Weber in terms of musical construction and orchestration. Neither was it Beethoven. Mendelssohn's orchestral music may be the most powerful sonic guide for inner sight, for an internal journey of associated symbolic and visual images. When, in rehearsal, one invokes this idea a new intensity in the playing emerges. The visual is a key to memory. Therefore the use of historical models, the evocation of Handel and Bach become keys to a central emotional experience shared by all: the fragmentary recall, from the ear to the eye, of past experience.

Although the "Pastoral" Symphony of Beethoven, or even Haydn's *The Seven Last Words of Christ*, can be understood as prefiguring a Romantic approach to using music to represent the temporal experience of the external world, these works remain squarely within a complex and subtle eighteenth-century tradition, as Richard Will has demonstrated. Instrumental ensemble music, notably symphonic music, was used in the act of representation of the material and the "ineffable." Sound alone, without text or picture, created a communicative medium of illustration between composer and listener. Instrumental compositions evoked static and dynamic experiences, as well as personal figures, and imaginary states of mind, using techniques such as tone painting. The infinite as well as the earth-bound were depicted. In the most complex versions of the eighteenth-century tradition of characteristic symphonic music, such as Beethoven's "Pastoral" (and perhaps even the "Eroica") music depicted real events – lighting, thunder, shepherd's pipes, processions, dances, battles, and scenes. Music developed rhetorical conventions designed to depict the characteristics of personalities. Even in the *Missa Solemnis*, Beethoven used rhythmic gestures and keys to characterize theological meaning.

It was Mendelssohn, more than Berlioz or Spohr, who redirected the way in which the experience of being in the world can be expressed through music. This innovation extended to the indirect encounter through literature. In the case of *Fingal's Cave*, the direct experience of a landscape takes on a musical language that effectively communicates personal response. Mendelssohn subordinates but does not eliminate musical gestures that imply natural events. But depiction is replaced by implication. The musical subject becomes the composer's reflection and response, not the event or object itself. The peaceful, the idyllic, the turbulent, the presence of water or mountains are evoked only with echoes of an earlier musical realism. But the composer's task, in Mendelssohn's hand, is no longer descriptive or painterly. The reaction to experience, its memory, or even its anticipation assumes musical form first and foremost in thematic and melodic construction. The thematic material is formed in a manner that does not reveal, in some illustrative fashion, the subject of its depiction, with the possible exception of moving water. For example, in the opening of *Calm Sea and Prosperous Voyage*, the sense of stillness and expanse is orchestrated and evoked by the tempo and sonority. The listener in the characteristic symphony of the eighteenth century would be invited to follow the narrative, as Beethoven did in his own setting of the Goethe text. Music acts in an illustrative manner offering a parallel experience. In Mendelssohn, however, the listener is introduced to composer's internal reaction evoked by visual scene. We encounter a musical diary, so to speak. We hear the composer as reader, or as dreamer, responding in the time of memory to images generated by poetry. This brings us closer to *Tristan*.

Nature in music, indeed external reality, is suggested by Mendelssohn, as are events and the act of reading in the "Italian" and "Scottish" symphonies only through the audible subjectivity. The use of music as the narrative medium for communicating characteristics of human experience is restricted to a species of psychological and autobiographical self-representation. The way Wagner constructs leitmotifs – invented, distilled, and repeated musical variables that signify everything from real objects (swords) to characters to metaphysical concepts (fate) – reveals a direct link to Mendelssohn's manner of creating themes in the orchestral music. As in *Fingal's Cave*, the "Scottish" and "Italian" symphonies, as well as in *Calm Sea* and *Melusine*, the composer tells of his experience by fashioning his own characteristic musical symbolism using distinct and pithy themes that are not illustrative but yet evocative, particularly of distance and light. Mendelssohn's thematic ideas mark the starting point in the development of parallels between the visual and the musical that are elaborated by Wagner and after, well into the era of sound film music. Mendelssohn's musical ideas orient the listener to the external referent explicitly through the subjective vantage point of the composer. Mendelssohn adapts the expectations of musical time of the Beethovenian symphony and alters it to fit the personal narrative. He does not borrow from a set of commonly understood rhetorical devices (e.g., keys) or clearly understood techniques of tone painting. The integration of the musical and visual imagination is achieved by Mendelssohn's exploitation of music's power to suggest associations, rather than its capacity to describe or compete with linguistic notions of clarity and specificity. Psychologically speaking music, as Wagner also believed, penetrated more deeply than language or pictures. But Mendelssohn achieves this result without the operatic apparatus. When an orchestra begins to think that it is projecting an internal sequence of visual experiences, then the obsession with neoclassical formalism recedes and the consideration of the emotional character of the music begins.

Nothing is more striking in this regard than Mendelssohn's brilliance and originality as an orchestrator of thematic material. From the first page of the Overture to *A Midsummer's Night's Dream* to the E minor Violin Concerto, the segregation of instrumental groupings, the employment of wide registration, the highlighting of single voices reveal the capacity to use the orchestra to evoke a sense of the encounter between the composer and lived experience. Therefore Mendelssohn perfects the use of music to create the illusion of three-dimensionality. The use of sound as evocative of the space in which the individual narrator found himself was path-breaking and essential to Wagner's craft. The residue of the tradition of music as evoking characteristics of reality persists in Mendelssohn as transfigured into the creation of theme and melody as markers of told experience. In contrast to the "Pastoral," the presence of the viewer, not the event, is primary. Although the connection to experience remains susceptible to translation into language by the listener with an accurate sense of the primary references (e.g. Goethe, Scotland), finding those references is not indispensable for the listener to enjoy or grasp the musical experience per se.

Wagner learned from Mendelssohn how to make music narrate independent of text; the referents can be garnered from a context in which the characterization of the narrator through music alone is required. Each of Wagner's characters gains a distinct musical personality through thematic and harmonic elaboration. This process of using music to mediate experience Wagner gleaned from Mendelssohn. The aesthetic gestures both composers use often refer to an object of extramusical meaning apart from the personality of the narrator that is not obvious in some tone painting sense. The same can be said for the musical characterization of ideas or mental states achieved by both composers. One can listen to Wagner without linking music to a precise representation of external action or inner thought, as in Mendelssohn. In this sense Mendelssohn did not write so-called "absolute music" in the manner in which it became defined in the mid 1850s. Rather he, as Wagner would, used music as a means of refracting ordinary meaning. The music that accompanies Wotan in the orchestra is dependent on the successful command of the Romantic habit of creating a song without words. Wagner's orchestra, using patterns of thematic construction, characterization, repetition, and transformation pioneered by Mendelssohn, narrates; the musical content of the drama extends a logic of thematic construction that is linked to the subjective representation of experience characteristic of Mendelssohn, not Beethoven.[9]

Turning to the way in which music in the nineteenth century managed to evoke humor and the playful – indeed, even the lyrical – Wagner, especially in *Die Meistersinger*, revealed another Mendelssohnian influence. The "Italian" Symphony and the *Midsummer Night's Dream* Overture have future parallels in the way in which Wagner characterizes joy and youthfulness. Wagner's evocation of how crowds gather and move about in apparently good spirits also reveals Mendelssohnian origins. With respect to the melodic characterization of optimism and lyrical beauty, a comparison of Walther's Prize Song – in terms of character rather than a fingerprint style match up – with the interlude between the second and third movements of the E Minor Violin Concerto might be suggestive. Indeed, that work, particularly in the first movement, demonstrates a long evolving melodic line that can be set alongside the Prize Song and the solo material given to Hans Sachs. The

close of Act III is indeed, ironically, Mendelssohnian in its employment
of the chorus; it also suggests some debt to Mendelssohn's experiments in
structuring drama. The stately elongated and affirmative uses of chorale-like
endings (and the use of the chorus in the "Lobgesang," and, for example, the
final moments of the symphonies, particularly the Third and the Fifth) are
models of the kind of Wagnerian closing found in *Meistersinger*. Indeed, one
of Wagner's greatest debts is in the manner in which he employs a chorus as
a dramatic vehicle. His ear betrays an adherence to the choral texture and
sonority cultivated by Mendelssohn.

If one returns to the comparison between the opening of *Tristan* and the
opening of the "Scottish," intensity and interiority of a similar nature can
be found. What this suggests is that one might resist, as an interpreter, conducting Mendelssohn with too much stylistic adherence to his neo-classical
models. Expressive intensity developed through use of varied colors in string
sound, some tempo rubato, and an effort to phrase the melodic material as
if it were narrating might lead to a less undifferentiated impression. It is not
that one wishes to make Mendelssohn sound more the way we are now used
to hearing Wagner; but more expressive freedom in delivering the dramatic
account of the subjective that the music narrates is necessary. This includes
the sense of awe. Consider the opening of *St. Paul*. Here, as in *Parsifal*, is
a stunning sonic transformation of the sense time is present. The piety is
personal, not doctrinal. The entire oratorio does not lack for operatic ambition. Performing it calls for highlighting the operatic contrasts and pacing
it as if it were a work for the stage. Indeed, *St. Paul* was performed with
tableaux vivants in the nineteenth century. The oratorio becomes, as does
Elijah, a far different medium than the one used by Handel or Haydn, and
as removed from the Bach of the *St. Matthew Passion*.

When one compares the two versions of the "Italian" Symphony one
is humbled by the standards the composer set himself. He had none of
Wagner's bravura. Why was Mendelssohn dissatisfied with what posthumously became regarded as a near-perfect work? That judgment was already
unsympathetic to a view of Mendelssohn as having an aesthetic ambition
that might have placed him closer to Liszt and Wagner. The 1834 version is
more elaborate, with more development of material, fuller recapitulations,
and a less light-hearted sensibility. Indeed, it appears that Mendelssohn
sought to shift the balance from a direct response to landscape and the
Grand Tour to creating an inward musical narration of the personal, if not
spiritual reflection on the experience of the people and culture of Italy. As
in *Calm Sea*, the place of Goethe, of a musical analogue to literary transformation, is suggested by the 1834 version in the composer's desire to provide
the work with gravity, interior intensity, greater formal balance, and wider
harmonic color that render the mood more differentiated. Furthermore,

Mendelssohn's determination to transform historical models without abandoning them and to modernize tradition is stronger in the 1834 version. The subjective and personal is not lost but rendered seemingly more universally accessible by corresponding more closely to aesthetic expectations, thereby building more points of reference for the audience.

The lesson for conductors, from both the comparisons to Wagner and the contrasts between the two versions of the "Italian," is indeed to follow Mendelssohn's lead as charted by his revisions. The music, first and foremost, must be understood as an aspect of religious faith and piety; its embracing and affirmative spiritual content is never far from the surface, audible in the transparency of the ease of communication. Second, the music is intensely personal and foregrounds the subjective experience of life through thematic construction and musical form. Third, the thematic content mirrors meaning and emotional valence. Mendelssohn's music cannot be understood from the vantage point of absolutist aesthetics or aestheticism. Fourth, transparency does not demand loss of intensity or gravity. The music, even in moments of rapid figuration, lightness, and grace (for which the composer is noted), benefits from deepening contrasts, highlighting expressivity and avoiding a mechanical application of a static model of neoclassicism immune from improvisation in interpretation. Mendelssohn did not write imitations of eighteenth-century music, even as a teenager. Fifth, Mendelssohn's orchestral music – like the choral music – utilizes its forces uniquely to evoke space and distance. Few composers have so commanded the shifts between far and near, the grand and the intimate, the monumental and the personal. Sixth and last, the intimacy and interiority of the music are optimistic and reflective. They are not manipulative or morbid and require both performer and listener to engage the musical experience with a personal spiritual commitment. There is, therefore, a less restricted set of adequate solutions vis à vis the musical texts. Profundity and emotional complexity are not necessarily tied to a Wagnerian sense of the tragic or of fatalism.

Conductors should not be afraid of taking risks with Mendelssohn. The first step is to reject the conventional contrast between Mendelssohn and Wagner and locate the expressive intensity they both share. The second is to articulate one's sense of Mendelssohn's dramatic and emotional character to players in rehearsal and to the audience. Conductors are advised, rightly so, against speech making or vague pronouncements in rehearsal. Yet in Mendelssohn there is an opportunity to make the point by changing the way phrases are shaped, balances set and, with choruses, texts delivered. Once the link between the musical and the visual and the spiritual is established in the musical materials, a different sound emerges. A few key words and detailed observations have worked in assisting musicians to locate in Mendelssohn's music the immediacy and depth it usually lacks in performance. Given the significance of the revival of a reactionary religious fundamentalism in contemporary life and politics, the balance between emotionalism and humanism in Mendelssohn's sacred music makes that portion of the repertory particularly timely for revival in concert.

There is in Mendelssohn that perhaps unique combination: a powerful control of time and the dramatic, an unerring sense of pace and arrival, and, in the choral music, an unrivaled capacity to move humanity through a Raphael-like translucent beauty and a palpable enthusiasm for the divine in the human community. An idealist, Mendelssohn wrote music for public performance that used the norms of the aesthetic, in the sense of Schiller, on behalf of civilization and tolerance, toward moral and ethical education and the betterment of community. There was never a greater composer who had as much confidence in continuities between past and present, human universals, and the potential of progress, tolerance, and reason. Delivering Mendelssohn's message in performance convincingly is something contemporary life might well benefit from. There is nothing naive or superficial at work. Owing to its resistance to spectacular theatricality there is more at stake in the effort to generate affection for the full range of Mendelssohn's large-scale works than the reputation of a composer or his music. Redeeming our affections for Mendelssohn can strengthen our belief that music and its performance can be forces on the side of enlightenment, tolerance, and peace. There is more at stake here than music.

Notes

Introduction: Mendelssohn as border-dweller

1. *Maus I: A Survivor's Tale* (New York, 1986). The sequel, *Maus II: And Here My Troubles Began*, appeared in 1991. The pair won a Pulitzer Prize, in 1992.

2. Friedrich Nietzsche, *Jenseits von Gut und Böse*, in *Friedrich Nietzsche: Gesammelte Werke* (Munich, 1925), XV, 202. See, however, Leon Botstein's warning against too simplistic a reading of Nietzsche's formulation in "The Aesthetics of Assimilation and Affirmation: Reconstructing the Career of Felix Mendelssohn," in *MhW*, 7.

3. *MNI*. The single most important collection of work on Mendelssohn's reception in Germany is *Felix Mendelssohn – Mitwelt und Nachwelt: Bericht zum 1. Leipziger Mendelssohn – Kolloquium am 8. und 9. Juni 1993*, ed. Leon Botstein (Wiesbaden, 1996).

4. Leon Botstein, "Aesthetics of Assimilation," 22. See, too, Botstein, "Songs Without Words: Thoughts on Music, Theology, and the Role of the Jewish Question in the Work of Felix Mendelssohn," *MQ* 77 (1993), 561–78; and Michael Marissen, "Religious Aims in Mendelssohn's 1829 Berlin-Singakademie Performances of Bach's St. Matthew Passion," *MQ* 77 (1993), 718–26.

5. Jeffrey Sposato, "Creative Writing: The [Self-] Identification of Mendelssohn as Jew," *MQ* 82 (1998), 190–209. See, however, Leon Botstein's subsequent rejoinder, "Mendelssohn and the Jews," *MQ* 82 [1998], 210–19).

6. See his letter of 16 July 1820, in Sebastian Hensel, *Die Familie Mendelssohn 1729–1847, nach Briefen und Tagebüchern*, ed. Konrad Feilchenfeldt (Frankfurt am Main and Leipzig, 1995), 126, trans. in *The Mendelssohn Family (1829–1847), From Letters and Journals*, trans. Karl Klingemann and an American collaborator, 2nd rev. edn., 2 vols. (London, 1882), I, 82.

7. See, in particular, his letter of 2 June 1837, in which he refuses his mother's plea that he encourage Fanny to publish, in *Briefe aus den Jahren 1833 bis 1847*, ed. Paul Mendelssohn Bartholdy and Carl Mendelssohn Bartholdy (Leipzig, 1863), 141–42; trans. in *Letters of Felix Mendelssohn Bartholdy from 1833 to 1847*, trans. Lady Wallace (London, 1863), 113–14. Landmarks in this literature, all bearing to some extent on the relationship between the two, include Marcia J. Citron, "Felix Mendelssohn's Influence on Fanny Mendelssohn Hensel as a Professional Composer," *Current Musicology* 37/38 (1984), 9–17; Nancy B. Reich, "The Power of Class: Fanny Hensel," in *MhW*, 86–99; and Sarah Rothenberg, " 'Thus Far, But No Farther': Fanny Mendelssohn's Unfinished Journey," *MQ* 77 (1993), 689–708; and Marian Wilson Kimber, "The Suppression of Fanny Mendelssohn: Rethinking Feminist Biography," *19th-Century Music* 26 (2002), 113–29. See also the important recent collection of essays gathered under the heading "Part IV: Felix and Fanny" in *TMH*, 233–88.

8. Sir Julius Benedict, *A Sketch of the Life and Works of the Late Felix Mendelssohn-Bartholdy*, appendix to W. A. Lampadius, *Life of Felix Mendelssohn Bartholdy*, trans. William Leonhard Gage (London, 1877 [1850]), 172.

9. Henry F. Chorley, *Modern German Music: Recollections and Criticisms*, 2 vols. (London, 1854), II, 417, 404.

10. *Ibid.*, 401.

11. K. Freigedank [Wagner's pseudonym], "Das Judenthum in der Musik," *NZfM* 33 (1850), 101–07 and 109–12.

12. Review of 23 February 1889; my immediate source is *Great Composers: Reviews and Bombardments by Bernard Shaw*, ed. Louis Crompton (Berkeley and Los Angeles, 1978), 122.

13. A highly thoughtful consideration of the particular critical tradition into which Shaw's remarks fit is Friedhelm Krummacher, "Composition as Accommodation? On Mendelssohn's Music in Relation to England," in *MSt*, 80–105.

14. The 1829 Liederspiel, *Die Heimkehr aus der Fremde*, was a fully mature work, but never intended to be put before the public, composed as it was for a private celebration of Mendelssohn's parents' silver wedding anniversary.

15. *The Romantic Generation* (Cambridge, MA, 1998), 589.

16. See in particular Douglass Seaton, "The Problem of the Lyric Persona in Mendelssohn's Songs," in *KBB*, 167–86; and Seaton, "Mendelssohn's Cycles of Songs," in *TMH*, 203–29.

17. Greg Vitercik, "Mendelssohn the Progressive," *The Journal of Musicological Research* 8 (1989), 372.

18. "Robert Schumann mit Rücksicht auf Mendelssohn-Bartholdy überhaupt: III. Mendelssohn," *NZfM* 27 (1845), 113. This translation is mine, though excerpts of this article appear, translated by Susan Gillespie, in *MhW*, 341–51.

19. *PM*, 7–9.

20. Botstein, "Aesthetics of Assimilation," 13. Botstein draws out further, and richly historicies, a number of this essay's central themes in his "Neoclassicism, Romanticism, and Emancipation: The Origins of Felix Mendelssohn's Aesthetic Outlook," in *MC*, 1–23.

21. "*Felix culpa*: Mendelssohn, Goethe, and the Social Force of Musical Expression," in *Classical Music and Postmodern Knowledge* (Berkeley and Los Angeles, 1995), 122–42. Closely related issues are confronted insightfully in Julie D. Prandi, "Kindred Spirits: Mendelssohn and Goethe, *Die erste Walpurgisnacht*," in *TMH*, 135–46.

22. "Mendelssohn's Babel: Romanticism and the Poetics of Translation," *Music & Letters* 80 (1999), pp. 23–49.

23. Thomas Christian Schmidt, *Die ästhetischen Grundlagen der Instrumentalmusik Felix Mendelssohn Bartholdys* (Stuttgart, 1996), 221.

24. On the relationship between Mendelssohn's concert overtures and contemporary operatic overtures, see in particular R. Larry Todd, *Mendelssohn: The Hebrides and Other Overtures* (Cambridge, 1993), esp. 38–51.

25. In a particularly dramatic recent case, Judith Silber Ballan's reading of the "Reformation" Symphony as "a narrative that . . . depicts, in order, the Catholic Church, a struggle, and then the victorious emergence of the Protestants" ("Marxian Programmatic Music: A Stage in Mendelssohn's Musical Development," in *MSt*, 155) – so sensible as to seem almost self-evident – is threatened with complete annihilation by James Garratt's clever reconsideration of the supposed "Catholicism" of the first movement's introduction in his "Mendelssohn's Babel" (1999). Wolfgang Dilinger has furthered considerably conversation on the topic of Mendelssohn's programmatic vision in his "The Programme of Mendelssohn's 'Reformation' Symphony, Op. 107," in *TMH*, 115–33.

26. A particularly insightful recent contribution to this conversation is Thomas Grey, "*Tableaux vivants*: Landscape, History, Painting, and the Visual Imagination in Mendelssohn's Orchestral Music," *19th-Century Music* 21 (1997), 38–76.

27. Robert Schumann, "Trio's für Pianoforte, Violine, und Violoncello," *NZfM* 13 (1840), 198.

1. Mendelssohn and the institution(s) of German art music

1. Mendelssohn garnered considerable public and critical notice, for instance, at a Stettin concert of 20 February 1827, at which his *Midsummer Night's Dream Overture* and Concerto for Two Pianos in A♭ were programmed alongside Beethoven's Ninth Symphony (that piece's north German premiere); Mendelssohn had also provided choral music for an 1828 Berlin commemoration of the 300th anniversary of Albrecht Dürer's death.

2. Joshua Rifkin challenged the presumed 1729 premiere of the piece, making a strong case for a date of two years earlier, in "The Chronology of Bach's St. Matthew Passion," *MQ* 61 (1975), 360–87.

3. *Briefwechsel zwischen Goethe und Zelter*, ed. Max Hecker, 3 vols. (Frankfurt am Main, 1987), III, 154; quoted in Arndt Richter, *Mendelssohn: Leben, Werke, Dokumente* (Mainz, 1994), 127.

4. See, in particular, Martin Geck, *Die Wiederentdeckung der Matthäuspassion im 19. Jahrhundert: Die zeitgenössischen Dokumente und ihre ideengeschichtliche Deutung* (Regensburg, 1967).

5. See Eduard Devrient, *My Recollections of Felix Mendelssohn-Bartholdy, and his Letters to Me*, trans. Natalia MacFarren (London, 1869), 47–55. On the dubious verity of Devrient's account, see R. Larry Todd, *Mendelssohn: A Life in Music* (Oxford, 2003), 194–95.

6. See Barry Bergdoll, *Karl Friedrich Schinkel: An Architecture for Prussia* (New York, 1994).

7. Wulf Konold, *Felix Mendelssohn Bartholdy und seine Zeit* (Laaber, 1984), 13.

8. The most accurate existing account (to which the present narrative is indebted) of Mendelssohn's spottily documented early education is Todd, *Mendelssohn*, 33–34.

9. See R. Larry Todd, *Mendelssohn's Musical Education: A Study and Edition of His Exercises in Composition* (Cambridge, 1983).

10. Review of a concert of 13 May 1833 in *The Harmonicon*, June 1833, 135; quoted in Roger Nichols, *Mendelssohn Remembered* (London, 1997), 127.

11. Dr. Ferdinand Hiller, *Mendelssohn: Letters and Recollections*, trans. M. E. von Glehn (New York, 1972 [1874]), 29.

12. Julius Benedict, *Sketch of the Life and Works of Felix Mendelssohn Bartholdy*, 2nd edn. (London, 1850), 24. The most penetrating discussion to date of Mendelssohn's role in

establishing musical "interpretation" as the conductor's central task is Donald Mintz, "Mendelssohn as Performer and Teacher," in *MC*, 87–134 (esp. 99–102).

13. The history of baton conducting throughout Germany is traced as far back as 1812, when Ignaz Franz Mosel conducted thus in Vienna, in Johannes Forner et al., *Die Gewandhauskonzerte zu Leipzig 1781–1981*, ed. Johannes Forner (Leipzig, 1981), 67–68. Important figures include Louis Spohr – who conducted an 1820 concert in London with a baton – and Weber, who habitually used a rolled-up page of a score.

14. For a range of contemporary reports on the subject, see Clive Brown, *A Portrait of Mendelssohn* (New Haven, 2003), 238–57.

15. Quoted in Sebastian Hensel, *The Mendelssohn Family (1729–1847), From Letters and Journals*, 2nd revised edn., trans Karl Klingemann and an American collaborator (London, 1882), I, 85.

16. For a fascinating discussion of the personal and (potential) political significance of this initial journey to England, particularly with regard to the question of anti-Semitism, see Paul Jourdan, "The Hidden Pathways of Assimilation: Mendelssohn's First Visit to London," in *Music and British Culture, 1785–1914* (Oxford, 2000), 99–119.

17. Philharmonic Society conductor George Smart's recollection is unaccountably at odds with the great bulk of reviews and letters surrounding Mendelssohn's English premiere, his journal entry on the subject reading, "A sinfonia by Mendelssohn was performed on May 25th at the Philharmonic Society; not much notice was taken of this composition" (*Leaves from the Journals of Sir George Smart* [New York, 1971], 271).

18. See Peter Ward Jones, "Mendelssohn and his English Publishers," in *MSt*, 240–55.

19. This was not altogether for lack of trying: Mendelssohn spent these months completing his "Reformation" Symphony, doubtless intended for performance at Berlin's Tercentenary Celebration of the Augsburg Confession. The celebration took place on 25 June without Mendelssohn's symphony. See Judith Karen Silber [Ballan], "Mendelssohn and His Reformation Symphony," *Journal of the American Musicological Society* 40 (1987), 310–36.

20. The most systematic handling this episode has yet received is Wm. A. Little, "Mendelssohn and the Berlin Singakademie: The Composer at the Crossroads," in *MhW*, 65–85.

21. *Felix Mendelssohn-Bartholdys Briefwechsel mit Legationsrat Karl Klingemann*, ed. Karl Klingemann (Essen, 1909), 100.

22. Martin Blumner, *Geschichte der Sing-Akademie zu Berlin* (Berlin, 1891), 93; see also Georg Schünemann, *Die Singakademie zu Berlin: 1791–1941* (Regensburg, 1941), 73–74.

23. *MNI*, 227.

24. Little sees Mendelssohn's failure to obtain the post, "in the final analysis, as one of his great triumphs, since it liberated him from the need to commit himself to a specific institution and specific goals at a time when the freedom to grow and develop was critical to the full realization of his genius" (81). Martin Blumner's early account of the event makes no mention whatever of the issue of anti-Semitism (*Geschichte der Sing-Akademie zu Berlin*, 93).

25. A glimpse of the glowing critical reception of these concerts, together with the program of the first two, appear in Susanna Großmann-Vendrey, *Felix Mendelssohn Bartholdy und die Musik der Vergangenheit* (Regensburg, 1969), 51–53.

26. Cecilia Hopkins Porter, "The New Public and the Reordering of the Musical Establishment: The Lower Rhine Music Festivals, 1818–1867," *19th-Century Music* 3 (1980), 211.

27. *Ibid.* 219.

28. Those that followed were the festivals of 1835, 1836, 1838, 1839, 1842, and 1846.

29. Richter, *Mendelssohn*, 189.

30. Cecilia Hopkins Porter, "The Reign of the Dilettanti: Düsseldorf from Mendelssohn to Schumann," *MQ* 73 (1989), 481–82.

31. The first comprehensive account of Mendelssohn's work in Düsseldorf is provided in [Wilhelm Joseph] v[on] W[asielewski], "Felix Mendelssohn-Bartholdy in Düsseldorf in den Jahren 1833–35," *Neue Berliner Musikzeitung* 1 (1847), 389–92. See also Wilhelm Hubert Fischer, "Der Musikverein unter Leitung von Felix Mendelssohn Bartholdy von 1833 bis 1835," in *Festschrift zur hundertjährigen Jubelfeier des Städtischen Musikvereins Düsseldorf . . .* (Düsseldorf, 1918).

32. Großmann-Vendrey, *Vergangenheit*, 54–66.

33. The impression made on Mendelssohn by Santini's collection is captured in Mendelssohn's letter of 8 November 1830, in *Felix Mendelssohn Bartholdy: Reisebriefe von 1830/31*, ed. Peter Sutermeister (Zurich, 1949), 163. Mendelssohn's desire to cultivate a relationship with Baini becomes clear in his letter of 7 December 1830 (*Ibid.*, 175).

34. Letter of 26 October 1833, in *Briefe aus den Jahren 1833 bis 1847 von Felix Mendelssohn Bartholdy*, ed. Paul Mendelssohn Bartholdy and Carl Mendelssohn Bartholdy (Leipzig, 1863), 10.

35. Großmann-Vendrey, *Vergangenheit*, 59–60.

36. On Immermann's role in Felix's appointment, see *MNI*, 232.

37. Letter of 28 March 1834, in *Briefe 1833 bis 1847*, 32.

38. His "salto mortale" is described in a letter of 4 November 1834, in *Ibid.*, 58.

39. A fascinating introduction to the history of the Gewandhaus building itself is Rudolf Skoda, *Das Gewandhaus Leipzig: Geschichte und Gegenwart* (Berlin, 1986), 10–55.

40. Important general surveys of the orchestra's concerts through the period of Mendelssohn's involvement include Alfred Dörffel, *Die Gewandhausconcerte zu Leipzig: Festschrift zur hundertjährigen Jubelfeier der Einweihung des Concertsaales im Gewandhause zu Leipzig*, 2 vols. (Leipzig, 1884; repr. Leipzig, 1980), 83–137; Großmann-Vendrey, *Vergangenheit*, 138–72; and Johannes Forner et al., *Die Gewandhauskonzerte zu Leipzig 1781–1981* (Leipzig, 1981), 67–88.

41. Mintz, "Performer," 103.

42. Beethoven's Fourth Symphony concluded the fourth and final concert of the first series, on 8 March. In the 1847 cycle, it was the third concert of the four-concert series that concluded with Beethoven – the Ninth Symphony – with the final concert dedicated to more recent work, including that of Spohr, Spontini, Rossini, and Donizetti. The complete programs of these concerts appear in Großmann-Vendrey, *Vergangenheit*, 161–69.

43. See Matthias Pape, *Mendelssohns Leipziger Orgelkonzert, 1840: Ein Beitrag zur Bach-Pflege im 19. Jahrhundert* (Wiesbaden, 1988). A reproduction of the original program for the event – in which Mendelssohn's name, at the top, stands in letters three times the size of Bach's, at the bottom – appears on 40.

44. "Reminiscences of Mendelssohn by His English Pupil," in *MhW*, 248. The reminiscences appeared originally in *Dwight's Journal of Music* 32 (1872), 345ff., 353ff., 361ff.

45. Letter of 30 October, *Bunsen aus seinen Briefen*, II, 142–43, quoted in *MNI*, 371.

46. Important accounts of this chapter in Mendelssohn's life are David Brodbeck, "A Winter of Discontent: Mendelssohn and the Berliner Domchor," in *MhW*, 1–32; and Wolfang Dinglinger, "Mendelssohn – General-Musik-Direktor für kirchliche und geistliche Musik," in *KBB*, 23–36.

47. This arrangement is described in Ludwig von Massow's report to the king of 20 May 1841, in *Briefe 1833 bis 1847*, 286–87.

48. Quoted in Georg Schünemann, "Zur Geschichte des Berliner Domchors: Ein vergessenes Jubiläum," *Die Musikpflege* 6 (1935/6), 382; my immediate source is Brodbeck, "Domchor," 3.

49. His reasons are laid out – in impressively restrained tones – in his letter of 23 October 1842, to von Massow, in *Briefe 1833 bis 1847*, 339–41.

50. On these works, and their complex relationship to the liturgical and ecclesiastical environment for which they were crafted, see Brodbeck, "Domchor," 15–32.

51. *Briefe 1833 bis 1847*, 230–31.

52. The most probing study of Mendelssohn's relationship with Friedrich August II, and of the course of their negotiations on the subject of the conservatory, is Klaus Häfner, "Felix Mendelssohn Bartholdy in seinen Beziehungen zu König Friedrich August II. von Sachsen," *Mendelssohn Studien* 7 (Berlin, 1990), 219–68.

53. Quoted in Mintz, "Performer," 116.

54. *Ibid.*, 120–21. A particularly valuable commentary on Mendelssohn's work as a teacher at the Gewandhaus is William Smyth Rockstro, *Mendelssohn* (London, 1884), 104–13; this excerpt appears, together with other relevant documents, in Brown, *Portrait*, 280–306.

55. The most authoritative account of Mendelssohn's final weeks is his wife's long-neglected testimony, recently brought to light in Peter Ward Jones, "Felix Mendelssohn Bartholdys Tod: Der Bericht seiner Frau," *Mendelssohn Studien* 12 (2001), 205–26.

56. *Briefe 1833 bis 1847*, 31.

57. *Ibid.*, 438.

2 Mendelssohn and Judaism

An earlier version of portions of this essay appeared as "Mendelssohn's Music and German-Jewish Culture: An Intervention," *MQ* 83 (1999), 31–44. © Oxford University Press.

1. Regensburg, 1974.

2. See Lars Ulrich Abraham, "Mendelssohns Chorlieder und ihre musikgeschichtliche Stellung," in *PM*, 83.

3. Arnaldo Momigliano, "J. G. Droysen between Greeks and Jews," in *Essays in Ancient and Modern Historiography* (Middletown, 1977), 310.

4. See Michael P. Steinberg, *Listening to Reason: Culture, Subjectivity, and 19th-century Music* (Princeton, 2004), Introduction and passim. Chapter 4, "Canny and Uncanny Histories in Biedermeier Music," contains a sustained treatment of Mendelssohn.

5. Peter Mercer-Taylor, *The Life of Mendelssohn* (Cambridge, 2000), 5–16. Mercer-Taylor's treatment here of Moses Mendelssohn's biography and its importance to his grandson is exceptionally strong. As my own argument will make clear, I am in disagreement with Mercer-Taylor's reasonable conclusion that "the Germans, not the Jews, were the Mendelssohns'

chosen people" (30). This binary misrepresents, in my view, both Abraham Mendelssohn's Hegelianism and Felix's multiculturalism. Particularly interesting is Mercer-Taylor's speculation that Felix "inherited Moses' [physical] constitution" (12). This speculation might presumably enable or inspire a psychoanalytic exploration of Felix's inheritance of his grandfather's "constitution" – physical and otherwise.

6. See the debate between David Sorkin ("The Mendelssohn Myth and Its Method") and Allan Arkush ("The Questionable Judaism of Moses Mendelssohn") in *New German Critique* 77 (1999), 7–44.

7. See Steven M. Lowenstein, *The Mechanics of Change: Essays in the Social History of German Jewry* (Atlanta, 1992), 24, 35; David Clay Large, *Berlin* (New York, 2000), 58; Lowenstein, *The Berlin Jewish Community* (New York, 1994), 121.

8. Deborah Hertz, *Jewish High Society in Old Regime Berlin* (New Haven, 1988), 230–32, cited in Lowenstein, *The Berlin Jewish Community*, 121.

9. Abraham Mendelssohn, "Why I have Raised You as a Christian: A Letter to His Daughter (c. July 1820)," in *The Jew in the Modern World: A Documentary History* ed. Paul Mendes-Flohr and Jehuda Reinharz (New York, 1995), 257–58.

10. *MQ* 82 (Spring 1998).

11. *MQ* 83 (Spring 1999), as indicated above, in the first (unnumbered) note in this chapter.

12. *MNI*, viii.

13. The original letter was written to Manfred Schloesser, editor of the Festschrift in which it was published. The letter explained why Scholem would not contribute an essay to the volume on the "German Jewish dialogue." See Gershom Scholem, "Wider den Mythos von deutsch-juedischen Gespraech,'" in *Auf gespaltenem Pfad: Festschrift fuer Margarete Suessmann*, ed. M. Schloesser (Darmstadt, 1964), translated as "Against the Myth of the German-Jewish Dialogue," in *On Jews and Judaism in Crisis: Selected Essays* (New York, 1976), 61–2.

14. See George Mosse, *German Jews Beyond Judaism* (Bloomington, 1985).

15. *MNI*, 44.

16. Scholem, "Jews and Germans" (1966), in *On Jews and Judaism in Crisis*, 80.

17. *MNI*, 37. I have duplicated the translation as provided by Werner but have made one change after comparing his translation with the German version used in his own, later edition of 1980. Where the letter says that the name Mendelssohn had acquired "great authority" (*ein grosses Gewicht*), Werner had translated hyperbolically "acquired a Messianic import." I

am grateful to Peter Ward Jones for pointing this issue out to me.

18. See my discussion of this issue in its relation to Mahler and other thinkers in the chapter "The Catholic Culture of the Austrian Jews," in *Austria as Theater and Ideology: The Meaning of the Salzburg Festival* (Ithaca, 2000).

19. Eduard Devrient, *Meine Erinnerungen an Felix Mendelssohn Bartholdy und seine Briefe an mich* (Leipzig, 1869), 62.

20. See *MNI*, 100.

21. *Ibid.*, 230–31.

22. William A. Little, "Mendelssohn and the Berlin Singakademie: The Composer at the Crossroads," in *MhW*, 78.

23. *Ibid.*, 80.

24. *MNI*, 171.

25. *Ibid.*, 203.

26. Paul Gilroy, *The Black Atlantic: Modernity and Double Consciousness* (Cambridge, 1993).

27. Friedhelm Kemp, "Mendelssohns Berliner Umwelt," in *PM*, 12.

3. Felix and Fanny: gender, biography, and history

1. 28 September 1840, in *The Letters of Fanny Hensel to Felix Mendelssohn*, ed. Marcia J. Citron (Stuyvesant, NY, 1987), 294, 572, translation modified.

2. 9 June 1847, *Briefe von Felix Mendelssohn-Bartholdy an Ignaz und Charlotte Moscheles*, ed. Felix Moscheles (Leipzig, 1888; repr. Walluf-Nendeln, 1976), 280.

3. J. T. [John Thomson], "Notes of a Musical Tourist," *The Harmonicon* 8 (3 March 1830), 99.

4. Carl Friedrich von Ledebur, *Tonkünstler-Lexikon Berlins von den Ältesten Zeiten bis auf die Gegenwart* (Berlin, 1861; repr. Tutzing, Berlin, 1964), 236; François Joseph Fétis, *Biographie universelle des musiciens et bibliographie générale de la musique*, 2nd edn. (Brussels, 1860–65; repr. Paris, 1883), IV, 296.

5. Francis Galton, *Hereditary Genius: An Inquiry into its Laws and Consequences* (London, 1869; repr. New York, 1870), 245.

6. "The Mendelssohn Family," *The Saturday Review* 53 (21 January 1882), 87.

7. "The Mendelssohn Family [Second Notice]," *The Musical Times* 23 (1 June 1882), 312–13.

8. E. Sergy (pseud. of Noémie Koenig), *Fanny Mendelssohn. D'après les mémoires de son fils* (Paris, 1888). Marian Wilson Kimber, "Zur frühen Wirkungsgeschichte Fanny Hensels," in *Fanny Hensel geb. Mendelssohn*, ed. Beatrix Borchard and Monika Schwarz-Danuser (Stuttgart, 1999), 248–62.

9. Sebastian Hensel, *Die Familie Mendelssohn 1729–1847, nach Briefen und Tagebüchern*, ed. Konrad Feilchenfeldt (Frankfurt am Main and

Leipzig, 1995), 131; Eduard Devrient, *Meine Erinnerungen an Felix Mendelssohn-Bartholdy und seine Briefe an mich* (Leipzig, 1869), 13.

10. Hans-Günter Klein, "Similarities and Differences in the Artistic Development of Fanny and Felix Mendelssohn Bartholdy in a Family Context: Observations Based on the Early Berlin Autograph Volumes," in *TMH*, 243.

11. Hensel, *Die Familie Mendelssohn*, 859.

12. Ferdinand Hiller, *Mendelssohn. Briefe und Erinnerungen*, 2nd edn. (Cologne, 1878), 94.

13. Quoted in James Robert Sterndale Bennett, *The Life of William Sterndale Bennett* (Cambridge, 1907), 126–27.

14. Mrs. [Sarah] Austin, "Recollections of Felix Mendelssohn," *Fraser's Magazine for Town and Country* 37 (April 1848), 427–28.

15. Fanny Hensel, *Tagebücher*, ed. Hans-Günter Klein and Rudolf Elvers (Wiesbaden, 2002), 86.

16. *Ibid.*

17. Hensel, *Die Familie Mendelssohn*, 169.

18. 15 May [1837], *The Mendelssohns on Honeymoon: The 1837 Diary of Felix and Cécile Mendelssohn Bartholdy, together with Letters to Their Families*, ed. and trans. Peter Ward Jones (Oxford, 1997), 156.

19. 25 August 1829, in *Felix Mendelssohn: A Life in Letters*, ed. Rudolf Elvers, trans. Craig Tomlinson (New York, 1986), 96.

20. 30 January 1836, in Felix Mendelssohn Bartholdy, *Briefe aus den Jahren 1833 bis 1847*, 5th edn., ed. Paul and Carl Mendelssohn Bartholdy (Leipzig, 1865), 114.

21. Marcia Citron, "Fanny Hensel's Letters to Felix Mendelssohn in the Green-Books Collection at Oxford," in *Mendelssohn and Schumann: Essays on Their Music and Its Content*, ed. Jon Finson and R. Larry Todd (Durham, NC, 1984), 102–04.

22. 30 July 1836, in *The Letters of Fanny Hensel to Felix Mendelssohn*, 209, 514.

23. c. August 1834, *Ibid.*, 151, 473.

24. 28 December 1831, in *Reisebriefe von Felix Mendelssohn Bartholdy aus den Jahren 1830 bis 1832*, ed. Paul Mendelssohn Bartholdy, 3rd edn. (Leipzig, 1862; repr. Mainz, n.d.), 310.

25. Marian Wilson Kimber, "'For Art has the Same Place in Your Heart as Mine': Family, Friendship and Community in the Life of Felix Mendelssohn," in *MC*, 30–33.

26. 2 June 1837, in *The Letters of Fanny Hensel to Felix Mendelssohn*, 234, 529, translation modified.

27. Devrient, *Erinnerungen*, 40.

28. *Aus Moscheles' Leben: Nach Briefen und Tagebüchern*, ed. Charlotte Moscheles, 2 vols. (Leipzig, 1872), II, 54; letter of 6 October 1831 in *Reisebriefe*, 287–88; *Briefe von und an Joseph*

Joachim, ed. Johannes Joachim and Andreas Moser, 3 vols. (Berlin, 1911–13), II, 78–79, quoted in Nancy B. Reich, *Clara Schumann, the Artist and the Woman*, 2nd edn. (Ithaca, 2001), 216.

29. See Mendelssohn's critique of a Lied by an unidentified woman in *Felix Mendelssohn: A Life in Letters*, 273.

30. Adolf Bernhard Marx recalled Abraham suggesting more "secure" careers to Felix in *Erinnerungen aus meinem Leben* (Berlin, 1865), I, portions reprinted as "From the Memoirs of Adolf Bernhard Marx," trans. Susan Gillespie, in *MhW*, 208 ff.

31. Hensel, *Die Familie Mendelssohn*, 126.

32. Nancy B. Reich, "The Power of Class: Fanny Hensel," in *MhW*, 86–99.

33. Henry F. Chorley, "Mendelssohn's Mother and Sister," in W. A. Lampadius, *Life of Felix Mendelssohn Bartholdy*, trans. William Leonhard Gage (Boston, 1865; repr. Boston, 1978), 210–11.

34. R. Larry Todd, "On Stylistic Affinities in the Music of Fanny Hensel and Felix Mendelssohn Bartholdy," in *TMH*, 258.

35. "Fanny Mendelssohn," *The Musical Times* 29 (1 June 1888), 341.

36. In fact, the Romantic myth frequently emphasizes the artist overcoming family resistance.

37. Whitney Chadwick and Isabelle de Courtivron, Introduction to *Significant Others: Creativity and Intimate Partnership* (London, 1993), 10.

38. Elise Polko, "Versunkene Sterne," in *Musikalische Mährchen, Phantasien und Skizzen* (Leipzig, 1852), 206–11.

39. Jules [sic] Benedict, *Sketch of the Life and Works of the Late Felix Mendelssohn Bartholdy* (London, 1850), 56.

40. William Rounseville Alger, *The Friendships of Women* (Boston, 1868), 76–77.

41. Gloria Kamen, *Hidden Music: The Life of Fanny Mendelssohn* (New York, 1996), 47.

42. 29 June 1829, in *The Letters of Fanny Hensel to Felix Mendelssohn*, 57, 407.

43. *MNI*, 76–77.

44. 11 June 1830, in Hensel, *Die Familie Mendelssohn*, 350–51. The reference at the end is to Wilhelm Hensel.

45. David Warren Sabean, "Fanny and Felix Mendelssohn-Bartholdy and the Question of Incest," *MQ* 77 (1993), 709–17. Sabean instead places the relationship in the context of early nineteenth-century ideas about the intimacy of siblings.

46. 28 September 1840, in *The Letters of Fanny Hensel to Felix Mendelssohn*, 296, 574.

47. Marian Wilson [Kimber], "Mendelssohn's Wife: Love, Art and Romantic Biography," *19th Century Studies* 6 (1992), 1–18.

48. Marian Wilson Kimber, "The Composer as Other: Gender and Race in the Biography of Felix Mendelssohn," in *TMH*, 335–51.

49. Marx, "From the Memoirs of Adolf Bernhard Marx," 210–11.

50. Hermann Zopff, "Characteristics of Felix Mendelssohn-Bartholdy," *Dwight's Journal of Music* 11 (15 August 1857), 154.

51. George Upton, *Woman in Music*, 2nd edn. (Chicago, 1886), 147.

52. "From My Study," *The Musical Times* 36 (1 September 1895), 590.

53. Chadwick and De Courtivron, *Significant Others*, 10.

54. The rest of this chapter is based on my "The Suppression of Fanny Mendelssohn: Rethinking Feminist Biography," *19th Century Music* 26 (2002), 113–29. © The Regents of the University of California.

55. For example, see Françoise Tillard, *Fanny Mendelssohn*, trans. Camille Naish (Portland, OR, 1996), and Marcia J. Citron, "Mendelssohn(-Bartholdy) [Hensel], Fanny (Cécilie)," in *The New Grove Dictionary of Music and Musicians*, 29 vols., ed. Stanley Sadie and John Tyrrell, 2nd edn. (London, 2001), XVI, 388.

56. Letter of 24 June 1837, in *Briefe 1833 bis 1847*, 141–42.

57. Letter of 10 December 1847, in Ingeborg Stolzenberg, "Paul Mendelssohn-Bartholdy nach dem Tode seines Bruders Felix," *Mendelssohn Studien* 8 (1993), 184.

58. Hensel, *Die Familie Mendelssohn*, 877.

59. Edward Dowden, Review of Sebastian Hensel's *The Mendelssohn Family (1729–1827 [sic]) from Letters and Journals*, in *The Academy* 21 (21 January 1882), 37.

60. 24 June 1837, New York Public Library, published in *The Mendelssohns on Honeymoon*, 165–68.

61. See Camilla Cai, Preface to Fanny Hensel (née Mendelssohn), *Songs for Pianoforte, 1836–1837*, Recent Researches in the Music of the Nineteenth and Early Twentieth Centuries 22 (Madison, 1994), viii–ix. Cai has suggested that Hensel's failure to publish in 1838 may have been due in part to the death of Adolph Schlesinger, her chief advocate at the Schlesinger publishing firm.

62. Johann Christian Lobe, *Fliegende Blätter für die Musik* 1 (1855); trans. Susan Gillespie as "Conversations with Felix Mendelssohn" in *MhW*, 191.

63. Felix Mendelssohn Bartholdy, *Briefe an deutsche Verleger*, ed. Rudolf Elvers and H.

Herzfeld (Berlin: de Gruyter, 1968); Peter Ward Jones, "Mendelssohn and His English Publishers," in *MSt*, 240–55.

64. Letter to Angelica von Woringen, 26 November 1846, quoted in *The Letters of Fanny Hensel*, 352n, translation modified.

65. Phyllis Benjamin, "A Diary Album for Fanny Mendelssohn Bartholdy," *Mendelssohn Studien* 7 (1990), 213. See Mendelssohn's letter to Fanny expressing his concern over her miscarriage, 14 April 1837 (*The Mendelssohns on Honeymoon*, 138–39).

66. *The Mendelssohns on Honeymoon*, 52.

67. These are nos. 2, 3, and 12 in Op. 8 ("Heimweh", "Italien", and "Suleika und Hatem") and nos. 7, 10, and 12 in Op. 9 ("Sehnsucht", "Verlust", and "Die Nonne").

68. Letter of c. 22 May 1830, *The Letters of Fanny Hensel*, 100, 436.

69. Letter to Lea Mendelssohn, 19 July 1842, in Hensel, *Die Familie Mendelssohn*, 650.

70. [Thomson], "Notes of a Musical Tourist," 99.

71. Hensel, *Die Familie Mendelssohn*, 480; F. Max Müller, *Auld Lang Syne* (New York, 1898), reprinted in *MhW*, 254–55.

72. Linda Nochlin, *Women, Art and Power and Other Essays* (New York, 1988), 155.

4 Mendelssohn and the rise of musical historicism

1. See Charles Rosen, "Mendelssohn and the Invention of Religious Kitsch," *The Romantic Generation* (London, 1996), 569–98.

2. Carl Dahlhaus, "Geschichtliche und ästhetische Erfahrung," in *Die Ausbreitung des Historismus über die Musik: Aufsätze und Diskussionen*, ed Walter Wiora (Regensburg, 1969), 243; Walter Wiora, "Grenzen und Stadien des Historismus," in *Die Ausbreitung des Historismus*, ed. Wiora 302.

3. See Friedhelm Krummacher, "Historismus," *Die Musik in Geschichte und Gegenwart*, 2nd edn., ed. Ludwig Finscher (Kassel and Stuttgart, 1994–), Sachteil, IV, 342–51.

4. A different perspective on the relation between (neo)classicism and historicism is provided in Leon Botstein, "Neoclassicism, Romanticism, and Emancipation: The Origins of Felix Mendelssohn's Aesthetic Outlook," in *MC*, 1–23.

5. Michel Foucault, *Les mots et les choses* (Paris, 1966), translated as *The Order of Things: An Archaeology of the Human Sciences* (New York and London, 2002), 401–02.

6. Winckelmann's significance for the development of historicism is discussed in my "Prophets Looking Backwards: German Romantic Historicism and the Representation of

Renaissance Music," *Journal of the Royal Musical Association* 125 (2000), 164–204.

7. Johann Gottfried Herder, *Denkmahl Johann Winkelmanns* (1777), *Sämtliche Werke*, ed. Bernhard Suphan, 33 vols. (Berlin, 1877–1913; repr. Hildesheim, 1967–68), VII, 481.

8. Johann Wolfgang von Goethe, draft of a letter to the architect Ludwig Friedrich Catel, April 1815, *Goethes Briefe*, ed. Karl Robert Mandelkow, 4 vols. (Hamburg, 1962–67), III, 627–28.

9. Heinrich Heine, *Die romantische Schule* (1835), *Heinrich Heine Säkularausgabe*, ed. Fritz Mende *et al.*, 27 vols. (Berlin and Paris, 1970–), VIII, 9.

10. Friedrich Schlegel, "Nachricht von den Gemälden in Paris" (1803), *Kritische Friedrich-Schlegel-Ausgabe*, ed. Ernst Behler *et al.*, 35 vols. (Munich, 1958–), IV, 13.

11. See especially Friedrich Schlegel, "Vom Raffael," *Kritische Friedrich-Schlegel-Ausgabe*, IV, 48–60.

12. Heinrich Heine, *Die Stadt Lukka* (1828), *Heinrich Heine Säkularausgabe*, VI, 143.

13. Goethe, letter to the architect Sulpiz Boisserée, 14 February 1814, *Goethes Briefe*, III, 605. At the time of this remark (which is echoed in other letters from the winter of 1813–14), Goethe's knowledge of the work of Overbeck and Cornelius was restricted to drawings on religious and mythological subjects; later in 1814, he acquired Overbeck's painting *Heilige Elisabeth*. See Richard Benz, *Goethe und die romantische Kunst* (Munich, [1940]), 211, 214–15.

14. Friedrich Schlegel, "Über die deutsche Kunstausstellung zu Rom, im Frühjahr 1819, und über den gegenwärtigen Stand der deutschen Kunst in Rom" (1819), *Kritische Friedrich-Schlegel-Ausgabe*, IV, 248.

15. Georg Wilhelm Friedrich Hegel, *Ästhetik*, ed. Friedrich Bassenge, 2nd edn., 2 vols. (Berlin and Weimar, 1965), I, 550–51 (all translations are based on *Aesthetics: Lectures on Fine Art*, trans. T. M. Knox, 2 vols. [Oxford, 1975]).

16. *Ibid.*, 577, 584.

17. *Ibid.*, 578.

18. *Ibid.*, 577.

19. *Ibid.*, 578.

20. *Ibid.*, 163.

21. See Andreas Huyssen, *Die frühromantische Konzeption von Übersetzung und Aneignung: Studien zur frühromantischen Utopie einer deutschen Weltliteratur* (Zurich and Freiburg im Breisgau, 1969).

22. Franz Brendel, *Geschichte der Musik in Italien, Deutschland, und Frankreich. Von der ersten christlichen Zeiten bis auf die Gegenwart*, 6th edn. (Leipzig, 1878), 128.

23. *Ibid.*, 129.

24. Ulrich Konrad, *Otto Nicolai: Studien zu Leben und Werk* (Baden-Baden, 1986), 69–70.

25. Heinrich Hübsch, *In welchem Style sollen wir bauen?* (Karlsruhe, 1828). This pamphlet, and other contributions to the debate which it stimulated, are translated in *In What Style Should We Build? The German Debate on Architectural Style*, ed. Wolfgang Herrmann (Santa Monica, 1992).

26. Anon. (Anton Springer), "Kritische Gedanken über die Münchner Kunst," *Jahrbücher der Gegenwart* (1845), 1022–34, as presented in *Realismus und Gründerzeit: Manifeste und Dokumente zur deutschen Literatur 1848–1880*, ed. Max Bucher *et al.*, 2 vols. (Stuttgart, 1976), II, 5–6.

27. Barry Bergdoll, *Karl Friedrich Schinkel: An Architecture for Prussia* (New York, 1994).

28. Alan Barfour, *Berlin: The Politics of Order 1737–1989* (New York, 1990), 30–39.

29. Karl Friedrich Schinkel, letter of January 24 1833 to Prince Maximilian of Bavaria, Margarete Kühn, *Schinkel Lebenswerk: Ausland: Bauten und Entwürfe* (Berlin and Munich, 1989), 4, as quoted in Bergdoll, *Karl Friedrich Schinkel*, 217.

30. The most detailed study of Mendelssohn's historical orientation in the different stages of his career remains Susanna Großmann-Vendrey, *Felix Mendelssohn Bartholdy und die Musik der Vergangenheit* (Regensburg, 1969); see also her "Mendelssohn und die Vergangenheit," in *Die Ausbreitung des Historismus*, ed. Wiora, 73–84.

31. Carl Friedrich Zelter, "Erste Denkschrift," 28 September 1803, as presented in Cornelia Schröder, *Carl Friedrich Zelter und die Akademie: Dokumente und Briefe zur Entstehung der Musik-Sektion in der preußischen Akademie der Künste* (Berlin, 1959), 76.

32. Carl Friedrich Zelter, unsent draft of a letter to Goethe, 6–11 April 1829, in *Briefwechsel zwischen Goethe und Zelter in den Jahren 1799 bis 1832, Johann Wolfgang von Goethe: Sämtliche Werke nach Epochen seines Schaffens*, ed. Edith Zehm (Munich, 1998), XX/3, 1001.

33. See R. Larry Todd, *Mendelssohn's Musical Education: A Study and Edition of his Exercises in Composition* (Cambridge, 1983), 2–11.

34. This aspect of Zelter's activities is explored in my "Performing Renaissance Church Music in Nineteenth-Century Germany: Issues and Challenges in the Study of Performative Reception," *Music & Letters* 83 (2002), 187–236 (esp. 189–92).

35. Carl Friedrich Zelter, "Zweite Denkschrift" (c. 1803), as presented in Georg Schünemann, *Carl Friedrich Zelter, der Begründer der Preussischen Musikpflege* (Berlin, 1932), 14–15.

36. See Carl Dahlhaus, "Mendelssohn und die musikalischen Gattungstraditionen," in *PM*, 55–60.

37. Zelter, letter of 28 May 1825, *Briefwechsel zwischen Goethe und Zelter*, XX/1, 847.

38. Felix Mendelssohn, letter of 20 September 1827 to his mother, as quoted in Großmann-Vendrey, *Vergangenheit*, 24.

39. Großmann-Vendrey, "Mendelssohn und die Vergangenheit," 78.

40. Wulf Konold, *Felix Mendelssohn Bartholdy und seine Zeit* (Laaber, 1984), 139. Similarly, Michael P. Steinberg contends that for the young Mendelssohn, Bach was "no antique or mere harbinger, but a modern composer" ("Das Mendelssohn–Bach–Verhältnis als ästhetischer Diskurs der Moderne," in *Felix Mendelssohn: Mitwelt und Nachwelt. Bericht zum 1. Leipziger Mendelssohn-Kolloquium am 8. und 9. Juni 1999*, ed. Leon Botstein [Wiesbaden, 1996], 84–88.

41. Lea Mendelssohn, letter of 19 October 1821 to Henriette von Pereira-Arnstein, as quoted in *Leipziger Ausgabe der Werke Felix Mendelssohn Batholdys*, ed. Hellmuth Christian Wolff, ser. I, I (Leipzig, 1972), v.

42. Zelter, letter to Goethe of 5–14 April 1827, *Briefwechsel zwischen Goethe und Zelter*, XX/1, 992.

43. Hans-Joachim Schulze, "Bach – Leipzig – Mendelssohn," in *Felix Mendelssohn: Mitwelt und Nachwelt*, ed. Botstein, 79–83. The view that this performance marked the initiation of a Bach revival had its roots in the reports and reviews of Adolf Bernhard Marx, all of which are presented in Martin Geck, *Die Wiederentdeckung der Matthäuspassion im 19. Jahrhundert: Die zeitgenössischen Dokumente und ihre ideengeschichtliche Deutung* (Regensburg, 1967).

44. See the letter to his family of 21 May 1830, Felix Mendelssohn Bartholdy, *Reisebriefe aus den Jahren 1830 bis 1832*, ed. Paul Mendelssohn Bartholdy, 5th edn. (Leipzig, 1863), 5.

45. See Thomas Schmidt, *Die ästhetischen Grundlagen der Instrumentalmusik Felix Mendelssohn Bartholdys* (Stuttgart, 1996), 59–60.

46. Goethe, diary entry of 24 May 1830, *Briefwechsel zwischen Goethe und Zelter*, XX/3, 1114; Mendelssohn, letter to his parents of 25 May 1830, *Reisebreife*, 9.

47. Mendelssohn, letter to Rebecka Dirichlet, 22 July 1844, in Sebastian Hensel, *Die Familie Mendelssohn*, 11th edn. (Leipzig, 1903), II, 328, as quoted in Großmann-Vendrey, *Vergangenheit*, 221.

48. Mendelssohn, letter to his father of 10–11 December 1830, *Reisebreife*, 89.

49. Mendelssohn, letter to Fanny Hensel and Rebecka Dirichlet of 28 May 1831, *ibid.*, 171.

50. Mendelssohn, letter to Zelter of 18 December 1830, *ibid.*, 97.

51. Mendelssohn, letter to Ernst Friedrich Bauer of 4 March 1833, *Briefe 1833 bis 1847*, 2.

52. See Friedhelm Krummacher, "Art – History – Religion: On Mendelssohn's Oratorios *St. Paul* and *Elijah*," in *MC*, 299–382 (esp. 304–05).

53. Abraham Mendelssohn, letter of 10 March 1835, Mendelssohn, *Briefe 1833 bis 1847*, 85–86.

54. Mendelssohn, letter of 15 July 1831, Eduard Devrient, *Meine Erinnerungen an Felix Mendelssohn-Bartholdy und seine Briefe an mich* (Leipzig, 1872), 115, as quoted in Krummacher, "Bach, Berlin und Mendelssohn," 63.

55. Mendelssohn, letter to Zelter of 18 December 1830, *Reisebriefe*, 96–97.

56. Schmidt, *Die ästhetischen Grundlagen*, 43; Johann Wolfgang von Goethe, "Maximen und Reflexionen," no. 813, *Goethes Werke*, XII, 767.

57. Großmann-Vendrey, "Mendelssohn und die Vergangenheit," 80.

58. Mendelssohn, letter to Otto von Woringen, 12 March 1836, as presented in Großmann-Vendrey, *Vergangenheit*, 81.

59. Eduard Krüger, "F. Mendelssohn Bartholdy, Drei Psalmen (2. 43. 22.) Opus 78," *Neue Berliner Musikzeitung* 4 (1850), 3–5 (3).

60. See my "Mendelssohn's *Antigone* and the Afterlife of Art" (forthcoming); see also Sinéad Dempsey, "Aesthetic and Ideological Trends in the Reception of Mendelssohn's Orchestral Music in the Mid-Nineteenth Century," Ph.D. thesis, University of Manchester (forthcoming).

61. Heinrich Heine, "Rossini und Felix Mendelssohn" (1842), "Musikalische Saison in Paris" (1844), *Lutezia: Berichte über Politik, Kunst und Volksleben*, in *Heinrich Heine Säkularausgabe*, XI.

62. Eduard Hanslick, "An Wien's Musikfreunde vor der Aufführung des 'Elias'" (1847), *Sämtliche Schriften*, ed. Dietmar Strauß (Vienna, 1993), I/1, 119–27; Franz Brendel, "Robert Schumann mit Rücksicht auf Mendelssohn-Bartholdy, und die Entwicklung der modernen Tonkunst überhaupt," *NZfM* 22 (1845), 63–67, 81–83, 89–92, 113–15, 121–23, 145–47, 149–50 (esp. 146). Cf. Richard Hohenemser, *Welche Einflüsse hat die Wiederbelebung der älteren Musik im 19. Jahrhundert auf die deutschen Komponisten?* (Leipzig, 1900), 66; Hans-Elmar Bach, "Mendelssohn als Komponist geistlicher a cappella-Musik," *Musica sacra* 88 (1968), 168.

63. Heine, *Lutezia*, 141.

64. Gottfried Wilhelm Fink, "Paulus. Oratorium nach Worten der heiligen Schrift componirt von Felix Mendelssohn-Bartholdy," *Allgemeine musikalische Zeitung* 39 (1837), 522.

65. Robert Schumann, "Fragmente aus Leipzig" (1837), *Gesammelte Schriften über Musik und Musiker*, 3rd edn. (Leipzig, 1875), I, 328.

66. See Theodor W. Adorno, "Toward a Reappraisal of Heine," *Gesammelte Schriften*, ed. Rolf Tiedemann (Frankfurt am Main, 1986), XX/2, 447–48.

67. Krummacher, "Art – History – Religion," 314–18; Peter Mercer-Taylor, "Rethinking Mendelssohn's Historicism: A Lesson from *St. Paul*," *The Journal of Musicology* 15 (1997), 208–29 (esp. 228–29).

68. James Garratt, "Mendelssohn's Babel: Romanticism and the Poetics of Translation," *Music & Letters* 80 (1999), 23–49; James Garratt, *Palestrina and the German Romantic Imagination: Interpreting Historicism in Nineteenth-Century Music* (Cambridge, 2002), 241–60.

5 Mendelssohn as progressive

1. Arnold Schoenberg, *Theory of Harmony*, trans. Roy E. Carter (Berkeley, 1978), 401.

2. Robert Schumann, "Trios für Pianoforte, Violine und Violoncello," *NZfM* 13 (1840), 197–98.

3. Charles Rosen, *The Romantic Generation* (Cambridge, MA, 1995), 589.

4. Donald Francis Tovey, *Essays in Musical Analysis*, 6 vols. and supplement (London, 1935–44), I, 145–46.

5. Viktor Urbantschitsch, "Die Entwicklung der Sonatenform bei Brahms," *Studien zur Musikwissenschaft* 14 (1927), 282.

6. Carl Dahlhaus, *Between Romanticism and Modernism: Four Studies in the Music of the Later Nineteenth Century*, trans. Mary Whittall (Berkeley, 1980), 43–44.

7. See, for example, Greg Vitercik, *The Early Works of Felix Mendelssohn: A Study in the Romantic Sonata Style* (Philadelphia, 1992), 47–70.

8. Vitercik, *Early Works*, 79ff. and 190ff., respectively. On op. 26, see R. Larry Todd, *Mendelssohn: The Hebrides and Other Overtures* (Cambridge, 1993), 64–68 and passim.

9. It is worth noting that some form of structurally goal-oriented acceleration shapes each section of the first movement: the multifaceted intensifications of pace in the exposition; an extended passage of purely schematic acceleration of the development; and the wholesale elimination of the transitional material in the recapitulation. On the development section, see Peter Mercer-Taylor, *The Life of Mendelssohn* (Cambridge, 2000), 155.

10. The term comes from Ernest Ansermet, "L'œuvre d'Igor Strawinsky," *La Revue Musicale* 10 (1921), 9, 17–27.

11. For a closer examination of the relation of motive and tonality in this movement, see Vitercik, *Early Works*, 180–90. On a similar interrelation of motive and tonality in the *Hebrides* Overture, see 190–200.

12. This is a characteristic strategy in Mendelssohn's finest works; the Octet, *Hebrides* Overture, and the "Italian" Symphony offer particularly striking examples. The coda to the last movement of the "Scottish" Symphony represents the most impressive, and probably at the same time the most controversial, example.

13. On the notion of closure, see Barbara Herrnstein Smith, *Poetic Closure: A Study of How Poems End* (Chicago, 1968).

14. See Leon Plantinga, "Schumann's Critical Reaction to Mendelssohn," in *Mendelssohn and Schumann: Essays on Their Music and Its Context*, ed. R. Larry Todd and Jon W. Finson (Durham, 1984), 17–18.

15. On Schubert's influence on Brahms, see James Webster, "Schubert's Sonata Forms and Brahms's First Maturity," *19th-Century Music* 3 (1978/79), 18–35; and 4 (1979/80), 52–71.

16. Donald Francis Tovey, "Brahms's Chamber Music," in *The Main Stream of Music and Other Essays* (New York, 1949), 230.

17. Kofi Agawu, "Formal Perspectives on the Symphonies," in *The Cambridge Companion to Brahms*, ed. Michael Musgrave (Cambridge, 1999), 133–55.

18. The terms are taken from Carl Dahlhaus, *Between Romanticism and Modernism*, 47; see also Agawu, "Formal Perspectives," 134.

19. Charles Rosen, *The Classical Style: Haydn, Mozart, Beethoven*, exp. edn. (New York, 1997), 460.

20. Vitercik, *Early Works*, 320–21, n. 18; and 226–67; see also Rosen, *Romantic Generation* 574–80.

21. The movement – and the work as a whole – repays close study; it is one of the composer's most original and distinctly characteristic conceptions; see Rosen, *Romantic Generation*, 581–86 and Vitercik, *Early Works*, 267–90.

22. Mercer-Taylor, *Mendelssohn*, 87.

23. *Ibid.*, 88.

24. On the concept of stratification, see Roman Ingarden, *The Literary Work of Art: An Investigation on the Borderlines of Ontology, Logic, and Theory of Literature*, trans. George Grabowicz (Evanston, 1973).

25. See note 18.

26. For a summary of Goethe's ideas see Nicholas Boyle, *Goethe: The Poet and the Age* (Oxford, 1991), I, 593–97. The present discussion is drawn from Boyle's commentary.

27. Cited in Boyle, *Goethe*, I, 593.

28. Mendelssohn to Adolf Fredrik Lindblad, cited in Friedhelm Krummacher, *Mendelssohn –*

der Komponist: Studien zur Kammermusik für Streicher (Munich, 1978), 72. Translation mine.
29. "Plot can be defined as the dynamic, sequential element in narrative." Robert Scholes and Robert Kellogg, *The Nature of Narrative* (Oxford, 1966), 207.
30. Krummacher, *Mendelssohn*, 72. Translation mine.
31. Mendelssohn to Abraham Mendelssohn, Paris, 31 March 1832, in *Reisebriefe von Felix Mendelssohn Bartholdy aus den Jahren 1830 bis 1832*, ed. Paul Mendelssohn Bartholdy (Leipzig, 1861), 52. Translation mine.
32. Mercer-Taylor, *Mendelssohn*, 104.
33. Donald Francis Tovey, *Beethoven* (London, 1944), 30.
34. Tovey, *Essays*, III, 178.
35. *Ibid.*, 6.
36. Mozart to his father, 28 December 1782; cited in H. C. Robbins Landon, "The Concertos: (2) Their Musical Origin and Development" in *The Mozart Companion*, ed. H. C. Robbins Landon and Donald Mitchell (New York, 1969), 227.

6 Symphony and overture
1. General studies of Mendelssohn's orchestral works include Thomas Grey, "The Orchestral Music," in *MC*, 395–550; R. Larry Todd, "Mendelssohn," in *The Nineteenth-Century Symphony*, ed. D. Kern Holoman (New York, 1997), 78–107; Wulf Konold, *Die Symphonien Felix Mendelssohn Bartholdys: Untersuchungen zu Werkgestalt und Formstruktur* (Laaber, 1992); Thomas Ehrle, *Die Instrumentation in den Symphonien und Ouvertüren von Felix Mendelssohn Bartholdy* (Wiesbaden, 1983).
2. R. Larry Todd, *Mendelssohn's Musical Education: A Study and Edition of His Exercises in Composition* (Cambridge, 1983).
3. For synopses and comments on the sinfonias, see Wulf Konold, "Mendelssohns Jugendsymphonien: Eine analytische Studie," *Archiv für Musikwissenschaft* 46 (1989), 1–41, 155–83; and Albert James Filosa, Jr., "The Early Symphonies and Chamber Music of Felix Mendelssohn Bartholdy," Ph.D. diss., Yale University, 1970, 6–9 and 44–89.
4. The Mendelssohn family had traveled to Switzerland for a family vacation in 1822, and this piece dates from the following spring.
5. For a detailed discussion of op. 11, see Wulf Konold, "Opus 11 und Opus 107: Analytische Bemerkungen zu zwei unbekannten Sinfonien Felix Mendelssohn Bartholdys," in *Felix Mendelssohn Bartholdy*, ed. Heinz-Klaus Metzger and Rainer Riehn, *Musik-Konzepte* 14/15 (Munich, 1980), 8–16.
6. Grey, "The Orchestral Music," 408–10. Filosa regards the thematic model as a Mendelssohnian

"fingerprint" in the early sinfonias; see Filosa, "Early Symphonies," 58.
7. At the London performances and again later in Munich in 1831 Mendelssohn substituted an orchestrated version of the scherzo from the Octet.
8. Wolfram Steinbeck deals with this decisive position of the overtures in "Der klärende Wendepunkt in Felix' Leben," in *KBB*, 232–56.
9. Adolf Bernhard Marx, a close friend of the composer at the time, takes credit for pressing Mendelssohn to this vivid programmaticism, in place of a more conventional, "musical" approach. See the translation from his *Erinnerungen aus meinem Leben* (Berlin, 1865) in "From the Memoirs of Adolf Bernhard Marx," trans. Susan Gillespie, in *MhW*, 216–17.
10. Thomas Grey has also described this as portraying "the sleeping household of the Duke"; Grey, "The Orchestral Music," 465.
11. Arnd Richter, "Beethoven, Mendelssohn, Hegel und Marx: Zur Poetik der Ouvertüre 'Meeresstille und glückliche Fahrt,'" *NZfM* 149, no. 7–8 (1988), 18–23, discusses the background of the overture in relation to Beethoven's choral cantata on Goethe's texts.
12. See the programmatic description from the *Signale für die musikalische Welt*, published in 1847 and translated in R. Larry Todd, *Mendelssohn: The Hebrides and Other Overtures* (Cambridge, 1993), 77.
13. Todd, *Mendelssohn: The Hebrides and Other Overtures*, 78; Grey, "The Orchestral Music," 470. Lawrence Kramer also hears this closing as "a grateful reminiscence of the calm sea of the opening," though one might question the rationale by which the sailor reminisces gratefully about having been becalmed; see his "*Felix culpa*: Goethe and the Image of Mendelssohn," in *MSt*, 76, reprinted as "*Felix culpa*: Mendelssohn, Goethe, and the Social Force of Musical Expression," in Lawrence Kramer, *Classical Music and Postmodern Knowledge* (Berkeley and Los Angeles, 1995), 137–38.
14. I owe this observation to the brief discussion of the concept in relation to Weber's operas in Carl Dahlhaus, *Nineteenth-Century Music*, trans. J. Bradford Robinson (Berkeley and Los Angeles, 1989), 69–71.
15. Letters of travelers with special literary talent could even be published, as were Goethe's or, later, Mendelssohn's own. The first German version of Mendelssohn's Grand Tour letters is Felix Mendelssohn Bartholdy, *Reisebriefe aus den Jahren 1830 bis 1832*, ed. Paul Mendelssohn Bartholdy (Leipzig, 1861), trans. Lady Wallace as *Letters from Italy and Switzerland by Felix Mendelssohn Bartholdy* (London, 1862). For a

more reliable text, see Felix Mendelssohn Bartholdy, *Briefe einer Reise durch Deutschland, Italien und die Schweiz und Lebensbild*, ed. Paul Sutermeister (Zurich, 1958).

16. "Ich glaube, ich habe heut da den Anfang meiner Schottischen Symphonie gefunden"; letter of 30 July 1829, quoted in Sebastian Hensel, *Die Familie Mendelssohn 1729 bis 1847*, (17th edn. Berlin, 1918), 268. English text quoted from Sebastian Hensel, *The Mendelssohn Family (1729–1847)*, trans. Carl Klingemann and an American collaborator (repr. New York, 1969), 198.

17. For a thorough description of the genesis of the work, see Todd, *Mendelssohn: The Hebrides and Other Overtures*, 26–37. See also Andreas Eichhorn, *Felix Mendelssohn Bartholdy: Die Hebriden – Overtüre für Orchester op. 26* (Munich, 1998).

18. See R. Larry Todd, "Of Sea Gulls and Counterpoint: The Early Versions of Mendelssohn's *Hebrides* Overture," *19th-Century Music* 2 (1979), 197–213.

19. See John Michael Cooper, "'Aber eben dieser Zweifel': A New Look at Mendelssohn's 'Italian' Symphony," *19th-Century Music* 15 (1992), 169–87, and his *Mendelssohn's "Italian" Symphony* (Oxford, 2003), based in part on his 1994 dissertation, "Felix Mendelssohn Bartholdy and the *Italian* Symphony: Historical, Musical, and Extramusical Perspectives," Duke University. Facsimiles of the sources and an edition of the 1834 revisions, edited by Cooper and Hans-Günter Klein, were published in 1997 (Wiesbaden). See also Wulf Konold, *Felix Mendelssohn Bartholdy: Symphonie Nr. 4 A-Dur Op. 90, "Die Italienische"* (Munich, 1987).

20. Thomas S. Grey, "*Tableaux vivants*: Landscape, History Painting, and the Visual Imagination in Mendelssohn's Orchestral Music," *19th-Century Music* 21 (1997), 38–76, discusses not only the "Italian" Symphony but other works, as well.

21. Grey creates a fairly detailed program, pointing out that development's new theme, like a "masked intruder," is at first driven away and then welcomed back into the carnival celebration, concluding that "Whatever unruly antagonisms are enacted in Mendelssohn's musical carnival, they are easily contained, at last, within the larger social order of the symphonic tradition." Grey, "The Orchestral Music," 442; complete discussion of the movement begins on page 439.

22. August Wilhelm Ambros, *Die Grenzen der Musik und Poesie* (Leipzig, 1855), 176.

23. Dale A. Olsen, "Ethnomusicology and Music History: Mendelssohn's Italian Journey – Field Work or 'A Runaway with the Rich and Famous?'"; paper presented to the Joint Annual Meetings of the American Musicological Society (Southern Chapter) and the Society for Ethnomusicology (Southeastern/Caribbean Chapter), Tuscaloosa, Alabama, 17 February 1989.

24. The history of the composer's unrealized hope for this performance is discussed in Judith Silber Ballan, "Mendelssohn and His *Reformation* Symphony," *Journal of the American Musicological Society* 60 (1987), 310–36.

25. Ferdinand Hiller, *Mendelssohn: Letters and Recollections*, trans. M. E. von Glehn (London, 1874; repr. New York, 1972), 21–22.

26. For an analytical study of the "Reformation" Symphony, see Konold, "Opus 11 und Opus 107: Analytische Bemerkungen zu zwei unbekannten Sinfonien Felix Mendelssohn Bartholdys," 16–28.

27. An interesting interpretation of the stylistic contrasts within this work is Ulrich Wüster, "'Ein gewisser Geist': Zu Mendelssohns Reformations-Symphonie," *Die Musikforschung* 44 (1991), 311–30. For a detailed study of the programmatic aspect of the symphony, emphasizing its relationship to Beethoven's Ninth Symphony, see Wolfgang Dinglinger, "The Programme of Mendelssohn's 'Reformation' Symphony, Op. 107," trans. John Michael Cooper, in *TMH*, 115–33.

28. Grey notes here the suggestion of a Gregorian intonation formula; "The Orchestral Music," 418.

29. See Alfred Heuß, "Das 'Dresdener Amen' im ersten Satz von Mendelssohns Reformationssinfonie," *Signale für die musikalische Welt* 62 (1904), 281–84, 305–06. James Garratt, "Mendelssohn's Babel: Romanticism and the Poetics of Translation," *Music & Letters* 80 (1999), 25–27, cautions against too specifically programmatic a reading of the symphony.

30. For example, Hermann Deiters, in his review of the symphony in the *Allgemeine musikalische Zeitung* 3 (1868) 349–50, 356–57, who compares the movement to Pamina's "Ach, ich fühl's" in Mozart's *Die Zauberflöte*. Grey hears the influence of the slow movement in Beethoven's Piano Sonata op. 110, which Beethoven labeled *klagender Gesang*; see Grey, "The Orchestral Music," 424.

31. A helpful discussion of levels of discourse is Robert Hatten, "On Narrativity in Music: Expressive Genres and Levels of Discourse in Beethoven," *Indiana Theory Review* 12 (1991), 75–98, esp. 86ff.

32. He explained the impetus for the work in a letter to his sister Fanny of 7 April 1834; see Felix Mendelssohn Bartholdy, *Letters of Felix*

Mendelssohn Bartholdy from 1833 to 1847, trans. Lady Wallace (London, 1863), 31–32.

33. Robert Schumann, "Ouverture zum Märchen von der schöne Melusine," in *Gesammelte Schriften über Musik und Musiker* (Leipzig, 1875), 138–40.

34. Letter to his mother of 18 March 1839, in Felix Mendelssohn Bartholdy, *Letters of Felix Mendelssohn Bartholdy from 1833 to 1847*, ed. Paul and Carl Mendelssohn Bartholdy, trans. Lady Wallace (London, 1863), 154–55.

35. William Lyle Pelto, "Musical Structure and Extramusical Meaning in the Concert Overtures of Mendelssohn," Ph.D. diss., University of Texas, 1993; Siegwart Reichwald, "Two Days in the Workroom of a Composer: Schubert's C Major Symphony, Mendelssohn's Ruy Blas, and the Development of the Romantic Symphony," paper presented at the 12th Biennial International Conference on Nineteenth-Century Music, University of Leeds, 4–7 July 2002.

36. The dedication of the symphony to Queen Victoria suggests that Mendelssohn continued to associate the work with the British Isles. To be sure, the identity of the symphony as Scottish eluded Schumann; he erroneously believed that it had originated during Mendelssohn's Italian sojourn and heard it accordingly. See Robert Schumann, "Symphonien für Orchester," *NZfM* 18, no. 39 (1843), 155–56. Peter Mercer-Taylor has made an interesting argument for the work's essential German character in his "Mendelssohn's 'Scottish' Symphony and the Music of German Memory," *19th-Century Music* 19 (1995), 68–82. Thomas Schmidt-Beste argues that the real significance of the work is that Mendelssohn suppressed its Scottish connections; see his "Just how 'Scottish' is the 'Scottish' Symphony? Thoughts on Form and Poetic Content in Mendelssohn's Opus 56," in *TMH*, 147–65.

37. Grey, "The Orchestral Music," 450.

7 The works of solo instrument(s) and orchestra

1. Donald Francis Tovey, *Essays in Musical Analysis, Volume III: Concertos* (London, 1936), 178.

2. Mendelssohn composed a number of other concerted works outside the purview of this article. In March of 1820, at eleven years of age, the composer began a work for piano and strings in D minor, his first attempt in the genre. This has not been published; the manuscript is in the Deutsche Staatsbibliothek zu Berlin, Preussischer Kulturbesitz, Mendelssohn Nachlass, Mus. Ms. Autogr. Mendelssohn 1. See Hans-Günter Klein, "Verzeichniss der im Autograph überlieferten Werke Felix Mendelssohn Bartholdys im Besitz der Staatsbibliothek zu Berlin," *Mendelssohn Studien* 10 (1997), 200ff.

In 1832 and 1833, Mendelssohn composed, and seems to have orchestrated, the Concertstücke for Clarinet, Basset-Horn, and Piano, with orchestral accompaniment, opp. 113 and 114, as concert vehicles for Heinrich and Karl Bärmann; they were not published in Mendelssohn's lifetime. See R. Larry Todd's "The Instrumental Music of Felix Mendelssohn-Bartholdy," Ph.D. dissertation, Yale University (abbreviated as Todd diss. hereafter), 384, n. 2. Todd includes substantial discussion of all of the Mendelssohn concertos, with particular focus on the D minor Violin Concerto (1822), the A♭ major Double Piano Concerto (1824), the *Capriccio brillant* (1832), and the D minor Piano Concerto op. 40 (1837).

In 1833, in collaboration with Ignaz Moscheles, Mendelssohn composed a *Duo Concertant* for Two Pianos and Orchestra (*Variations brillantes*) on a March from Carl Maria von Weber's opera *Preciosa*, listed as Moscheles' op. 87b.

3. As Marian Wilson [Kimber] notes ("Felix Mendelssohn's Works for Solo Piano and Orchestra," Ph.D. dissertation, Florida State University, 1993 [abbreviated as Wilson diss. hereafter], 9–10), Mendelssohn's autograph for the A minor Concerto is not dated. The year 1822 is given for this work in Sebastian Hensel, *The Mendelssohn Family (1729–1847) from Letters and Journals*, 2nd edn., trans. Karl Klingemann (New York, 1882; repr. New York, 1969), I, 117. A performance of the work was noted in the *Allgemeine musikalische Zeitung* 4 (22 January 1823).

4. R. Larry Todd's "An Unfinished Piano Concerto by Mendelssohn," *MQ* 68, no. 1 (1982), 80–101, argues that op. 64 was initially conceived for piano during the years 1842–44. However, see Grey, "The Orchestral Music," in *MC*, 516.

5. R. Larry Todd, "Mendelssohn: Orchestral Works," *New Grove* online.

6. Thomas Grey, "The Orchestral Music," in *MC*, 503.

7. Letter to Moscheles of 10 August 1832, in *Letters of Felix Mendelssohn to Ignaz and Charlotte Moscheles*, ed. Felix Moscheles (1888; repr. edn. Freeport, NY, 1970), 30.

8. See R. Larry Todd, "Piano Music Reformed: The Case of Felix Mendelssohn Bartholdy," in *MC*, 580–81.

9. Edwin. J. Simon, "The Double Exposition in Classic Concerto Form," Ph.D. dissertation, University of California, 1954.

10. Daniel N. Leeson and Robert D. Levin, "On the Authenticity of K. Anh. C 14.01 (297*b*), a *Sinfonia Concertante* for Four Winds and Orchestra," *Mozart-Jahrbuch* 1976 / 77 (Kassel, 1978), 70–96. Leeson and Levin are responsible for this seven-part delineation of the form of the first movement. For a more complete historical discussion of the development of concerto form in the eighteenth and nineteenth centuries, see my *Structural Novelty and Tradition in the Early Romantic Piano Concerto* (Stuyvesant, NY, 1999). The book contains timeline analytical graphs of the first movements of all of the Mozart concertos, as well as many early nineteenth-century composers, including Beethoven, Chopin, Schumann, Liszt, Sterndale Bennett, Field, Steibelt, and many others.

11. Karl-Heinz Köhler, "Felix Mendelssohn (-Bartholdy)," *The New Grove Dictionary*, ed. Stanley Sadie, 20 vols. (London, 1980), VII, 134–59.

12. *Leipziger Ausgabe der Werke von Felix Mendelssohn Bartholdy, Herausgegeben von der Sächsischen Akademie der Wissenschaften zu Leipzig*, Serie II: *Konzerte und Konzertstücke*, Band I, ed. Christoph Hellmundt (Wiesbaden, 1999), "Introduction," xv.

13. Wilson diss., p. 9. See her analytical chart of the first movement on p. 14.

14. Todd diss., pp. 351ff. See his diagram of the first movement, p. 352. See also *Leipziger Ausgabe der Werke von Felix Mendelssohn Bartholdy, Internationale Felix-Mendelssohn-Gesellschaft*, Serie II: *Instrumentalkonzerte*, Band VI, *Konzert d-Moll für Violine und Streichorchester, Erste und zweite Fassung*, ed. Renate Unger (Leipzig, 1960; repr. 1973), "Zum Vorliegenden Band," v.

15. Peter Mercer-Taylor, *The Life of Mendelssohn* (Cambridge, 2000), 33.

16. Todd, "Piano Music Reformed," 582.

17. *Leipziger Ausgabe der Werke von Felix Mendelssohn Bartholdy, Herausgegeben von der Sachsischen Akademie der Wissenschaften zu Leipzig*, Serie II: *Konzerte und Konzertstücke*, Band VIII, *Konzert für Violine, Klavier und Orchester (Bläser und Pauken ad libitum) d-Moll*, ed. Christoph Hellmundt (Wiesbaden, 1999), "Introduction," xvii.

18. Todd, "Piano Music Reformed," 584.

19. Friedhelm Krummacher, "Art – History – Religion: On Mendelssohn's Oratorios *St. Paul* and *Elijah*," in *MC*, 303.

20. Eric Werner, "Two Unpublished Mendelssohn Concertos," *Music & Letters* 36 (1955), 135. See also Peter John Roennfeldt, "The Double Piano Concertos of Felix Mendelssohn," DMA thesis, College-Conservatory of Music, Cincinnati, 1985, p. 92.

21. *Felix Mendelssohn: A Life in Letters*, ed. Rudolf Elvers, trans. Craig Tomlinson (New York, 1986), 18.

22. For an in-depth discussion of this see my *Felix Mendelssohn: Concerto for Two Pianos and Orchestra in E major (1823): Original Version of the First Movement* (Madison, 1999), and "Mendelssohn and Moscheles: Two Composers, Two Pianos, Two Scores, One Concerto," *MQ* 83 (1999), 51–74.

23. *NZFM* 10 (January 1839), 5.

24. Werner, "Unpublished Concertos," 92.

25. Todd diss., 358–59.

26. Roennfeldt, "Double Piano Concertos," 92.

27. Todd, "Piano Music Reformed," 583.

28. See my *Structural Novelty* for more discussion of the influence of Weber's *Konzertstück*.

29. See Wilson diss., 104-83, for a complete discussion of the publication history and compositional process in op. 25.

30. Todd, "Piano Music Reformed," 584–85.

31. R. Larry Todd, *Mendelssohn: The Hebrides and Other Overtures* (Cambridge, 1993), 21.

32. Todd, "Piano Music Reformed," 611.

33. Peter Mercer-Taylor's unpublished paper, "Taming the Romantic Weber: Mendelssohn's *Capriccio brillant* as Self-Mythology," contains a fascinating and insightful perspective on Mendelssohn's debt to Weber, and analysis of op. 22. I am grateful to Dr. Mercer-Taylor for permitting me access to his paper. See the reading of op. 22 in his *Mendelssohn*, 105–06.

34. Mercer-Taylor, *Mendelssohn*, 105–06.

35. Wilson diss., 47–48.

36. *Ibid.*, 184–96.

37. Todd, "Mendelssohn: Orchestral Works."

38. Wilson diss., 194, letter written to Moscheles from Düsseldorf, 7 February 1834, *Briefe an Ignaz und Charlotte Moscheles* (Leipzig, 1888), 74, with Wilson's modified translation from that in *Letters to Ignaz and Charlotte Moscheles*, 98.

39. The review is cited and quoted in Wilson diss., 278, under the name F. L., "Das Musikfest in Birmingham," *NZfM* 3 (13 October 1837), 119.

40. See Marian Wilson, "Felix Mendelssohn's Piano Concerto no. 2 op. 40: A Study of the Autograph Sources," M.M. thesis, Florida State University, 1989, and Wilson diss., 275–384.

41. Todd diss., 372.

42. Todd, "Piano Music Reformed," 600–01.

43. *On Music and Musicians*, ed. Konrad Wolff, trans. Paul Rosenfeld (New York, 1946), 207.

44. Quoted in Mercer-Taylor, *Mendelssohn*, 153.

45. Wilson diss., 392.

46. The E minor Violin Concerto op. 64, as Todd argues, may have been initially conceived for piano during the years 1842–44. See his "An Unfinished Piano Concerto by Mendelssohn,"

MQ, 68, no. 1 (January 1982), 80–101. However, see discussion of op. 64 later in this chapter.

47. As quoted in Wilson diss., 385, from *Briefe aus den Jahren 1833 bis 1847 von Felix Mendelssohn Bartholdy*, ed. Paul Mendelssohn-Bartholdy and Carl Mendelssohn-Bartholdy (Leipzig, 1863) 106; the translation is Wilson's modification of that in *Letters of Felix Mendelssohn Bartholdy from 1833 to 1847*, trans. Lady Wallace (London, 1863), 135.

48. Mercer-Taylor, *Mendelssohn*, p. 154.

49. Grey, "Orchestral Music," 522–23.

50. Wilson diss., 386, quoting D. L., in *NZfM* 8 (13 April 1838), 120.

51. Wilson diss., 386, quoting G. W. Fink, in the *Allgemeine musikalische Zeitung* 41 (18 April 1838), 262–63.

52. Grey, "Orchestral Music," 516.

53. *Ibid*.

54. Todd, "Mendelssohn: Orchestral Works." For discussion of the op. 64 sketches, see H. C. Worbs, "Die Entwürfe zu Mendelssohns Violinkonzert e-moll," *Die Musikforschung* 12 (1959), 79–81; Reinhard Gerlach, "Mendelssohns Kompositionsweise – Vergleich zwischen Skizzen und Letztfassung des Violinkonzerts opus 64," *Archiv für Musikwissenschaft* 28 (1971), 119–33; Gerlach, "Mendelssohns schöpferische Erinnerung der 'Jugendzeit.' Die Beziehungen zwischen dem Violinkonzert op. 64, und dem Oktett für Streicher, op. 20," *Die Musikforschung* 25 (1972), 142–52; and Gerlach, "Mendelssohns Kompositionsweise (II). Weitere Vergleiche zwischen den Skizzen und der Letztfassung des Violinkonzerts op. 64," in *PM*, 149–67. Todd discusses the sketches at some length in his dissertation, 384–95. See also his "An Unfinished Piano Concerto by Mendelssohn," 80–101.

55. Joseph Kerman, *Concerto Conversations: The Charles Eliot Norton Lectures, 1997–98* (Cambridge, MA, 1999), 91.

56. Krummacher, "Art – History – Religion," 331.

57. Grey, "Orchestral Music," 519.

58. Krummacher, "On Mendelssohn's Compositional Style: Propositions Based on the Example of the String Quartets," trans. Douglass Seaton, in *MC*, 556.

8 Mendelssohn's chamber music

1. R. Larry Todd, *Mendelssohn's Musical Education: A Study and Edition of his Exercises in Composition* (Cambridge, 1983), 62.

2. *Ibid.*, 77–80.

3. "as I repeat that we have learned and profited hardly at all from textbooks, but first and foremost from your talent and our mutual abilities," Carl Friedrich Zelter to Felix Mendelssohn Bartholdy, 3 August 1824; see Thomas Schmidt-Beste, "'Alles von ihm gelernt?' Die Briefe von Carl Friedrich Zelter an Felix Mendelssohn Bartholdy," *Mendelssohn-Studien* 10 (1997), 25–56, quote on 42. All translation from German into English is the author's.

4. Cf. the memoirs of one of Mendelssohn's pupils, the violinist Wilhelm Joseph von Wasielewski: Wilhelm Joseph von Wasielewski, *Aus siebzig Jahren. Lebenserinnerungen* (Stuttgart/Leipzig, 1897), 34–36.

5. In a letter of 16 July 1824, Zelter even sent his pupil a riddle with two melodies he himself composed as countersubjects of fugues from Bach's *Well-Tempered Clavier* – Felix was to find the original fugues. Felix of course accepted the challenge and answered with the solved riddle in his next letter (as it turned out, both countermelodies even belonged to the same fugue, the B minor from Book I). Both letters are edited in Schmidt-Beste, "'Alles von ihm gelernt?'" 37–41.

6. Goethe, Conversation with Eckermann, 12–14 January 1827; Johann Peter Eckermann, *Gespräche mit Goethe in den letzten Jahren seines Lebens*, ed. Fritz Bergemann (Leipzig, 1968), 178.

7. Gottfried Heinz, *Die Geschichte des Klavierquintetts von den Anfängen bis Robert Schumann* (Neckargemünd, 2001). The addition of a double bass to large-ensemble chamber works in itself was no rarity; R. Larry Todd points out parallels between the sextet and Johann Nepomuk Hummel's Septet op. 74 for flute, oboe, French horn, viola, violoncello, double bass, and piano of 1816 which was also published in a version for string quartet (violin, viola, violoncello, double bass) and piano. See R. Larry Todd, "The Chamber Music of Mendelssohn," in *Nineteenth-century Chamber Music*, ed. Stephen E. Hefling (New York, 1998), 180.

8. *MNI*, 63.

9. See Friedhelm Krummacher, *Mendelssohn – der Komponist. Studien zur Kammermusik für Streicher* (Munich, 1978), 154–57. Krummacher's magisterial study remains the standard work on Mendelssohn's chamber music, and all of the conclusions presented here draw heavily on this book.

10. Sebastian Hensel, *Die Familie Mendelssohn 1729–1847*, 3 vols. (Berlin, 1879), I, 151; the English version of the passage from Goethe's *Faust* is taken from the translation by George Madison Priest (New York, 1941).

11. English translation after *MNI*, 119.

12. See Friedhelm Krummacher, *Das Streichquartett. Teilband II: Von Mendelssohn bis zur Gegenwart*, Handbuch der musikalischen Gattungen 6,2 (Laaber, 2003), 11–30.

13. See Ludwig Finscher, *Studien zur Geschichte des Streichquartetts*, I: *Die Entstehung des klassischen Streichquartetts. Von den Vorformen zur Grundlegung durch Joseph Haydn*, Saarbrücker Studien zur Musikwissenschaft 3 (Kassel etc., 1974), 285–301.

14. Felix Mendelssohn Bartholdy to Adolf Fredrik Lindblad, [February 1828], *Bref till Adolf Fredrik Lindblad fran Mendelssohn . . . och andra*, ed. L. Dahlgren (Stockholm, 1913), 19–20. The letter is not dated, but the subsequent letter from Mendelssohn, dated 22 April, mentions that the last letter had been written nine weeks previously.

15. *MNI*, 118.

16. *Ibid.*, 308.

17. *Ibid.*, 358.

18. *Ibid.*, 308.

19. Fanny Hensel to Felix Mendelssohn Bartholdy, 17 February 1835, *The Letters of Fanny Hensel to Felix Mendelssohn*, ed. Marcia J. Citron (Stuyvesant, NY, 1987), 490; translation the author's, considerably revised from Citron's on 174.

20. Krummacher, *Mendelssohn – der Komponist*, 467.

21. See Thomas Christian Schmidt, *Die ästhetischen Grundlagen der Instrumentalmusik Felix Mendelssohn Bartholdys* (Stuttgart, 1996), 155–209.

22. Felix Mendelssohn Bartholdy to Wilhelm von Boguslawski, 19 April 1834; Bruno Hake, "Mendelssohn als Lehrer. Mit bisher ungedruckten Briefen Mendelssohns an Wilhelm v. Boguslawski," *Deutsche Rundschau* 140 (1909), 465.

23. Felix Mendelssohn Bartholdy to Johann Heinrich Lübeck, 20 August 1836; unpublished, copy in Staatsbibliothek zu Berlin – Preußischer Kulturbesitz, Musikabteilung, Mendelssohn-Archiv Nachlass 7,42.

24. Felix Mendelssohn Bartholdy to Bernhard Schüler (pseudonym "Silphin vom Walde"), 22 January 1841; *Briefe aus den Jahren 1833 bis 1847*, ed. Paul and Carl Mendelssohn Bartholdy (Leipzig, 1863), 265.

25. See Schmidt, *Die ästhetischen Grundlagen*, 55–56.

26. *Ibid.*, 306–10.

27. Robert Schumann, "*Trios für Pianoforte mit Begleitung*", in *Gesammelte Schriften über Musik und Musiker*, 5th edn., ed. Martin Kreisig (Leipzig 1914), I, 500.

28. Felix Mendelssohn Bartholdy to Ignaz Moscheles, 7 February 1834; *Briefe an Ignaz und Charlotte Moscheles*, ed. Felix Moscheles (Leipzig, 1888), 74.

29. See Armin Koch, *Choräle und Choralhaftes im Werk von Felix Mendelssohn Bartholdy*

(= Abhandlungen zur Musikgeschichte 12) (Göttingen, 2003), 124–30.

30. Friedhelm Krummacher, "Mendelssohn's Late Chamber Music: Some Autograph Sources Reconsidered," in *Mendelssohn and Schumann. Essays on Their Music and Its Context*, ed. Jon W. Finson and R. Larry Todd (Durham, NC, 1984), 76–80.

31. Felix Mendelssohn Bartholdy to Karl Emil von Webern, 24 May 1847; *Briefe 1833 bis 1847*, 483.

32. *MNI*, 496.

33. Krummacher, "Mendelssohn's Late Chamber Music," 80–84.

9 The music for keyboard

1. This essay will focus on the keyboard pieces published by Mendelssohn; he left very many unpublished works. For work lists see the Mendelssohn article in the *The New Grove Dictionary of Music and Musicians*, ed. Stanley Sadie and John Tyrrell, 29 vols. (London, 2001) and *MC*, 748–65.

2. R. Larry Todd, "Piano Music Reformed," in *MC*, 582.

3. Mendelssohn composed a "Scottish Sonata", most probably c. 1828, but did not publish it in this guise; a revised version of its three movements appeared in 1834 as the *Fantasia in F♯ minor* op. 28.

4. Cited in *MNI*, 52.

5. Letter to Franz Brendel (18 September 1849), cited by Christa Jost in "In Mutual Reflection: Historical, Biographical and Structural Aspects of Mendelssohn's *Variations sérieuses*," in *MSt*, 95, from *Robert Schumanns Briefe*, neue Folge, ed. Th. G. Jansen, 2nd edn. (Leipzig, 1904), 312.

6. Wulf Konold, *Felix Mendelssohn Bartholdy und seine Zeit* (Laaber, 1984), 256.

7. Hauptmann in a letter to Franz Hauser in October 1834. Cited in Christa Jost, *Mendelssohns Lieder ohne Worte*, Frankfurter Beiträge zur Musikwissenschaft 14 (Tutzing, 1988), 27. Mendelssohn took some pride in the songs, but already in 1832 he complained to his father about the "endless piano songs" (*die ewigen Clavierlieder*).

8. *Ibid.*, 14–15 and passim after 68.

9. *Ibid.*, 20–24. Among the composers are Stephen Heller, Sigismund Thalberg, Hans von Bülow, Max Reger, and Schoenberg(!). In France, Fauré, d'Indy, and Gounod composed *Romances sans paroles* or some variation on that title.

10. Cited in *Felix Mendelssohn: Letters*, ed. G. Selden-Goth (New York, 1945; repr. 1973), 266.

11. On this question and the *Songs without Words* in general see John Michael Cooper,

"Words without Songs: Of Texts, Titles, and Mendelssohn's 'Lieder ohne Worte,'" in *Bericht über den Internationalen Kongreß der Gesellschaft für Musikforschung, "Musik als Text," Freiburg, September 1993*, II, Freie Referate, ed. Hermann Danuser und Tobias Plebuch (Kassel, 1998), 341–46, and Todd, "Piano Music Reformed," 593–99, especially 594, where Todd cites the Leipzig theorist and Cantor of the Thomaskirche Moritz Hauptmann: "What is it all about? Is he really in earnest? . . . Songs without Words must be uncanny, I think."

12. Fanny Mendelssohn, *The Letters of Fanny Hensel to Felix Mendelssohn*, ed. and trans. Marcia J. Citron (Stuyvesant, NY, 1987), 261. Years later, in a review of volume II, Schumann echoes the creative spontaneity that Fanny's description implies, but without its levity: "Who of us in the twilight hour . . . in the midst of improvising has not unconsciously begun to sing a quiet melody? Should one happens to be able to play the cantilena along with the accompaniment, above all, when one happens to be a Mendelssohn, the loveliest 'song without words' would result." Cited in Todd, "Piano Music Reformed," 594.

13. The distribution of the lower voices between the two hands in this piece presents another classic pianistic problem, as seen in mm. 18–23, which introduce a minor-mode version of the antecedent phrase of the main theme in the lower voice that makes a fleeting but highly evocative allusion to the tragic D minor slow movement of Beethoven's String Quartet in F op. 18 no. 1, a duet between the first violin and the cello.

14. Todd is very interested in relating textures to texted-song forms and in his enthusiasm forces the issue somewhat. He establishes a "duet" category that includes the "Duetto" and also the *Gondellieder* and other pieces that contain parallel melodic lines. As we have seen, the "Duetto" presents an interaction between two distinct voices that is typical of vocal duets, which certainly present voices moving together but also emphasizes dialogue. Authors going back to Schumann associate the homorhythmic songs with polyphonic Romantic part songs. This seems misguided, in part because of the large registral space between the bass and upper voices in many of the piano works, in part because the bass and inner voices do not have as much melodic integrity as is typical of a part-song, in part because the number of voices changes within a songs, and also because these are very pianistic textures in their own right. Schumann's comment, "Mendelssohn has progressed from the simple Lied through the duet to the polyphonic and choral style," should

be understood in general terms; he does not link specific songs to the specific vocal genres and he uses the general term style. Citation *from Robert Schumann: On Music and Musicians*, trans. Paul Rosenfeld, ed. Konrad Wolff (New York, 1946), 212.

15. Jost, *Lieder ohne Worte*, 73, n. 254, cites a remark in a German popular music guide about these pieces: "Perhaps they are based on the idea of a [German] courtly love song (Minnelied), imagining a troubadour who preludes on his harp before he begins to sing."

16. Based on an unpublished letter to Eduard Devrient of 14 January 1837. See *MNI*, 279.

17. Cited in Ferdinand Hiller, *Mendelssohn: Letters and Recollections*, trans. M. E. von Glehn, intr. by Joel Sachs (New York, 1972), 81.

18. See R. Larry Todd on this and other aspects of the preludes and fugues in "'Me voilà perruqué': Mendelssohn's *Six Preludes and Fugues* op. 35 reconsidered," in *MSt*, 162–99. Todd considers op. 35 to be Mendelssohn's most important work for the piano.

19. On Mendelssohn's stylistic mediations see Charles Rosen's discussion of no. 7 of the *Seven Characteristic Pieces* (op. 7), a binary-form andante movement evocative of an allemande, in *The Romantic Generation* (Cambridge, MA, 1998), 587–88.

20. Cited, with minor revisions, in *Robert Schumann: On Music and Musicians*, 215.

21. The first Prelude has been associated with the first Prelude of the *Well-Tempered Clavier*, Book I in C major. This exaggerates the importance of the single common feature, the arpeggiations; otherwise the movements could not be more different, and the arpeggiations of the later piece do not, in my view, create an allusion to the former that can be heard. At best we have *Augenmusik*.

22. Rosen, *The Romantic Generation*, 590–95.

23. For a survey of Mendelssohn's organ music see Robert C. Mann, "The Organ Music," in *MC*, 625–56.

24. Susanne Großmann-Vendry, "Stilprobleme in Mendelssohns Orgelsonaten Op. 65," in *PM*, 185–94.

25. Henry Gauntlett in *The Musical World*, 15 September 1837; cited in Grossman-Vendry, "Stilprobleme," 190.

26. Cited in Jost, "*Variations sérieuses*," 34.

27. Mendelssohn played the variations for the first time in November 1841 at the Gewandhaus; he also played them privately for Spohr and Wagner in 1846. Spohr remembers "He played a fearsomely difficult and highly idiosyncratic composition of his own . . . with monstrous bravura . . ." (*Selbstbiographie* [Kassel and Göttingen], 1861, II, 306–07).

28. Letters to Rebecka and to Karl Klingemann convey his excitement about variations. To Klingemann, "I vary every theme that occurs to me . . . passionately . . . as though I had to make up for never having written any before." Rebecka learns that he has already finished two variation sets – the second consisting of twelve "sentimental" variations in E♭ (a less substantial but interesting work, published posthumously as op. 82 in 1850) and has plans for further piano variations and some "with and for" orchestra as well. Mendelssohn did complete two further sets of piano variations, but no variations in other genres were composed.

29. Jost, "*Variations sérieuses*," 44–57.

30. *The Classical Style: Haydn, Mozart, Beethoven* (London, 1971), 401.

31. Suite no. 3 in D minor: see Peter Rummenhöller, *Romantik in der Musik* (Kassel, 1989), 178–81.

32. Todd sees a spiritual connection between Mendelssohn's use of "sérieuses" and Beethoven's Quartet in F minor op. 95 ("Piano Music Reformed," 606).

33. The copy belongs to the Mendelssohn Nachlaß in the Bodleian Library in Oxford.

34. See the commentary in the Norton Critical Score: *Johann Sebastian Bach, Cantata No. 4 "Christ lag in Todesbanden." An Authoritative Score, Backgrounds, Analysis, Views and Comment*, ed. Gerhard Herz (New York, 1967).

35. Letter to Moscheles in 1835 on new mazurkas (probably op. 17) and other new pieces "so mannered that they are hard to stand." *Letters of Felix Mendelssohn to Ignaz and Charlotte Moscheles*, ed. F. Moscheles (Boston, 1888), 129 and 156.

36. Mendelssohn praises Liszt's playing; "The only thing that he seems to me to want is true talent for composition, I mean really original ideas . . ." Cited in *ibid.*, 203–04.

37. Todd, "Piano Music Reformed," 178–79.

38. This information is taken largely from Donald Mintz, "Mendelssohn as Performer and Teacher," in *MC*, 109.

39. See Robert C. Mann, "The Organ Music," in *ibid.*, 625–56.

40. See Matthias Pape, *Mendelssohns Leipziger Orgelkonzert 1840: Ein Beitrag zur Bach-Pflege im 19. Jahrhundert*, Jahresgabe 1987 der Internationalen Bach-Gesellschaft Schaffhausen (Wiesbaden), 15–16.

41. Jost, "*Variations sérieuses*," 37.

42. Cited by Mintz from Sir George Grove in his article "Mendelssohn" in the first edition of the *Dictionary of Music and Musicians*, reprinted in Grove, *Beethoven, Schubert, Mendelssohn* (London, 1951), 374.

43. This passage has been translated by Nancy Reich for her forthcoming translation of a German edition of the diaries, which will be published in German by Breitkopf & Härtel und in English by the Northeastern University Press. The remark is recorded in Diary 6a, 16. The original manuscript diaries are located in the Robert-Schumann Haus in Zwickau, Germany. The author wishes to thank Dr. Gerd Nauhaus, the director of the Haus, for permission to publish this excerpt.

10 On Mendelssohn's sacred music, real and imaginary

An earlier version of this paper was read at the conference A Sense of Place: Seventy Years of Musical Scholarship at Yale, in New Haven in December 2001.

1. Camille Selden, *Mendelssohn* (Paris, 1867), 125.

2. Hippolyte Barbedette, *Félix Mendelssohn, sa vie et ses œuvres* (Paris, 1869), 132.

3. *Dictionary of Music and Musicians*, ed. George Grove, 2nd edn. (London, 1890), II, 304.

4. Jack *Werner*, "The Mendelssohnian Cadence," *The Musical Times* 97 (1956), 17–19; repr. in Werner, *Mendelssohn's "Elijah"* (London, 1965), 86–87.

5. *MNI*, 471.

6. Jeffrey S. Sposato, "The Price of Assimilation: The Oratorios of Felix Mendelssohn and the Nineteenth-Century Anti-Semitic Tradition," Ph.D. diss., Brandeis University, 2000, 20–21.

7. Staatsarchiv der Hansestadt Hamburg; see Rudolf Elvers, "Frühe Quellen zur Biographie Felix Mendelssohn Bartholdys," in *KBB*, 18.

8. Zelter to Goethe, 23 October 1821; the passage originally read, "Er [Felix] ist zwar ein Judensohn aber kein Jude. Der Vater hat mit bedeutender Aufopferung seine Söhne nicht beschneiden lassen und erzieht sie wie sichs gehört." But when the Goethe–Zelter *Briefwechsel* was published in 1834, the sentence was doctored to read "Der Vater hat mit bedeutender Aufopferung seine Söhne etwas lernen lassen und erzieht sie wie sich's gehört." See further, Elvers, "Frühe Quellen," 18–19.

9. Jacob Bartholdy to Abraham Mendelssohn, n.d., in Sebastian Hensel, ed., *The Mendelssohn Family (1729–1847) from Letters and Journals*, trans. C. Klingemann (London, 1882; repr. 1969), I, 75.

10. *Wiener Zeitschrift für Kunst* 7 (1822); facs. in *Das verborgene Band: Felix Mendelssohn Bartholdy und seine Schwester Fanny Hensel*, ed. H.-G. Klein (Wiesbaden, 1997), 65.

11. Rudolf Elvers, "Einleitung" to Fanny Hensel, *Tagebücher*, ed. H.-G. Klein and Rudolf Elvers

(Wiesbaden, 2002), viii. Similarly, when Felix's sister Fanny Hensel began to publish her compositions toward the end of her life, she was identified as "Fanny Hensel geb. Mendelssohn Bartholdy."

12. See Alexander Altmann, "Moses Mendelssohns gesammelte Schriften, neuerschlossene Briefe zur Geschichte ihrer Herausgabe," *Bulletin of the Leo Baeck Institute* 11, no. 42 (1968), 73–115.

13. In the introductory essay "Die Familie Mendelssohn in historischer Sicht" to *Bankiers, Künstler und Gelehrte: Unveröffentlichte Briefe der Familie Mendelssohn aus dem 19. Jahrhundert*, ed. Felix Gilbert (Tübingen, 1975), xxiv.

14. Wilhelm to Luise Hensel, 1 December 1823, *Unveröffentlichte Briefe*, 57–61.

15. Hensel, *The Mendelssohn Family*, I, 131.

16. "Lebensgeschichte Moses Mendelssohn" in Moses Mendelssohn, *Gesammelte Schriften*, ed. G. B. Mendelssohn (Leipzig, 1843), I, 43–44 ("Es war Mendelssohn's auf unerschütterliche Ueberzeugung gegründete Meinung, daß die Verschiedenheit religiöser Ansichten unter den Menschen nicht unterdrückt werden müsse und daß die Welt in grausenhafte Barbarei verfallen würde, wenn es möglich wäre eine Religion zur einzigen zu machen").

17. See the edition by Barbara Mohn (Stuttgart, 1997), *Neun Psalmen und Cantique*. The melody appeared, without attribution to Mendelssohn, as *Cantique* no. 103 in the *Recueil de cantiques chrétiens*, introduced to the Frankfurt congregation in 1849.

18. *MNI*, 415–16, and the revised German version in *Mendelssohn: Leben und Werk in neuer Sicht* (Zurich, 1980), 443–44; and Werner, "Felix Mendelssohn's Commissioned Composition for the Hamburg Temple: *The 100th Psalm* (1844)," *Musica Judaica* 7, no. 1 (1984/85), 54–57.

19. Including five letters from the director of the Temple to Mendelssohn (14 November 1843, and 8 and 21 January, 29 March, and 12 April 1844), in the Green Books of the M. Deneke Mendelssohn Collection of the Bodleian Library, Oxford, XVIII, 185 and XIX, 15, 48, 192, and 223; and the composing autograph of Psalm 100 in an *a cappella* version, dated 1 January 1844 (Kraków, Biblioteca Jagiellońska, *Mendelssohn Nachlass* 39, 43–45).

20. Oxford, Bodleian Library, M. Deneke Mendelssohn, Green Books XVIII, 185.

21. 8 January 1844, Fränkel to Mendelssohn.

22. Felix's letter does not survive, but is mentioned in Fränkel's letter of 21 January,

which permits us to infer the context of the correspondence.

23. Again, Mendelssohn's letter does not survive, though it is mentioned in Fränkel's letter of 12 April.

24. See David Brodbeck, "A Winter of Discontent: Mendelssohn and the Berliner Domchor," in *MSt*, 1–32.

25. Thus in Caput 16 of Heine's *Deutschland: Ein Wintermärchen* (1844), appears the quatrain: "Abraham had begotten with Lea / A little boy, Felix. The youngster / Has made great strides in the Christian world – / Has already become *Kapellmeister*." See further Leon Botstein and Susan Gillespie, "Heinrich Heine on Mendelssohn," in *MhW*, 352–63. On Heine's conversion, see Jeffrey L. Sammons, *Heinrich Heine: A Modern Biography* (Princeton, 1979), 107ff.

26. The *Konfirmations-Bekenntnis* is printed in *Felix Mendelssohn-Bartholdys Briefwechsel mit Legationsrat Karl Klingemann in London*, ed. Karl Klingemann [Jr.] (Essen, 1909), 358–62.

27. Felix to Julius Schubring, 18 November 1830, in *Briefwechsel zwischen Felix Mendelssohn Bartholdy und Julius Schubring, zugleich ein Beitrag zur Geschichte und Theorie des Oratoriums*, ed. Julius Schubring (Leipzig, 1892), 15. The Calvinist Schleiermacher preached at Trinity Church (Dreifaltigkeitskirche) in Berlin, where Mendelssohn worshiped. According to Hans-Jürgen Sievers, the congregation was an example of a *Simultangemeinde*, with a blend of Calvinist and Lutheran members, the result of Friedrich Wilhelm III's efforts beginning in 1817 to unify the Reformed and Lutheran branches of the Protestant Church in Prussia. See Hans-Jürgen Sievers, "Die Familie Mendelssohn Bartholdy in den Kirchenbüchern der Evangelisch-reformierten Kirche zu Leipzig," in *In der Mitte der Stadt: Die Evangelisch-reformierte Kirche zu Leipzig von der Einwanderung der Hugenotten bis zur friedlichen Revolution*, ed. H.-J. Sievers (Leipzig, 2000), 100.

28. "Il croit fermement à sa religion luthérienne, et je le scandalisais quelquefois beaucoup en riant de la Bible." Hector Berlioz, *Correspondance générale I: 1803–1832*, ed. Pierre Citron (Paris, 1972), I, 441 (6 May 1831).

29. See Sposato, "The Price of Assimilation," Chapter 5, and Martin Staehelin, "*Elijah*, Johann Sebastian Bach, and the New Covenant: On the Aria 'Es ist genug' in Felix Mendelssohn-Bartholdy's Oratorio *Elijah*," in *MhW*, 121–36.

30. See R. Larry Todd, *Mendelssohn's Musical Education: A Study and Editions of His*

Exercises in Composition (Cambridge, 1983), 27–39.

31. Two other works based on chorales, *Aus tiefer Noth* and *Mitten wir im Leben sind*, appeared as nos. 1 and 3 of the *Drei Kirchenmusiken* op. 23 in 1832.

32. Eduard Devrient, *Meine Erinnerungen an Felix Mendelssohn-Bartholdy und seine Briefe an mich* (Leipzig, 1969), 62.

33. Michael Marissen, "Religious Aims in Mendelssohn's 1829 Berlin-Singakademie Performances of Bach's *St. Matthew Passion*," *MQ* 77 (1993), 718–26.

34. Sposato, "The Price of Assimilation," 131.

35. Martin Geck, *Die Wiederentdeckung der Matthäuspassion in 19. Jahrhundert: Die zeitgenössischen Dokumente und ihre ideengeschichtliche Deutung* (Regensburg, 1967), 38.

36. *Allgemeine musikalische Zeitung* 39 (1837), 522.

37. Friedhelm Krummacher, "Art – History – Religion: On Mendelssohn's Oratorios *St. Paul* and *Elijah*," in *MC*, 310.

38. Abraham to Felix, 10 March 1835, in *Letters of Felix Mendelssohn Bartholdy from 1833 to 1847*, ed. Paul Mendelssohn Bartholdy, trans. Lady Wallace (London, 1863), 67. On the relationship between *St. Paul* and Bach's music, see further Glenn Stanley, "Bach's *Erbe*: The Chorale in the German Oratorio of the Early Nineteenth Century," *19th-Century Music* 11 (1987), 127ff.; and Peter Mercer-Taylor, "Rethinking Mendelssohn's Historicism: A Lesson from *St. Paul*," *Journal of Musicology* 15 (1997), 208–29.

39. See "From the Memoirs of Adolf Bernhard Marx," trans. Susan Gillespie, in *MhW*, 214; and Karl Klingemann, "Account of the Musical Festival at Düsseldorf," *Musical World*, 17 June 1836, 1.

40. In the following discussion, movements of *St. Paul* (1–45) are identified by numbering the Overture as 1.

41. For Peter Mercer-Taylor, the progression of chorales suggests not so much a dependence "on an established language" as a "thoughtful, wholly original metalinguistic impulse" through which the oratorio "sets out to critique its own compositional premises." Mercer-Taylor, "A Lesson," 229.

42. Felix to William Bartholomew, 30 December 1846, in F. G. Edwards, *The History of Mendelssohn's Oratorio "Elijah"* (London, 1896), 106.

43. See further Sposato, "The Price of Assimilation," Chapter 5.

44. Leon Botstein, "The Aesthetics of Assimilation and Affirmation: Reconstructing the Career of Felix Mendelssohn," in *MhW*, 23.

45. See the Vorwort to my edition of *Christus* (Stuttgart, 1994).

46. Isaac Nathan, *A Selection of Hebrew Melodies, Ancient and Modern: Reprint of the 1815–1816 Edition*, ed. Frederick Burwick and Paul Douglass (Tuscaloosa, 1988), 29.

47. Felix to Charlotte Moscheles, 17 July 1833, in *Letters of Felix Mendelssohn to Ignaz and Charlotte Moscheles*, trans. and ed. Felix Moscheles (Boston, 1888), 74.

48. See further Monika Hennemann, "Mendelssohn and Byron: Two Songs Almost without Words," *Mendelssohn Studien* 10 (1997), 142ff.

49. See my *Mendelssohn: A Life in Music* (New York, 2003), 506.

50. Other examples include the trio of the scherzo from the *Lobgesang* (see below), and the Organ Sonata op. 65 no. 5. In a related sub-group are the early "Gellert" Chorales of 1820, completed as studies for Zelter, in which Felix composed new melodies to which he set texts from the *Geistliche Oden und Lieder* of C. F. Gellert.

51. Charles Rosen, *The Romantic Generation* (Cambridge, MA, 1995), 590.

52. See Julius Schubring, "Reminiscences of Felix Mendelssohn-Bartholdy," *Musical World* 31 (18 May 1866), repr. in *MhW*, 227.

53. Carl Dahlhaus, "Mendelssohn und die musikalischen Gattungstraditionen," *PM*, 58; see also Georg Feder, "On Felix Mendelssohn Bartholdy's Sacred Music," in *MC*, 272–73.

54. For accounts of the festival, see Mark Evan Bonds, *After Beethoven: Imperatives of Originality in the Symphony* (Cambridge, MA, 1996), 80ff.; and R. Larry Todd, *Mendelssohn: A Life in Music* (New York, 2003), 395.

55. Including the Fugue in E♭ for string quartet op. 81 no. 4, the opening of the "Reformation" Symphony, and the choral fugue that opens the second part of *St. Paul*.

56. Concerning the new liturgy, or *Agende*, see Brodbeck, "A Winter of Discontent," especially 1–15.

57. This version is available in the edition by David Brodbeck (Stuttgart, 1998).

58. Kraków, Biblioteca Jagiellońska, Mendelssohn Nachlass 38 (*bis*), 235–37.

59. *MNI*, 257. Though the first autograph of the symphony is dated March 1833, and thus postdates Zelter's death (May 1832), Mendelssohn's letter of 11 June 1831 to Thomas Attwood established that the symphony was "finished" (i.e., conceptualized though not written out in score) before the composer left Italy.

60. Considerable mystery surrounds this composition, finished in Berlin on 5 February 1833, and thus *before* Mendelssohn's

appointment in Düsseldorf, where he conceivably may have introduced the piece in a service in one of the city's Catholic churches. According to Fanny Hensel, A. B. Marx performed the work in Berlin, probably c. July 1834. See Fanny's letter to Felix, c. 1 August 1834, in *The Letters of Fanny Hensel to Felix Mendelssohn*, ed. and trans. Marcia J. Citron (Stuyvesant, NY, 1987), 152.

61. Mendelssohn to Klingemann, 19 January 1847, in *Felix Mendelssohn-Bartholdys Briefwechsel mit Karl Klingemann*, ed. Klingemann, 319.

62. Mendelssohn to Magis, 13 March 1846, in Albert van der Linden, "Un Fragment inédit du 'Lauda Sion' de F. Mendelssohn," *Acta Musicologica* 26 (1954), 52.

63. The fugue is reinstated in my edition of *Lauda Sion* (Stuttgart, 1996).

64. "Learned in the sacred institutions, we consecrate the bread and wine as the host of salvation."

65. H.-F. Chorley, *Modern German Music* (London, 1854), II, 325.

66. *Ibid.*, 326–27.

11 Mendelssohn's songs

1. His earliest known song is the "Lied zum Geburtstag meines guten Vaters, den 11ten December" of 1819, now in the Bodleian Library, Oxford (GB-Ob, MDM c. 21, fol. 107). A facsimile can be found in Ernst Wolff, *Felix Mendelssohn Bartholdy* (Berlin, 1906), facing 13. See Peter Ward Jones, "Mendelssohn's First Composition," in *TMH*, 101–02.

2. John Michael Cooper, "Of Red Roofs and Hunting Horns: Mendelssohn's Song Aesthetic, with an Unpublished Cycle (1830)" forthcoming in *The Journal of Musicological Research* 21/4 (2002), 277–317.

3. Many works have been lost, and there are privately owned manuscripts which may contain either alternate versions of known songs or unknown songs with a generic title such as "Frühlingslied." See Ralf Wehner, "'It seems to have been lost': On Missing and Recovered Mendelssohn Sources," in *TMH*, 3–25.

4. Eduard Otto's so-called "translations" offended Mendelssohn to such an extent that he wrote a blistering letter of rebuke, including the statement, "And hence there is scarcely a line [in your poems] whose meaning I can ascertain with any certainty. What is going on here?" This comes from an unpublished letter of 26 April 1841 in the Heinrich-Heine-Institut in Düsseldorf (shelfmark 62.5657).

5. Christern's letter of 17 July 1841 is in the Bodleian Library, Oxford (MS M. Deneke Mendelssohn d. 40, no. 9). See also Karl Christern, *Sechs Lieder ohne Worte von Felix Mendelssohn Bartholdy, mit entsprechender Dichtung für Gesang und Pianoforte übertragen von Christern* (Bonn: N. Simrock, [1842]).

6. The autograph manuscript of this letter written on 15 November 1842 is in private hands. There is a contemporary copy in the Bodleian Library, Oxford (MS M. Deneke Mendelssohn c. 32, fols. 56–57).

7. See *Felix Mendelssohn Bartholdy: Reisebriefe aus den Jahren 1830 bis 1832*, ed. Paul Mendelssohn Bartholdy, 5th edn. (Leipzig, 1863), 205–06.

8. Adolph Bernhard Marx's review of the *Zwölf Gesänge* op. 8 appeared in the Berlin *Allgemeine musikalische Zeitung* 4, no. 23 (6 June 1827), 178–80.

9. The Mendelssohn–Klingemann solo songs are "Im Herbst" op. 9 no. 5; "Frühlingslied" op. 34 no. 3; "Sonntagslied" op. 34 no. 5; "Der Blumenstrauss" op. 47 no. 5; "Bei der Wiege" op. 47 no. 6; "Frühlingslied" op. 71 no. 2; "Herbstlied" op. 84 no. 2; and "Es lauschte das Laub" op. 86 no. 1. The child prodigies Felix and Fanny were, of course, famously the apples of Goethe's eye, and both brother and sister set the great poet's verse as songs on occasion; see Lawrence Kramer, "*Felix culpa*: Mendelssohn, Goethe, and the Social Force of Musical Expression" in Kramer, *Classical Music and Postmodern Knowledge* (Berkeley, 1991), 122–42 and Kramer, "The Lied as Cultural Practice: Tutelage, Gender and Desire in Mendelssohn's Goethe Songs" in *ibid.*, 143–73.

10. See Leon Botstein, "The Aesthetics of Assimilation and Affirmation: Reconstructing the Career of Felix Mendelssohn," in *MhW*, 26–27.

11. *Felix Mendelssohn: A Life in Letters*, ed. Rudolf Elvers, trans. Craig Tomlinson (New York, 1986), letter of 25 August 1829 to his father Abraham Mendelssohn Bartholdy, 143.

12. Felix Mendelssohn Bartholdy, *Briefe aus den Jahren 1833 bis 1847 von Felix Mendelssohn Bartholdy*, ed. Paul Mendelssohn-Bartholdy and Carl Mendelssohn-Bartholdy (Leipzig, 1863; 2nd edn. 1864; final edn. 1870), 36.

13. See Douglass Seaton, "The Problem of the Lyric Persona in Mendelssohn's Songs," in *KBB*, 167–86.

14. See Adolf Bartels, *Heinrich Heine. Auch ein Denkmal* (Dresden and Leipzig, 1906), 139. See also Bartels, *Heine-Genossen. Zur Charakteristik der deutschen Presse und der deutschen Parteien* (Dresden and Leipzig, 1908).

15. See Thomas Schmidt-Beste, "Felix Mendelssohn Bartholdy and Heinrich Heine," *Heine-Jahrbuch* 39 (2000), 111–34. Heine mocked Mendelssohn in Caput 16 of

Deutschland: Ein Wintermärchen; see *MhW*, 352–63.

16. See Ignace Feuerlicht, "Heines 'Auf Flügeln des Gesanges,'" *Heine-Jahrbuch* 21 (1982), 30–49.

17. Heine first mentions the poem in a letter of 24 December 1821. See Heinrich Heine, *Historisch-kritische Gesamtausgabe der Werke*, vol. I/2, ed. Pierre Grappin (Hamburg, 1975), 784–86. The poem was first published in the *Tragödien, nebst einem lyrischen Intermezzo, von H. Heine* (Berlin, 1823), where it was the eighth poem, and again in the first edition of the *Buch der Lieder* (Hamburg, 1827), where it is the ninth poem.

18. See Heinrich Heine, *Sämtliche Schriften*, vol. IV, ed. Klaus Briegleb, 2nd edn. (Munich, 1978), 313 (*Neue Gedichte*) and vol. III, 3rd edn. (Munich, 1996), 652 (*Elementargeister*).

19. *Gedichte von Ludewig Heinrich Christoph Hölty, neu besorgt und vermehrt von Johann Heinrich Voss* (Weissenfels, 1814), 242–44.

20. Douglass Seaton, "Mendelssohn's Cycles of Songs," in *TMH*, 203–29.

21. In Friedrich Spee, TRVTZ-NACHTIGAL. Oder GEISTLICHES POËTISCH LVST-WAELDLEIN, facsimile edn. Berne, 1985: "Der trübe Winter ist fürbey, / Die kranich wider kehren; / Nun reget sich der Vogelschrey, / Die Nester sich vermehren: / Laub mitt gemach / Nun schleicht an tag, / Die blümlein sich nun melden, / Wie Schlänglein kreum / Gehn lächelnd vmb / Die Bächlein kühl in wälden. / / Wo nur man schawt, fast alle welt / Zum frewden thut sich rüsten: / Zum schertzen alles ist gestelt, / Schwebt alles fast in lüsten. / Nur Jch allein, / Jch leyde pein, / Ohn end ich werd gequeelet, / Seit ich mitt dir, / Vnd du mitt mir, / O JESV, dich vermählet."

22. On a visit to the singer Livia Frege on 9 October 1847, Mendelssohn reportedly stated that the "Altdeutsches Frühlingslied" referred to his sister Fanny.

23. See also Monika Hennemann, "Mendelssohn and Byron: Two Songs almost without Words," *Mendelssohn-Studien* 10 (1997), 131–56; Luise Leven, "Mendelssohn als Lyriker unter besonderer Berücksichtigung seiner Beziehungen zu Ludwig Berger, Bernhard Klein und Adolf Bernhard Marx," Ph.D. diss., University of Frankfurt am Main, 1926; and Leven, "Mendelssohn's Unpublished Songs," *Monthly Musical Record* 88 (1958), 206–11.

12 Felix Mendelssohn's dramatic composition: from Liederspiel to *Lorelei*

1. See for example Wulf Konold's chapter "Scheitern an der Oper?" in his biography *Felix Mendelssohn Bartholdy und seine Zeit* (Laaber, 1984), 225–45.

2. In his third "Berlin letter" from 7 June 1822, Heinrich Heine summarized the Berlin public opinion: "Except for the young Felix Mendelssohn, who is, in the judgment of all musicians, a musical miracle and could become a second Mozart, I would not be able to find a single musical genius among the autochthones living in Berlin." Quoted in Heinrich Heine, *Sämtliche Schriften*, vol. II ed. Klaus Briegleb (Munich, 1968), 59–60. Unless otherwise noted, all translations are by the author

3. Eduard Devrient, *My Recollections of Felix Mendelssohn-Bartholdy and His Letters to Me*, trans. Natalia Macfarren (London, 1869).

4. Letter of Oettinger to Mendelssohn, Berlin, 11 November 1841, Oxford, Bodleian Library, MS. M.D.M. d.50, item 172.

5. Letter of Becher to Mendelssohn, Vienna, 18 May 1842, quoted in Renate Federhofer-Königs, "Der unveröffentlichte Briefwechsel Alfred Julius Becher (1803–1848) – Felix Mendelssohn Bartholdy (1809–1847)," *Studien zur Musikwissenschaft* 41 (1992), 69–70.

6. Letter of Mendelssohn to Devrient, Frankfurt, 26 April 1845, quoted in Devrient, *Recollections*, 259.

7. With Liszt the parallel is especially striking, as a child-prodigy opera in the 1820s (*Don Sanché*) was followed by a lengthy search for a suitable libretto in the 1840s, only to result in one unfinished mature opera (*Sardanapale*, 1849) and a subsequent concentration on orchestral music and dramatic oratorio.

8. Letter of Lea Mendelssohn Bartholdy to Henriette von Pereira-Arnstein, 20 July 1820, quoted in pre-release of Ruldolf Elvers, *Felix Mendelssohn Bartholdy: Briefe*, vol. I (1817–1829), 17.

9. Since only the first two acts of the spoken dialogue survive, the work still awaits publication.

10. Quoted in Sebastian Hensel, *Die Familie Mendelssohn 1729–1847* (Frankfurt, 1995), 175.

11. The authorship of this libretto (or at least of a major portion) has only recently been established. See Rudolf Elvers, " 'Nichts ist so schwer gut zu componiren als Strophen.' Zur Entstehungsgeschichte des Librettos von Felix Mendelssohns Oper 'Die Hochzeit des Camacho,' " (Berlin and Basel, 1976). For the public performance, the text was dramatically revised by Freiherr Carl von Lichtenstein.

12. Elvers, "'Nichts ist so schwer gut zu componiren als Strophen,'" 11.

13. Devrient, *Recollections*, 24.

14. Review in *Allgemeine musikalische Zeitung* 29, no. 24 (June 1827), cols. 410–12, quoted in *MC*, ed. and trans. Douglass Seaton, 245.

15. Georg Schünemann, "Mendelssohns Jugendopern," *Zeitschrift für Musikwissenschaft* 23 (1922), 545.

16. Letter of Mendelssohn to Devrient, 13 July 1831, quoted in Devrient, *Recollections*, 114.

17. The genre was particularly popular in Berlin, where it had originated with Reichardt's *Lieb und Treu* in 1800.

18. Letter to Friedrich Rosen, Berlin, 9 April 1830, quoted in *Felix Mendelssohn-Bartholdys Briefwechsel mit Legationsrat Karl Klingemann in London*, ed. Karl Klingemann (Essen, 1909), 78.

19. The resemblance to the opening of Act I, scene 3 in Weber's *Freischütz*, which Mendelssohn heard at its premiere on 18 June 1821, is certainly not coincidental.

20. Review in *NZfM* 54 (January–June 1861), trans. Douglass Seaton, quoted in *MC*, 244.

21. Letter of Mendelssohn to his father, Paris, 21 February 1821, quoted in, *Letters from Italy and Switzerland by Felix Mendelssohn Bartholdy*, ed. Paul Mendelssohn Bartholdy, trans. Lady Wallace (London,1862), 341.

22. Letter of Mendelssohn to his father, Paris, 19 December 1831, quoted in *ibid.*, 307.

23. Letter of Planché to Mendelssohn, London, 20 July 1838, Oxford, Bodleian Library, MS. M.D.M. d.34, item 14.

24. Memorandum of Mendelssohn to William Chappell, Leipzig, 29 December 1838, quoted in James Robinson Planché, *The Recollections and Reflections of J. R. Planché* (London, 1872), 311.

25. Letter of Mendelssohn to Klingemann, Leipzig, 2 January 1840, quoted in *Briefwechsel*, ed. Klingemann, 241–42.

26. Planché, *Recollections*, 315.

27. *The Morning Herald*, 21 January 1847, 5.

28. Letter of Mendelssohn to Klingemann, 18 February 1847, quoted in *Briefwechsel*, ed. Klingemann, 321.

29. Letter sketch of Mendelssohn to Lumley, no date, Oxford, Bodleian Library, M.D.M. d.51, item 303.

30. Letter sketch of Mendelssohn to Beale, 1 January 1847, *ibid.*, item 1.

31. For an extensive discussion, see my forthcoming dissertation on Mendelssohn's operatic projects (Johannes Gutenberg-Universität, Mainz).

32. Letter of Mendelssohn to Kinkel, 2 April 1843, Bonn, Universitäts-und Landesbibliothek, S 2662.

33. Letter of Gollmick to Mendelssohn, Frankfurt, 21 June [18]37, Oxford, Bodleian Library, MS. M.D.M. d.32, item 48.

34. Letter of Zuccalmaglio to Mendelssohn, Franzensbad, 30 July 1838, Oxford, Bodleian Library, MS. M.D.M. d.34, item 23.

35. See letter of Mendelssohn to Adolf Böttger, 10 December 1841, quoted in Dr. Karl Mendelssohn-Bartholdy, *Goethe and Mendelssohn (1821–1831)*, trans. M. E. von Glehn (London, 1874), 156–58.

36. Letter of Mendelssohn to Devrient, Frankfurt, 26 April 1845, quoted in Devrient, *Recollections*, 260.

37. Devrient, *Recollections*, 43.

38. *Ibid.*, 43.

39. Considering that the libretto was written by one of the better-known German authors, it is surprising that it has remained unpublished (and is not even included in the otherwise reliable complete critical edition of Immermann's works). Only the second and third acts of the libretto are still extant, but Julius Rietz's (Mendelssohn's successor in Düsseldorf) interest in the text suggests that it was completed by Immermann.

40. Wilhelm Stahl, *Emanuel Geibel und die Musik* (Berlin, 1919), 15.

41. Letter of Mendelssohn to Geibel, 27 August 1847, Washington, D.C., Library of Congress, Music Division. There is no evidence of a complete manuscript of Act 1.

42. For a more extensive discussion, cf. R. Larry Todd, "Mendelssohn's Operatic Destiny: *Die Loreley* Reconsidered," in *KBB*, particularly 126–37.

43. Henry F. Chorley, *Modern German Music* (London, 1854), II, 388.

44. John Warrack's acerbic comment that the music "suggest(s) not so much the gathering of a host of spirits as girls joining a new school" amusingly sums this up. See John Warrack, "Mendelssohn's Operas," in *Music and Theatre: Essays in Honour of Winton Dean*, ed. Nigel Fortune (Cambridge, 1987), 297.

45. Mendelssohn describes his libretto preferences in several instances; see, for example, his letter to Devrient, 26 April 1845, quoted in Devrient, *Recollections*, 260: "It [the libretto] should be German, and noble, and cheerful; let it be a legend of the Rhine, or some other national event or tale; or let it be a powerful type of character (as in Fidelio)" or his letter to Julius Becher, Berlin, 13 October 1841, quoted in Federhofer-Königs, "Der unveröffentlichte Briefwechsel Alfred Julius Becher (1803–1848) – Felix Mendelssohn Bartholdy (1809–1847)," 61: "I would like to have something truly passionate, humane, natural, touching to all people, basic . . . In one word: the most beautiful!"

46. Eduard Krüger, 'Ueber die heutige Oper', *NZFM* 20, no. 12 (18 February 1840), 58–59.

47. For example, *Elijah* was performed in the 1912–13 season for the "first time in America as music drama" by the Majestic Grand Opera Company in New York.

48. Cf. Ralf Wehner, "Mendelssohns Musik zu Immermanns 'Kurfürst Johann Wilhelm im Theater,'" *Die Musikforschung* 2/ 2002, 145–61.

49. Quoted in Michael Steinberg, "The Incidental Politics to Mendelssohn's *Antigone*," in *MhW*, 137.

50. Cf. Ernst Wolff, *Felix Mendelssohn Bartholdy* (Berlin, 1906), 152.

51. Letter of Mendelssohn to Droysen, 2 December 1841, quoted in *Ein tief gegründet Herz: Der Briefwechsel Felix Mendelssohn-Bartholdys mit Johann Gustav Droysen*, ed. Carl Wehmer (Heidelberg, 1959), 71–72.

52. Förster, quoted in Peter Andraschke, "Felix Mendelssohns *Antigone*," in *KBB*, 165.

53. Quoted in Peter Ranft, *Felix Mendelssohn Bartholdy: Eine Lebenschronik* (Leipzig, 1972), 100–01.

54. Unlike those in German and most other modern European languages, the patterns of Greek poetry depend for much of their effect on syllabic length, rather than word-stress.

55. Wolff, *Felix Mendelssohn Bartholdy*, 166–67.

56. Letter of Mendelssohn to Kinkel, 2 April 1843, D-BNu S 2662.

13 Mendelssohn received

1. The literature on Mendelssohn's reception history is voluminous. For an overview of recent contributions that is closely keyed to a classified bibliography, see Friedhelm Krummacher, "Aussichten im Rückblick: Felix Mendelssohn Bartholdy in der neueren Forschung," in *KBB*, 279–96. See also Chapter 3 of my *Felix Mendelssohn Bartholdy: A Guide to Research* (New York, 2001), 107–17.

2. For a survey of these recent developments in primary-source scholarship, see my "Knowing Mendelssohn: A Challenge from the Primary Sources," *Notes* 61 (2004), forthcoming.

3. *Allgemeine musikalische Zeitung* (Leipzig) 20, no. 45 (11 November 1818), col. 791; see Rudolf Elvers, "Frühe Quellen zur Biographie Felix Mendelssohn Bartholdys," in *KBB*, 22.

4. See Thomas Grey, "The Orchestral Music," in *MC*, 460.

5. See R. Larry Todd, *Mendelssohn: The Hebrides and Other Overtures* (Cambridge, 1993), 16.

6. The surviving correspondence suggests an approximate date of mid-February 1828 for this commission. See Kent Eugene Hatteberg, "*Gloria* (1822) and *Große Festmusik zum Dürerfest* (1828): Urtext Editions of Two Unpublished Choral-Orchestral Works by Felix Mendelssohn, with Background and Commentary," D.M.A. diss., University of Iowa, 1995, I, 139.

7. See Martin Geck, *Die Wiederentdeckung der Matthäuspassion im 19. Jahrhundert: Die zeitgenössischen Dokumente und ihre ideengeschichtliche Deutung* (Regensburg, 1967).

8. Only one contemporary source – Eduard Devrient's memoir, published forty years after the fact – indicates that anti-Semitism played a role in this decision, and Wm. A. Little has argued that other considerations were more influential. See Peter Mercer-Taylor, *The Life of Mendelssohn* (Cambridge, 2001), 110–13; further, Wm. A. Little, "Mendelssohn and the Berlin Singakademie: The Composer at the Crossroads," in *MhW*, 65–85.

9. See David L. Brodbeck, "A Winter of Discontent: Mendelssohn and the *Berliner Domchor*," in *MhW*, 1–32; further, Wolfgang Dinglinger, "Mendelssohn: General-Musik-Director für kirchliche und geistliche Musik," in *KBB*, 23–37.

10. The Leipzig conservatory, which first opened its doors in 1843 and still flourishes as the Hochschule für Musik und Theater "Felix Mendelssohn Bartholdy."

11. "Felix Mendelssohn-Bartholdy," in *The Musical Gem: A Souvenir for [1834]* (London, [1833]), 68–70.

12. *Ibid.*, 70.

13. That some of the information was derived from private sources is clear from the references to Mendelssohn's then-unpublished youthful operas and from the inaccurate accounting for the tepid reception of *Camacho*. The author smooths over the rather unsavory tale in a fashion such as might well have been offered by one of the young composer's London acquaintances to avoid tarnishing the recounting of his successes. For a discussion of the *Camacho* premiere, see Mercer-Taylor, *Mendelssohn*, 60–62.

14. *The Musical Gem*, 68.

15. *Ibid.* "Some of Luther's hymns" probably refers to the series of chorale cantatas (which are decidedly Lutheran and employ texts from Luther's translation of the Bible). The reference to "an *Ave*" remains unclear; it may refer to the setting of "Ave Maria" composed in 1830 and published in 1832 or to the setting of "Ave maris stella" for soprano and orchestra, composed in 1828 and published posthumously.

16. Johann Peter Lyser, "Felix Mendelssohn Bartholdy," in *Allgemeine Wiener Musik-Zeitung* 154 (24 December 1842); repr. in *Ein unbekanntes Mendelssohn-Bildnis von Johann Peter Lyser*, ed. Max F. Schneider (Basel, 1958), 37–43.

17. Lyser, *Ein unbekanntes Mendelssohn-Bildnis*, ed. Schneider, 38. These remarks echo those

offered by Schumann in his review of *St. Paul* and *Les Huguenots*; see discussion below.

18. *Ibid.*, 39.

19. *Ibid.*

20. See Leon Plantinga, "Schumann's Critical Reaction to Mendelssohn," in *Mendelssohn and Schumann: Essays on their Music and its Context*, ed. Jon W. Finson and R. Larry Todd (Durham, NC, 1984), 11–19.

21. Robert Schumann, "Fragmente aus Leipzig, 4," *NZfM* 7 (1837), 75.

22. Robert Schumann, "Trio's für Pianoforte, Violine und Violoncello," *NZfM* 13 (1840), 198. See also R. Larry Todd, "Mozart according to Mendelssohn: A Contribution to *Rezeptionsgeschichte*," in *Perspectives on Mozart Performance*, ed. R. Larry Todd and Peter Williams (Cambridge, 1991), 158–203.

23. Robert Schumann, "Aufzeichnungen über Mendelssohn," in *Felix Mendelssohn Bartholdy*, ed. Heinz-Klaus Metzger and Rainer Riehn (Munich, 1980), 102.

24. Schumann, "Trio's," 198.

25. Leon Botstein, "The Aesthetics of Assimilation and Affirmation: Reconstructing the Career of Felix Mendelssohn," in *MhW* 5–42, esp. 32–37.

26. See, for example, Joel Lester, "Substance and Illusion in Schumann's 'Erinnerung,' Op. 68: A Structural Analysis and Pictorial (*geistliche*) Description," *In Theory Only* 4 (1978), 9–17; Bernhard R. Appel, "'Actually, taken directly from family life': Robert Schumann's *Album für die Jugend*," in *Schumann and his World*, ed. R. Larry Todd (Princeton, NJ, 1994), 171–202; Michael P. Steinberg, "Schumann's Homelessness," in *Schumann*, ed. Todd, 47–79.

27. See Donald Mintz, "1848, anti-Semitism, and the Mendelssohn reception," in *MSt*, 126–48.

28. "K. Freigedank," [pseudonym Richard Wagner], "Das Judenthum in der Musik," *NZfM* 33 (1850), 101–07, 109–12. The usual English translation for the title is "Judaism in Music" (suggesting above all the Jewish religion), but Wagner's uses the term *Judentum* as a conceptual counterpart to "Christentum," meaning the community of Christendom.

29. Wagner, "Judenthum," 102. The English translation is lightly modified from that presented W. Ashton Ellis's translation (*Richard Wagner's Prose Works*, vol. III: *The Theatre*, 82).

30. Wagner, "Judenthum," 102; Ellis trans., 82.

31. Wagner, "Judenthum," 103; Ellis trans., 84.

32. Wagner, "Judenthum," 103; Ellis trans., 84.

33. Wagner, "Judenthum," 103; Ellis trans., 84.

34. Wagner, "Judenthum," 104; Ellis trans., 84–85.

35. Wagner, "Judenthum," 104; Ellis trans., 87.

36. Franz Liszt, *Des Bohémiens et de leur musique en Hongrie* (Paris, 1859). There is to date no evidence to refute Liszt's authorship of these words, but Mendelssohn is never mentioned by name in the original 1859 publication (the source from which the material presented in this text is quoted). In Liszt's defense, however, it should be added that at least the second, significantly expanded and substantially more vitriolic edition (1881) of this text and its contemporaneous English translation, like many other texts published under Liszt's name, was demonstrably corrupted by Princess Carolyne von Sayn-Wittgenstein. In any case, the book's influence was certainly enhanced because many readers associated these ideas with an artist of Liszt's impressive credentials.

37. See Jonathan Bellman, *The "Style hongrois" in the Music of Western Europe* (Boston, 1993), esp. 175–99.

38. Liszt, *Des Bohémiens*, 37. In the second, corrupt French edition (1881) and the English translation by Edwin Evans (*The Gipsy in Music*, 2 vols. [London, 1926]) the textual interpolations expand this material considerably: the first sentence is found on 40 of the English edition, the next two on 44.

39. Liszt, *Des Bohémiens*, 39–40.

40. Wagner, "Judenthum," 105–06; Ellis trans., 95.

41. Wagner, "Judenthum," 107; Ellis trans., 93–94.

42. Although Mendelssohn's works abound with examples of this stylistic dialectic, the most often discussed examples are the Prelude and Fugue in E minor op. 35 no. 1, and the finale of the Piano Trio in C minor op. 66. See R. Larry Todd, "'Me voilà perruqué': Mendelssohn's Six Preludes and Fugues op. 35 reconsidered," in *MSt*, 162–99; Thomas Schmidt-Beste, *Die ästhetischen Grundlagen der Instrumentalmusik Felix Mendelssohn Bartholdys* (Stuttgart, 1996), 318–33. See also Charles Rosen, "Mendelssohn and the Invention of Religious Kitsch," in *The Romantic Generation* (Cambridge, MA, 1995), 569–98, esp. 595–97; and James A. Garratt, "Mendelssohn's Babel: Romanticism and the Poetics of Translation," *Music & Letters* 80 (1999), 23–49.

43. For a splendid overview of these theories of progress, see John Williamson, "Progress, Modernity and the Concept of an Avant-garde," in *The Cambridge History of Nineteenth-Century Music*, ed. Jim Samson (Cambridge, 2001), 287–317; further, Glenn Stanley, "Historiography," in *The New Grove Dictionary of Music and Musicians*, 2nd edn., ed. Stanley

Sadie and John Tyrrell (London, 2001), XI, 546–61, esp. 568–56.

44. See Jurgen Thym, "Schumann in Brendel's *Neue Zeitschrift für Musik*," in *Mendelssohn and Schumann*, ed. Finson and Todd, 21–36. Another important advocate of this approach to music history was Adolph Bernhard Marx, a composer and former friend of Mendelssohn. See, for example, his widely disseminated book *Die Musik des neunzehnten Jahrhunderts und ihre Pflege* (Leipzig, 1855, with numerous subsequent editions and translations).

45. Franz Brendel, *Geschichte der Musik in Italien, Deutschland und Frankreich: Von den ersten christlichen Zeiten bis auf die Gegenwart*, 5th edn. (Leipzig, 1875), 347.

46. Anonymous [Richard Wagner], "Rossini's Stabat Mater," *NZfM* 15 (1841), 205.

47. Richard Wagner, *Oper und Drama*, in *Richard Wagner: Dichtungen und Schriften: Jubiläumsausgabe in zehn Bänden*, ed. Dieter Borchmeyer (Frankfurt am Main, 1983), VII, 246.

48. Wagner, "Über das Dirigieren," *Jubiläumsausgabe*, VIII, 135.

49. Wagner, *Über das Dichten und Komponieren*, *Jubiläumsausgabe*, IX, 294.

50. Viewed as a whole, the works published during Mendelssohn's lifetime do not portray him as a *Kirchenkomponist*: out of seventy-three works prepared for publication and provided with opus numbers by Mendelssohn, only nine are sacred, and out of the remaining twenty-four works published without opus numbers during his lifetime, only four are sacred. It is worth noting that Mendelssohn himself published none of his *a cappella* sacred music.

51. Indeed, Botstein has argued that Wagner's emphasis on the genre of opera was a self-affirmative reaction against Mendelssohn's influence in other genres. See "The Aesthetics of Assimilation and Affirmation," 12.

52. For an amateur but conceptually representative application of this historiographic method, see Adolf Schubring, "Schumanniana No. 4: The Present Musical Epoch and Robert Schumann's Position in Music History (1861)," trans. John Michael Cooper in, *Schumann and his World*, ed. Todd, 362–74. Ironically, Brendel, Wagner, Liszt, and others emphatically resisted the notion that Mendelssohn's brilliantly composed incidental music to the dramatic literature of classical antiquity constituted dramatic music.

53. Most importantly, *Felix Mendelssohn Bartholdy: Reisebriefe aus den Jahren 1830 bis 1832*, ed. Paul Mendelssohn-Bartholdy (Leipzig, 1861); *Briefe aus den Jahren 1833 bis 1847 von Felix Mendelssohn Bartholdy*, ed. Paul and Carl Mendelssohn-Bartholdy (Leipzig, 1862); and

Sebastian Hensel, *Die Familie Mendelssohn, 1729–1847: Nach Briefen und Tagebüchern* (Berlin, 1879). All of these sources were published in numerous subsequent editions and translations. For an annotated survey of these memoirs and collections of correspondence, see Chapter 2 (69–93) of my *Guide to Research*.

54. See Jim Samson, "The Great Composer," in *The Cambridge History of Nineteenth-Century Music*, 259–84. For an exploration of the mechanisms by which this historiographic method has materially affected perceptions of Mendelssohn's contributions to the genre of the string quartet and the nineteenth-century history of that genre, see Friedhelm Krummacher, "Epigones of an Epigone? Concerning Mendelssohn's String Quartets – and the Consequences," in *TMH*, 303–34.

55. The qualifier "selected" is important because those compositions that were chosen as the proper starting points for subsequent musical projects by no means represent the emphatically trivial style that Beethoven also cultivated in the last years of his life.

56. See Stephen Jay Gould, *The Mismeasure of Man*, 2nd edn. (New York, 1996), esp. Chapters 2 and 3 (105–75).

57. See Marian Wilson Kimber, "The Composer as Other: Gender and Race in the Biography of Felix Mendelssohn," in *TMH*, 335–51.

58. See Botstein, "Assimilation and Affirmation," esp. 32–37; Botstein, "Neoclassicism, Romanticism, and Emancipation: The Origins of Felix Mendelssohn's Aesthetic Outlook," in *MC*, 1–27.

59. See Wilson Kimber, "Composer as Other," esp. 344–51.

60. George Grove, "Mendelssohn," article in *Grove's Dictionary of Music and Musicians*, ed. George Grove (London, 1880), II, 253–310.

61. Especially commendable in this regard are *Briefe von Felix Mendelssohn-Bartholdy an Ignaz und Charlotte Moscheles*, ed. Felix Moscheles (Leipzig, 1888); Johannes Eckardt, *Ferdinand David und die Familie Mendelssohn-Bartholdy: Aus hinterlassenen Briefschaften* (Leipzig, 1888); and *Felix Mendelssohn-Bartholdys Briefwechsel mit Legationsrat Karl Klingemann*, ed. Karl Klingemann (Essen, 1909).

62. For example, Eduard Hanslick, "Briefe von Felix Mendelssohn-Bartholdy an Aloys Fuchs," *Deutsche Rundschau* 57 (1888), 65–85; and Bruno Hake, "Mendelssohn als Lehrer: Mit bisher ungedruckten Briefen Mendelssohns an Wilhlem v. Boguslawski," *Deutsche Rundschau* 140 (1909), 453–70.

63. Alfred Dörffel, *Geschichte der Gewandhausconcerte zu Leipzig vom 25. November 1781 bis 25. November 1881* (Leipzig, 1884).

64. Ernst Wolff, *Felix Mendelssohn Bartholdy* (Berlin, 1906; 2nd edn., 1909).

65. Three important contributions should be mentioned here: Joseph Esser, "Felix Mendelssohn Bartholdy und die Rheinlande," Ph.D. diss., Universität Bonn, 1923; Wilhelm Hubert Fischer, "Felix Mendelssohn-Bartholdy: Sein Leben und Wirken in Düsseldorf," in *95. Niederrheinisches Musikfest, Düsseldorf, 1926: Festschrift mit Angaben der Konzerte des Städt. Musikvereines und seiner Geschichte . . . nebst einer Schilderung der Düsseldorfer Musikfeste 1833 und 1836 unter Leitung von Felix Mendelssohn-Bartholdy* (Düsseldorf, 1926); and Rudolf Werner, *Felix Mendelssohn Bartholdy als Kirchenmusiker* (Frankfurt am Main, 1930).

66. The literature on this period is voluminous. For an introduction, see Thomas Schinköth, "'Es soll hier keine Diskussion über den Wert der Kompositionen angeschnitten werden': Felix Mendelssohn Bartholdy im NS-Staat," *Mendelssohn-Studien* 11 (1999), 177–205.

67. Julius Alf, *Geschichte und Bedeutung der Niederrheinischen Musikfeste in der ersten Hälfte des neunzehnten Jahrhunderts* (Düsseldorf, 1940), passim.

68. Wolfgang Boetticher, *Robert Schumann: Einführung in Persönlichkeit und Werk* (Berlin, 1941).

69. For example, Karl Blessinger, *Mendelssohn, Meyerbeer, Mahler: Drei Kapitel Judentum in der Musik als Schlüssel zur Musikgeschichte des 19. Jahrhunderts* (Berlin, 1939); Blessinger, *Judentum und Musik: Ein Beitrag zur Kultur- und Rassenpolitik* (Berlin, 1944).

70. The quotations given here are from the English translation (Alfred Einstein, *A Short History of Music* [New York: Alfred A. Knopf, 1937], 196–97). These translations concur with the German text as it is given in all editions through 1948 (1918, 1920, 1927, 1934, 1948).

71. In the German editions of this text, this phrase reads: "Er ist ein Meister der äußerlichen formalen Gestaltung" ("He is a master of the arrangement of external form") – thus stating an additional idea that is only implicit in the English translation: that Mendelssohn falls short in the category of "internal" form (i.e., ideas and content). Alfred Einstein, *Geschichte der Musik*, 2nd edn. (Leiden, 1934), 119–20.

72. Einstein, *Short History*, 196.

73. *Ibid.*, 197.

74. On Mendelssohn's relationship to this myth, see Marian Wilson Kimber, "'For art has the same place in your heart as in mine': Family, Friendship, and Community in the Life of Felix Mendelssohn," in *MC*, 29–85, esp. 61–63.

75. Paul Henry Lang, *Music in Western Civilization* (New York, 1941), 811.

76. For surveys of these problematical portrayals, see Albrecht Riethmüller, "Das 'Problem Mendelssohn,'" *Archiv für Musikwissenschaft* 59 (2002), 210–21; further, Hans-Werner Boresch, "Neubeginn mit Kontinuität: Tendenzen der Musikliteratur nach 1945," in *Die dunkle Last: Musik und Nationalsozialismus*, ed. Brunhilde Sonntag, Hans-Werner Boresch, and Detlef Gojowy (Cologne, 1999), 286–317, esp. 304–06.

77. Bernhard Bartels, *Mendelssohn-Bartholdy: Mensch und Werk* (Bremen, 1947); George Grove, *Beethoven, Schubert, Mendelssohn* (London, 1951).

78. *Felix Mendelssohn Bartholdy: Lebensbild mit Vorgeschichte* (Zurich, 1949), ed. Peter Sutermeister; 2nd rev. edn. as *Felix Mendelssohn Bartholdy: Briefe einer Reise durch Deutschland, Italien und die Schweiz, und Lebensbild* (Zurich, 1958).

79. Eric Werner, "Mendelssohn," article in *Die Musik in Geschichte und Gegenwart*, ed. Friedrich Blume (Kassel, 1961), IX, 59–98; *MNI*.

80. Donald Monturian Mintz, "The Sketches and Drafts of Three of Felix Mendelssohn's Major Works," Ph.D. diss., Cornell University, 1960.

81. The symposium, held in Berlin in 1972, produced the first of a series of important collections of essays devoted to various aspects of Mendelssohn's life, works, and posthumous reception. See *PM*.

82. The journal *Mendelssohn-Studien*, published by Duncker & Humblot (Berlin).

83. For example, the early string *sinfonie* (see Wulf Konold, "Mendelssohns Jugendsinphonien: Eine analytische Studie," *Archiv für Musikwissenschaft* 46 [1989], 155–83); the chorale cantatas (see Pietro Zappalà, *Le "Choralkantaten" di Felix Mendelssohn-Bartholdy* [Venice, 1991]); the "Paris" Kyrie in D minor (see Ralf Wehner, *Studien zum geistlichen Chorschaffen des jungen Felix Mendelssohn Bartholdy* [Cologne, 1996], 155–87); *Die Heimkehr aus der Fremde* (see Thomas Krettenauer, *Felix Mendelssohn Bartholdys "Heimkehr aus der Fremde": Untersuchungen und Dokumente zum Liederspiel op. 89* [Augsburg, 1994]); or the concert aria *Infelice! / Ah, ritorna, età dell'oro* (see John Michael Cooper, "Mendelssohn's Two *Infelice* Arias: Problems of Sources and Musical Identity," in *TMH*, 43–97).

84. For annotated commentaries on these important studies, see Chapter 5 (137–77) of my *Guide to Research*.

85. The last ten years have witnessed the appearance of two "new" compositions: the 1838 *Festgesang* "Möge das Siegeszeichen" (first

published Wiesbaden, 1997), and the
still-unpublished orchestral prelude to Karl
Immermann's play *Kurfürst Johann Wilhelm im
Theater* (see Ralf Wehner, "'. . . das sei nun alles
für das Düsseldorfer Theater und dessen Heil
. . .': Mendelssohns Musik zu Immermanns
Vorspiel 'Kurfürst Johann Wilhelm im Theater'
(1834)," *Die Musikforschung* 55 [2002],
145–61).

86. Clive Brown, *A Portrait of Mendelssohn*
(New Haven, 2003); R. Larry Todd,
Mendelssohn: A Life in Music (New York, 2003).

87. See *MNI*, and esp. its significantly improved
revision (*Mendelssohn: Leben und Werk in neuer
Sicht* [Zurich, 1980]).

88. See Jeffrey Sposato, "The Price of
Assimilation: The Oratorios of Felix
Mendelssohn and the Nineteenth-Century
Anti-Semitic Tradition," Ph.D. diss., Brandeis
University, 2000; Sposato, "Creative Writing:
The [Self]-Identification of Mendelssohn as
Jew," *MQ* 92 (1998), 190–209.

89. Most obviously important here (and
perhaps surprising) are Mendelssohn's personal
and artistic relationships with Franz Liszt. On
this issue, see Wm. A. Little, "Mendelssohn and
Liszt," in *MSt*, 106–25; further, Martin Geck,
"Im Dienst der Volksbildung: Franz Liszt und
Felix Mendelssohn Bartholdy," in *Von Beethoven
bis Mahler: Leben und Werk der großen
Komponisten des 19. Jahrhunderts* (Reinbek,
2000), 212–79.

90. See Leon Botstein, "Neoclassicism,
Romanticism, and Emancipation: The
Origins of Felix Mendelssohn's Aesthetic
Outlook," in *MC*, 1–27; further, Peter
Mercer-Taylor, "Mendelssohn and the Musical
Discourse of the German Restoration," Ph.D.
diss., University of California at Berkeley,
1995.

**14 Wagner as Mendelssohn: reversing habits
and reclaiming meaning in the performance of
Mendelssohn's music for orchestra and chorus**
1. There are two new important books on
Mendelssohn that can provide the reader with
the most compelling and up-to-date account of
biography and reception, particularly with
respect to issues of interpretation. These two
works each contain a bibliography and critical

apparatus sufficient for any further reading and
research. See R. Larry Todd, *Mendelssohn: A Life
in Music* (New York, 2003) and John Michael
Cooper, *Mendelssohn's "Italian" Symphony*
(Oxford, 2003).

2. The obvious sources are Nietzsche, *The Birth
of Tragedy* and Mann on Wagner and the novels
The Magic Mountain and *Doctor Faustus*.

3. See Leon Botstein, "Neoclassicism,
Romanticism, and Emancipation: The Origins
of Felix Mendelssohn's Aesthetic Outlook," in
MC, 1–27. It should be noted that modern
scholarship has revealed new perspectives on
how to understand Mendelssohn in ways that
are helpful to performance considerations. See
for example Thomas Grey's "*Tableaux vivants*:
Landscape, History Painting and the Visual
Imagination in Mendelssohn's Orchestral
Music," *19th Century Music* 21 (1997) 42–55.

4. See Barry Bergdall, *Karl Friedrich Schinkel: An
Architecture for Prussia* (New York, 1994); the
new installation at Berlin Nationalgalerie.

5. In order to dispense with the personal
dimension behind this essay in as discreet a
manner as possible, brief disclosure as to the
author's experience as a performer with
Mendelssohn is appropriate. I recorded the
complete *St. Paul* in the mid 1990s, with the
extra numbers Mendelssohn removed from the
final version and have, since the mid 1980s,
performed in a variety of public professional
concert venues with different orchestras in
Europe and America, *St. Paul*, *Antigone*, all five
symphonies, the overtures, the Violin Concerto,
the two piano concertos, the string symphonies,
and a good bit of sacred music. The Bard Music
Festival was devoted to Mendelssohn in 1991.

6. Carl Dahlhaus, *Nineteenth Century Music*
(Berkeley, 1989) 157; see also Cooper,
Mendelssohn's "Italian" Symphony, 1.

7. Ian Watt, *The Rise of the Novel: Studies in
Defoe, Richardson and Fielding* (Berkeley, 1957).

8. See Mendelssohn's praise for his father's
comments on Bach in the exchange of letters in
March 1835. In *Felix Mendelssohn: Letters*, ed. S.
Selden-Goth (New York, 1945) 239–44.

9. This discussion owes much to Richard Will,
*The Characteristic Symphony in the Age of Haydn
and Beethoven* (Cambridge, 2002), an
outstanding analysis and survey.

Select bibliography

Benedict, Julius, *Sketch of the Life and Works of the Late Felix Mendelssohn Bartholdy* (London, 1850; 2nd edn. [revised and enlarged] 1853).

Blunt, Wilfred, *On Wings of Song* (London, 1974).

Botstein, Leon, "Songs without Words: Thoughts on Music, Theology, and the Role of the Jewish Question in the Work of Felix Mendelssohn," *MQ* 77 (1993), 561–78.

Botstein, Leon, ed., *Felix Mendelssohn – Mitwelt und Nachwelt: Bericht zum 1. Leipziger Mendelssohn-Kolloquium am 8. und 9. Juni 1993* (Wiesbaden, 1996).

Brown, Clive, *A Portrait of Mendelssohn* (New Haven, 2003).

Citron, Marcia J., "Felix Mendelssohn's Influence on Fanny Hensel as a Professional Composer," *Current Musicology* 37/38 (1984), 9–17.

Cooper, John Michael, *Felix Mendelssohn Bartholdy: A Guide to Research, With An Introduction to Research Concerning Fanny Hensel* (New York, 2001).
  Mendelssohn's "Italian" Symphony (Oxford, 2003).

Cooper, John Michael, and Julie D. Prandi, eds., *The Mendelssohns: Their Music in History* (Oxford, 2002).

Dahlhaus, Carl, ed., *Das Problem Mendelssohn* (Regensburg, 1974).

Devrient, Eduard, *Meine Erinnerungen an Felix Mendelssohn-Bartholdy und seine Briefe an mich* (Leipzig, 1869); trans. Natalia MacFarren as *My Recollections of Felix Mendelssohn-Bartholdy, and his Letters to Me* (London, 1869).

Dinglinger, Wolfgang, *Studien zu den Psalmen mit Orchester von Felix Mendelssohn Bartholdy* (Cologne, 1993).

Edward, F. G., *The History of Mendelssohn's Oratorio "Elijah"* (London, 1896).

Ehrle, Thomas, *Die Instrumentation in den Symphonien und Ouvertüren von Felix Mendelssohn Bartholdy* (Wiesbaden, 1983).

Finson, Jon W., and R. Larry Todd, eds., *Mendelssohn and Schumann: Essays on Their Music and Its Context* (Durham, NC, 1984).

Garratt, James, "Mendelssohn's Babel: Romanticism and the Poetics of Translation," *Music & Letters* 80 (1999), 23–49.
  Palestrina and the German Romantic Imagination: Interpreting Historicism in Nineteenth-Century Music (Cambridge, 2002).

Geck, Martin, *Die Wiederentdeckung der Matthäuspassion im 19. Jahrhundert: Die zeitgenössischen Dokumente und ihre ideengeschichtliche Deutung* (Regensburg, 1967).

Gerhartz, Leo Karl, ed., *Felix Mendelssohn Bartholdy: Repräsentant und/oder Außenseiter? Fünf Vorträge zu den "Kasseler Musiktagen 1991"* (Kassel, 1993).

Gilbert, Felix, *Bankiers, Künstler und Gelehrte: Unveröffentlichte Briefe der Familie Mendelssohn aus dem 19. Jahrhundert* (Tübingen, 1975).

Grey, Thomas S., "*Tableaux vivants*: Landscape, History Painting, and the Visual
  Imagination in Mendelssohn's Orchestral Music," *19th-Century Music* 21
  (1997), 38–76.
Großmann-Vendrey, Susanna, *Felix Mendelssohn Bartholdy und die Musik der
  Vergangenheit* (Regensburg, 1969).
  "Mendelssohn und die Vergangenheit," in *Die Ausbreitung des Historismus über
  die Musik: Aufsätze und Diskussionen*, ed. Walter Wiora (Regensburg, 1969),
  73–84.
Hensel, Fanny, *The Letters of Fanny Hensel to Felix Mendelssohn*, ed. and trans.
  Marcia J. Citron (Stuyvesant, NY, 1987).
  Tägebucher, ed. Hans-Günter Klein and Rudolf Elvers (Wiesbaden, 2002).
Hensel, Sebastian, *Die Familie Mendelssohn 1729–1847: Nach Briefen und
  Tagebüchern*, 3 vols. (Berlin, 1879); trans. Karl Klingemann and an American
  collaborator as *The Mendelssohn Family (1729–1847): From Letters and Journals*
  (New York, 1881).
Hiller, Ferdinand, *Felix Mendelssohn-Bartholdy: Briefe und Erinnerungen* (Cologne,
  1874); trans. M. E. von Glehn as *Mendelssohn: Letters and Recollections* (London,
  1874).
Jacob, Heinrich Eduard, *Felix Mendelssohn and his Times*, trans. Richard and Clara
  Winston (London, 1959).
Jenkins, David, and M. Visocchi, *Mendelssohn in Scotland* (London, 1978).
Jost, Christa, *Mendelssohns Lieder ohne Worte* (Tutzing, 1988).
Kaufman, Schima, *Mendelssohn: "A Second Elijah"* (New York, 1934).
Klingemann, Karl, ed., *Felix Mendelssohn-Bartholdys Briefwechsel mit Legationsrat
  Karl Klingemann in London* (Essen, 1909).
Köhler, Karl-Heinz, *Felix Mendelssohn Bartholdy* (Leipzig, 1963).
Konold, Wulf, *Felix Mendelssohn Bartholdy: Symphonie Nr. 4 A-Dur Op. 90, "Die
  Italienische"* (Munich, 1987).
  *Die Symphonien Felix Mendelssohn Bartholdys: Untersuchungen zu Werkgestalt und
  Formstruktur* (Laaber, 1992).
  Felix Mendelssohn Bartholdy und seine Zeit (Laaber, 1984).
Kramer, Lawrence, "*Felix culpa*: Mendelssohn, Goethe, and the Social Force of
  Musical Expression," in *Classical Music and Postmodern Knowledge* (Berkeley
  and Los Angeles, 1995), 122–42.
Krummacher, Friedhelm, *Mendelssohn – der Komponist: Studien zur Kammermusik
  für Streicher* (Munich, 1978).
Lampadius, Wilhelm Adolf, *Felix Mendelssohn Bartholdy: Ein Denkmal für seine
  Freunde* (Leipzig, 1848).
Marek, George, *Gentle Genius: The Story of Felix Mendelssohn* (New York, 1972).
Mendelssohn Bartholdy, Felix, *Briefe aus den Jahren 1833 bis 1847 von Felix
  Mendelssohn Bartholdy*, ed. Paul Mendelssohn-Bartholdy and Carl
  Mendelssohn-Bartholdy (Leipzig, 1863); trans. Lady Wallace as *Letters of Felix
  Mendelssohn Bartholdy from 1833 to 1847* (London, 1863).
  Briefe von Felix Mendelssohn-Bartholdy an Ignaz und Charlotte Moscheles (Leipzig,
  1888); trans. Karl Klingemann as *Letters of Felix Mendelssohn to Ignaz and
  Charlotte Moscheles* (London, 1888).

Felix Mendelssohn Bartholdy: Briefe, ed. Rudolf Elvers (Frankfurt, 1984); trans. Craig Tomlinson as *Felix Mendelssohn: A Life in Letters* (New York, 1986).

Felix Mendelssohn Bartholdy: Briefe einer Reise durch Deutschland, Italien und die Schweiz und Lebensbild, ed. Peter Sutermeister (Zurich, 1958).

Felix Mendelssohn Bartholdy: Reisebriefe aus den Jahren 1830 bis 1832, ed. Paul Mendelssohn Bartholdy (Leipzig, 1861); trans. Lady Wallace as *Letters from Italy and Switzerland by Felix Mendelssohn Bartholdy* (Boston, 1862).

Felix Mendelssohn Bartholdy, Werke, ed. Julius Rietz (Leipzig, 1874–77).

Felix Mendelssohn: Letters, ed. and trans. G. Selden-Goth (New York, 1945).

Leipziger Ausgabe der Werke Felix Mendelssohn Bartholdys, ed. Internationale Felix-Mendelssohn-Gesellschaft (Leipzig, 1960–).

Mendelssohn-Studien (1972–).

Mercer-Taylor, Peter, *The Life of Mendelssohn* (Cambridge, 2000).

Mintz, Donald Manturean, "The Sketches and Drafts of Three of Felix Mendelssohn's Major Works," 2 vols., Ph.D. diss., Cornell University, 1960.

Nichols, Roger, *Mendelssohn Remembered* (London, 1997).

Pelto, William Lyle, "Musical Structure and Extramusical Meaning in the Concert Overtures of Mendelssohn," Ph.D. diss., University of Texas, 1993.

Porter, Cecilia Hopkins, "The Reign of the Dilettanti: Düsseldorf from Mendelssohn to Schumann," *MQ* 73 (1989), 476–512.

Radcliffe, Philip, *Mendelssohn* (London, 1954; 3rd edn., rev. Peter Ward Jones, London, 1990).

Richter, Arndt, *Mendelssohn: Leben, Werke, Dokumente* (Mainz, 1994).

Rosen, Charles, "Mendelssohn and the Invention of Religious Kitsch," in *The Romantic Generation* (Cambridge, MA, 1995), 569–98.

Rudolph, Eberhard, "Mendelssohns Beziehungen zu Berlin," *Beiträge zur Musikwissenschaft* 14 (1972), 205–14.

Schmidt, Christian Martin, ed., *Felix Mendelssohn Bartholdy: Kongreß-Bericht Berlin 1994* (Wiesbaden, 1997).

Schmidt, Thomas, *Die ästhetischen Grundlagen der Instrumentalmusik Felix Mendelssohn Bartholdys* (Stuttgart, 1996).

Schumann, Robert, *Erinnerungen an Felix Mendelssohn Bartholdy*, ed. Georg Eismann (Zwickau, 1947); trans. James A. Galston as *Memoirs of Felix Mendelssohn-Bartholdy: From Private Notes and Memoranda, Letters, and Dairies [sic] of Robert Schumann* (Rochester, NY, 1951).

Seaton, Douglass, "A Study of a Collection of Mendelssohn's Sketches and Other Autograph Material: Deutsche Staatsbibliothek Mus. Ms. Autogr. 19," Ph.D. diss., Columbia University, 1977.

Seaton, Douglass, ed., *The Mendelssohn Companion* (Westport, 2001).

Shepard, Elizabeth, *Charles Auchester* (London, 1853).

Sposato, Jeffrey, "Creative Writings: The [Self-] Identification of Mendelssohn as Jew," *MQ* 82 (1998), 190–209.

Tillard, Françoise, *Fanny Mendelssohn* (Paris, 1992); trans. Camille Naish as *Fanny Mendelssohn* (Portland, OR, 1996).

Todd, R. Larry, "The Instrumental Music of Felix Mendelssohn Bartholdy: Selected Studies Based on Primary Sources," Ph.D. diss., Yale University, 1979.

  Mendelssohn's Musical Education: A Study and Editions of His Exercises in Composition (Cambridge, 1983).

  Mendelssohn: The Hebrides and Other Overtures (Cambridge, 1993).

  Mendelssohn: A Life in Music (New York, 2003).

Todd, R. Larry, ed., *Mendelssohn and His World* (Princeton, 1991).

  Mendelssohn Studies (Cambridge, 1992).

Vitercik, Greg, "Mendelssohn the Progressive," *The Journal of Musicological Research* 8 (1989), 333–74.

  The Early Works of Felix Mendelssohn: A Study in the Romantic Sonata Style (Philadelphia, 1992).

Ward Jones, Peter, ed. and trans., *The Mendelssohns on Honeymoon: The 1837 Diary of Felix and Cécile Mendelssohn Bartholdy, together with Letters to Their Families* (Oxford, 1997).

Werner, Eric, *Mendelssohn: A New Image of the Composer and his Age*, trans. Dika Newlin (London, 1963); rev. as *Mendelssohn: Leben und Werk in neuer Sicht* (Zurich, 1980).

Wolff, Ernst, *Felix Mendelssohn Bartholdy* (Berlin, 1906).

Worbs, Hans Christoph, *Felix Mendelssohn Bartholdy in Selbstzeugnissen und Bilddokumenten* (Rheinbek, 1974).

Index

abbreviations, xv
absolute music, 265
acceleration, 278
Aeneid (Virgil), 39
Aeschylus, 226
aestheticians, 67, 68
aesthetics, Hegel's lectures on, 64
"Aesthetics of Assimilation and Affirmation,
    The" (Botstein), 6–7
Agawu, Kofi, 81, 83
Agricola, Alexander, 61
Albert, Prince of England, xiii
Alexis und Dora (Goethe), 65
Alf, Julius, 246
Alger, William, 47
Allgemeine musikalische Zeitung, 160, 214, 234,
    235
Altes Museum, 12
Ambros, A. W., 103
Anglican church music, 169
Antigone (Sophocles), 22, 68, 225, 227
anti-Semitism, 2, 4
    Berlin Singakademie directorship and, 16, 36
    classification and, 27–28
    criticism of Mendelssohn and, 26, 238–40,
        246–48, 253, 260, 292
    gender role restrictions and, 50
    language and, 189–90
    Liszt and, 239–40
    Third Reich, 246
    Wagner and, 238–39
architecture
    Gothic, 60
    historicism in, 60
    unifying style in, 60
Arlès-Dufour, 218
Arnstein Pereira, Henriette von, 190
arpeggiation, 285
art
    Catholicism and, 59
    historicism in, 56–57, 58–59
    Italian, 57
    Nazarenes, 58–60
    objectification of, 257
    subjectivity in, 256
assimilation, 29
*Ästhetishen Grundlagen der Instrumentalmusik
    Felix Mendelssohn-Bartholdys, Die*
    (Schmidt), 6–7
Athalie (Racine), 225

Austen, Jane, 255–56, 258, 260
Austin, Sarah, 43

Bach, Carl Philipp Emanuel, 61, 113–14
Bach, Johann Christian, 113–14, 149
Bach, Johann Sebastian, xi, xiii, 11, 13, 17, 19,
    21, 61, 62, 63–64, 66, 91, 94, 252, 277
    Bach revival, 11, 63–64, 172, 277
    influence on Mendelssohn, 95, 130–48, 156,
        164, 172, 259
    Mendelssohn's interest in, 62
    Mendelssohn's performance of works of, 165
Bach, Johann Sebastian, works
    Ascension Oratorio (BWV 11), 17
    Cantata no. 4, *Christ lag in Todesbanden*
        (BWV 4), 164
    choral music, 11, 63–64, 164, 172
    Concerto, keyboard, in D-minor (BWV
        1052), 150
    St. Matthew Passion (BWV 244), 11, 14, 35,
        36, 61, 63, 159, 172–73, 174, 175, 234,
        266
    Well-Tempered Clavier (BWV 846-893), 43,
        61, 62, 283
Bach, Wilhelm Friedemann, 61
Baillot, Pierre, x, 115
Baini, Giuseppe, 19, 65
Ballan, Judith Silber, 270
ballet music, 214
Barbedette, Hippolyte, 167
Bardin, Abbé, 14, 16
Bärmann, Carl, 130
Baroque music, 61
    church sonatas, 159
    ritornello concerto style, 115
    trio sonata, 131
Bartels, Adolf, 192
Bartels, Bernhard, 248
Barthody name, 35
Bartholdy, Jacob (*olim* Jacob Salomon), 168,
    169
Bartholomew, William, 169, 175
baton conducting, 15, 271
battle music, 110
Beale, T. F., 217
Becher, Alfred Julius, 207
Beethoven, Ludwig van, xi, 12, 16, 17, 18, 19,
    20, 21, 62, 81, 82, 91, 95, 149, 165, 244,
    252, 255, 256, 257, 258
    album in tribute to, 160, 164

Beethoven, Ludwig van (*cont.*)
  influence on Mendelssohn, 95, 115, 120, 130,
      136, 138–39, 140, 141, 142, 257
  Mendelssohn as heir to, 255
  Mendelssohn compared to, 251
  Mendelssohn's early exposure to, 150
  Mendelssohn's performance of works
      of, 165
  monumentality of, 258, 260
  Wagner as heir to, 258
Beethoven, Ludwig van, works
  Concertos, 114
  Concertos, piano
      No. 3 in C minor, op. 37, 114, 117
      No. 4 in G major, op. 58, 114, 165
      No. 5 in Eb major, op. 73 ("Emperor"),
          15, 16, 114, 120, 165
  Missa Solemnis op. 123, 263
  Quartets, piano, 132
  Quartets, strings
      op. 18, no. 1 in F major, 285
      op. 74 in Eb major ("Harp"), 81, 138
      op. 95 in F minor ("Serious"), 163
      op. 131 in C# minor, 84, 138
      op. 132 in A minor, 81, 138
      op. 135 in F major, 138, 139–40
  Quintet, strings, in C major op. 29, 77, 137
  Sonatas, piano
      No. 28 in A major, op. 101, 150
      No. 29 in Bb major, op. 106
          ("Hammerklavier"), 150
      No. 30 in E major, op. 109, 151
      No. 31 in Ab major, op. 110, 111, 280
      No. 32 in C minor, op. 111, 166
  Symphonies
      No. 3 in Eb major op. 55, 109
      No. 4 in Bb major op. 60, 85, 272
      No. 5 in C minor op. 67, 85, 95, 109, 166
      No. 6 in F major op. 68, "Pastoral", 17,
          257, 263, 265
      No. 7 in A major op. 92, 102
      No. 9 in D minor op. 125, 181, 234, 256,
          258, 270, 272
  Variations, 164
      in C minor (WoO 80), 163
      op. 120 ("Diabelli"), 163
Befreiungsdom, 60
Bellini, Vincenzo, 21
Benedict, Sir Julius, 3, 15, 47
Benjamin, Phyllis, 51
Bennett, Sir William Sterndale, 43
Berger, Ludwig, x, 13
Berlin
  architecture, 12
  conversions from Judaism, 29–30
  opera projects in, 219
Berlin Academy of Arts, 22–23
Berlin Cathedral, 171

Berlin Freitagskollegium, 61
Berlin Singakademie, 11, 14, 61, 63, 172
  architecture of, 11
  directorship of, 16, 36, 234
  Fanny's participation in, 43
  Mendelssohn's participation in, 43, 63
  significance of, 36
Berlioz, Hector, 12, 172
  Harold en Italie, op. 16, 103
  Symphonie fantastique, op. 14, 72, 81
Biedermeier generation, 31, 32
Bigot, Marie, x
Bildung, 33, 34, 36
biographies, 46–52
Birmingham Music Festival, 17, 123
Blummer, Martin, 271
Blümner, Heinrich, 23
Bodleian Library, 31
Boeckh, Philipp August, 225
Boguslawski, Wilhelm von, 144
botanical metamorphosis, 83
Botstein, Leon, vi, 2, 3, 6–7, 30, 31, 176, 192,
      237, 294
Bötticher, Wolfgang, 246
Brahms, Johannes, 17, 47, 80–81, 254
  Mendelssohn's influence on, 80, 82
Brahms, Johannes, works
  Serenades
      No. 1 in D major, op. 11, 80
      No. 2 in A major, op. 16, 80
  Sextet, strings
      No. 1 in Bb major, op. 18, 80, 81
      No. 2 in G major, op. 36, 80, 81
  Symphonies
      No. 2 in D major, op. 73, 80
      No. 3 in F major, op. 90, 82
Breitkopf & Härtel, 243
Brendel, Franz, 5, 59, 68, 166, 241, 242
Brentano, Clemens, 221
Brotherhood of St. Luke (Nazarenes). *See*
      Nazarenes
Bruch, Max, 221
Brugmüller, Friedrich August, 18
Brühl, Graf, 209
Brunswick Music Festival, 17
Buch der Lieder (Heine), 192–95
Bunsen, Christian Karl Josias von, 22
Byron, George Gordon, Baron, 178

cadence, 76–79, 82
cadenzas, 114, 128
canons, 3
Casper, Johann Ludwig, 208–09
Catholic Church
  art and, 57, 59
  Mahler and, 36
  music for, 18–19, 169
  programmatic music and, 270

Cervantes, 209
Chadwick, Whitney, 46, 49
chamber music, 130–48. *See also* Mendelssohn,
        Felix, works
    instrumental chorales, 180
    late works, 147–48
    Mendelssohn's early works, 130–34
    Mendelssohn's "first maturity" works, 130,
        134–40
    Mendelssohn's mature works, 130, 141–47
    musical design, 76
    phases in, 130
    "practice works", 131
    string quartets, 137–40
    string quintets, 137
characteristic music, 98–104, 110, 279
    preludes and fugues, 157–58
Cherubini, Luigi, 18, 19, 21, 97
Chézy, Helminie von, 221
Chopin, Frederic, 12, 113, 165, 252
chorales. *See also* Mendelssohn, Felix,
        works
    criticism of use of, 174–75
    in *Elijah*, 175
    "imaginary", 180, 182
    Lutheran, 175
    Mendelssohn's Christian faith and, 2
    Mendelssohn's use of, 172, 174, 175, 180
    in Organ Sonatas op. 65, 159
    in *Paulus*, 174
    progression of, 288
choral music. *See also* Mendelssohn, Felix,
        works
    Bach, 11, 63–64, 164
    criticism of, 5, 6–7
    historicism and, 55
Chorley, Henry Fothergill, 3–4, 45, 46, 188,
        217, 220
Christern, Karl, 190
Christian church music, 2
Cimarosa, Domenico, 21
Citron, Marcia, 43, 44
classical imitation, 56–57
Classical Music and Postmodern Knowledge
        (Kramer), 6
classicism, 81
classification
    anti-Semitism and, 27–28
    Mendelsohhn's Jewish identity and, 27–28
"Clavier-Concert, Das" (Schumann), 116
Clementi, Muziio, 149
climax, in Romantic music, 72
coda, 76, 79, 83
concertmasters, 20
concerto form, 88
    Baroque ritornello concerto style, 115
    cadenzas, 114
    concerto style, 113–14

double-exposition, 113, 116, 117, 118
    orchestral ritornellos, 113
    single-exposition, 127
concertos, 112–29. *See also* Mendelssohn, Felix,
        works
    early, 113–17
    Mendelssohn's attitude toward, 112
    Mozart and, 113–14
    revision of, 116
    Romantic music, 112
conducting
    with baton, 15, 271
    Gewandhaus Orchestra, 20–21, 23, 24, 234
    by Mendelssohn, 11, 14, 15, 19, 20, 43, 261
    Mendelssohn's influence on, 15, 271
    works of Mendelssohn, 254–55, 260, 267–68
contrapuntal devices, 132
Cooper, John Michael, vi, 3
Cornelius, Peter von, 58, 276
Courtivron, Isabelle de, 46, 49
Coventry, 159
Cramer, Johann Baptist, 114
Creation, The (Haydn), 18
"Creative Writings: The [Self-] Identification of
        Mendelssohn as a Jew" (Sposato), 30
creativity
    compositional historicism and, 70
    gender and, 45
    Goethe's philosophy on, 67
    of women, 45, 49
cultural identity, 32, 40
Cummings, William Hayman, 181
cyclic design, 83, 86

Dahlhaus, Carl, 6, 26, 41, 56, 72, 181
David, Ferdinand, 20, 24, 127, 245
"dehistoricism," 56
"developing variation" technique, 130
development, 76, 135
Devrient, Eduard, 11, 14, 16, 36, 42, 66, 155,
        172, 206, 211, 220, 221, 292
    Hans Heiling, 221
    Recollections of Mendelssohn, 206, 219
Dictionary of Music and Musicians (Grove), 245
Dinglinger, Wolfgang, 270
Dirichlet, Rebecka Henriette (née
        Mendelssohn, later Mendelssohn
        Bartholdy), 13, 211
Döhler, Theodor, 113
Dohm, Christian Wilhelm, 29
Donizetti, Gaetano, xii, 21
Don Quixote (Cervantes), 209
Dörffel, Alfred, 245
Dostoevsky, Fyodor, 255
double bass, 283
"double consciousness," 40
"double-exposition" concerto form, 113, 116,
        117, 118

Dowden, Edward, 50
dramatic music, 206–29. *See also* opera
  Berlin projects, 216–18
  London projects, 216–18
  Munich projects, 216
  operatic projects and ideas, 219–24
  Paris projects, 218
  unsolicited plot suggestions, 219–20
"Dresden Amen", 105
Dreyschock, Alexander, 21
Droysen, Gustav, 13, 27, 220
DuBois, W. E. B., 40
duet form, 38
duets, 285
Dürer, Albrecht, 234, 235, 270
Dussek, Jan, 114
Düsseldorf
  Catholic church music in, 18–19
  incidental music composed in, 225
  Lower Rhine Music Festival, 16–17
  Mendelssohn's musical directorship of,
    18–19, 20, 25, 234
  musical culture, 18
  opera, 19
Duveyrier, Charles, 218
Dvorak, Antonin, 252

early music, 55, 61–62
Edward III and the Siege of Calais (Planché), 221
"Ein' feste Burg ist unser Gott" (chorale), 106
Einsten, Albert, 246–47, 248
El Cid, 221
elfin style, 98
  "Elfin fugue," 137
  "Elfin Scherzo," 139
  in piano quartets, 132, 133
  in String Octet op. 20, 136
Elvers, Rudolf, 27, 168
England, opera projects in, 216–18
epic-historical music, 109, 110
"Erste Walpurgisnacht" (Goethe), 37
Ertmann, Baroness Dorothea von, xii
Eumenides (Aeschylus), 226
exposition, 76

Family Mendelssohn, Die (Hensel), 42, 49
Fasch, Christian Friedrich Carl, 11
Faust (Goethe), 67, 136
Fétis, François-Joseph, 42, 65
Fichte, Johann Gottlieb, 13
Field, John, 114, 149
  Piano Concerto no. 2 in Ab major, 117
Fink, Gottfried Wilhelm, 69, 173
Flemming, Paul, 201
folk dances, 139
folk songs, 151, 192
Foucault, Michel, 56
Fouqué, Friedrich de la Motte, 107

Fränkel, Maimon, 170–71
Freischütz, Der (Weber), 12, 214
Frederick the Great (Friedrich II), 61, 62
French violin school, eighteenth century, 115
Frescobaldi, Girolama, 149
Freud, Sigmund, 39
Friedrich, Caspar David, 256–57, 258
Friedrich August II, Saxon King, xiii, 23
Friedrich-Werdesche church, 60
Friedrich Wilhelm IV, King of Prussia, xiii, 18,
    23, 171, 182, 219, 287
  appoints Mendelssohn as music director,
    225, 234
  coronation of, 22
  works ordered by, 229
Frisch, Walter, 81
fugues, 94, 283
funeral marches, 109, 110

Gade, Neils, xiv, 21, 24, 25
Garratt, James, vi, 6, 270
Gedaechtniskirche, Kaiser Wilhelm, 30
Geibel, Emanuel, 221–24
Gelobet seist du Jesu Christ (chorale), 145
gender. *See also* women
  in biography, 46–52
  creativity and, 45
  role restrictions, 45–46, 49–50
genre, 62
German-Flemish Choral Festival, 17, 25
German Jews Beyond Judaism (Mosse), 33
Germany
  anti-Semitism in, 246–48
  Christian–Jewish relations, 33, 34, 36, 40
  German–Jewish relations, 32–34, 37,
    238–40
  historical mission of, 59
  Jewish assimilation in, 35
  Lutheran music, 169
  "Reformation" symphony and, 104
  Third Reich, 246
Geschichte der Kunst des Altertums (*History of
    Ancient Art*) (Winckelmann), 56–57
*Geschichte der Musik in Italien, Deutschland und
    Frankreich* (*History of Music in Italy,
    Germany, and France*) (Brendel), 241
Gewandhaus Orchestra, 20–21, 23, 24, 108,
    127, 234
Gilbert, Felix, 169
Gilroy, Paul, 40
Gluck, Christoph Willibald, 18, 21
Gnomen und Elfen (Schüller), 144
Goethe, Johann Wolfgang von, x, xi, xii, 6, 11,
    37, 57, 58, 61, 63, 64, 65, 67, 83,
    99–100, 114, 136, 137, 166, 168, 241,
    254, 263, 276
Gollmick, Carl, 219, 221
Gothic architecture, 60

Gounod, Charles, 45
Goya, Francisco de, 257
Graetz, Heinrich, 29
Greek art, historicism and, 57
Greek drama
    Antigone (Sophocles), 225–26, 227
    language patterns, 292
    Oedipus at Colonos (Sophocles), 225, 227
    verse rhythms, 227
Grey, Thomas, 97, 100, 110, 111, 112, 125, 126,
    128, 138, 234, 280
Griepenkerl, Wolfgang Robert, 220
Großmann-Vendrey, Susanna, 63
Grove, Sir George, 167, 245, 248, 249
Gugel, Heinrich, x
Gutenberg quadricentennial, 181
Gypsies, 239

Halévy, Fromental, 221
Handel, George Frideric, 17, 21, 62, 163, 252,
    266
    oratorios, 18
        Alexander's Feast, 18
        'Dettingen' Te Deum, 18
        Israel in Egypt, 17, 18
        Judas Maccabaeus, 18
        Messiah, 18, 183
        Solomon, 18
Hanslick, Eduard, 68
Hanstein, August, 180
"Hark! The herald angels sing" (C. Wesley), 181
Harmonicon, The, 14, 42–51
harmony, 139
Härtel, Raimund, 181
Hauptmann, Moritz, 24, 151
Haydn, Franz Joseph, 19, 21, 92, 131, 149, 266
    Creation, The, 18
    Seasons, The, 18
    Seven Last Words of Christ, The, 263
Hebrew Melodies (Nathan), 178
Hegel, Georg Wilhelm Friedrich, xi, 13,
    58–59, 63, 64, 67, 144, 172, 226,
    241
Heine, Heinrich, 57, 58, 68, 171, 172, 192–98,
    202, 290
Hennemann, Monika, vi, 4
Henning, Carl Wilhelm, x, 13
Hensel, Fanny Cäcilia (née Mendelssohn, later
    Mendelssohn Bartholdy), 136, 138,
    208, 210, 211, 285, 287
    biographies of, 43
    birth of, 13
    character, 43–44
    childhood, 43
    as child prodigy, 43
    Cholera Cantata, 44
    conversion of, 28, 30
    cultural norms and, 50

death of, xiv, 24, 25, 42, 45, 147, 202
diaries of, 51
Felix's compositions for, 116
gender role restrictions, 45–46, 49–50
health of, 51
influence on Felix, 45, 46, 48
letters of, 42, 44, 47, 50, 141
marriage, xi, 48, 169, 211
as pianist, 13, 43–44
publication of music by, 46, 49, 50
relationship with Felix, 42, 43–45, 46, 47–48,
    52
reputation of, 42–43, 45, 46
Sebastian's descriptions of, 43, 44
social class restrictions on, 45, 46
Songs without Words and, 152
as suppressed, 2–3, 49, 51, 52
writings of, 42, 43
Hensel, Sebastian Ludwig Felix, 42, 43, 44,
    49–50, 51
Hensel, Wilhelm, 48, 169
    Fanny's letters to, 47
    marriage, xi
Herder, Johann Gottfried, 57
Hereditary Genius (Galton), 42
"Herr Gott dich alle loben wir" (chorale), 145
Hertz, Deborah, 30
Herz, Henriette, 13, 45, 113
Heyse, Carl Wilhelm Ludwig, x, 13
High Classic style, 92
Hiller, Ferdinand, 14, 16, 21, 24, 42, 43, 44, 155,
    165
historical concerts, 21, 59, 64
historical processes. *See also* progress
    criticism of Mendelssohn and, 241
    musical history and, 241–43
    musical values and, 244–45
historicism, 6. *See also* musical historicism
    in architecture, 60
    in art, 56–57, 58–59
    authentic expression of age *vs.*, 57, 58–59
    "dehistoricism," 56
    as false veneration of past, 57
    modernism *vs.*, 56, 61
Hitzig, Henriette, 30
Holly, Ludwig, 198
L'homme automate, 207
Horsley, Charles Edward, 22
Hübsch, Heinrich, 60
Hugo, Victor
    Ruy Blas, 107–08, 220, 225
Hullah, John, 185
humanism, 34
Humboldt, Alexander von, 13
Humboldt, Wilhelm von, 13
Hummel, Johann Nepomuk, 283
    Piano Concerto in A minor op. 89, 114
    Septet op. 74, 283

idée fixe, 81
"imaginary" chorales, 180
"imaginary church music," 181
Immermann, Karl Leberecht, xii, 19, 216, 221, 225
   Kurfürst Wilhelm im Theater, 296
International Felix-Mendelssohn-Gesellschaft, 249
Italian art, historicism and, 57
Italienische Reise (Goethe), 67
Itzig, Daniel, 12, 30

James, Henry, 255
Janissary band, 93
Jeanrenaud, Cécile-Sophie-Charlotte. *See*
   Mendelssohn Bartholdy, Cécile
   (née Jeanrenaud)
Jerusalem (M. Mendelssohn), 28, 29, 168
Jews and Judaism. *See also* anti-Semitism
   arts and, 239, 248
   Christian-Jewish relations, 33, 34, 36
   conversion from, 29–30, 31, 39
   as cultural "other," 27–28, 243
   gender role restrictions and, 50
   German-Jewish relationship, 32–34, 37, 238–40
   Jewish identity, 28, 29–30
   "Jewish problem", 26, 27
   Jews as mice metaphor, 1
   language and, 239
   Mendelsohhn's Jewish identity, 2, 26–28, 31, 35–36, 37, 39, 248, 249–50
   modern life and, 29
   New Year's celebrations and, 37
   pseudo-scientific views on, 245
Joachim, Joseph, 21
Joan of Arc (Schiller), 218
Jones, Peter Ward, 31, 51
Jost, Christa, 160, 164
Judaism. *See* Jews and Judaism
"*Judenthum in der Musik, Das*" (Wagner), 26, 238–39, 253, 293

Kalkbrenner, Friedrich, x, 113
Kamen, Gloria, 47, 48
Kaufhaus des Westens (KaDeWe), 30
Kerman, Joseph, 127–28
Keudell, Robert von, 45
Kiesewetter, Raphael Georg, 65
Kimber, Marian Wilson, vii, 3, 244
Kinkel, Gottfried, 220, 228
   Assassinen, Die, 221
Kinkel, Johanna, 221
Kirchenlied, 164
Kirnberger, Johann Philipp, 13, 61, 172
   Kunst des reinen Satzes, 172

Klingemann, Karl, 15–16, 101, 109, 174, 191, 202, 210, 211, 217, 220, 245, 285
Köhler, Karl-Heinz, 114
Königliche Schauspiele, Berlin, 209
Konold, Wulf, 62
Kramer, Lawrence, 6, 110, 279
Kreutzer, Conradin, 106, 115
Krommer, Franz, 137
Krüger, Eduard, 67, 225
Krummacher, Friedhelm, 69, 115, 128, 129, 142, 148, 173
Kunt, Karl, 160

Lady of the Lake, The (Scott), 189
Lang, Josephine, 45
Lang, Paul Henry, 247–48
language
   anti-Semitism and, 189–90
   Mendelssohn's views on, 189–92
Laocoön (Lessing), 38
Lavater, Johann Caspar, 29
Ledebur, Carl von, 42
Leeson, Daniel N., 282
Leipzig
   "historical concerts," 21
   incidental music composed in, 225
   Marktplatz, 181
   Mendelssohn as musical director of, 20–22
   music academy, 23–24
   musical culture, 23, 24
leitmotifs, 264
Lessing, Gotthold Ephraim, 33, 38–39, 189
Levin, Rahel. *See* Varnhagen von Ense, Rahel
   Antoine.
Levin, Robert D., 282
Lind, Jenny, 217
Lindblad, Adolf Frederik, 84, 138
Lindeman, Steve, vi, 4
listeners, role of, 252, 258, 265, 267
Liszt, Franz, 12, 17, 21, 113, 165, 251, 258, 266, 286, 290, 293
   anti-Semitism of, 239–40
   criticism of Mendelssohn by, 240, 247
literature
   musical inspiration from, 98–100
   reception of, 255–56
Little, William, 16, 36, 271, 292
logical form, 81, 82
London, opera projects in, 216–18
London Philharmonic Society, 15–16
Loewe, Carl, 117
Lowenstein, Steven, 29
Lower Rhine Music Festival, 16–17, 25, 246
Ludwig I, King of Bavaria, 60
Luise, Queen of Prussia, 60
Lutezia (Heine), 68
Lutheran church, 28, 35

Lutheran music, 169
   chorales, 175
   function of, 258
   Psalms, 170
lyricism
   in Brahms Sextets, 81
   as main theme, 76
   musical form and, 72, 75–76
   in sonata form, 72, 75–76
Lyser, Johann Peter, criticism of Mendelssohn
   by, 235–36, 237, 241, 242

Macpherson, James, 101
Magis, Henri-Guillaume-Marie-Jean-Pierre,
   187
Mahler, Gustav
   Catholic church and, 36
   "Der Einsame im Herbst" (The Lonely Man
      in Autumn"), 203, **204**
   Lied von der Erde, Das, 203
   performance of works of, 260
   reputation of, 26
Mann, Thomas, 252, 255
Mantius, Eduard, 211
Marissen, Michael, 173
Marschner, Heinrich August, 97, 221
Marx, Adolph Bernhard, 13, 48, 174, 181, 191,
   277, 294
Marx, Karl, 39
Mary, Queen of Scots, 101, 109
Maus (Spiegelman), 1
Mechetti, Pietro, 160
Méhul, Étienne Nicolas, 21
melodic counterpoint, 139
*Mendelssohn: A New Image of the Composer and
   his Age* (Werner), 2, 30
Mendelssohn, Brendel. *See* Schlegel,
   Dorothea
Mendelssohn, Henriette, 13
Mendelssohn, Joseph, 169
Mendelssohn, Moses, 13, 167, 168, 169, 170,
   189, 235
   Germany Jewish relationship and, 32
   humanism and, 34
   Judaism and, 28, 29–30, 33–34
   language and, 189
   name change, 35
   religious views, 169
Mendelssohn, Nathan, 30
"Mendelssohn and the Berlin Singakademie:
   The Composer at the Crossroads"
   (Little), 36
"Mendelssohn and the Jews" (Botstein), 30
Mendelssohn Bartholdy, Abraham, 12, 13, 168
   on Bach, 174
   baptism of, 168
   on Beethoven, 138
   chamber music and, 131

   children's religion and, 28, 30, 168
   on compositional historicism, 66
   conversion of, 28, 30
   criticism of Felix by, 84
   death of, xii, 21, 38
   influence on Felix, 208, 209
   letters to Fanny, 30
   letters to Felix, 35
   on name change, 35
   oppression of Fanny by, 3
   religious beliefs, 30, 38, 39
Mendelssohn Bartholdy, Carl Wolfgang Paul,
   xiii
Mendelssohn Bartholdy, Cécile (née
   Jeanrenaud), xii, 2, 22, 48, 123, 141,
   170
Mendelssohn Bartholdy, Fanny Cäcilia. *See*
   Hensel, Fanny Cäcilia.
Mendelssohn Bartholdy, Felix (Jacob Ludwig
   Felix), 137
   Abraham's letters to, 35
   as an artist, 13, 101
   Bach and, 62, 94, 130, 156, 172, 259
   baptised, x, 168
   Beethoven and, 91, 95, 115, 120, 130, 136,
      138–39, 140, 141, 142, 150, 164, 257
   as Berlin Academy of Arts director, 22–23
   Berlin Singakademie directorship and, 16,
      36, 234
   biographical research on, 249
   birth of, x, 13
   character of, 25, 43–44, 235, 267
   as child prodigy, 40, 43
   children, 22
   chronology, x
   classification of, 27–28
   composer/virtuoso role, 3
   compositions for Fanny, 116
   conducting works of, 254–55, 260, 267–68
   as a conductor, 11, 14, 15, 20, 43, 261
   as conductor of Gewandhaus Orchestra,
      20–21, 23, 24, 234
   as conductor of opera, 19
   as court composer, 225
   creative women and, 45
   creativity of, 4–7, 70
   criticism of, 4–7, 68, 233
      by Abraham
      anti-Semitic, 2, 4, 238–40, 246–48, 253,
         260
      constructive, 237
      contemporary, 234–37
      current reception of, 233, 249, 250
      depth of music, 252–53, 255, 258–59,
         260
      early twentieth century, 245–48
      failure to complete a mature opera,
         206–07, 210, 224, 228–29, 242

Mendelssohn Bartholdy, Felix (*cont.*)
    "feminine" music, 261
    late nineteenth/early twentieth century,
        243–45
    by Liszt, 240, 247
    by Lyser, 235–36, 237
    posthumous, 233–43, 251
    by Schumann, 236–37, 241, 242
    by Wagner, 238–39, 252, 261
  culture and, 32, 50
  death of, xiv, 25, 47
  as Düsseldorf musical director, 18–19, 20,
    25, 234
  early compositions, 11, 13, 43, 189, 207–15
  early music and, 55, 61–62
  early recognition of, 234
  educational performances, 165–66
  education of, 13
  European travel, 15–16, 36, 64, 100–04, 109,
    118, 149, 210
  family, 12
  Fanny's influence on, 45, 46, 48
  on folk melodies, 151
  German influence on, 104
  health of, 24
  ideological, 233
  incidental music commissions, 22
  influence of female relatives on, 48
  influence on Brahms, 80, 82
  influence on Wagner, 62, 261, 262, 265
  interpretive fallacies, 32
  Jewish identity of, 2, 26–28, 31, 35–36, 37,
    39, 248, 249–50
  Jewish influences on music, 28–29, 167
  at Leipzig academy, 24
  as Leipzig musical director, 20–22
  letters
    on composition, 84
    to Devrient, 66, 155
    to family, 125, 192
    to Fanny, 42, 44, 49, 111, 280
    to Wilhelm Hensel, 151
    to Hiller, 155
    to Klingeman, 191, 285
    to Lea, 51
    to Lindblad, 138
    to Charlotte Moscheles, 42
    to Ignaz Moscheles, 113, 123
    to Rebecka, 160, 285
    while traveling, 64, 101, 110, 279
    to Zelter, 65, 66
  libretti written for, 208–09, 216–17, 219–24,
    229
  Lutheran identity of, 35
  Lutheran music of, 169
  marriage, xii, 22, 48, 141, 170
  as modern composer, 55
  monumental music and, 257, 258

  Moses and, 273
  Mozart and, 206
  musical concerns of, 67, 117
  musical culture and, 12
  musical historicism of, 55, 60–65, 66–68,
    155, 236, 242–43, 246, 254, 267
  musical memory, 14–15
  musical style, 32, 63, 71–72, 76, 92, 96,
    97–98, 104–05, 155, 159, 227, 242–43,
    259–60
  on musicians as public figures, 244
  music theory and composition studies, 13
  name change, 35, 168
  neoclassical and, 252–53, 254, 267
  as "Neuchrist," 31, 171, 188
  opera and, 19, 207, 210
  "oppression" of Fanny by, 3, 49, 51, 52
  organ performance, 149, 165
  originality of, 202, 256
  performance of works of, 261
  piano performance, 14, 149, 165, 166, 235
  piano repertories, 165
  piano studies, 13
  piano style, 145, 154
  posthumously published work, 238
  progressiveness of, 71–88
  Protestant music, 35–36, 171–72
  publication of Fanny's music and, 49, 50, 51
  publication of memoirs and letters, 243,
    245
  publication of works of, 50–51, 238, 243
  public performances, 131–32
  relationship with Fanny, 42, 43–45, 46,
    47–48, 52
  religious beliefs, 2, 168–70, 176, 179–80,
    258–59
  religious conversion, 28, 29
  religious expression through music, 267
  religious identity, 29, 167–69, 170, 176, 235
  religious music, 65–68, 167–88
  reputation of, 3–4, 26, 91, 228–29, 233, 238,
    253
  revision by, 116
  revisionist work on, 6
  Romantic music and, 110–11, 236, 242,
    246–47, 249, 256
  scholarly studies on, 245, 248–50
  secondary studies on, 243
  on *Songs without Words*, 151–52
  St. Matthew Passion and, 172–73
  stereotyping of, 26
  "student compositions" for piano, 149
  subjectivity in works of, 256–58, 260, 264,
    267
  Sunday musicales, 114, 115, 116
  tribute to Beethoven, 160, 164
  understanding of history by, 63, 64
  unpublished works, 50

violin studies, 13
virtuosity and, 113, 132, 259
Wagner and, 251–52, 267
as wall-dweller, 1–2
Weber's influence on, 117–18
on words in songs, 189–92
works as visual experience, 258
works evoking nature, 62
works in amateur repertoire, 253
works in profession repertoire, 253, 254
Mendelssohn Bartholdy, Felix, works
  chamber music
    fugues (twelve), string quartet, 131
    Octet, strings, in Eb major, op. 20, 14, 75,
      120, 130, 134–37, 196, 254, 278
    Quartets, piano, 132–33: D minor, 131,
      No. 1 in C minor, op. 1, 131, 132, 133,
      No. 2 in F minor, op. 2, **73**, **74**, 72–75,
      131, 132, **133**, No. 3 in B minor, op. 3,
      130, 131, 132–33, 134
    Quartets, strings, 137–40: No. 1 in Eb
      major, op. 12, 81–84, 137, 138, 139,
      No. 2 in A minor, op. 13, 62, 81,
      82–83, 84, 137, **140**, 138–40, Nos. 3–5,
      op. 44, 130, 141–44, No. 4 in E minor,
      op. 44, no. 2, **143**, No. 6 in F minor,
      op. 80, 5, 147–48, op. 81, 147
    Quintets, strings, 137: No. 1 in A major,
      op. 18, **77**, **79**, 76–80, 81, 82, 85, 137,
      No. 2 in Bb major, op. 87, 147
    Sextet, piano, in D major, op. 110, 120,
      133–34
    Sonatas, cello: No. 1 in Bb major, op. 45,
      141, 145–47, No. 2 in D major, op. 58,
      145, 147, 180
    Sonatas, violin: F major, 141, 145, op. 4 in
      F minor, 115, 131, 145
    Trios, piano: No. 1 in D-minor, op. 49, 5,
      130, 141, 144–45, 236–37, No. 2 in
      C minor, op. 66, 85, 130, 131, 144,
      146, 180, 293
  choral music, 167–88, 252, 294
    Cantique pour l'Eglise wallonne, 170
    chorale cantatas, 172, 292
    "Christ lag in Todesbanden," 164
    Christus (fragment), op. 97, 176, **177**, **179**
    Elijah (*Elias*), op. 70, 25, 37, **176**, 175–77,
      225, 253, 254, 258, 266
    Erste Walpurgisnacht, Die, op. 60, 6, 108
    Festgesang ("Gutenberg"), 181
    Festgesang "Möge das Siegeszeichen", 295
    Hear My Prayer, 169
    Hora est, 169
    Lauda Sion, op. 73, 169, **186**, **187**, 185–88
    Lobgesang. *See* symphonies, no. 2
    Motets: *Drei Motetten*, op. 69, 170, No. 1,
      Nunc dimittis, 169, No. 2, *Jubilate Deo*,
      169, No. 3, *Magnificat*, 169

Three Motets op. 39, 169
Psalms, 181–82: *Drei Psalmen*, op. 78, 23,
  171; No. 2, Psalm 43, 183, **184**, No. 3,
  Psalm 22, 183
Psalms: "Lord hear the voice of my
  complaint" (Psalm 5), 145, Psalm 24,
  170, 171, Psalm 42 op. 42, 183, **184**,
  Psalm 84, 170, Psalm 98 op. 91, 23,
  171, 183, **184**, Psalm 100, 170, 171,
  Psalm 114 op. 51, 167, 257, Psalm 115
  op. 31, 169, 174
Responsorium et Hymnus, op. 121, **185**, 185
St. Paul (*Paulus*), op. 36, 37–39, 44, 61, 62,
  66, 67, 68–69, 173–75, 181, 224–28,
  236, 253, 254, 255, 258, 266, 296
Te Deum, 63
Tu es Petrus, 63, 169
dramatic music, 206–24, 229
  Beiden Neffen, Die, 209
  Beiden Pädagogen, Die, 208, 209, 211
  Heimkehr aus der Fremde, Die, (*Son and
    Stranger*), op. 89, 210–11, 215, 269:
    "Lisbeth's song" (no. 12), 211
  Hochzeit des Camacho, Die, op. 10, 4,
    209–10, 211, 214, **215**, 219, 223, 235,
    292
  Ich J. Mendelssohn - Ich A. Mendelssohn,
    207
  incidental music, 224–28: *Antigone*, op. 55,
    22, 225–26, 227, 255, *Athalie*, op. 74,
    180, 228; "War March of the Priests,"
    228; *Midsummer Night's Dream, A*,
    incidental music, op. 61, 5, 22, 151,
    196, 227–28, 254, wedding march, 227,
    228, *Oedipus at Colonus*, 227, 255
  Lorelei, Die, op. 98, 206, **223**, 221–24,
    228–29
  Onkel aus Boston, Der, 209, 214
  Pervonte (sketches), 220
  "Quel bonheur pour mon coeur"
    (dramatic scene), 207
  Soldatenliebschaft, Die, 208, 211
  Wandernden Komödianten, Die, 209,
    211–14
Lieder and Gesänge, 189–205
  "Altdeutsches Frühlingslied" ("Old
    German Spring Song"), op. 86, no. 6,
    204, 202–5
  "Andres Maienlied" ("Another May
    Song") op. 8, no. 8, 189, 191, 198–99
  "Auf Flügeln des Gesänges" ("On Wings of
    Song"), op. 34, no. 2, 192–95, 196
  Der erste Frühlingstag (*The First Day of
    Spring*) op. 48, nos. 1–3, 202
  Drei Volkslieder (*Three Folk Songs*) op. 41,
    nos. 2–4, 202
  "Erntelied" ("Harvest Song"), op. 8, no. 4,
    199–201, **201**

Mendelssohn Bartholdy, Felix, works (*cont.*)
"Frühlingslied" ("Spring Song"), op. 8, no. 6, 201
"Frühlingslied" ("Spring Song"). op. 34, no. 3, 202
"Frühlingslied" ("Spring Song"). op. 47, no. 3, 202
Gesänge, Zwölf, op. 8, 51
"Herbstlied" ("Autumn Song") op. 63, no. 4, 191
"Im Grünen" (In the Green Woods), op. 8, no. 11, 202
"Im Grünen" (In the Green Woods), op. 59, 202
Lieder, Zwölf, op. 9, 51
Lieder, Sechs (male part-songs), op. 50, 202
Lieder, Vier (male part-songs), op. 75, 202
"Neue Liebe" ("New Love"), op. 19a, no. 4, 195–98, **197**
"Pilgerspruch" ("Pilgrim's Proverb"), op. 8, no. 5, 201
"Raste Krieger, Krieg ist aus", 189
"Reiselied" ("Journeying song"), op. 34, no. 6, 189
"Schlafloser Augen Leuchte," **178**
orchestral, 91, 112–29
Calm Sea, Prosperous Voyage Overture, op. 27, 6, 7, 20, 85, 99–100, 106, 120, 262, 263, 264, 266
Capriccio brillant, piano and orchestra, in B minor, op. 22, 113, 117, 118, 122
Concerto, piano, in A minor, 112, 114, 115
Concerto, piano, no. 1 in G minor, op. 25, 85, **87**, 88, 113, 116, 117, 118–20, 121, 122, 254
Concerto, piano, no. 2, in D minor, op. 40, 113, 122, 124–25
Concerto, two pianos, in Ab major, 115–17, 120, 270
Concerto, two pianos, in E major, 115–16, 119, 121
Concerto, violin, in D minor, 115
Concerto, violin, in E minor, op. 64, 5, 88, 112, 113, 122, 126–28, 246, 254, 264, 265, 282
Concerto, violin and piano, in D minor, 115
Hebrides, The, Overture, op. 26, 7, 75, 101–02, 103, 262, 278
Konzerstücke, clarinet, basset-horn, and piano, opp. 113 and 114, 281
Lobgesang. See symphonies, no. 2
Midsummer Night's Dream, A, Overture, op. 21, 6, 98–99, 128, 219, 234, 235, 246, 254, 264, 265, 270
Rondo brillant, piano and orchestra, op. 29, 113, 122

Ruy Blas Overture, 107–08, 225
Schöne Melusine, Die, Overture, op. 32, 44, 106–07, 262, 264
Serenade und Allegro giojoso, piano and orchestra, op. 43, 113, 120, 122, 125–26
sinfonias, strings, 62: No. 1 in C major, 92, No. 2 in D major, 2, 92, No. 3 in E minor, 92, No. 4 in C minor, 92, **93**, 95, No. 5 in Bb major, **93**, 95, No. 6 in Eb major, 92, 95, **96**, No. 8 in D major, 92, 96, No. 9 in C major, 92, 95, **95**, No. 10 in B minor, 92, No. 11 in F major, 92, 96, No. 12 in G minor, 93, No. 13 in C minor, 96
symphonies, 91: No. 1 in C minor, op. 11, **97**, 96–98, 110, 279, No. 2 in Bb major, op. 52 ("Lobgesang"), 95, 108, **182**, 180–82, 183, 256, 257, 266, No. 3 in A minor, op. 56 ("Scottish"), 5, 7, 85, 107, 108, 109–10, 111, 254, 257, 266, 278, 280, 281, No. 4 in A major, op. 90 ("Italian"), 7, 44, 50, 95, 101, 102–04, 138–40, 184–85, 254, 262, 264, 265, 266–67, 278; "Saltarello", 139; No. 5 in D major, op. 107 ("Reformation"), 7, 50, 85, 86, 95, 104–06, 111, 179, 270, 271, 280
work for piano and strings in D minor, 281
organ music, 149
Fugue in E minor, 85
Sonatas, op. 65, 159, 180: No. 1 in F minor/major, 159, No. 3 in A major, 159, No. 4 in Bb major, 159, No. 6 in D minor/major, 159
Three Preludes and Fugues, op. 37, 155, 158
piano solo, 149
Capriccio in F-Sharp minor, op. 5, 150
Etude in Bb minor, op. 104b, no. 1, 124
Fantasia in F# minor ("Scottish Sonata") op. 28, 284
"Fantasy on 'The Last Rose of Summer'" op. 15, 151
Kinderstücke, op. 72, 155
Lieder ohne Worte (Songs without Words), 5, 48, 114, 139, 151–53, 155, 190–92, 236: Vol. 1, op. 19b, no. 4, 153, Vol. 1, op. 19b, no. 6 (*Venetianisches Gondellied*), 152, Vol. 2, op. 30, no. 3, 153, Vol. 2, op. 30, no. 5, 153, Vol. 2, op. 30, no. 6 (*Venetianisches Gondellied*), 152, Vol. 3, op. 38, no. 4, 153, 154, Vol. 3, op. 38, no. 6 (*Duetto*), 153, Vol. 4, op. 53, no. 5, 152, 154, Vol. 4, op. 53, no. 6 (*Volkslied*), 152, 154, Vol. 5, op. 62, no. 4, 153, **155**, 154–55,

Vol. 5, op. 62, no. 5 (*Venetianisches Gondellied*), 152, Vol. 5, op. 62, no. 6 (*Frühlingslied*), 152, Vol. 6, op. 67, no. 4 (*Spinnerlied*), 153, Vol. 6, op. 67, no. 5, 153, Vol. 7, op. 85, no. 5, 153
piano composition in C minor, 145
Perpetuum mobile in C major, op. 119, 117
Sieben Charakterstücken (Seven Characteristic Pieces), op. 7, 61, 150, 155, 156, 157
Six Preludes and Fugues op. 35, 61, 124, 155–56, 158: No. 1 in E minor, 124, 158, 180, **180**, 293, No. 2 in D major, 158, No. 5 in F minor, 156, **157**, No. 3 in B minor, 156
sonatas: op. 6 in E major, 62, 138, 150, op. 106 in Bb major, 120, 138, 150
Three Fantasies or Caprices, op. 16, 151
Variations in Eb op. 82, 164, 286
Variations sérieuses, op. 54, 5, 156, **161**, **162**, **164**, 160–65, 246
Mendelssohn Bartholdy, Lea Felicia Pauline (née Salomon), 12, 13, 61, 207
baptised, 168
conversion of, 28, 30
influence on Felix, 208, 209
religious views, 169
Mendelssohn-Bartholdy, Paul Hermann, 13, 27, 49–50, 131, 145, 211
Mendelssohn Bartholdy, Rebecka Henriette. *See* Dirichlet, Rebecka Henriette
Mendelssohn Bartholdy name, 168
"Mendelssohnian project," 237
"Mendelssohn problem," 26, 27, 249
Mendelssohn Problem, The (Das Problem Mendelssohn) (Dahlhaus), 1, 6, 26, 41
Mendelssohn renaissance, 26
Mercer-Taylor, Peter, vi, 33, 69, 82, 85, 86, 121, 125, 272–73, 281, 288
Meyerbeer, Giacomo, 225, 227, 236, 238
Le Prophète,, 218
Midsummer Night's Dream (Shakespeare), 22, 225
Milder-Hauptmann, Anna, 168
Mintz, Donald, 21, 24, 248
model productions ("Mustervorstellungen"), 19
Modern German Music (Chorley), 3
modernism, 39, 59, 61
Momigliano, Arnaldo, 27
monothematic sonata form, 131
monumentality, 257, 258
Moritz, Carl Philipp, 84
Moscheles, Charlotte, 178
Moscheles, Emily, 45, 116
Moscheles, Ignaz, xi, 21, 24, 25, 42, 113, 114, 122–23, 245, 281
Mosel, Ignaz Franz, 271

Mosse, George Lachmann, 33
motivic development, 144
Mozart, Wolfgang Amadeus, 19, 20, 21, 88, 92, 123, 149, 165, 252, 261
concerto style, 113–14
influence on Mendelssohn, 211, 215
Mendelssohn compared to, 144, 206
Mendelssohn's repertory of, 165
Mozart, Wolfgang Amadeus, works
Quartets, piano, 132
Quartet, strings, G major (K. 387)
Quartet, strings, A major (K. 464)
Quintets, strings, 137
Symphony no. 41 in C major (K. 551, "Jupiter"), 182
Müller, Friedrich Max, 52
Munich opera projects, 216
Musica sacra, 171
musical communication
ideal of, 252
role of listeners in, 252, 258, 265, 267
subjectivity and, 257–58
musical design, 76, 81, 85
Musical Gem, The, 235
musical historicism, 55–70. *See also* historicism
creativity and, 70
criticism of, 68, 242–43
defined, 56
of Mendelssohn, 55, 60–65, 66–68, 155, 236, 246, 254, 267
musical progress *vs.*, 241
musical styles, 59
religious music, 65–68
of Schinkel, 254
views on, 56–57, 68–70
Musical Quarterly, The, 30, 31, 250
musical style
as authentic expression, 58
culture and politics and, 253–54
eclecticism, 60
Einstein's analysis of, 246–47
historical eras of, 241–43
historicism, 59
stylistic pluralism, 69
Musical Times, The, 42, 46–47
Music & Letters, 6
musicology (*Musikwissenschaft*), 244
anti-Semitism and, 246–48
Musik in Geschichte and Gegenwart, Die, 248

"Die nächtliche Heerschau" (Zedlitz), 190
narrative music, 104–06, 111, 280
Nathan, Isaac, 178
Nathan der Weise (Lessing), 189
natural selection, 244
nature, music evoking, 62
Naumann, Johann Gottlieb, 21
Nazarenes, 58–60, 64, 66, 67, 68

Nazi Germany, 246
Neeb, Heinrich, 221
neoclassicism, 58, 80–81, 252–53, 254, 267
"neo-pre-Classicism," 92
"Neue Liebe" ("New Love") (Heine), 195–98
Neues Tempel, 170–71
Neue Zeitschrift für Musik, 4, 5, 116, 124, 126, 160, 166, 241
Nicolai, Otto, 59
Nietzsche, Friedrich, 252
Nochlin, Linda, 52
North German Music Festival, 17
Novalis (Baron Friedrich von Hardenberg), 57
Nun danket alle Gott (chorale), 182

O Jesu Christe, wahres Licht (chorale), 174
O Gott, du frommer Gott (chorale), **176**
Oedipus in Colonos (Sophocles), 225, 227
Oettinger, Eduard Maria, 207
opera, 4. *See also* dramatic music
    Berlin projects, 219
    Düsseldorf projects, 19
    European projects, 215–19
    Leipzig projects, 21
    London projects, 216–18
    Mendelssohn's failure to complete a mature opera, 207, 210, 224, 228–29, 242
    Munich projects, 216
    Paris projects, 218
    Romanticism and, 207
    Wagner and, 294
operatic overture, 7
originality, 241
Ossian, 101
Otto, Eduard, 190, 289
Overbeck, Johann Friedrich, 58, 276

Paganini, Nicolò, 172
Palestrina, Johannes Pierluigi von, 19, 62, 65
Paris opera projects, 218
Pelto, William, 108
perpetuum mobile, 136–37, 139
Pforr, Franz, 58
Philharmonic Society
Planché, James Robinson, 216–17, 221
Pleyel, Ignaz Josef, 137
"poetic" instrumental writing, 140
"poetic meaning," 138
poetic unity, in string quartets, 142
Poissl, Baron von, 216
pôle harmonique, 78
Polko, Elise, 47
Porter, Cecelia Hopkins, 17
"post-Classic" sinfonias, 92
postmodernism, 27, 39–40

Prechtler, Otto, 220
    Braut von Venedig, Die, 221
Problem Mendelssohn, Das (Dahlhaus), 1, 6, 26, 41
programmatic music, 7, 139–40
    Catholic Church and, 270
    Mendelssohn's views on, 107
progress. *See also* historical processes
    criticism of Mendelssohn and, 241, 243
    evolution and, 244
    in music, historicism and, 241
progressivism, 6
Prölz, Adolf, 181
Protestant Cathedral, Berlin, 182
Protestant music
    Mendelssohn's interest in, 35–36, 171–72
    programmatic, 270
Proust, Marcel, 255
Prussia. *See also* Germany
    cultural vitality of, 12, 22
    salon culture, 13
Prussian *Agende*, 171
publishing
    of Fanny's music and, 49, 50, 51
    gender role restrictions, 46
    of Mendelssohn's music, 46, 49, 50–51
"purple passage," 77

Racine, Jean Baptiste, 225, 228
recapitulation, 76
"recapitulation problem", 72
Recollections of Mendelssohn (Devrient), 206
redundancy, 118
Reformwille, 6
Reger, Max, 254
Reich, Nancy B., 45, 46
Reichel, Adolf, 221
Reichwald, Siegwart, 108
religious tolerance, 168–70
Rellstab, Ludwig, 189
Rietz, Eduard, xii, 115, 134, 137
Rietz, Julius, 221, 243
Rifkin, Joshua, 270
Righini, Vincenzo, 21
Rizzio, David, 109
Robert, Friederike, 201
"Robert Schumann with Reference to Mendelssohn-Bartholdy and the Development of Modern Music Generally" (Brendel), 5
Rode, Pierre, 115
Romani Gypsies, 239
Romantic fantasy, 193
Romantic Generation, The (Rosen), 5
Romantic literature, 48
Romantic music
    climax in, 72

coda in, 76, 79, 83
concertos, 112
creative theory, 83
Einstein's analysis of, 246–47
experience represented in, 263
harmony, 114
Mendelssohn and, 91, 100–04, 110–11, 236,
    242, 246–47, 249, 262
musical form, 71–72
narrative, 104–06, 111, 280
opera and, 207
poetic language of, 194
sonata form in, 71–72
Romberg, Bernhard, 21
rondo form, 117
Rösel, Gottlob Samuel, 13
Rosen, Charles, 5, 71, 81, 158, 163–65,
    180
Rosen, Friedrich August, 13
Rossini, Gioacchino, 21, 94
Rousseau, Johann Baptiste, 221
Rubens, Peter Paul, 257
Rungenhagen, Karl Friedrich, xii, 16,
    36
Ruy Blas (Hugo), 107–08, 220, 225

sacred music, 65–68, 167–88
    divide between concert music and,
        184–85
    "imaginary", 181
    for Jewish services, 170–71
    Mendelssohn's publication of, 294
    Mendelssohn's religious identity and,
        168–70
    uniting concert music with, 180, 181,
        182–84
Salieri, Antonio, 21
Salomon, Bella, 169
salon culture, 13
Santini, Fortunato, 19
Scarlatti, Domenico, 149
Schadow, Johann Gottfried, xi
Schauroth, Delphine von, 48, 118
Schauspielhaus, Berlin, 12
Schelble, Johann Nepomuk, 22
Schiller, Friedrich von, 218
Schinkel, Karl Friedrich, 12, 60, 61, 254, 257
Schlegel, August Wilhelm von, 13, 57
Schlegel, Dorothea (née Brendel Mendelssohn),
    13, 168–69, 170
Schlegel, Friedrich, 13, 57, 58, 59, 100, 168
Schleiermacher, Friedrich, 13, 172, 259
Schlesinger, Adolph Martin, 275
Schloesser, Manfred, 273
Schmidt, Thomas Christian, 6–7, 67
Schmidt-Beste, Thomas, vi, 4, 281
Scholem, Gershom, 33–34, 273
Schönberg, Arnold, 71

Schubert, Franz Peter, xi, 12, 109, 165, 205, 246
    "Gretchen am Spinnrade" (D118), 153
    "Gruppe aus dem Tartarus" (D396), 199
    "Gute Ruh', gute Ruh" ("Des Baches
        Wiegenlied") (D795/20), 109
    Schöne Müllerin, Die (D795), 109
    "Schwestergruss" (D762), 196
    Symphony no. 9 in C major (D944, "Great"),
        21, 108, 182
Schubring, Julius, 172
Schüller, Bernhard
    Gnomen und Elfen, 144
Schumann, Clara née Wieck, 21, 24, 45, 47, 152
    on Mendelssohn's piano skills, 166
Schumann, Robert, 5, 7, 12, 17, 24, 47, 107,
    116, 154, 155, 238, 246, 252, 285
    critical commentary on Mendelssohn by, 69,
        71, 80, 124–25, 144, 152, 156, 158,
        236–37, 241, 242, 285
    Piano music, 165
    Symphonies, 21
    Davidsbündler, 235
Scott, Sir Walter, 189
Scribe, Eugène, 217, 218, 220
Seasons, The (Haydn), 18
Seaton, Douglass, vii, 7
Selden, Camille, 167
shadow cycle, 202
Shakespeare, William, 19, 217, 225
Shaw, George Bernard, 4
sinfonias, 91–96. *See also* Mendelssohn, Felix,
        works
    development of, 91–92, 95
    High Classic style, 92
    Italinate, 92
    models, 92
    musical style, 96
    "neo-pre-Classicism," 92
    "post-Classic," 92
    style, 92
"single-exposition" concerto form, 127
Smart, George, 271
Smart, Henry, 221
social class roles, 45, 46
sonata form, 81
    Baroque church, 159
    in *A Midsummer Night's Dream* Overture
        op. 21, 98
    lyricism in, 72, 75–76
    Mendelssohn's use of, 71, 83, 142
    monothematic, 131
    in romantic music, 71–72
    in *Die schöe Melusine* Overture op. 32, 107
    structural processes and, 80
    in Symphony no. 5 in D minor [op. 107]
        ("Reformation"), 105
    thematic expression in, 72
sonata for solo instrument and piano, 145–47

songs, 189–205
  imitating folk songs, 192
  Mendelssohn's view of words in, 189–92
  reputation of, 189
  shadow cycle, 202
  song cycles, 201
  as "translation" of poetry, 195
Sonntagsmusik (Sunday salon concerts), 43
Sophocles, 225, 227
Souchay, Marc André, 190
Spee, Friedrich, 202
Spiegelman, Art, 1
Spiegelman, Vladek, 1
Spinoza, Baruch, 29
spirituality
  in modern performance, 260
  in works of Mendelssohn, 259
Spohr, Louis, 17, 21, 271, 285
  Symphony no. 6 in G, 59
Spontini, Gaspare, 17, 172, 209–10
Sposato, Jeffrey, 30, 31, 168, 172, 173, 250
Staehelin, Martin, 172
Stanley, Glenn, vii, 4
Steinberg, Michael P., vii, 2, 277
Strauss, Richard, 17
string quartets, 137–40
subjectivity
  Jewish, 28–29
  musical communication and, 257–58
  in works of Mendelssohn, 256–58, 260, 264, 267
Sur les Bohémiens et de leur musique en Hongrie (attr. Liszt), 239–40
Sutermeister, Peter, 248
symphonic form, 256
symphony orchestras, 20

tarantella, 139
Taubert, Wilhelm, 23, 225
Taufepidemie (baptism epidemic), 29
Taufhaus des Westens, 29
Tchaikovsky, Pyotr Ilich, 252
Tempest, The (Shakespeare), 19, 216, 217, 220
tempos, 261
Thalberg, Sigismund, 21, 113, 124
theme
  lyricism and, 76
  Mendelssohn's concept of, 144, 264
  Mendelssohn's use of, 264–65, 267
  presentation of, 144
  reintroduction of, 132
  in string quartets, 142
  in works of Brahms and Mendelssohn, 80, 81
Thibaut, Anton Friedrich Justus, 18, 62
Thomson, John, 42
"three-hand" technique, 124
Tieck, Ludwig, 57, 107, 219, 225, 227

Todd, R. Larry, vii, 46, 100, 102, 112, 115, 117, 120, 122–24, 127, 131, 149, 163, 192, 282, 283, 285
tonal processes, 71–72, 78–79, 88
Tovey, Donald Francis, 71, 80, 86, 88, 112
Tragödie (Heine), 202
Trutz-Nachtigall (Spee), 202

Über die bildende Nachahmung des Schönen (Moritz), 84
Über Reineheit der Tonkunst (On Purity in Music) (Thibaut), 18, 62
Undine (Fouqué), 107
Upton, George, 49
Urbantschitsch, Viktor, 72

variations, 160–65
Varnhagen von Ense, Rahel (née Levin), 13, 172
"Vater unser in Himmelreich" (chorale), 159
"vaudeville," 208, 209
Veit, Simon, 168
Velazquez, Diego, 257
verse-rhythms, 227
Versuch, die Metamorphose der Pflanzen zu erklären (Goethe), 83
"Versunkene Sterne" (Polko), 47
Victoria, Queen of England, xiii, 51, 281
Viotti, Giovanni Battista, 21, 115
Virgil, 39
virtuosity, 113, 132, 259
Vischer, Friedrich Theodor, 68
Vitercik, Greg, vii, 6
Vogler, Abbé Georg Joseph, 21
Voigts, Friedrich, 209
Volkstümlichkeit, 192
"Voluntaries," 159
Voss, Johann Heinrich, 198–99, 202

Wackenroder, Wilhelm Heinrich, 57, 58
Wagner, Richard, 4, 26, 27, 47, 294
  chorus use by, 266
  criticism of Mendelssohn by, 238–39, 240, 242, 247, 252, 253, 258, 261
  as heir to Beethoven, 258
  leitmotifs, 264
  Mendelssohn and, 251–52, 267
  Mendelssohn's influence on, 62, 261, 262, 265
  originality of, 261
  performance of works of, 260, 261–62
  religious views, 258–59
  works evoking nature, 62
Wagner, Richard, works
  "Das Judenthum in der Musik," 239, 253, 293
  Liebesmahl der Apostel, 258, 262
  Lohengrin, 261, 262
  Meistersinger von Nürnberg, Die, 265

Parsifal, 259, 262
Tannhäuser, 259
Tristan und Isolde, 261
"walking bass," 103
Warte, Jacob von der, 199
Was mein Gott will (chorale), 159
Watt, Ian, 256
Weber, Carl Maria von, xi, 12, 16, 18, 19, 21, 94, 97, 114, 121, 149, 262, 271
    influence on Mendelssohn, 117–18, 215
Weber, Carl Maria von, works
    Der Freischütz, 12, 214
    Konzertstück, Piano and Orchestra, F minor op. 79, 16, 117–18, 120, 121
    Piano Concerto no. 2 in Eb major, 114
    Piano Sonata in C major op. 24, 117
Weltmusik ("world music"), 59
Werner, Eric, 2, 16, 30–33, 36, 37, 39, 40, 41, 47–48, 134–40, 141, 147, 167, 170, 184, 248, 249, 250, 273
Werner, Jack, 167
Wesley, Charles, 181
Wesley, Samuel, 149
Wiedergutmachung, 248
Will, Richard, 263

Winckelmann, Johann Joachim, 56–57
Winterfield, Carl von, 65
Winter's Tale, A (Shakespeare), 217–18
Wiora, Walter, 56
Wolff, Ernst, 245, 249
women. *See also* gender
    creativity of, 45
    influence on great composers, 46–47
    influence on Mendelssohn, 48
    role restrictions, 49
Woolf, Virginia, 255
Woringen, Angelica von, 50

Youens, Susan, vii, 5

Zedlita, Johann Christian, 190
Zelter, Carl Friedrich, x, xii, 11, 13, 16, 61, 62, 63, 64, 66, 72, 91, 99, 114, 115, 130, 131, 132, 168, 172, 184, 208, 209, 214, 254, 283, 288
Zionism, 33
Zopff, Hermann, 48
Zuccalmaglio, Anton Wilhelm von, 219
Zuruckspinnung, 80
Zweibrücken Music Festival, 17